Tamoxifen Tales

Tamoxifen Tales
Suggestions for Scientific Survival

V. Craig Jordan

Professor of Breast Medical Oncology,
Professor of Molecular and Cellular Oncology,
The University of Texas MD Anderson Cancer Center,
Houston, TX, USA

ELSEVIER

ACADEMIC PRESS
An imprint of Elsevier

Academic Press is an imprint of Elsevier
125 London Wall, London EC2Y 5AS, United Kingdom
525 B Street, Suite 1650, San Diego, CA 92101, United States
50 Hampshire Street, 5th Floor, Cambridge, MA 02139, United States
The Boulevard, Langford Lane, Kidlington, Oxford OX5 1GB, United Kingdom

Notices
Knowledge and best practice in this field are constantly changing. As new research and
experience broaden our understanding, changes in research methods, professional
practices, or medical treatment may become necessary.

Practitioners and researchers must always rely on their own experience and knowledge in
evaluating and using any information, methods, compounds, or experiments described
herein. In using such information or methods they should be mindful of their own safety
and the safety of others, including parties for whom they have a professional responsibility.

To the fullest extent of the law, neither the Publisher nor the authors, contributors, or
editors, assume any liability for any injury and/or damage to persons or property as a
matter of products liability, negligence or otherwise, or from any use or operation of any
methods, products, instructions, or ideas contained in the material herein.

Library of Congress Cataloging-in-Publication Data
A catalog record for this book is available from the Library of Congress

British Library Cataloguing-in-Publication Data
A catalogue record for this book is available from the British Library

Hardback ISBN: 978-0-323-85051-3
Paperback ISBN: 978-0-323-99617-4

For information on all Academic Press publications visit our website at
https://www.elsevier.com/books-and-journals

Publisher: Stacy Masucci
Acquisitions Editor: Andre G. Wolff
Editorial Project Manager: Pat Gonzalez
Production Project Manager: Kiruthika Govindaraju
Cover Designer: Greg Harris

Typeset by TNQ Technologies

"We are in it for life"
Tamoxifen Team motto

"But you, of course, went on to become a real (and very eminent) chemist, and one whose discovery has saved half a million people—I remember how excited I was when I first read about tamoxifen."

Oliver Sacks, MD, 2002
Author of "Uncle Tungsten"

"I congratulate you on your scientific discovery of tamoxifen—you will certainly be responsible for saving far more lives than any soldier in the SAS, territorial or regular!"

General Sir Michael Rose, KCB, CBE, DSO, QGM, 2007
Former commander 22nd SAS regiment at the time of the Iranian Embassy Siege and Falklands War

"To Craig Jordan my friend and my Teammate! Thanks for all you have done for UT, the United States and the United Kingdom"

Admiral Bill McRaven, 2015
Chancellor of the University of Texas
Overall Commander in the hunt for Osama Bin Laden

"What an extraordinary life you have led, and what a contribution you have made."

David Cornwell, 2016
(a.k.a. John le Carré)
"Smiley's People"

"A fellow Pilgrim and Adventurer."

Lt. Colonel Alistair MacKenzie, PhD, 2019
New Zealand SAS
"Pilgrim Days: from Vietnam to the SAS"

Dedicated to the women

who shaped my life

and without whom this memoir could

not have been written

S. Cynthia Jordan, Helen M. Y. Jordan, and Alexandra K. L. Jordan

Coat of Arms and Citation

Virgil Craig Jordan of Kenly Lodge Bramhall in the County of Cheshire and of Lakeshore Plaza, Chicago in the State of Illinois in the United States, Esquire Officer of the Most Excellent Order of the British Empire, Doctor of Philosophy, Doctor of Science, and honorary Doctor of Medicine of the University of Leeds, Diana Princess of Wales Professor of Cancer Research at Northwestern University Medical School, lately Captain in the Special Air Service Regiment (Territorial and Army Volunteer Reserve), and sometime Captain in the Intelligence Corps (Territorial and Army Volunteer Reserve).

Assigned Badge or Device

A Sagittary statant the human puts armoured at each elbow a Mullet, the bow in the dexter gauntlet fully extended and charged with an arrow all Argent rising from helm wreathed Argent and or manteled or doubled Argent two Goosefeathers also Argent the equine parts girthed or leading therefrom, a line also or reflexed between forelegs and terminating in an Escalop Argent (the goose feathers and bow plus arrow refers to status as horse-archers (sagitarius), the silver escalop refers to the symbol of Diana, the Princess of Wales' family the Spencers).

Contents

About the author

V Craig Jordan was born in New Braunfels, Texas, United States, in 1947. He traveled to England with his English mother, who remarried, and his stepfather adopted him to become a British citizen. Jordan had an unimpressive early career, except for a passion for chemistry. His mother allowed him to convert his bedroom into a chemistry laboratory. He was educated in England obtaining his BSc (1969) and PhD in Pharmacology (1973) studying a group of failed antifertility agents called nonsteroidal antiestrogens. He received his DSc (1985) and the first awarded honorary Doctor of Medicine (2001) all from Leeds University. There was little interest in drug development of antiestrogens in the early 1970s, but his work in academia blossomed into the tamoxifen we have today that saved millions of women's lives. Over a 40-year career, he researched all aspects of antiestrogens and discovered selective estrogen receptor modulators (SERMs). He used structure−function relationships to investigate molecular mechanisms, developed laboratory models of human disease, studied metabolism, developed the first clinically relevant models of SERM resistance in vivo, and translated all of his concepts into clinical trials. He is known as the "Father of Tamoxifen," but it is the discovery of SERMs that has shown the greatest potential for the future. During his work, Jordan has held Professorships at Wisconsin (1985−93) where he was director of the Breast Cancer Program, Northwestern University, Chicago (1993−2004) (also the Diana, Princess of Wales Professor of Cancer Research) where he was the director of the Breast Cancer Research Program, the Fox Chase Cancer Center (2004−09) (also the Alfred G Knudson Chair of Cancer Research) where he was Vice President of Medical Sciences and Research Director, Georgetown Lombardi Cancer Center (the Vincent T. Lombardi Chair of Translational Cancer Research) where he was the scientific director. Currently, he is a professor of Breast Medical Oncology and professor of Molecular and Cellular Oncology at the University of Texas, MD, Anderson Cancer Center in Houston (also the Dallas/Ft. Worth Living Legend Chair for Cancer Research). He has contributed more than 1000 scientific articles with more than 38,000 citations (h-index 118 and the 2184th cited biomedical scientist in the world). His work on SERMs has been recognized with 50 international awards including the American Cancer Society Medal of Honor, the Bristol Meyers Squibb Award, the General Motors Kettering Prize, the Karnofsky Award (ASCO), the Dorothy P. Landon Award (AACR), and the St. Gallen Prize (Switzerland). He is a member of the National Academy of Sciences, member of the National Academy of Medicine, fellow of the Academy of Medical Sciences (UK), and one of only 90 honorary fellows of the Royal Society of Medicine worldwide. He received the Order of the British Empire (OBE) from Her Majesty Queen Elizabeth II for Services to International Breast Cancer Research in 2002. This was for developing the laboratory principles for the treatment and prevention of breast cancer with tamoxifen. In 2019, he was appointed Companion of the Most Distinguished Order of St. Michael and St. George for Services to women's health, i.e., the discovery and development of

SERMs. In his parallel world, during his PhD at Leeds, he was recruited to be a captain in the Intelligence Corps (top secret security classification) and trained to be an authority on nuclear, chemical, and biological warfare on the advisory staff of the Deputy Chief Scientist (Army). The US government took away his US citizenship in 1972 for being an officer in the Army of a Foreign Power. He was attached by the British to the American Army (1972–74) to be the nuclear, biological, and radiological officer for Region I in the United States (New England, New York State, Puerto Rico, and the US Virgin Islands) to report on the operational state of American cities in Region I in the time of nuclear war. He is the only person, not a law enforcement officer, to be trained as a Drug Enforcement Administration Agent in the United States. He was recruited to the Special Air Service (SAS) and remained an SAS regular Army Reserve Officer in America, the land of his birth, until 9/11 when his American citizenship was returned with the words "we are all on the same side now."

Acknowledgments

I would like to first thank my publisher Elsevier for inviting me to present my academic journey, from which experience, I have been able to distill a number of suggestions for scientific survival. Mine was not a conventional path of effortlessly transitioning from Grammar School in England to success at the University of Leeds. As you will read in these pages, success in pharmacology and therapeutics required honest mentors to create the right intervention at the right time in my development. These individuals include my mother, S Cynthia Jordan, father Geoffrey Webster Jordan, grandfather James Fredrick Mottram, staff at Moseley Hall Grammar School Mr Bescoby (zoology master/career master), Mr Radford, and Mr Anderson, chemistry teachers, staff at the Department of Pharmacology, University of Leeds Medical School: Dr Ronnie Kaye (tutor and mentor), Dr Edward Clark (Medicinal Chemistry Lecturer and PhD Supervisor), Dr George Mogey (eventually colleague in the Department of Pharmacology, Leeds University), and Edward and Jeannie Klaiber my "boss" at the Worcester Foundation for Experimental Biology in Shrewsbury, MA, United States, for making the stay for me and my family in Shrewsbury a wonderful experience. My collaborators and colleagues Thomas B Pokoly, MD, for delivering my first daughter Helen Melissa Yvonne in Worcester, MA, and Mr Ronnie MacDonald at the University of Leeds for delivering my second daughter Alexandra Katherine Louise.

I thank the late Sir James Black (Nobel Laureate) and Dr Bert O'Malley (Chancellor of Baylor College of Medicine) for their interlinking support during the span of my life. Bert ensured our friendship flourished in Houston with regular dinner meetings at his favorite restaurant Antica Osteria, regrettably now a pandemic casualty. My friends and colleagues for 50 years, Harry and the late Angela Brodie, I thank for our adventures in endocrine therapy, around the world and in life. I thank Dr Nizar Tannir who led the change in attacking my statistically fatal diagnosis of Stage IV renal carcinoma, and Dr Andrea Califano who stepped forward to work with Dr Tenir "to save the life of Craig Jordan who has saved the lives of millions of breast cancer patients worldwide."

I particularly wish to thank Dr. Robert Clarke, then Dean of Science at Georgetown University, for his friendship and for organizing an outstanding leaving party for me at Georgetown. He and his wife Lena then took me out to dinner where I was presented with a portrait of Colonel Blair ("Paddy") Mayne, 1SAS Regiment. Robert had acquired the portrait at the Ypres Gate in Belgium as both "Paddy" and he (obviously in different generations!) had attended the same Grammar School, Regent House, in Northern Ireland. This was to be my farewell gift from Georgetown, which now hangs proudly on my "SAS wall of honor" at my home in Houston.

I thank all the members of my six consecutive Tamoxifen Teams at the University of Leeds, the University of Wisconsin, Northwestern University, the Fox Chase Cancer Center, Georgetown University, and the MD Anderson Cancer Center. By investing in their career development, therapeutics was advanced dramatically for women with breast cancer, and breast cancer could now be prevented (by direct and indirect approaches). A new group of medicines was discovered called selective estrogen receptor modulators (SERMs), but by investigating "the good, the bad, and the ugly of tamoxifen" at Wisconsin, the returns for women's health were enormous. By chance or fate, my Tamoxifen Team defined the molecular mechanisms of estrogen-induced apoptosis, a paradox in the clinical treatment of breast cancer with high-dose estrogen before tamoxifen, but my Tamoxifen Teams at Fox Chase Cancer Center, Georgetown, and the MD Anderson deciphered molecular mechanisms and resolved the paradoxical results of the Women's Health Initiative trial.

I would like to thank Professor William Wood of Emory University for his spiritual support and thank Patti Conklin, medical intuitive and vibrational healer, for contributing to my journey of spiritual growth and healing.

Last, but never least, and really most importantly, I thank Balkees Abderrahman MD, PhD, and Philipp Maximov MD, PhD, for their assistance assembling this book, Marcus Greene of Leeds University for assistance selecting the "perfect photograph" for our front cover that for me, best represents the University of Leeds. Jayne Glennon, of Leeds University Alumni Association, helped and assisted me with my sponsorship of student education and awards over decades. Most importantly, she and Professor John Ladbury ensured that my last PhD student, Balkees Abderrahman obtained her split-site PhD for students of very high ability within the 3-year limit in the midst of the coronavirus pandemic!

The scope and foundation steps in a career

At the start of an invited lecture, I often state "I am the least likely person to be standing before you today." I owe an enormous debt of gratitude to my teachers. I cannot repay them, but their indispensable contribution to guide my career development lives on through the philosophy they taught me: invest in the next generation. I thank my mentor Sir James Black, FRS (Nobel laureate) for this direct support of my career and for his philosophy "invest in the young." At the age of 32, he nominated me to become the Chair of Pharmacology at King's College, London. But I already had plans to go to America. Undaunted, he successfully nominated me for the Gaddum Award. His nomination letter was direct. "I nominated him to be the Chair of Pharmacology at King's College, London. He chose to go to America!" I received the Gaddum Award that led to further opportunities.

At Moseley Hall Grammar School in Cheadle, Cheshire, my chemistry teachers Mr Radford and Mr Anderson were inspirational. I remember at lunchtimes, sitting with Mr Radford chatting about chemistry when he allowed me to do A-level organic synthesis experiments, often alone, in his school chemistry laboratories. This was when I was in the fifth form (a 15 year old) waiting for my suboptimal results in the "O"-level exams but already doing sixth form chemistry studies. Mr Bescoby, my zoology and careers master, did more than was required to help me by investing in my future. He taught me the new science of molecular biology, twice a week at lunchtime, to address questions that might arise in my S-level zoology examination. I won the school prize for zoology in 1965. I bought a chemistry book! Each took time to listen and encouraged my success. At the University of Leeds, Dr Clark, Dr Kaye, and Dr Mogey had a profound effect on my life and career in pharmacology. They taught and encouraged my ascent in science. From Dr Mogey, I learnt to be an honest advocate for young talented students. It is their example that I have always sought to emulate in giving my "Tamoxifen Team" members opportunities to excel. I thank all my staff, PhD students, postdocs, and medical and surgical team fellows, especially those that agreed to contribute to this memoir, with a short account of their careers.

The University of Leeds changed my life in an exceptional and positive way. For this, I will be forever grateful. I thank their staff and my teachers for my first-class Honours Degree, my Doctor of Philosophy, Doctor of Science, and the first Honorary Doctor of Medicine (given by the University) degrees. It is said that it is fatal to obtain a bachelor's degree and a PhD at the same university, but maybe it is the exception that makes that rule. The University of Leeds was my academic beginning and my first tenured job as a faculty member in the Department of Pharmacology. This is that story.

The university is not the buildings but the embodiment of the vision and leadership of the faculty and student body. For this reason, I am honored to have Lord

Melvyn Bragg, my Chancellor, to contribute a Foreword to my memoir. The path to progress for the University is demonstrated through the successes of new discovery and from the education of the students who come from around the globe. This accumulative achievement bodes well for the future. Lord Bragg is a living legend, and I am proud to call him a friend. It was he who handed me my honorary Doctor of Medicine degree that started a continuing friendship over the past decades.

But Leeds University gave me more than just an education and opportunities to create the Medean Society (see Chapter 2). I was determined to seek a commission in the Army through Leeds University Officers Training Corps (LUOTC). I was commissioned as an infantry officer in 1969, but was then "talent-spotted" by the Intelligence Corps to become a Captain and Technical Intelligence Staff Officer in a small group of senior faculty nationally advising the Deputy Chief Scientist (Army). I was, however, a PhD student! As a lecturer in Pharmacology, I wanted my knowledge also to aid Society. I was trained as a Drug Enforcement Administration (DEA) Officer in Meridan, Connecticut, United States, at the State Police Barracks by the DEA training team. I subsequently helped to train 60% of British drug squads at Bishopgarth in Wakefield (1974–79). My knowledge and formal training in international law enforcement techniques was one way that I could reinvest in the future of the United Kingdom. I subsequently organized a visit of a DEA training team to Bishopgarth to present their whole law enforcement training course (3 weeks) for British police forces. Later, I was talent spotted by 23SAS, remained a Regular Army Reserve Officer in the SAS until my 50th birthday, but retain my links through the SAS Regimental Association. I am grateful to General Sir Michael Rose (he was the SAS Officer in overall charge of settling the Iranian Embassy hostage crisis in 1980. Watch "6 days") for his generosity in recommending me to be a member of the SAS Regimental Association.

During my time as an Officer Cadet at the LUOTC in the 1960s, I met, then Major Alan Roberts who ultimately became the Pro Chancellor at Leeds University. He rose to the academic rank of Professor and was promoted to the rank of Colonel in the Royal Artillery (V). Many years later, we met again when he was Vice President of the Royal Society of Medicine and he talent-spotted me for honorary Fellowship of the Royal Society of Medicine, the award of their Jephcott Gold Medal, and my election as President of the Royal Society of Medicine Foundation of North America. Through the University of Leeds, Alan has remained a true friend, and I thank him for all he has done for my career. He encouraged me to reconnect with LUOTC, which I have been happy to do, with the Jordan Prize for the best LUOTC cadet each year (Chapter 13). The Prize started in 1996 as an investment in the next generation. I was honored to be appointed as the honorary Colonel of LUOTC as part of the Yorkshire Officers Training Regiment. This appointment, approved by her Majesty Queen Elizabeth II, retained my connection with the unit that trained me. For me, LUOTC first introduced me to the 4 aces of leadership that must be held to excel in any major struggle of consequence. This may be the defense of the realm or a struggle for knowledge to vanquish disease.

1. The leader must have the imagination to see the problem, isolate it, and create a solution.
2. To advance the solution to the problem, the leader must have the ability to inspire others to accomplish the task.
3. The leader must share his ideas and ensure that others are given credit when the task is successfully completed.
4. Throughout, the leader must be resolute with a spirit of enthusiasm and have the will to accomplish the task despite all difficulties.

Equally important (but actually essential for enhancing your morale after an exhausting 3-day army exercises with little sleep and comfort) is the deploying of triple S. Infantry Sergeant Major Jim Erswell at LUOTC, trained us as infantry officers, and swore by triple S (s***, shave, and shower) to revive us all after exhausting exercises with no sleep. It works!

These lessons are the foundation for the scientific survival suggestions within this book.

I am most grateful to my academic colleagues on both sides of the Atlantic. Simultaneously, I was nominated for election to the National Academy of Sciences in the United States (by nominator unknown) and Fellowship of the Academy of Medical Sciences in the United Kingdom nominated by Professor Terrance Rabitts FMedSci, FRS from the University of Oxford. I am deeply grateful for their generosity.

But now, by a twist of fate, or led by my DNA, I find myself back in Texas at the MD Anderson Cancer Center. I thank Ron DePinho MD, the then President, and Ethan Dimitrovsky, MD, the Provost, for their commitment of purpose to consummate my recruitment to the premier cancer care center in the United States (and the World). By coincidence, during my induction ceremony to become a member of the Academy of Medicine, Engineering and Science of Texas, I met my new Chancellor at the University of Texas, William McRaven. I thank Admiral McRaven for his continuing friendship and support. He was the NAVY Seal Admiral in overall command of the operation to kill Osama Bin Laden. As Special Forces soldiers, we bonded.

Foreword—Melvyn Bragg

Universities are places of learning and opportunity, where individuals can gain the knowledge and experience to change society in a positive way. I have seen universities work their magic but rarely have I witnessed such a "play of chance" for an individual to come to a university, seize the opportunity, and change the lives of millions of families in such a positive way.

In the mid1960s, Craig Jordan had his opportunity when he was admitted to Leeds University and he seized it. He excelled at chemistry and, by chance won a scholarship to read for his PhD at Leeds University because, as you will discover within these pages, he liked the challenge of the research topic. Perhaps fortunately for society, his project failed and he turned to study the pharmacology of "failed contraceptives." These "failures," however, should now be viewed as Craig's training to be successful in science.

This period at Leeds University was essential for him to gather the knowledge he was to use as a foundation to reinvent a "failed contraceptive" to be a lifesaving medicine for millions of women. Craig mentions the quote from Churchill "Success is the ability to go from one failure to another with no loss of enthusiasm". You will see that Craig has always exhibited enthusiasm for his quest, and this is evidenced by the section, called "In Their Own Words" (Chapter 18) written by some of his trainees. Tamoxifen, it now appears, was initially viewed as a failure, but by chance and by spotting opportunity, a pioneering medicine was reinvented to become one of the most successful cancer therapies of all time.

I first met Craig one evening in Leeds during a dinner party on July17, 2001. It was the day before the degree ceremony for the undergraduate students, but I was also, as Chancellor of the University, to present the honorary degrees on behalf of the university. On this occasion, the honorary graduates (see Figure below) were Baroness Boothroyd, former Speaker of the House of Commons, Baroness Greenfield, President of the Royal Institution, Seamus Heaney, Nobel Prize for Literature (1995), and Professor Craig Jordan, Diana Princess of Wales Professor of Cancer Research at Northwestern University, United States. Craig was to receive the first honorary Doctorate in Medicine for humanitarian research at Leeds University.

His citation starts with these ringing words, "Craig Jordan is one of the most distinguished medical scientists of the last hundred years" and closes with the statement "Craig Jordan is one of those medical research scientists whose persistence and faith in the results of his investigations have had a profound impact on the quality and duration of the lives of so many people that it is difficult to exaggerate their true worth to mankind."

In medical science, one needs evidence as proof of statements, and in Craig's case, the evidence for his citations was his earlier award of the Cameron Prize by the University of Edinburgh. One cannot apply for the award, but it is awarded by the selection committee to those "who have made a highly important and valuable addition to practical therapeutics." The list of recipients since its inception in

1879 includes, Pasteur (1884), Paul Ehrlich (1914), Madame Curie (1931), Sir Alexander Fleming (1945), and Sir James Black (1980). Craig received the Cameron Prize in 1993. Craig's life's work, researching "the good, the bad, and the ugly" of tamoxifen is perhaps unique, as the medicine has gone from strength to strength over the past 40 years. Unlike other medicines, it did not "have its time and vanish," as other more potent derivatives were discovered. It became a part of the fabric of medicine and our society as an inexpensive and effective way to save lives. Should this memoir from Craig of the "Tamoxifen Tales" capture the imagination of even a few young scientists in a new generation, who then go on to succeed, he will have contributed yet another success for our society.

Melvyn Bragg
(Lord Bragg of Wigton)
March 14, 2020
London

Honorary Degree recipients at the summer ceremony 2001. Left to right: Vice Chancellor Sir Alan Wilson, Professor V. Craig Jordan; Diana, Princess of Wales Professor of Cancer Research, Northwestern University, Chicago, United States; Baroness Boothroyd, former Speaker of the House of Commons; Lord Melvyn Bragg, Chancellor of the University of Leeds; Baroness Greenfield, President of the Royal Institution; and Seamus Heaney, Nobel Laureate (Literature, 1995). Professor Jordan was to receive the first honorary Doctorate in Medicine for humanitarian research at Leeds University.

Why write this book?

This personal memoir has its origins over the past decade, with the realization that there was a need to set down some simple principles as a guide for young scientists wanting to succeed. Talented individuals want to contribute to the future of medical science and healthcare despite the indifference of governments to invest in the future of discovery. Enthusiastic and committed young undergraduates are our most precious assets that ensure the survival of nations. A nation that does not invest in the quest for new knowledge cannot succeed. Knowledge results in economic strength and, in the case of medicine, citizens that are healthy, engaged, and productive. The United States and the United Kingdom continue to contribute with a wealth of new knowledge. Both nations have contributed landmark achievements in science in the past, but the keywords here are—the past. The changing economy of the world and a pandemic has forced cutbacks in the investment in medical science at a time of extraordinary opportunity for our next generation. The past 40 years of my career has seen a remarkable change in our knowledge of breast cancer, treatment, and prevention. Forty years ago, there was only rudimentary knowledge of breast cancer biology, treatment was barbaric, and prevention was science fiction. All changed with the investigation of a failed contraceptive ICI 46,474, and its application as a long-term adjuvant therapy to treat breast cancer. Prevention became a clinical reality—twice—with tamoxifen and another abandoned failure raloxifene. Progress is possible and can be achieved. But regrettably, I have seen many incorrect versions of the "discovery and development of tamoxifen." They have only a passing resemblance to reality. This is the story that I have been asked by many, to recount. It is a human story and one to be read by patients who should like to know how advances in medicine occur and by the thousands of aspiring medical research scientists (or in fact any trainee in science) who wish to guide themselves to contribute to Society.

Let me first, briefly, describe where we were some 50 years ago when the US National Cancer Act was passed in 1971. The goal was to create an organization to encourage discovery in cancer and translate these findings from the environment of the laboratory, as rapidly as possible, to patient care. The vehicle in the United States was the Comprehensive Cancer Center that was mandated to compete for research grants and save lives. This process was described as "the War on Cancer."

The analogy with war is not embraced by all, but I believe there is a ring of truth to the struggle against an adaptable and unrelenting enemy. Indeed, much knowledge to fight cancer came out of advances and discoveries made in World War II: cytotoxic chemotherapy has its origins in chemical warfare agents and radioisotopes were used (the offshoot of the atomic bomb) to create radiolabeled compounds and drugs. These are but two examples of swords being beaten into ploughshares.

The massive commitment the United States made to medical science in the 1960s and 1970s consolidated the extraordinary advances made by the pharmaceutical industry, during their halcyon days of expansion, triggered by accelerated new drug development required by World War II. It is unlikely that penicillin G would have been mastered from mold without the need to save the lives of millions of wounded soldiers. Incidentally, Prime Minister Winston S Churchill who contracted pneumonia was cured with sulfadiazine, a synthetic compound of a group known as sulfonamides. The sulfonamides were discovered by Domagk in Germany in the 1930s and received the Nobel Prize in 1939. Hitler was already angry at the Nobel committees because Carl von Ossietzky, a critic of the Nazi regime, had previously received the Nobel Peace Prize in 1935. This resulted in the German Government not permitting German Nationals from receiving the Nobel Prize. Domagk received his certificate for his Nobel Prize in 1947 (incidentally the year of my birth in Texas), but without his Prize money! New synthetic analgesics, mass morphine production, and antimalarials (necessary for troops to fight in the tropics) such as paludrine would not have occurred. The scientists who received the Nobel Prize for penicillin, Alexander Fleming, Ernst Chain, and Howard Florey would not have received their landmark Prize, and there would have been no antibiotics for quite a while.

To build on their success, and maintain their trajectory at the forefront of science as the world's most powerful nation in the 1960s, the US government created a bold plan for immediate action. The philosophy of the government of the United States was "If you have succeeded in a competitive system of education elsewhere and you have unique scientific knowledge we can develop, you can come to America." In the United Kingdom, it was referred to as the Brain Drain.

When I was invited to go to the University of Wisconsin Comprehensive Cancer Center (Madison) in 1980, the grant system for the government with its peer-reviewed funding had a pay line of 25%. That is, 25 out of every 100 submitted grants from qualified scientists working in the world's best medical centers were being funded by the government. Generous overhead costs were also paid by the government to universities to "pay the expenses" of faculty doing research. There was massive investment in the future of the United States. That investment in science in the 1980s was amazing, and the world benefited from American scientific leadership, healthcare benefited worldwide, the economy benefited, and the pharmaceutical industry benefited from expanding menu of new drugs for diseases never before believed possible. Molecular biology was replacing biochemistry with new techniques to manipulate DNA—the biotechnology industry was born. The world changed, and we all benefited. The government review process was transparent, balanced, and helpful. Reviewers provided sound advice, and if followed, any scientist could successfully progress toward the pay line. Though not perfect, the system was the best in the world.

Today, the pay line has all but evaporated. It has become 7%. In other words, 7 out of every 100 grants from qualified professional scientists at the best universities in the country will be funded. Now you only have two chances to succeed, and then your project has to be abandoned for federal funding support. There are valiant efforts by the American Association for Cancer Research (AACR) Foundation and the equivalent organization of the American Society of Clinical Oncology (ASCO) to invest in young medical scientist for training. The American Cancer

Society (ACS) continues to contribute their commitment to research grants for the best and the brightest scholars with ideas that promote progress in cancer research, but about 25 years ago, the ACS chose to focus funding of the young researcher. While this is a laudable strategy, in the short term, there is a strategic problem with the current crisis in funding that may last for decades. With whom will the next generation train if there are no senior accomplished medical scientists whose life's work has deciphered all we know today?

Susan G Komen for the Cure has a clear vision for harnessing all of our nation's talent at every stage of their career. Their approach is innovative as the most talented and accomplished scientists, with a proven record of advancing cancer research, and has a core investment in senior scientists as scholars. In return, the scholars must dedicate time evaluating and selecting the best research projects that have the best chance of scientific success in priority areas. I believe this is an excellent model, but it relies on the creation of a pact between the citizens and business to be sustained. The Komen organization reinvests funds raised to conquer cancer that covers a broad front with donations to the AACR, ASCO, and major awards for both basic and clinical research, i.e., the Brinker International Award. There are both individual research and team research grants.

So, I hear you saying, what is the problem we need to solve to participate in first-class research? You tell us there are unprecedented opportunities and at least some investments in the future. We have the best scientific infrastructure with the best centers of learning and powerful pharmaceutical companies. Our science created the atomic bomb in a national emergency, and we rose to the challenge of the USSR, beating us into space with Sputnik and then the first man in space, Yuri Gagarin. President Kennedy stated, "We choose to go to the moon in the next decade"—and we succeeded in doing just that in July 1969 with 6 months to spare! Already billions have been spent on cancer research, why haven't we cured cancer?

Well, in my view, medical research is not a "moon shot" as everyone believes. Our German rocket scientists knew where the moon was, and where it would be so you could aim the rocket at the appropriate target area. The rockets were tested, often failing, over and over by a new organization, called the National Aeronautics and Space Administration (NASA), charged with creating and training teams of astronauts for achievable goals using developing technology: orbiting the earth with extravehicular activities (space walks), going around the moon and back and then the big one—landing on the moon and (fortunately) coming back. A magnificent achievement within a decade. However, the physics was mostly known, resources were huge, it was our national priority, and the near tragedy of Apollo 13 proved that men could survive in the face of disaster without a lot of help. Again, magnificent, as theirs is one of the stories of men succeeding in the face of certain death. But none of this is Nature, the variation of biology and the adaptability of disease.

With disease, the rules change in response to the environment created. The ability of either infectious disease or cancer to replicate indefinitely makes disease a moving target that must be destroyed but without destroying the life of the patient at the same time. It is targeted therapy that will not remain the same for the disease as, in the case of cancer, self-replication must occur indefinitely with no off switch to survive as the treatment environment changes. These cells spread from an innocuous site like the breast where cancerous growth does little immediate harm, to sites in the brain, bones, and lungs where metastases invade, dominate, destroy normal tissue, and kill the patient.

We have more knowledge about the cancer, its vulnerable targets, and targeted therapies than ever before, but we need trained people to decipher the machinery of normal and cancer cells. Once deciphered, the new knowledge needs to be deployed for public health. That, however, is the essential role of the pharmaceutical industry—their role is not discovery. Discovery is often an individual event by committed scientists in universities and medical research institutes.

Our knowledge is abundant, and our training and skills are better than at any time in human history but other economic crises, most notably the coronavirus pandemic; by necessity, have changed political priorities. Decades of preventive wars have drained our resources. Afghanistan is a glaring example of history repeating itself as no one has mastered that land yet. As a simplistic analogy regarding war, it is as if during World War II, the allies had already spent years in training, deployed to England, and successfully achieved the D-Day landing and then—the government said "Well done, but we have had to change our plans as the victory in Europe is no longer a priority. All our resources will now go to the Pacific War. You will receive no replacements for your casualties, no supplies, no ammunition, no gasoline, and no new fighting vehicles, warships or aircraft. You now hold on and figure out how to win the war in Europe." As we know the enemy was far from capitulating, but the Russian army was advancing fast in 1944. All of Europe could well have become communist. So the strategy of "not investing in success" would have had dire consequences for the future of western democracies and changed the whole of the remaining years of the 20th century.

This is what cancer research (and the spin off for medical research) now faces through a policy of "not investing in success" for our nation and the future well-being of our citizens. Knowledge is our most important commodity to survive. But when I talk to those in the business world who understand the concept of investing in success, they are perplexed and somewhat shocked that there is no stability for science in our nation. One retort is "join a pharmaceutical company, get paid, and get a budget for research."

Regrettably, again, this is not the role of the pharmaceutical company. The roles are development, safety, clinical trials, and large-scale production after FDA approval and reliable distribution to patients. Again. discovery is essentially outside the pharmaceutical industry with innovation in universities and by the individual. It is not a right to participate in the quest for knowledge; it has always been an Olympic event depending entirely on the gifted individual making the right decisions at the right time. So how do you begin to contribute successfully? The answer to my question is the journey we will travel together through the pages of this book based on my personal experiences. It is an unexpected opportunity to "develop a drug (tamoxifen) to improve women's health." This one discovery led to others to create a new group of medicines called selective estrogen receptor modulators (SERMs) to treat multiple diseases in women with a single tablet, and then, by studying acquired resistance to tamoxifen, we discovered how estrogen kills specially adapted breast cancer cells.

When I had completed my memoir, I discovered there were many other "self-help guides," but I selected just two recent contributions as the authors have, and continue to contribute to our view of scientific discovery or to leadership for a new generation. Their advice has resonance for me through different aspects of my life that are intertwined. I found the principles for success and survival in life and science are the same.

Jim Watson was one member of a cluster of interconnected exceptional scientists at Cambridge and King's College London that created the world of DNA we live in today. He and I have had numerous chance meetings at Cold Spring Harbor (discussing breast cancer treatments), the annual celebrations for the Bristol Myers Squibb Awards for Distinguished Achievement in Cancer Research (discussing his honorary knighthood), and the American Association for Cancer Research Foundation President's Circle dinners (on the occasion of my award for raising $1,000,000 for our Foundation as the Chairperson of the President's Circle; Fig. 1). We are colleagues in the National Academy of Sciences.

FIGURE 1

James Watson and I on the occasion when the AACR recognized me for helping to raise $1,000,000 for the AACR Foundation in 2010.

Jim's book entitled "Avoid Boring People (Vintage books, a division of Random House Inc NY 2010)" is excellent. He correctly states that his research group was his family; as are the generations of my "Tamoxifen Teams." Our motto, "We are in it for life" is a double entendre stating we are contributing lifesaving research and we remain loyal to our Tamoxifen Team members forever. Here are just a few of Jim's many (108) suggestions! Read out loud your written words (I do this all the time or dictate as the flow is often better). Immediately, write up a big discovery (good advice, get it out there or others will). Teaching can make your mind move on a big problem (I found, in my early university career at Leeds University, getting back to basics can help with new discoveries—principles emerge). Have your students master subjects outside your expertise (works every time for me—I bring the clinical relevance and history and they bring the latest papers in Nature or a new technique) and finally, choose an objective apparently ahead of its time (everything we did in the laboratory with tamoxifen, SERMs, raloxifene, antihormone resistance and estrogen-induced apoptosis are our examples).

The recent book by Bear Grylls "A Survival Guide for Life" (Barton Press, 2012) is an excellent list of 75 suggestions from his extensive store of his short life's experience. He is the Chief Scout in the United Kingdom and internationally known adventurer with many TV series to his credit. For me, he is a former member of 21 SAS, the sister regiment of my Special Forces Regiment 23 SAS. We have never met, but he continues to do much good and is an ideal role model for a new generation. Here I quote several "rules" he makes in his book because these are excellent and will amplify what the young medical scientist will now read in this memoir.

Number 1: "Have a dream" (mine was to develop a drug, any drug, to treat cancer)

"All men dream; but not equally. Those who dream by night in the dusty recesses of their minds wake in the day to find that it was vanity: but the dreamers of the day are dangerous men, for they may act their dreams with open eyes to make it possible."

T.E. Lawrence (Lawrence of Arabia)

Number 5: "Be the most enthusiastic person you know" (I am a bit too enthusiastic for most people)

"Imagine interviewing a candidate who says they love to get up early and being the first into work, and they love warming up peoples' days with a smile and getting their colleagues a cup of tea to cheer them up. That all they want is the chance to show how hard they can work and how they go the extra mile." Bear Grylls

How do you teach that?—you lead by example.

Number 8: "Them that stick it out are them that win" (I never stop trying)

"To see things through to the very end is frequently an important factor in being successful." So what is success? "Success is the ability to go from one failure to another with no loss of enthusiasm." Winston S. Churchill

Number 9: "That little bit extra" (My life's philosophy is total commitment to achieve the goal)

When Bear Grylls passed selection to the SAS (for the current medical scientist, it is like getting peer reviewed grants from the government, i.e., a 7% success rate against the best competitors and then a tenured job at a University), the commanding officer said these words to the handful of survivors.

"From this day on you are part of a family. I know what you have had to give to earn the right to be here. The difference between the four of you and the rest of those who failed (there were 140 outstanding volunteers at the start) is very simple: it is the ability to give that little bit extra when it hurts. You see, the difference between ordinary and extraordinary is often that little word extra."

Buy the book "A Survival Guide for Life". Bear Grylls, Barton Press, London 2012.

How did the "Tamoxifen Tales: Suggestions for Scientific Survival" really happen? Over dinner at an American Association for Cancer Research (AACR) Prize Award Ceremony 10years ago, Nance Guilmartin from the Landon Foundation enthusiastically endorsed the proposal of crediting the individual scientific success, as of my Tamoxifen Teams, to their personal accomplishments during their PhD training. I have now expanded this concept to ask trainees from different perspectives to comment on their experiences "Case Studies in their own words" (Chapter 18). They are PhD students, postdoctoral fellows, surgical residents, or medical oncology fellows. Suddenly, THIS book took on a life of its own!

Dr Hiltrud Brauch, Deputy Director of Dr Margaret Fischer Bosch, Institute for Clinical Pharmacology in Stuttgart, Germany (see Fig. 4.5), generously invited me to be the Scientific Mentor on her European Union Graduate Student Grant entitled Defeating Drug Resistance. At their annual meeting, in 2012 on the campus of the University of Liverpool, England, I was asked to present a lecture on my Scientific Survival Suggestions. Scientists from the Food and Drug Administration (FDA) in the United States were also there to present lectures to the students about the process for drug approval in the United States. At the break, they enthusiastically invited me to address FDA scientists in their Women's Health Program and they started this process of publication with "requests for the book." Who should read this book? Anyone who has the desire to change medicine, invest in new generation of young scientists, and conquer diseases. This memoir is now the distillate of my life's scientific experience "being self-taught by pictures" as I often put it. If the memoir encourages the success of just a few committed individuals to do what can be done to advance medical science, then I will have succeeded.

This year, 2021, is the 50th anniversary of the passing of the National Cancer Act. To mark this milestone in cancer medicine, the National Cancer Institute (NCI) has selected those medical scientists who created our progress in cancer care. I was delighted to be named by the NCI for my work on SERMs and breast cancer prevention with SERMs (link to be added in two weeks during proofs).

The American Association for the Advancement of Science (AAAS) chose to create an award to highlight the value of independent research grants to address subjects not immediately seen as relevant for investment by taxpayer money. In 2021 (https://www.goldengooseaward.org/01awardees/serms), I was selected to be the recipient of the "Golden Goose Award" (i.e., that lays a Golden Egg). The work that you will read about in these pages was completed by the investment of $30 million of Federal Grants and $35 million in philanthropy from the Lynn Sage Foundation in Chicago, the Avon Foundation, and the Susan G. Komen Foundation. The goal of the award is to educate Congress about the benefits to nations of discoveries that result in citizens who are healthier, have longer lives, and do not suffer the trauma of fractured families. In the case of my award, I never took patents out of my discoveries, as this was financial support from the Nation. The economic benefits for the United Kingdom (AstraZeneca) created a world-class cancer care company. As you will read, tamoxifen alone had an unplanned patent life in lucrative markets for nearly 35 years and was a billion dollar a year medicine. Raloxifene, a failed breast cancer treatment, became a billion dollar in annual sales winner for a decade. These benefits for nations and their citizens created the world we enjoy today.

Prelude

What creates the directions in our lives? What is it that allows each of us to address challenges and overcome potential catastrophic situations? In my case, it was a small, but committed group of immediate family members who, unguided and unknowingly, ensured my success. This was structured and subtle. There were no compulsory activities for children like today. I was to decide my own path and create my own environment. These were different times in the wake of World War II. As a foreign national (American citizenship, born in America in New Braunfels, Texas in 1947) who, in England, was required to have an identity card, I was not aware of the problems, to be resolved, that were to come. These issues were dealt with calmly by my mother and stepfather Geoffrey Webster Jordan. Problems of my faltering path toward an education and career were dealt with diplomatically by my mother with my school masters. She deployed charm and diplomacy, and I learned that quality. Catastrophic issues with my education were solved by my mother and grandfather who ensured I went to job opportunities in the event I was not allowed to continue to study at Moseley Hall Grammar School in Cheshire, England. But it is the life and death of close family members that make their impression. This is not only when it occurs in early life but also at the time, that I was establishing a family of my own.

As I grew up, my mother was periodically debilitated with migraine headaches. She was bedridden for days, and there were no effective treatments. These migraines continued throughout the 1960s, but then, at menopause, the migraine never occurred again. In my teens, I discovered I was also getting migraine headaches, in retrospect, probably induced by my stress at a competitive school of one thousand pupils—Moseley Hall Grammar School in Cheshire. This condition extended into the first year of my University education. Early on, I discovered that the headaches would abate once the pain made me vomit. I coped at school and the early years of University by making myself vomit. My migraine never returned once I was successful at Leeds University, and I had success as a British Army officer. It may be that success and self-confidence were essential to cure my "learned" migraine episodes. But I do wonder about the role of my mothers sex steroids in the genesis of her migraine headaches. Someone should answer that question.

However, there was a catastrophe I was shielded from by my mother's hospitalization in the early 1960s. I was send to my grandfather's house at 4 King Close in Wilmslow. My mother had severe abdominal pain and was rushed to hospital for an emergency appendectomy. Recovering the following day, she told the staff there was still excruciating pain, but no immediate action was initiated. Finally, she was reoperated on (leaving a 2-foot long scar with horrible bootlace stitching forever destroying her abdomen) to discover she had an ectopic pregnancy that had burst her fallopian tube. She had a prolonged hospital and nursing home recovery with the fear of death from thrombosis. She and my father went away to Llandudno where they had had their honeymoon in Northern Wales. To prevent a fatal thrombosis, she forced my father to walk her the length of the Llandudno pier every day. Decades later, toward the end of her life, she told me: "I had to live to protect you" was her simple reply.

My mother, as a child, had a very close relationship with her grandmother in Wilmslow. To everyone in the village, this was a mystery as my grandfather's mother had a reputation as a tough, no nonsense disciplinarian. Toward the end of her life (she died at 95 years of age in Addlington, Cheshire), my mother and I became very close as I visited her in Cheshire, for a week every other month for 8... years. She spontaneously told me the family story that her mother, my grandmother Edith Mottram, had been very ill postpartum and had to remain in hospital for 6 months in 1923. Baby Cynthia was given to my grandfather's (Fredrick James Mottram's) mother to care for. Clearly, this bonded the two together.

When my mother died and was cremated, I scattered some of her ashes in Wilmslow Parish Church (Fig. 1) to be close to her father. She had "illegally" buried his ashes in the churchyard of Wilmslow Parish Church so he could be close to the place that was important to him. He carried the cross each week at services as a boy and attended the Church of England School next door.

For myself, my farewell to my mother occurred as I emptied the last of her ashes from the bridge into the river Bolin (Fig. 1), which would take her into the Styal woods she loved. I was tipping the jar when a breath of wind blew up from the river. Something told me not to move, and a breath of her ashes kissed my cheek. My daughter Alexandra told me that on the night her grandmother died, she heard an unusual hooting of a lone owl. She knew it was her grandmother saying goodbye.

My father Geoffrey Jordan was educated at the Leys School in Cambridge, and following 5 years of service in the Royal Air Force during World War II, he chose a career in banking. He had an orderly and routine life first commuting daily to his work at Martin's Bank in Manchester and then as branch manager for Barclay's Bank in Altringham, Cheshire. He and my grandfather provided the glue for our small family.

My father had his first heart attack in 1971. He never fully recovered and he became what was referred to as a "cardiac cripple." Treatment options were few. My father had complained of heart problems at home, the doctor had been informed, and my father was admitted to Stepping Hill hospital in Stockport. I was required to join a military exercise in West Germany called "Summer Sales" in the summer 1972. I was off to Germany. I had to maintain complete security as no one, not even my family could know where I was or what I was doing. At that time, I was a Reserve Captain in a Unit of Technical Intelligence Staff Officers on the staff of the Deputy Chief Scientist at the Ministry of Defense. I was a PhD student at Leeds University.

After a stop for an official briefing in Rheindahlen (Headquarters of the British Army of the Rhine), I arrived at the Ententeich hotel in Bielefeld, my operational area. The exercise was to train Headquarter's staff of BAOR for the eventuality that overwhelming Russian and East German armored forces would cross the West German border. The overall plan was to slow the invading forces by falling back across Germany so that a truce and peace negotiations could engage. Alternatively, the land war would go nuclear.

FIGURE 1

Above: Wilmslow Parish Church. My mother and father were married here on November 1, 1944, I and my daughter Helen were christened here. The bridge where I am standing crosses the River Bolin into Styal Woods. **Below:** Another important church for my family is Adel, outside Leeds, Norman Church where my daughter Alexandra was christened. I was present when Kate Middleton's grandfather's ashes were scattered at Adel Church, but little did I ever imagine that Prince William would be the one to present me with Companion of the Most Distinguished Order of St. Michael and St. George for services to women's health, at Buckingham Palace in November 2019 (Fig. 1.3).

The exercise was to be 10 days, and then I was to make my way to Lindau am Bodensee in Southern Germany. In my real world, I was a Medical Research Council Scholar completing my PhD and had been selected to attend the annual meeting of Nobel Laureates for lectures and cultural exchanges. An unusual combination for a month: practicing for the outbreak of World War III and then attending the largest assembly of Nobel Laureates outside the Stockholm Nobel Prize ceremony, with West German Chancellor, Willi Brandt. In those days being a German speaker was a requirement.

The BAOR exercise started, and the test of one's resolve would start: move every 12 h and take over from the other team as we fell back over the German countryside by night; sleeping the best we could for a few hours, brief the Generals, and move again. It was Bellenberg wood that everything would change.

I was woken at 3:30 a.m. by a polite Major who asked to talk to me outside my command tent. On the third or fourth attempt, I decided to comply. It was like a film. The low light illuminating the towering pine trees in the wood as we walked together. He explained that my father had died days earlier and I was to be extracted and flown back to Manchester to attend my father's funeral.

Once back in Cheshire, I learned that my father had spent the week in Stepping Hill hospital and he was scheduled for discharge on the morning he died at 5 a.m. It seems he responded poorly to be woken up at 5 a.m., and his explosive temper caused a second heart attack. This was when I learned of my errors (never to be made again) when one is required to be clandestine about one's movements and travel arrangement.

Upon learning of my father's death, my wife Marion went to meet with Professor Michael Barrett, Chairman of Pharmacology at Leeds University Medical School. She stated that she had no idea where I was. What is to be done, as his father's funeral is delayed until he can be there?

The old Medical School in Thorsby Place in Leeds had a system of phones in the offices for all Faculty and staff, but everyone else used a phone in the corridor at the entry to the Department. As a PhD student, that was my only option as I could not use my home phone. One picked up the phone and identified yourself to the Medical School operator, who wrote down the number to be called and how much you must pay for the call. Then you paid at the conclusion of your call.

Professor Barrett searched the phone records and found one I had called a couple of times in Ashford in Kent. Professor Barrett called and received the answer "Colonel Amlott". I am sure Colonel Amlott thought: "Never do that again Captain Jordan." The plan worked but I never was able to attend the Nobel Laureate meeting in Lindau 1972. Today, the consolation is that Dr Balkees Abderrahman, my current talented PhD student and Breast Medical Oncology Fellow, has been selected to attend the Lindau meeting in 2020. But then coronavirus struck and the meeting and flights were cancelled. Nevertheless, she was reselected in 2021 and invited to be on a 90-minute panel discussion with a selection of Nobel Laureates (https://www.mediatheque.lindau-nobel.org/videos/39161/why-trust-science/meeting-2021), and develop a published paper (https://www.lindau-nobel.org/blog-6-tools-to-supercharge-your-science-communication). But what of my Grandparents in Wilmslow?

My grandmother, Edith Mottram (Fig. 2) was diagnosed with congestive heart failure and placed on cardiac glycosides and bed rest. This was in 1962 when I was 15 years old. We visited my grandmother regularly, but one night was very different. I heard my mother get up at our home in Bramhall and go down stairs to answer the phone in the hall. No one was there. As she was ascending the stairs, the phone rang and it was my grandfather. My grandmother had died in the night, and he was asking my mother to come to Wilmslow for help and support. I was told to remain at home, but I insisted on traveling with my mother and father to Wilmslow. It was about 2 a.m.

Until that moment, I had never seen a person who had died. My grandmother (Fig. 2) had been a tall lady of sturdy build but what I saw was a small frail woman in the bed. I did not recognize her. We caught a few hours of sleep, and the doctor came around to the house. We gathered in the dining room as he announced that she had died of pneumonia, and not congestive heart failure. She was being treated for the wrong ailment! Shocked silence, but I learned that, in England, families had to carry on in the early 1960s. It was as it was. There was no alternative and blame was of no value now.

In 1968, my grandfather (Fig. 2) was diagnosed with problems in his bowels. I remember he was required to eat raw liver—a lot. But with time, he could not look after himself, so his house at 4 Kings Close, Wilmslow, was sold, and he

FIGURE 2

My grandmother and grandfather at the entrance to Wilmslow Parish Church.

went to live in a retirement home near where my parents lived. He had a colostomy, but he never complained. When I visited, we were both required to stand to talk; he was proud former army officer; I was an army officer too.

James Fredrick Mottram died at Easter in 1972, and my mother had to endure his funeral at Wilmslow Parish Church with a broken ankle. She was on crutches. Prior to his death, the board of the Manchester United Football Club wrote a letter to him as he was a shareholder in the football club and for each home game he would be seated in the stands near the board members (Fig. 3). My father Geoff Jordan died when I was away in the Army in Germany in June 1972 and I as a newly appointed lecturer in Pharmacology at the University of Leeds was required to go to America for 2 years to complete my "Been to America (BTA)" before resuming my teaching and research responsibilities at the University of Leeds in 1974. My mother would be left completely alone, as her parents, husband, son, and daughter-in-law would all be gone.

In just 10 years, all of my small family was gone except for my mother. It was 1972, but a surprise was in store. One day, a car drew up to my mother's home and an elderly, but spritely gentleman declared "Hellow Motty" (her maiden name was Mottram). Jack Baker was an early friend from before World War II, and they were both in the same Cheshire Unit of the Fire Service. For the next 30 years, Uncle Jack (as he was known to my children and I) would drive from his home in Southern Cheshire, 3 times a week to have adventures around Cheshire reliving old memories with my mother from before the war. He provided adventure, stability, and most importantly fun for decades. My mother would be safe while I traveled to Worcester, Massachusetts, to start my academic career.

Although I had witnessed the suffering and deaths of my grandmother, grandfather, and father in less than 5 years, I was never to have any serious illnesses. In fact, as you will read, I chose extremes in military service.

The life of that strong, indestructible Craig Jordan was all to change in 2018.

Life is what happens to you when you are making plans to do something else!

The year was 2018. I found myself, during the night, in the emergency room of my primary care physicians hospital in the Texas Medical Center, Houston. For the past year, I had been treated for hypertension, and because I had dangerously elevated red cell counts, I was having a unit of blood drawn at monthly intervals. Then I coughed up blood during the night and called my Breast Medical Oncology Fellow, Balkees Abderrahman for advice. "I will get you an Uber and we will go to the emergency room," she decided. I was met there by my primary care physician who had a chest X-ray taken followed by a whole body scan. My doctor stated I was to be checked into their "Presidential suite" for the night, and we would discuss this in the morning. He went home.

Dr Abderrahman assumed command once my physician had left. She demanded to see my X-rays and scans. She came into the room I was occupying in the emergency room, with tears in her eyes, and showed me my X-ray. There were large white

Telegraphic Address: 'STADIUM' Manchester
Telephone: 061-872 1661/2

MANCHESTER UNITED Football Club Ltd
OLD TRAFFORD, MANCHESTER
M16 0RA

Manager:
F. O'FARRELL.

Secretary:
L. OLIVE.

LO/AC

19th November 1971

Mr. P. Mottram
Dalraeg Nursing Home
Chester Road
Hazel Grove
Stockport
Cheshire

Dear Mr. Mottram,

We have had a telephone call informing us that you have been taken to hospital and we are sorry to learn about this. Mr. Edwards, Sir Matt and everyone at Old Trafford have asked me to send best wishes for a speedy recovery and hope it will not be too long before you are out and about again.

With kindest personal regards.

Yours sincerely,

Leslie Olive

Secretary

FIGURE 3

Grandfather was a shareholder and lifelong supporter of Manchester United football team. For every home game at Old Trafford, he invited three of his friends to accompany him to sit in the stands to watch the game with others of the Manchester United family.

dots all over both lungs; my first reaction was F#*K, I have never been a smoker and I have lung cancer! The whole body scan revealed a fist-sized tumor on my right kidney pressing into my liver. I had stage IV renal cancer. From recollections of my lectures to medical students at Wisconsin in the 1980s, this was rapidly fatal.

The next day I immediately contacted my friend and colleague Dr Christopher Logothetis, the Chairman of Urology at the MD Anderson Cancer Center. He was already monitoring indolent, noninvasive prostate cancer with regular PSA determinations. He passed me as a patient to the Deputy Chair of Urology Dr Nizar Tannir who immediately organized my treatment plan starting with removal of my right kidney by Dr Christopher Wood. I had an excellent result and rapidly recovered, but now for the plan to destroy the metastases in my chest and beat the odds of certain death.

Immunotherapy was tried first. I should mention that Drs Jim Allison and Tasuku Honjo, Kyoto, Japan, had just received the Nobel Prize for their pioneering work. Jim is a colleague at MD Anderson. By another strange coincidence Dr Hanjo, the corecipient from Japan, had just presented the Craig Jordan lecture in Translational Research at the Weatherall Institute at Oxford that I endow to "encourage young medical scientists to excel."

Progress was made for the first few months but, the severe gastrointestinal side effects I had recurrently during therapy saw me regularly in the emergency room. I refused to stop work, and my administrative assistant Vickie had to get me to the emergency room on more than one occasion. Then one weekend, my rounding junior physician, for emergency room inpatients, decided to put me out of my misery with large injections of a glucocorticoid. The immunotherapy was terminated, and I was sent home. However, I was not finished with the glucocorticoids because once high-dose therapy is initiated, one cannot just stop; one has to go through weeks of dose deescalation!

High-dose glucocorticoids makes the patient hyperaware of their surroundings and an insomniac. I had spent 2 years at the Worcester Foundation (1972–74) in Massachusetts as a visiting scientist. This is the home of the oral contraceptive and was a world center for steroid hormone research. It was here that I learned, that during World War II, one of the cofounders of the Worcester Foundation had worked on the application of glucocorticoids to aid American bomber pilots stay awake on night missions from Britain to bomb German war production facilities.

Once I had returned home to recuperate, I discovered that I could not sleep and decided to go down to the ground floor of my home, where I had commissioned workmen to build my library. I had 5000 hardback books on science (a minority) or the history of nations and warfare over the past 4000 years. I would sort out and create my new library. This frenzied activity lasted for weeks, as I titrated myself off the glucocorticoids every 10 days. The Craig Jordan library is an accomplishment to be proud of in this time of therapeutic side effects!

Next Dr Tannir tried targeted therapies. We made further progress with the destruction of some of my metastases in my chest. I should mention that in the summer of 2019, I was appointed as Companion of the Most Distinguished Order of St.

FIGURE 4

In November 2019, I was presented with my Companion of the Most Distinguished Order of St. Michael and St. George by William, the Duke of Cambridge in Buckingham Palace.

Michael and St. George for services to women's health by Her Majesty Queen Elizabeth II. My two daughters Helen and Alexandra and Dr Abderrahman (one is permitted only three guests) attended the ceremony at Buckingham Palace. My neck badge was presented by Prince William (Fig. 4), and we had an excellent conversation about his mother, Diana, Princess of Wales whom I had met, corresponded with and, upon her death, I held the Diana, Princess of Wales Professorship in Cancer Research, at Northwestern University, Chicago. My Palace visit was made wearing a "nappy" to avoid any "accidents" at the palace or celebrations at the Savoy, my favorite London hotel.

Once back in Houston Dr Abderrahman planned to stay one trial ahead of my cancer. She found a new trial in radiotherapy, designed to use an investigatory agents to facilitate the immune destruction of my metastases following low-dose field radiation to my chest for a few days. She forced me to sign a consent form. Never in a million years could anyone have foreseen the coronavirus pandemic hitting the

United States with such savagery. My disease became resistant to the targeted therapy with Dr Tannir and clinical trials closed down. ONLY consented patients would be considered for new and ongoing trials. Thank you Dr Abderrahman!

My doctor Jim Welsh, a radiotherapist, destroyed two "angry" lymph nodes that had declared themselves in my chest. The introductory treatment cycles were beneficial, but a mass behind my fifth left rib was also biopsied and destroyed with radiotherapy. All was going well but all good things come to an end, and the treatment was no longer effective. I returned to Dr Tenir who again put me on different targeted therapies.

Dr Tannir and Dr Abderrahman continued to discover new treatment approaches. We made excellent progress with large regressions of my lung metastases, and we killed off a bone metastasis in my sacrum with radiotherapy. However, I was humbled by a turn of events for which one could never anticipate or planned. An eminent scientist at Cornell in New York, Dr Caliphano, was contacted by Dr Abderrahman. He had published curative procedures for solid cancers in prestigious journals. He volunteered to assist MD Anderson with these words: "I do not do this as a rule, but I volunteer to help Dr Jordan beat his renal cell carcinoma as he has saved the lives of millions of women with breast cancer." It is August 21, 2021, and I am in New York for biopsies. I will be their first renal carcinoma patient. He is growing my renal carcinoma cells, studying the gene abnormalities, and he will complete in vitro and in vivo animal therapeutic studies with known targeted therapies to define the combination that will cure my stage IV renal cell carcinoma. The battle to destroy my enemy within will continue and as my Regimental Motto states: "Who Dares Wins."

So how did a schoolboy of modest/poor academic achievements at Neville Road County Primary School and Moseley Hall Grammar School in Cheshire become Professor V Craig Jordan CMG, OBE, PhD, DSc, FMedSci, member of the National Academy of Sciences, and National Academy of Medicine, honorary fellow of the Royal Society of Medicine, Dallas/Ft. Worth Living Legend Chair of Cancer Research, Department of Breast Medical Oncology, MD Anderson Cancer Center, Houston, Texas, at the top cancer center in the World? This is that story, with a subsequent distillation of Scientific Survival Suggestions, intended to advise anyone with the courage and determination to succeed in their chosen career.

What follows is the story of how I was guided through life by my teachers and how I applied my knowledge and imagination to educate scores of talented graduate students, postdoctoral fellows, and overseas visiting professors who changed medicine multiple times. We must now begin at the beginning.

Beginnings

The Mottrams are an ancient family from North Cheshire. The word means "meeting place" in Anglo Saxon and the Town of Mottram-St. Andrew is but a short distance from Wilmslow where our journey begins (Fig. 1.1).

My mother, Sybil Cynthia Mottram, was born in Wilmslow on May 17, 1921, to Edith Mottram and her husband James Frederick Mottram (born September 9, 1894,

FIGURE 1.1

The date of foundation for Mottram-St. Andrew as recorded on the village sign post is 1086. My own coat-of-arms is based on the Mottram coat-of-arms and is recorded as seen at the beginning of this book, at the Royal College of Arms in London.

Tamoxifen Tales. https://doi.org/10.1016/B978-0-323-85051-3.00001-4

FIGURE 1.2

On the left: My mother as a teenager on the tennis courts next to her home at 4 Kings Close, Wilmslow, Cheshire. On the right: Outside Grandfather's home at Kings Close, Wilmslow. A very happy home. My mother was 14 years old when she lived there, now demolished. Left to right: Helen Melyssa Yovonne Jordan, Alexandra Katherine Louise Jordan, myself, my mother (January 26th, 1990).

in Wilmslow). She grew up in Wilmslow having the advantage of tennis courts alongside the Mottram house at 4 Kings Close (Fig. 1.2). She was the Captain of the Wilmslow women's tennis team, and I grew up with her retelling whom she beat, when, and in what final, as we met other mothers out shopping.

My grandfather served in the Cheshire Regiment in World War I (see Chapter 9 "Sliding Door"). He found himself in Officer's training school and then assigned to the Regimental Headquarters at Chester Castle in 1917. Grandfather would train the musketry instructors. This meant that continuous classes of soldiers would be trained to perfection in the skills necessary to kill up to a mile away from the rifleman. The skill of the British soldier, at the time, was legendary. Four rounds a minute, each to hit a human target at half a mile was required. Often the soldiers could achieve hits regularly at 1 mile.

My mother informed me that Grandad only survived World War I because his mother (Old Granny) had given him such a tough upbringing. Old Granny had a tough upbringing herself. At the age of 15, she was left in charge of bringing up the other children when her parents died suddenly.

With the coming of World War II (1939–45), Grandfather was called again, but this time to be the training officer with the newly formed Home Guard in Wilmslow and Alderley Edge. My mother, by contrast, volunteered for the fire service to be a dispatch control officer. At this time in 1940, there were nightly bombing raids on Manchester and flights of bombers, flew overhead on the way to bomb the docks in Liverpool. Grandfather was routinely leading his men up into the woods around Alderley Edge a prominent craggy rock overlooking the Cheshire plain, to hunt down reported parachutists. None were found! Undaunted, they would regroup to "defend" the pub called the Wizard and recount the nights' adventure.

By 1942, the tide had turned in favor of the Allies (Great Britain, the countries of the Empire, the United States, Free France, and Russia). Russians were getting the edge of the invading German troops, and General Erwin Rommel (the Desert Fox) had been defeated at the battle of El Alamein in North Africa. This had prompted Prime Minister Winston Churchill to remark: "This is not the end or the beginning of the end, but it is perhaps, the end of the beginning." After El Alamein, the British never lost a battle. Italy was invaded by the allies, the Italians surrendered, but the resourceful German army poured troops into Italy and started a stubborn defense around Monte Cassino in mid-Italy.

The all-important second front was anticipated to be initiated to invade France across the English Channel. Hundreds of thousands of American troops poured into Southern England to train and prepare for the biggest seaborne invasion in history. But the German high command had already prepared a double-defensive strategy. German scientists created the V-1, a flying rocket plane full of explosive that would be "pointed" over the English Channel at London. Once the V-1 ran out of fuel, death would rain from the sky. The next surprise was the V-2, the first true ballistic missile that would fly too high for effective defense. Indeed, this was such a successful technological innovation that, at the end of the war in 1945, Werner von Braun, the head of the German missile program and his scientists, would negotiate to surrender their secrets and to go to Huntsville, Alabama! There they would establish the American space program in rocket technology that would result in the first men landing on the moon on July 20, 1969. By coincidence, my eldest daughter Helen went to work in a radiostation in Huntsville. We went around the space museum there—well worth a visit.

In 1944, clearly, a plan was needed for the fire service to protect the south of England and London effectively. The call went throughout England for fire service teams to volunteer to come south. My mother stepped forward to take her unit of 20, as she put it, "girls" from Wilmslow to Bray, outside London. But the plan was to go horribly wrong.

In Cheshire, the fire service dispatchers knew all the roads and routes to get the fire engines to where the bombs were falling. They knew the roads of Cheshire like the back of their hand. The firemen could phone back to base from a telephone box and inquire if they were getting close. The reply would be: "Yes, keep going down the road lined with trees until you get to the *Old Admiral Rodney Pub*, take a left and the bombs were reported to fall a mile down that road." Not so outside London. The dispatchers have no local knowledge, and they could not even learn any, as all road signs have been removed just in case the Germans had invaded England after 1940. This followed the evacuation of the army from Dunkirk earlier the same year. Mother's unit was told to occupy a large country house and "stay out of the way." But this comical situation turned into my beginning.

In the manor house next door (well, a mile or so away on another country estate) stationed an American Combat Engineer's Unit. Here my mother met Master Sargent Virgil Walter Johnson from Dallas, Texas. His unit was training for D-day. After several false starts, he and his unit landed in France on D+3 i.e.,: 3 days after the initial D-day landing. However, it was not easy going for the troops who had landed on the first 2 days as they had not yet got off the beaches, and the Germans were continuing to put up fierce resistance. To give you an idea of the intensity of fighting, I suggest watching "Saving Private Ryan." This was D+3!

Virgil returned after the intense fighting in Normandy to marry my mother at Wilmslow Parish Church, Cheshire on November 1, 1944. I was interested to discover, on the their marriage certificate, that my father-to-be's cousin Lieutenant Luther Trammel was a witness at the ceremony. We will meet the Trammel's from Houston, Texas, again. Virgil returned to France and found himself in the Battle of the Bulge; the last throw of the dice by the Germans to defend their Western border. This huge attack by the German army nearly succeeded but for three factors: (1) the German tanks ran out of fuel, (2) the bad weather prohibited allied air reconnaissance, but when the skies cleared and the German tanks were discovered and destroyed, (3) America's best fighting General, George Patton saved the defending and retreating American forces.

Going to America

With the war ending, my mother, as the wife of an American serviceman, left the fire service and planned her great adventure. Two things stuck in my mind of the stories she told. When asked what was her most memorable accomplishment in the war, without a moment's hesitation she replied: "I brought back my 20 girls to Cheshire with no pregnancies or VD!" What about arriving in America? "We first stayed on a ranch in Texas that had a peach orchard. I had not seen fresh fruit for 6 years and I had never eaten a peach; I ate peaches all day and I was in heaven!" (Fig. 1.3).

Virgil became a manager for the Chambers of Commerce in towns around Texas. Their Odyssey began in Virgil's home town of Dallas and then went consecutively over the 5 years (1945–50) to Mount Pleasant (East Texas), New Braunfels (near San Antonio), Wellington (the panhandle), and finally Houston.

I was born in New Braunfels, Texas, in the hospital at 5:25 a.m. on July 25, 1947. The hospital was demolished a year later, as it was no longer suitable to be a hospital so things were a little primitive. This was an original settlement from Braunfels in Germany sponsored by Count von Braunfels who wished to start communities on land he purchased in America to ease the problems of overpopulation and famine back in his lands in Germany. The attending physician at my birth was Dr. Karbach

FIGURE 1.3

My mother in her new life in Texas. Lower right: This image always reminded me of my time in Texas, as I was growing up. I did not remember anything of my first 3 years of life, but this image spoke to me with a favorite toy.

(I later found, on a visit to New Braunfels in the 1990s, Dr. Karbach's faded name on the door in town) who proclaimed: "What a beautiful German boy with long blond hair!" Having experienced the war, my mother heaved herself up from her bed and retorted: "He is not German, he is English." It was unclear to my mother, during her time in New Braunfels, that the inhabitants were not sure that the correct side had won! In 2010, I, with a German colleague Professor Hiltrud Brauch, went on a visit to Braunfels near Frankfurt in Germany. This is a beautiful (rebuilt) town and well worth a visit for a day! (Fig. 1.4).

My mother told of the difficult climate in Texas and how she missed the gentle breezes and green of the English countryside. Instead, she was sheltering from tornadoes, with me, in the storm cellar and terrible thunderstorms. What did seem exciting to me was the fact that in one house she could go on the land at the rear of our house and find Indian arrowheads; now that sounds great to any child!

By 1949, my mother was no longer able to continue in her marriage and she filed for divorce in Houston while staying with Luther and Loraine Trammel (Fig. 1.5). Decades later, Luther told me he carried a pistol when he drove my mother to the airport. Perhaps, Virgil would not surrender his son. However, he never made any effort to contact me. I believe this was a good thing as I was supposed to spend

FIGURE 1.4

The beautiful town of Braunfels in Germany where Hiltrud Brauch and I went for a day's adventure. Over the years we went on many adventures throughout Europe but none more challenging that a march along the 100 miles of Hadrian's Wall. This defensive wall in what is now the border between England and Scotland, was a defensive measure by the Romans to keep out the northern Celtic tribes. The total journey from coast to coast takes approximately 5 or 6 days with daily intermediate overnight stops.

3 months in the summers with him. He chose Thailand and two more marriages. He died in 1990 and is buried in a military cemetery outside Dallas.

My mother and I returned to England, with me having no recollection of these events. I took with me three books: (1) Johnny Appleseed, (2) a child's book on New York with prominent yellow cabs (my favorite color), and (3) a book about red squirrels. The sea voyage back to England was unknown to me (Fig. 1.7), but my mother told me that for breakfast everyday, I asked for "I ceem, I ceem." I love ice cream to this day. On arrival in England, we were met by my grandfather and grandmother in Southampton and taken to visit London. Stories would be retold, and a single photograph would become part of my family history in the 21st century. We went to Westminster Abbey and, apparently, I wandered off and got lost. No one could find me until someone had the bright idea to look behind a curtained alcove. There I was sitting on the Coronation Throne as natural as can be.

Outside Westminster Abbey, on the way back to our hotel, grandad decided to have a family photograph to record our visit for posterity (Fig. 1.8). Many street photographers were available to the tourists. We were not to know that, half a century

FIGURE 1.5

A historic family photograph in London. The saga begins when I received an early morning call in Madison, Wisconsin, from Luther Trammel (far left). Though we have never met, my mother had tracked the Trammels down (Loraine between my mother, next to Luther and Jack Baker far right) while I was in Bern, Switzerland, for a year creating a Ludwig Institute for Cancer Research. It was her intention that I should have someone in America to turn for help if circumstances required that course of action. Luther was my father's cousin (and the best man at my parent's wedding at Wilmslow Parish Church in 1944 in a gap in the fighting in Europe between D-day and the Battle of the Bulge). Based on these heroic efforts by my mother and Luther, I reconnected with my blood family in America. Jack painted my portrait in Fig. 1.6.

later, I was to choose this same spot for photographs, on my 50th birthday and with my daughters twice after I had been honored by Her Majesty Queen Elizabeth II at Buckingham Palace (Fig. 1.9). What better spot than the one recorded after I arrived in England as a 3-year-old Texan in 1950.

My early years in Cheshire

While we were living with my grandparents in Wilmslow at 4 Kings Close, I was christened in Wilmslow Parish Church. One of my mother's selected Godparents was Geoffrey Webster Jordan. This concept of Godparents is to provide security for a child if the parents die. My mother chose a direct route. Within a couple of years, my mother and Geoff Webster Jordan, from Bramhall, Cheshire, got married

FIGURE 1.6

When I was awarded my Doctor of Science degree from the Department of Pharmacology (by examination) in 1985, we considered this to be the pinnacle of my academic career. The DSc is awarded based on your publications in the scientific literature, which is examined by both internal and external members of the academic community. It is usually awarded when the candidate is in their 50s, and Departments in the United Kingdom were judged for academic excellence by the number of Faculty on staff with a DSc. I was 38 years old at the University of Wisconsin as Professor of Human Oncology and Pharmacology. My mother commissioned a portrait in my DSc academic robes with her life-long friend Mr. Jack Baker (see Fig. 1.5) to commemorate the "crossing of the Rubicon" in academic life.

FIGURE 1.7

My mother and I on board a ship on the way to England in 1950 to meet my grandparents in London.

FIGURE 1.8

Top: My first day in England in 1950 with my grandmother, mother, and grandfather photographed outside Westminster Abbey. The line of people can be seen top right waiting to go through the door into the Abbey. This spot became part of my history. Below: Me standing in the same spot outside Westminster Abbey in 1997. Monica and I celebrated my 50th birthday in London, and she recorded me at the same spot as in the top photograph. The lines are longer, visiting the Abbey, and the tree has grown taller!.

FIGURE 1.9

Top: In 2002, Her Majesty, Queen Elizabeth II recognized my contributions to International Breast Cancer Research with the Award of Officer of the Most Excellent Order of the British Empire (OBE). My daughters, Alexandra and Helen, with me holding my OBE in 2002 immediately after my investiture at Buckingham Palace, now "memorializing" the family place outside the Abbey! Below: In 2019, Her Majesty recognized my contributions to Women's Health with the appointment of Companion of the Most Distinguished Order of St. Michael and St. George (CMG). Although the majority of appointees are members of the security services (in my ceremony the head of MI6 was being advanced from CMG to KCMG). To be eligible for a CMG as a British citizen, one has to achieve a "First" in a foreign country. My "First" was Selective Estrogen Receptor Modulators (SERMs) in America (1990s and 2000s).

(Fig. 1.10), not at Wilmslow Parish Church, but at the Stockport Registry Office. It was prohibited to remarry in the high Church of England, as my mother had been divorced. How the Church of England has changed as both the sovereign to be, Charles III who will be head of the Church of England, and his wife are both divorced!

My father in name Geoffrey Webster Jordan lived at 10 Linney Road, near Bramhall Park, but the bungalow was rather small (Fig. 1.10). Two factors changed the future plans for the family, and we stayed in that area near Bramhall Hall: (1) a new primary school was being built in fields at the end of North Park Road and (2) on Central Drive, new houses were being built. The decision was made that I would attend the new Neville Road County Primary School (its badge was a bear rampant chained to a pole—the coat of arms of the Neville family—who were "King makers"), and we would buy a new home at 10 Central Drive. At the back of the houses, there were fields with horses and in the distance was "the Adswood brick works," which would provide hours on fun and adventure for the children of the neighborhood.

My first love, at around 6 years old, was Helen McKay whose parents lived at 1 Central Drive. Her parents would allow her to sleep over at my parent's house when they went out for the evening. In the late evening, Helen and I would talk to each other in loud whispers from our separate bedrooms, and my parents downstairs would continuously tell us to be quiet and "go to sleep!" My first daughter is named Helen.

Years later, when I was at the Royal Military Academy at Sandhurst, doing courses on the Soviet Army over the summer, I reconnected with Helen and her husband who, at the time were both British Airways cabin staff. They invited me round to dinner after picking me up in their car at Sandhurst. I will never forget their back bedroom that was piled full of drinks "liberated" from the planes! The evening did not go well. It turned out that Helen had decided views on the military establishment and its relevance in the 1970s. Clearly, that would not have worked for the life I had before me!

We had a small black-and-white TV at 10 Central Drive, and we held a party for our neighbors to watch the coronation of Queen Elizabeth II at Westminster Abbey in 1953. More than once, my mother noted "Craig has sat on the Coronation throne." Who would have ever predicted that my mother and I would visit Buckingham Palace in 2002 for me to be presented with my Officer of the Most Excellent Order of the British Empire (OBE) for services to international breast cancer research from Her Majesty Queen Elizabeth II?

Growing up in Bramhall

With social progress comes change, and so it was in rural Bramhall. The bombed houses of central Manchester were being leveled, and the change in the 1950s was the relocation of the population to the rural suburbs. It was social integration

FIGURE 1.10

Left: My mother and soon-to-be stepfather Geoffrey Webster Jordan at the Deanwater Hotel in Adlington, outside Wilmslow in Cheshire. They were required to have a civil ceremony, as the Church of England did not permit the marriage of people, following divorce, in church. Right: The Jordan Wedding Group at the Deanwater Hotel reception. Left to right: Wynnie Jordan, wife of Ken Jordan (brother of Geoff center) who is in the back in front of the "matriarch" Bertha Jordan with my "stepfather-to-be" Geoffrey Jordan. To the right of my mother are Mary Jordan and her husband Richard (Dick) Jordan. Their sons Robert and Ian currently live in Prestbury area of North Cheshire. In the early years of the 19th century, the Jordan Family can credit the accomplishments of the London Surgeon Mr. Joseph Jordan for initiating the first medical school, outside London. This was to evolve into the University of Manchester Medical School. I was already endowing prizes, 20 years ago, at the University of Leeds, so I decided to travel to Manchester to offer financial support to the medical school, to have an annual Joseph Jordan Memorial Lecture, to be presented by one of the medicals "Great and the Good" annually. I arrived at the Dean's office to discover there was a bust of Joseph Jordan prominently displayed. A good start I thought. However, without hesitation of discussion, the Dean declined the suggestion as an irrelevant contribution to his medical school. Taken aback, I chose to invest my philanthropy elsewhere (see Chapter 15). Richard and Mary Jordan are the parents of Robert and Ian Jordan, who live in North Cheshire in Prestbury. Robert is the head of the Jordan Family and he has completed a valuable volume of the Jordan Family members over the centuries. The family were originally Huguenots, who, after generations of religious persecutions in France, settled in Manchester two centuries ago. Robert has the original records of Joseph Jordan, the Founder of Manchester Medical School. Family history has it that he declined a knighthood, in favor of a family coat of arms for his blood relatives. He remained unmarried so there were no direct descendants. The family motto is "Arte non vie" (skill and not strength) with a depiction of three knotted ropes on the coat of arms to represent his surgeon's trade (in the early 1800s, a surgeon was not a prestigious profession) to save life. Upon the surprise award of my OBE, for service to international breast cancer

on a national scale. In Bramhall, it was a new housing estate on the fields behind our home at 10 Central Drive. The solution, by my parents, to this dilemma was to plan to move to 13 Central Drive across the road. I was settled at Neville Road County Primary school and it was now 11+ time to decide whether I would go to a grammar school. The grammar schools provided an academic track to "O" levels taken at the age of 16 and depending upon achieving 5 "O" levels, one could stay in school to take three "A" levels and try for a place at the 10 or so universities. Success rates in 1965 were 4 in 100 in my day (it is 60 in 100 today), but the idea of going to university never occurred to me or my parents.

My mother was determined that I should pass the 11+, so she decided that I would go to a tutor in Bramhall Village. Each Saturday morning, I was trained for the English, Mathematics, and General Studies examinations. This was a big help. I passed the 11+ and I went to Moseley Hall Grammar School in Cheadle (Fig. 1.11), but not before fracturing my arm on the new building site for the new housing estate behind our old house at 10 Central Drive! I was swinging under concrete blocks cemented onto small walls in the foundations of the new houses. Unknown to me, the concrete had not set yet and I pulled a concrete block onto me, missing my head by inches, but pining me to the ground. It would have been "end of story!"

I was off to Moseley Hall Grammar School 2 weeks later sporting a broken left arm. Nevertheless, this inconvenience passed quickly, and once the cast was removed, I ensured that my left arm was even stronger than my right. I needed to trust my left arm. It was also then that I decided on a course of action that would prepare me for organization and leadership throughout the rest of my life.

At Moseley Hall Grammar School at the age of 11 in 1958, I discovered a book called the *Small Army* written by Michael Marshal. It was damaged and was being thrown out, so I "liberated" my find. The book tells the story of Guernsey schoolboys who were evacuated to Buxton in Derbyshire, and settled in large, available premises

---

research in 2001, Her Majesty approved my eligibility to create a family coat of arms for myself and my heirs (Helen and Alexandra). As I was adopted by my stepfather Geoffrey Webster Jordan, I was not of the Jordan bloodline, so I set to work with the staff of the Royal College of Arms to create my own coat and motto (depicted within the front cover). It's based on the Mottram coat of arms, my bloodline. The whole process takes 6–9 months to ensure that every fact on the final pigskin (obtained only from the finest French pigs!) is verified as correct. Then for the motto that must not be replicated by any other family for the past 600 years. I devised "per scientium vires," which immediately delighted the staff at the Royal College of Arms as this motto, which means "strength through knowledge," had never before been used in their 600-year history. Clearly, the warriors of old were not impressed by "new knowledge in the world!" I will forever be thankful to Ian Jordan for being with my mother when it was time for her to join her parents in Heaven. Ian had told me how, when he was a small boy, my mother would always make a point of talking to him at family occasions at Mary and Dick's home. I, eventually, arrived in Cheshire, to put my mother's affairs in order; it only seemed appropriate to thank Ian and Patsy with dinner at the Deanwater Hotel, the site of my mother's wedding.

FIGURE 1.11

Mosely Hall Grammar School main building in Cheadle, Cheshire. The school was knocked down to build a sports complex in the 1970s. It is fair to say the Village sports complex is much more popular.

to continue their schooling in safety. They started different gangs with the intent of seeking out spies and collaborators in Guernsey after the war. It was a private army in the making.

In the late 1950s in England, the enemy was Russia, and the fear of nuclear war was real. What if we woke up 1 day and all the adults were gone; how would we survive and become the resistance? I would organize a "*Small Army*," and I took the name Der Dietrich (the Picklock) from the book I had liberated.

My first task was to create an organization: I would be the Colonel, Robert McGregor (major), Andrew Black (Captain), Michael Nash (Lieutenant), Graham Noden (second Lieutenant), the Slea brothers (sergeants), and Adrian Cowen (private). It was an officer heavy army!

I organized a magazine to be typed by Michael Nash's sister, and instructional pamphlets on the weapons we had available to us, i.e.,: our air rifles and pistols. However, we also created a cache of weapons: clubs we called El Cabongs, spears and bows and arrows were all to be hidden in various locations in case of an emergency. Our safe area, to train and if necessary defend, was in a wooded valley by the Ladybrook river in farmland near the Bramhall tennis club and the swimming baths on Bramhall Park Road. During the 4 years of Der Dietrich, we engaged in three battles: the battle of Rushton Drive, the second battle of Rushton Drive, and the battle of Memorial Hill. These battle honors were sewn into the battle standard of Der Dietrich (made from one of my mother's "liberated" silk underskirts). As we advanced into our teens, I organized a more effective defensive force with regular exercises such as "How quickly could we run to the sports shop in Stockport to purchase shotgun cartridges and return?" We were going to be ready.

In the wake of World War II, there were many firearms in our family houses. My grandfather in Wilmslow had his .455 Webley service revolver and ammunition from World War I, his father's .22 target rifle, and Mr. McGregor had a pair of German

Lugers and boxes of 9-mm ammunition. Robert, his son, had a .410 shotgun. We had our weapons, and we would defend our Homeland from Russian invaders. But where to disappear to and become an effective resistance group? The *Small Army* made the decision for us; we would travel to Buxton in time of war and invasion.

We need a medical organization should we be wounded. Bandages and slings were no problem, as I "liberated" a white sheet and ripped it up to create the required medical supplies. However, I decided to go through the drawers in my parents' bedroom just in case there was something I could use in our medical kits. There they were, packets containing waterproof coverings for bandages on the fingers. I liberated the whole box and distributed the contents to the members of Der Dietrich for their medical kits. Then all hell broke loose, as parents in the neighborhood descended on our home at 13 Central Drive. I had never heard of "Durex" (condoms) but was never to forget that evening with angry parents returning the offending "Durexes." Not the sort of thing that was discussed with 12 year olds in Central Drive! On reflection, perhaps it should have been, as three of the girls in the road became pregnant during their teens. The "pill" had yet to arrive in the 1950s but was not intended for schoolchildren.

As we all grew up, year by year, there was never a dull moment in Bramhall. I have lost track of all except two members of Der Dietrich: Adrian Cowan, had a successful career in the local Government in England, but in recent years, he payed me a wonderful compliment: "Thank you for Der Dietrich. I look at all the other children who have wasted their teenage years hanging around shopping centers. You gave us purpose every day." Michael Nash went to university and became a hydrologist in Hong Kong. I visited him there on two occasions: once when I was made an honorary fellow of the Royal Hong Kong Surgical Society and the second time was when "I was a spy for ICI Pharmaceuticals."

The Chinese government was keen to have American scientists visit China in the years after President Nixon and Henry Kissinger surprised the world by embracing China as a counterpoint to the USSR. It was the early 1980s, and I was invited to visit China on a lecture tour for a month. I was a tenured Full Professor at the Wisconsin Comprehensive Cancer Center. Alec Pleuvry, at ICI Pharmaceuticals at Alderley Park, offered to sponsor my visit if I would agree to two requests: find out if the nascent Chinese pharmaceutical industry was planning to flood the market with generic tamoxifen. At that time, all ICI tamoxifen (Nolvadex) was purchased by the Chinese in Hong Kong to treat their patients. The second request was: will you go to Tokyo and we will organize a weekend meeting at the New Ohtani Hotel with all of Japans breast cancer surgeons? Will you be the Keynote speaker?— Yes! In the audience was a breast surgeon Dr. Yiuchi Iino from Gunma University. He told me the following year, when he came to Madison, Wisconsin, for a year to work with my Tamoxifen Team, that at the Tokyo event he decided immediately that "I will go to the Wisconsin Comprehensive Cancer Center to learn from this man and his Tamoxifen Team." And so he did. He became the Chairman of Breast Surgery at Gunma University and President of the Japanese Breast Cancer Society. He was our Tamoxifen Team "point person" for Tamoxifen Team East sending faculty to be trained with me. All (Drs. Takei, Hozumi, Horiguchi, Park, and Lee) became professors in either Japan or South Korea. Dr. Eun-Sook Lee became President of the National Cancer Research Institute and Secretary of the Asian National Cancer Center Alliance in Seoul, South Korea. I have many happy memories of Tamoxifen Team East on the many return visits to Japan and South Korea.

On reflection, my future Tamoxifen Teams (Leeds, Wisconsin, Northwestern University, Fox Chase Cancer Center, Georgetown/Lombardi, and MD Anderson Cancer Center) were a result of my biological father's wandering genes. My mother told me, when she was in her later years, that she and he would walk around the small Texas town, and a train would pass through. He would say "let's jump on and see where it gocs", a philosophy I held in academia for 50 years. My experience by forming Der Dietrich as an 11/12-year-old in Bramhall, Cheshire, taught me leadership of small teams. Most importantly, Mr. Bescoby, my zoology master and school careers master, allowed me to have a science laboratory twice a week at lunchtime to teach other junior boys university-level biochemistry without supervision. Different world. We will meet Mr. Bescoby again soon.

Leeds University: foundation of a career

As a teenager, a love of chemistry and what chemistry could achieve to cure disease drew me toward pharmacology, with a specific interest in cancer therapeutics. My mother, perhaps in a moment of weakness, had allowed me to convert my bedroom into a real chemistry laboratory. On many occasions, an experiment would "get out of hand," and I would have to throw it out of the window and then set about extinguishing the burning curtains! Life was not simple in the Jordan household in Bramhall, Cheshire, but my mother would say "At least we know where he is!" Well, this was only partially true, as one experiment gave me a life-threatening moment.

For reasons that are now unclear, I decided to make chlorine gas. I can say now this in not to be recommended, but living through the "experiment that got out of hand" taught me several important lessons. My intension was to make just a bit (silly) of chlorine to see if the experiment would work, but one cannot make "a bit"—the reaction does not stop! My bedroom filled with the gas quickly, as I again heaved the glassware through the window and ran coughing my lungs out downstairs and into the garden. I have never coughed so violently before or since—it was never to end, or so it seemed. I hooked my arms over the garden gate for support if I should pass out. The first lesson I learned about myself was that I did not panic in a life-threatening crisis, i.e., inhaling significant quantities of a lethal World War I poisonous gas! Chlorine gas was the pioneer chemical weapon created by the German Nobel laureate Fritz Haber who considered war gases to be a "higher form of killing." Chlorine kills by irritating the lungs that respond by filling up with fluid. Hence, you eventually drown. The second lesson I learned was the first-hand experience of chemical warfare—this would give me an invaluable perspective in my "other world" 10 years later as an officer in the Intelligence Corps and then the SAS. Finally, and most importantly "never do that again." Back to the ascent in science.

I had successfully passed the 11+ exam, and I found myself at Moseley Hall Grammar School in Cheadle, Cheshire. However, my parents discovered that if I did not stay in school by not doing well at my "O" levels, I would be deported back to America, as an illegal alien with no work permit. In postwar Britain, it was an unforgiving world, as there were millions of displaced people. If you had no right of citizenship, you were deported to your country of origin. My stepfather solved the problem by adopting me as his legal son. My real father never contacted me but, apparently, led a secretive life in the Far East, but headquartered in Silver Spring, near Washington, D.C. He died in 1990.

It is fair to say that I was not initially successful at Grammar School. I did poorly in the GCE "O" levels with only three passes out of seven subjects. By rights, and I think by law, I was destined to leave school and go into the work force at the age of 16. My three "O"-level subjects were chemistry (of course), French, and Geography. I had secured a chemistry technician's job at Imperial Chemical Industries (ICI) Ltd., Pharmaceuticals Division in Alderley Park near where we lived. However, the gentleman who interviewed me recommended that someway should be found for me to stay for a further 2 years at Moseley Hall and take "A"-level chemistry and also "O"-level physics (I had dropped physics early as it was too mathematical for me). I was excited about becoming a synthetic organic chemist at ICI. Perfect! But how could the Headmaster, Mr. Armishaw at Moseley Hall, be convinced to break the law?! Mr. Armishaw did not stand a chance—against my mother's logic (and charm!). That July in 1963, we had gone to his office. She would guarantee that I would get two more "O" levels at the November 1963 resits, if I could move into the sixth form and do A-level chemistry and O-level physics. "If he could do this," she said "ICI will give him a job as a chemistry technician. He is very good at chemistry. I have allowed him to turn his bedroom into a chemistry laboratory. He collects chemistry books and memorizes university biochemistry books from Stockport library." Mr. Armishaw wisely agreed but I had to do at least two A levels so I selected zoology. I declined botany as I had no interest in plants. On reflection, I believe facing failure at a young age is good. It focuses you to have goals. I now had two academic topics. I liked both chemistry and zoology so that would be the basis of my future career— testing chemicals or medicines in animal models of human disease.

When I was in the lower sixth form (16−17 years old), my careers master and zoology teacher, Mr. Bescoby, provided me with a laboratory and allowed me to teach younger boys biochemistry. I even set examinations, and boys willingly took them! Remarkably, one boy (Andrew Mawson) went into medicine at Leeds Medical School. I very much enjoyed creating and developing my own interests in teaching and leadership.

Mr. Bescoby was an important mentor in my life and recommended to my parents that I should apply for a place at university. In those days, only 4 out of 100 qualified individuals succeeded (today, it is 60 out of 100 qualified individuals). In 1964, Mr. Bescoby chose to enhance my chances for examination success by tutoring me each week on the new science of DNA. In the 1950s, the structure of DNA had been proposed based on X-ray crystallographic results, and these data had been reported earlier in Nature [1,2]. In 1962, Watson, Crick, and Wilkins had received the Nobel Prize for Physiology and Medicine so this was the new "hot topic." He gave me a book to read on DNA and how cells make proteins. I love books, and they are a treasured part of my life.

I received only one invitation for an interview at one university—the University of Leeds Department of Pharmacology to read Special Studies Pharmacy. My academic record was weak, so far, but this was an opportunity. I traveled on the train to Leeds in mid-1964 for my interview at "the old Medical School" in Thoresby Place, next to Leeds General Infirmary. On the train, I read a Penguin paperback called "Organic Chemistry Today" (I still have the paperback book in my library) to focus and gain any new knowledge that might be useful at the interview. I found the Department of Pharmacology, but discovered I was the last to be interviewed and the schedule was already an hour behind. This was a tense time as I had already calculated that I had missed my train back to Stockport Edgeley Station!

After what seemed like hours, it was my turn and I was greeted by two gentlemen, Dr. Edward Clark, senior lecturer in the Department of Pharmacology who was responsible for all Pharmaceutical Chemistry teaching (Fig. 2.1) and Dr. Ronald (Ronnie) Kaye, Head of the Special Studies Pharmacy course at Leeds. The interview did not go well from the start as they asked me about—guess what—physics! I had no idea what they were talking about! But then, Dr. Clark changed tack (he was actually an accomplished yachtsman) and asked me about a chemical reaction. I came alive with excitement and stated "this is my lecture next week in the classes I teach in biochemistry at Moseley Hall during lunchtime." The interview continued for longer than planned as we exchanged chemical knowledge and I returned home—eventually (much to the relief of my mother). I remember the day the letter came to our home one morning. I had received an offer to read for a 4-year course in Special Studies Pharmacy in the Department of Pharmacology. I knew now that I had only to get the grades.

FIGURE 2.1

Dr. Edward Clark, senior lecturer in pharmacological chemistry, the University of Leeds.

In, or around, 1962, a group of classmates at Moseley Hall Grammar School decided to form a rock group. The members were Paul Bygraves (base), myself (drums), John Tabone (lead guitar), and our talented singer and rhythm guitar Bud Mather. We called ourselves "The Top Cats" after a popular children's TV program on the BBC. John's father financed the group with, for example, the purchase of my drum set. All we had to do was play events as often as possible to repay the loan.

We rented space in Cheadle Hulme Parish Hall to practice. I remember the excitement and sense of achievement we experienced, the first time we all started together and all finished together! The song was "Glad all over" by the Dave Clark Five. The total commitment to the group was achieving positive results, and suddenly, we were playing three or four evening a week. Several events will remain in my memory forever in, what I now realize, for me, was a confidence building experience. We featured at many dances at Cheadle Hulme Parish Hall, but for me the memory of starting off our set playing the very popular surfing number "Wipe Out." I would play the opening drum solo as the stage curtains slowly opened. Very exciting with all the teenage girls in the audience screaming!

On another occasion, we were playing at Bramhall Parish Hall when the local newspaper (the Stockport Advertiser) reporter asked me for an interview. He then wanted a photograph for his story, so in an uninhibited moment, I went into the audience and grabbed the hand of a very pretty teenager to be taken with me, to "spice things up" a little! I was thrilled when the story and photograph were published. By contrast, my mother was horrified!—"who is that girl?" I had no idea, but my mother rationalized the family shame, with the words: "well at least you are not wearing your glasses, so no one will know its you!" Not only was I learning teamwork with the group, but also the publicity from being in a group was having its own rewards.

Moseley Hall Grammar School in Cheadle was a boys' school of a thousand pupils. The girls' school was nearby, built about a mile away. One day, as I was walking past the girls school, there was about a dozen teenage girls waiting for a bus, on the other side of the road, to take them home. One shouted out: "That's the drummer from the "Top Cats" and they all screamed! To say I felt thrilled was an understatement! But all good things must come to an end. This was the time that a line in the sand had to be drawn, by my mother.

I had a chance to go to University if I secured the required grades for my entrance examinations. However, my commitment to the Top Cats, with evening performance three or four times a week out until after midnight was not compatible with academic success. On the fateful night, I was challenged by my mother blocking the stairs at home with the words: "University or remain a drummer in a rock group? Decide now." I chose to work toward my one chance to attend university. But what if my mother had not intervened at this moment on the stairs?

The life story you are about to read would not have played out in the way that is now documented and women's health would have evolved in a very different way. There would have been no translational strategy for the treatment and prevention of breast cancer with tamoxifen, no selective estrogen receptor modulators, no understanding of the mechanism of estrogen as an anticancer agent, no understanding of the results of the Women's Health Initiative trial, and no mentoring of talented research student and postdoctoral fellows. On the other hand, the Top Cats may have succeeded, and we would all be fabulously rich and famous internationally! We will never know.

That June in 1965, my school friend Tim Higenbottam and I went to Fishbourne to participate in an archeological dig at the Roman Palace near Chichester on the south coast of England, organized by the famous archeologist Professor Barry Cunliffe (I have retained a passion for history and archaeology all my life). I phoned home to discover I had succeeded with the required grades for Leeds. I had passed the "S"-level zoology exam, and I had won the school prize for zoology. With the money, I bought a chemistry book! Years later in 2013, I arranged to meet Professor (now Sir) Barry on one of my trips to Oxford. We had a wonderful lunch at a seafood restaurant (now sadly disappeared) in Jericho, and we exchanged inscribed books. He is an excellent lunch companion and remains a pillar of the academic archeology community. Tim won his place to Guy's Hospital Medical School (he was also a star rugby player at Moseley Hall Grammar School) and has had a very successful professional career in thoracic medicine with MD and DSc degrees, a Professorship in Medicine at Sheffield University Medical School and election as President of the Faculty of Pharmaceutical Medicine in the UK.

I arrived in Leeds in October 1965 to start my 4-year course, but this was initially daunting as I now had to complete a year of "A"-level physics, which I had never done, competing against over a hundred other students who had done "A"-level physics but had failed to achieve the appropriate grade required for their degree course. I also chose to take the advanced organic chemistry class called 3E that was part of my required course in year 2, and I elected to take 2A biochemistry that was not my degree requirement. Remember, I had been teaching university-level biochemistry at lunchtime at Moseley Hall.

With much effort, I survived the Christmas exams just passing everything, but in the next term, I had doubts about my degree choice for a future career in research. I debated whether I should transfer to take the Pharmacology degree and move away from Special Studies Pharmacy. I consulted my tutor Dr. Kaye, and he agreed to organize a meeting with Dr. George Mogey (Fig. 2.2), the faculty member responsible for admissions to Pharmacology. Dr. Mogey was stern and frightening as he announced over his half-moon glasses, after glancing at my slender academic record, that "I don't think you're good enough!" I rose to my feet and announced that I would come top in the class in 3E organic chemistry (120 students), get a first class pass in 2A biochemistry (100 students), and get the appropriate grade required in physics (100+ students). I turned and then strode out of the room slamming the glass door behind me. Fortunately, it did not smash.

I did all I said I would do in the examinations at the end of the first year, but I had second thoughts about transferring to Pharmacology because—I would do much less synthetic medicinal chemistry and this was my strong suit and passion. When the

FIGURE 2.2

Medean Society meeting. Lecture Theatre One, Old medical school. Speaker Mr. R. R. MacDonald. Front row left to right: Craig Jordan (President), Dr. George Mogey, Dr. Ronnie Kaye, and Teresa McCarthy (Treasurer).

phone call came inviting me to transfer, I decided to decline the enthusiastic offer from the professor of Pharmacology, Derek Wood. After putting the phone down, I realized I had probably made a fatal mistake and lost faculty support. But, as we will see later, I was in for a surprise about the quality and integrity of faculty with high ideals about their responsibilities to guide careers.

Having succeeded in getting into the second year of Special Studies Pharmacy, I found I now had some time on my hands (remember I took 3E organic chemistry a year early). I chose to start a Pharmacology Society for students called the Medean Society (Fig. 2.2) (the sorceress of Greek mythology who provided protective potions for Jason and the Argonauts to complete Jason's tasks). My plan was to recruit professors (heads of departments) or other senior medical researchers from the university, to address us each week, and we would follow that up with tea and biscuits so that we could chat to the "celebrity faculty member" (Fig. 2.3). I would introduce each speaker and lead the questioning after the talk. My first guest was Professor David Clayson, the famous head of the Yorkshire Cancer Research Campaign Laboratories at Leeds and well known for his then recent book on "Chemical Carcinogenesis." I had met him in the summer of 1966 when he allowed me to work with his Ph.D. students on liver carcinogenesis for a summer job. At last, I was doing cancer research! Professor Clayson spoke at the inaugural Medean Society

FIGURE 2.3

Members of Leeds Medean Society's committee (left to right) Messrs. R. Clarke, T. McCarthy, S. Hamilton, D. Bishop, Dr. Nelson, Mr. MacDonald (second from right: our guest speaker Mr. MacDonald with a talk on "Progestins and Endometrial Cancer" who years later would deliver my daughter Alexandra), and Mr. V. Craig Jordan (President).

lecture to a standing-room only audience in lecture theater 1 in the Old Medical School. The Medean Society became a great success during the 1960s at Leeds with a fabulous list of speakers and our annual dinner with the Department of Pharmacology faculty at a hotel in the Leeds City Center.

One talk to our Society made a lasting impression on me. I had recruited a pathologist, from our Chemical Pathology Department, who had published in the Lancet one of the first reports on the effects of thalidomide on fetal development. This was a safe drug to the mother but catastrophic to the developing embryo. It was anti-angiogenic (i.e.,: stopped blood vessel development). Our speaker stated, "you are pharmacologists so 1 day you may be in a leadership position when you see a bad result from a drug you are developing for a company. You must have the courage of your convictions to speak up." My moment in the late 1980s was tamoxifen and endometrial cancer (Chapter 8). My clinical colleagues did not initially embrace the concept that their patients should be prescreened by a gynecologist for uterine problems and endometrial cancer, which would be encouraged to grow during long-term tamoxifen treatment. I spoke up at a major clinical meeting in Bologna, Italy, and this triggered correspondence in the Lancet. Clinical practice changed, and lives were spared.

I learned many lessons in public speaking by introducing faculty at the Medean Society. I would spend the afternoon before our 5 p.m. meeting each Wednesday, memorizing the background education and career path of each celebrity faculty member, but this was not always enough. I recall one occasion, as I was reciting my introduction at the front of the General Lecture Theatre at the old Medical School, my mind suddenly went blank! I am told that I then turned to my right and walked slowly along the back of the front bench and ran my finger along the surface examining it at the end for dust. Afterward, everyone said, "Well, how did you manage to do that, making us all wait for your next words—perfect introduction." I never told anyone it was sheer panic! But I learned—write down prompt word on your hand and **always** have the first sentence for your talk and one word prompts just in case you freeze! I never used a sheet of paper but a small notepaper hidden in my palm. I wanted to develop spontaneity in public speaking.

I had read in the journal *Nature* [3] that a cell biologist named Dr. Steven Carter at ICI Pharmaceuticals division (Alderley Park) had discovered a new class of natural products called cytochalasins. There were several members of the class, but different concentrations would do strange things to mouse L cells (cancer cells): low concentrations would create multinuclear cells, and high concentrations would cause extrusion of the nucleus that was still surrounded by the cell membrane. Put simply, there was a blob of all the cytoplasm surrounded by cell membrane connected by a long thread of cell membrane to the nucleus surrounded by cell membrane. Imagine it looks like a dumbbell under the microscope. I decided to find a way to work with Dr. Carter so I took the bus from my home in Bramhall to Alderley Park near Alderley Edge and phoned him from the phone box outside in the road. I got through and proposed **my** plan to work for him during the summer and he replied "next time you are back in Cheshire come and see me." "I'm outside the front gate of Alderley Park now" I replied, and I was in! It was a great summer experience with the staff and almost daily, lectures on exciting topics in medicinal chemistry. To me, their library at Alderley Park was Aladdin's cave, and I found many medicinal chemistry books I could not live without. I bought copies for my studies at Leeds. I still use them for lectures on the "history of drug development." The time at Alderley Park was enhanced by whom I interacted with each day. Across the corridor from Dr. Carter's laboratory was Dr. Arthur Walpole's (Fig. 2.4) laboratory that was

FIGURE 2.4

Dr. Arthur Walpole, head of the Fertility Control Program at ICI Pharmaceuticals Division Alderley Park, Cheshire.

focused on the endocrinology of reproduction. They had just reported the antifertility properties of the isomers of ICI 46,474 (not known as tamoxifen until the 1970s as it was not destined to be a drug to treat cancer) [4–6]. More importantly, every Friday, the technicians from both Dr. Carter's lab and Dr. Walpole's lab would go to the Alderley Rose, a Chinese restaurant in Alderley Edge. It was fun, and we all got along very well together. Next door to Dr. Carter's laboratory was Dr. Mike Barrett's laboratory. He was studying new β-blockers for heart disease. ICI pharmaceuticals was still focused on β-blockers, initially discovered at Alderley Park by Jim Black later to be Sir James Black—Nobel Laureate. We will meet Mike Barrett and Arthur Walpole again. Nearly 20 years later, Jim Black would successfully nominate me for the Gaddum Award from the British Pharmacological Society in 1993, and in 2015, I received their Sir James Black Award for contributions to drug discovery.

It is sad to say that Alderley Park is now closed, but it gave tamoxifen and I our chance. This leading research center set in the Cheshire countryside gave both Britain and me personally much. An excellent history of Alderley Park is available [7]. A new Molecular and Genetics Research Park has been created outside Cambridge. Alderly Park is a vibrant biotech park.

Postscript on Career Preparation for a Degree in Pharmacy from the Department of Pharmacology at Leeds

My teachers did extraordinary things to help me. At the time, all would have said, and did, that they were only doing their job. This made a lasting impression on me to help the individuals in my Tamoxifen Teams to excel to their full potential. Supporting and investing in people works, but they must be challenged to succeed for their own careers—not feel "just like technicians being told what to do." Opportunity requires their will to win as it is their life.

Mr. Bescoby and Mr. Armishaw at Moseley Hall Grammar School made decisions to help me find my way. Mr. Bescoby gave me the zoology laboratory to teach once a week. I led practical classes alone and set exams. This would not happen today. It was then a trusting, responsible, but competitive world. Now there are constant fears of accidents and liability—different world. Mr. Bescoby tutored me each week in DNA and ensured I could pass the zoology S-level exam. I kept in touch with Mr. Bescoby, over the decades, since I left Moseley Hall to go to the University of Leeds in 1965. I told him of my career ascent and sent him copies of my books on antiestrogens and tamoxifen. The last letter I received from his address in Oldham: "It is very pleasing to me to realize that I have apparently had some little responsibility for your greatly successful career—though I feel that you attribute too much to my influence. I remember one of my own teachers telling me (years later) that as a teacher one could not expect any thanks from one's pupils if they become successful—but in my case he seems to have been wrong.". I chose to dedicate my first molecular biology publication to him. We were the first [8] to stably insert the estrogen receptor (ER) gene into an ER negative breast cancer cell line. Our question was "could the ER again take control of an ER-negative breast cancer cell?" The answer was yes. This led to a whole new biology of estrogen-induced apoptosis. Results, in turn, deciphered the current results of the Women's Health Initiative and aided in the design of better hormone replacement therapies for women around the world. When he died, Mr. Bescoby's daughter found me at Northwestern University in Chicago and told me how proud he had been of the success of my career. I sent my paper to her as I feel strongly that those who made our lives successful should be given the credit publicly

Mr. Bescoby and Mr. Armishaw aided me to get into Leeds University. In those days, letters of recommendations needed to be eye catching—no invitation to interview—no place at university. You will recall that Dr. Kaye and Dr. Clark interviewed me for a place at Leeds. Dr. Kaye later told me that their decision to do that was based on my Headmaster's letter. It started "Craig Jordan is an unusual young man. A VERY UNUSUAL YOUNG MAN." "We just had to interview you to see what that meant," Dr. Kaye said. Years later, when I was surprised and thrilled to receive the first honorary Doctor of Medicine degree from Lord Bragg our chancellor in 2002, I was overjoyed that both Dr. Kaye and Dr. Clark were there to witness the ceremony and to meet my family (Fig. 2.5).

I will now mention the unusual meeting I had at the dinner at Leeds during the evening celebration for my honorary Doctor of Medicine degree. The British have a wonderful tradition of rotating hosts from table to table after each course. In that

FIGURE 2.5

Dr. Clark, Dr. Kaye, and I at the reception prior to the award of my honorary Doctor of Medicine degree in 2001.

way, you meet everyone. I found myself next to a physicist/astronomer from the honorary degree committee and told him my tale of coming to Leeds without A-level physics and how hard it was for me to succeed back in 1965–66. "It was awful," I said "But I got an upper second class pass." He then announced that he, as a new faculty member, had taught that course then, and after the dinner he secured permission to look for and found my marks for the year (1966 1A Physics) with the line across the page by hand that decided the classes of pass. The line passed above JORDAN just keeping me out of a first! Small world! I received the actual record of the marks for my 1A physics final exam in 1966 from the Vice Chancellor of the University of Leeds Sir Alan Wilson (figure following the Foreword from Lord Bragg in the beginning of this book).

Remember Dr. Mogey with me declining the offer to change from Pharmacy to Pharmacology in early 1966? Years later, I accidentally saw a letter he wrote supporting me for a faculty position in the Department of Pharmacology at Leeds in 1972. I was at the Worcester Foundation in America, and they have a freedom of information act that permitted employees, each year, to see their personnel file. There it was, Dr. Mogey's letter that Professor Barrett had used to support my 2 years at the Worcester Foundation as a visiting scientist. Imagine my surprise to learn that not only was he supportive of me joining the faculty as his colleague, but also he had successfully nominated me for an Ackroyd Scholarship from the University that recognized their best and brightest students. For me it was money to buy books but 40 years later, as I was reading the biography of Sir George Porter (Nobel Laureate, 1967), Director of the Royal Institution and regular scientific TV star in the 1960s, I learned that he too had been an Ackroyd Scholar in the chemistry department at Leeds and this had given him a gentle push forward. For me, it was to enhance my self-confidence as I was now starting to receive recognition for my academic success: the zoology prize at Moseley Hall Grammar School and now an Ackroyd Scholarship at Leeds!

I am fortunate to have been given the opportunity in the Department of Chemistry at Leeds University to endow the Jordan Prize in Medicinal Chemistry. The prize is very important to me as I have great respect for, and very happy memories of chemistry at Leeds. The prize is awarded annually to the best student with this process arranged by my late friend and research colleague Professor Ron Grigg, FRS. Remarkably, the Prize would reconnect with me years later.

In closing the reflections on my years as an undergraduate, I wish to recount the process required for a path to progress to the next stage. I believe in a competitive process that is defining. Only by selecting the best, can our society succeed. At Leeds University in the 1960s, there was a week of examinations for your finals; the grade for which, would define the course of the rest of your life. In the case of Special Studies Pharmacy, this was a total of six daily 3-hour exams (no multiple choice but the choice to answer three essay questions with 1 h writing for each). The exams finished on Saturday lunchtime. It was very competitive with only the top few percent getting a first class pass. It was said a "First" opened all the doors, and I needed a "First" in Special Studies Pharmacy to get a grant from the Medical

Research Council to read for a PhD. On the last day of exams, it was pharmaceutical chemistry with the compulsory "drug degradation analysis" question. I could usually do these in my head, but this time the answer was a structure of a drug I had never seen before. The drug, in my experience, did not exist, so—do not panic—answer the other two selected questions and come back and try again. Horror, same answer as before, but I described it on paper and then those terrible words "stop writing." I was very angry that, in my mind, I was going to fail and not get the required "First" class honors degree. Then it was the wait in the run up to the obligatory *viva* by a Professor from another University who established fair play and set standards of excellence. The *viva* could raise your grade, but never lower it. It was the time to clarify the words in your answers. Obviously, it was my time to correct my answer of the drug analysis question—but I could not recognize my answer as any drug I knew! The *viva* committee ushered me in and the question was "what do you consider to be the future major advances in pharmacology"? After 15 min of oration, I was asked to leave in my now confused state. Over lunch, one of my cancer research Ph.D. student friends, Terry Lawson (who went on to be a professor at the University of Nebraska Medical Center Eppley Cancer Center) said simply "Because you have got a 'First.'" That afternoon, the final year students all gathered in the pharmaceutical chemistry laboratory to go through the archaic system of publically reading out the results in alphabetical order. JORDAN, VIRGIL CRAIG (short pause) FIRST.

I immediately found Dr. Clark to find out what the "mystery drug" was in his examination question. I explained it was no drug I had ever seen. He replied—" Exactly! For the first time, we decided to create a compound in the question that did not exist. This would be the reality in research. You were exactly right." This is another lesson in the confidence to excel by performance under stress.

References

[1] Watson JD, Crick FH. Genetical implications of the structure of deoxyribonucleic acid. Nature 1953;171:964−7.

[2] Watson JD, Crick FH. Molecular structure of nucleic acids: a structure of deoxuribose nucleic acid. Nature 1953;171:737−8.

[3] Carter SB. Effects of cytochalasins on mammalian cells. Nature 1967;213:261−4.

[4] Harper MJ, Walpole AL. Contrasting endocrine activities in cis and trans isomers in a series of substituted triphenylethylenes. Nature 1966;212:87.

[5] Harper MJ, Walpole AL. A new derivative of triphenylethylene: effect on implantation and mode of action in rats. J Reprod Fertil 1967;13:101−19.

[6] Harper MJ, Walpole AL. Mode of action of I.C.I. 46,474 in preventing implantation in rats. J Endocrinol 1967;13:83−92.

[7] Hill GB. Alderley park discovered. Lancaster, UK: Carnegie Publishing Ltd; 2016.

[8] Jiang SY, Jordan VC. Growth regulation of estrogen receptor-negative breast cancer cells transfected with complimentary DNAs for estrogen receptor. J Natl Cancer Inst 1992;84: 580−91.

The chance to be a Ph.D. student at the University of Leeds

3

In the late 1960s, cancer therapeutics was not a popular choice for a career and, in my case, would require some effort to become involved with the science behind developing drugs to treat cancer. There was little or no interest, either in academia or in the pharmaceutical industry. However, in 1969, armed with a First Class Honors degree from the Department of Pharmacology at the University of Leeds and supported by a research scholarship from the Medical Research Council (incidentally, someone declined their scholarship and I was elevated from the waiting list to the last funded student at the last minute—it was an opportunity!). I had had three opportunities to read for a Ph.D.: after my results in the chemistry courses, I was considering organic chemistry but decided against it because there was no immediate application to cancer treatment. I interviewed with Professor David Clayson, the Director of the Yorkshire Cancer Research Center at Leeds University, but he felt it was inappropriate to "steal me" from the Department of Pharmacology. I decided to study the estrogen receptor (ER) with Dr. Edward Clark (Fig. 2.1) in the Department of Pharmacology at the University of Leeds. Remember? He interviewed me to be an undergraduate in 1964.

Dr. Jack Gorski in the United States had published an exciting series of reports [1,2] showing that the ER could easily be extracted from the rat uterus and isolated by sucrose density gradient analysis. Dr. Clark filled me with enthusiasm for his proposal because he pointed out the ER was the only extractable drug receptor; all others were membrane bound. My project was going to be simple: I was to establish the new technique of sucrose density gradient analysis, isolate the ER, and crystallize the protein with an estrogen and an antiestrogen. Through X-ray crystallography in the Astbury Department of Biophysics at the University of Leeds, we would then establish the three-dimensional shape of the complexes to explain antiestrogenic action. The goal was to solve a fundamental question in pharmacology: What is the molecular mechanism of action for a drug?

Progress was slow in establishing the receptor purification technique of sucrose gradient analysis, and I switched my thesis topic to study the structure–activity relationships of antiestrogens. As it turned out, this was a good strategic decision, as it took the best efforts of the research community nearly 30 years to achieve partial success! The structure of the ligand-binding domain of the ER complexed with either estradiol or the antiestrogen raloxifene was solved by Dr. Rod Hubbard and scientists at York University, England, in 1997 [3]. However, the whole ligand ER complex has yet to be crystallized and resolved.

Tamoxifen Tales. https://doi.org/10.1016/B978-0-323-85051-3.00003-8

29

In 1972, there was little academic interest in the pharmacology of antiestrogens. Enthusiasm in the pharmaceutical industry had chilled because these drugs had not fulfilled their promise as contraceptive "morning after" pills. In fact, they did the exact opposite in subfertile women; they induced ovulation, and the women could then become pregnant [4,5] (obviously with help from a friend!). This was not the plan for the pharmaceutical industry as the market was so small and another medicine clomiphene was already the standard of care for the previous 10 years. It was clear that no one was recommending antiestrogen research as a sound career choice; it was perceived as a dead end. To make matters worse, the University of Leeds encountered difficulty in securing a qualified examiner for my thesis. Sir Charles Dodds, the discoverer of the synthetic estrogen, diethylstilbestrol (DES) [6], declined, with regrets, because he had not kept up with literature during the 20 years since his retirement. If only I had kept that letter! This led the Chairman of the Department of Pharmacology, Professor Barrett (he had moved from industry at ICI to be my future Head of Department), to suggest Dr. Arthur Walpole (Fig. 2.4), the Head of Fertility Control Research at ICI Pharmaceutical Division. As you recall, Michael Barrett had worked at ICI Pharmaceuticals with Walpole. I had met Dr. Walpole previously in 1967 when I was a summer student at ICI's Alderley Park, Cheshire. Thus, indirectly, the door was opened for the future development of ICI 46,474 into tamoxifen.

I was recruited to a tenure track faculty position at the University of Leeds in 1972 when I was still a graduate student, but I was first required to obtain additional research experience elsewhere. Professor Barrett solved this problem by arranging for me to work with Dr. Michael Harper (Fig. 3.1) at the Worcester Foundation

FIGURE 3.1

Dr. Michael J. K. Harper, reproductive endocrinologist in contraception program at ICI Pharmaceuticals, Alderley Park and the Worcester Foundation, Shrewsbury, MA.

for Experimental Biology in Massachusetts. Dr. Harper is a reproductive biologist, who, some years earlier, had worked with Dr. Arthur Walpole at ICI Pharmaceuticals Division. He is also the copatent holder for ICI 46,474 [7—9]. However, at that time, Dr. Harper was heading a team at the Worcester Foundation working on the potential of prostaglandins to be used as a "once-a-month" contraceptive pill. I remember the transatlantic telephone call when he offered me a 2-year Visiting Scientist job: "… can you come in September, will $12,000 a year be OK, and will you work on prostaglandins … ?" "YES, YES, YES" I said and headed for the library to find out what prostaglandins were!

Not to repeat the story in Chapter 9, I was as a Captain, Technical Intelligence Staff Officer, in the Intelligence Corps with a Top Secret security classification. I was also, technically an American citizen born in New Braunfels, Texas of an American father Virgil Walter Johnson, adopted by my British stepfather Geoffrey Webster Jordan, thereby also giving me British nationality.

On learning of my required 2-year Visiting Scientist position at the Worcester Foundation for Experimental Biology in Shrewsbury, MA, I called the US Consulate in Liverpool for guidance "do I travel on a renewed American passport or on my British passport?"

The Vietnam War was still winding down, and the telephone call went something like this: "Hello, my name is Virgil Craig Johnson and I am on the faculty of the University of Leeds. I am required to spend 2 years as a Visiting Scientist at the Worcester Foundation in Massachusetts and then return to my Faculty appointment at the University of Leeds." After a long pause the unemotional male voice replied "We were waiting for you to call." Although I had an enormous urge to put the phone down, I persisted with my dual nationality status and then declared my officer status in the British Intelligence Corps with Top Secret security clearance. The voice replied: you must immediately resign your commission in the British Army. If you do not, we will take away your US citizenship as a result of your service "in the Army of a foreign power."

Although this all seemed reasonable if I was serving in an East European army in the Warsaw pact, rules were rules. The commandant of the Intelligence Corps supported my action to "deswear my allegiance to the American Flag." This occurred in the American Consulate in Liverpool with my official letter from the Intelligence Corps confirming my military status in the British Army on the staff of the Deputy Chief Scientist (Army) at the Ministry of Defense. I would travel to America on a visitor's visa and retain my Reserve Officer status of call up in the time of war, while I was in America. As you will see, I used this time wisely with the American Army, but they only let me have "Secret" security clearance with their forces!

With a 2-year position assured at the WFEB, I decided to use all my savings to travel first class to New York on the QEII with my wife Marion. We were going to arrive in style for this adventure. I completed my Ph.D. thesis by essentially working 20 h a day 7 days a week (I also had to spend a week at the Porton Down Chemical Defense Establishment to complete my military service, see Chapter 9). I drove over to the Alderly Park one Friday to deliver my manuscript to Dr. Walpole in his laboratory but he was not there! Fortunately, one of his staff offered to take my precious thesis manuscript to his home.

My whole-day examination with Drs. Walpole, Clark, and Barrett went smoothly but became rather stressful as the hours passed. Professor Barrett then got up and returned with a bottle of sherry and glasses—he had had enough of "failed contraceptives"—I had passed. Now my wife and I were off to America on the QEII. But out of the blue, other complications occurred upon which we had not planned: family tragedies, nationality issues, and most importantly my wife was pregnant!

At Easter, earlier in the year, my grandfather had died of colon cancer after a long illness, and in June, my father had died unexpectedly from a heart attack as he was being discharged hospital after a weeks' observation. Now I was off to America with no health insurance in place and no medical infrastructure equivalent to the National Health Service. But solutions were on the way.

My mother was about to find herself alone with all her family now gone. Then came a surprise that occurred when I was visiting my mother in Cheshire. A car drew up to the house and a spritely gentleman jumped out of his car and exclaimed "Hellow Motty!" This was Jack Baker her friend from their World War II days in the North Cheshire Fire Service (see Prelude and Chapter 1).

They grew old together reminiscing about times past in "the war."

My mother solved the problem for Marion and I, concerning medical care in America. As luck would have it, my mother's friends were traveling first class on the QEII as well (what are the chances of that?). They were visiting their daughter, Libby, who was married to an American doctor—an obstetrician in Boston. It turned out that he had a colleague who he trained with at the Boston Lying-In Hospital. He was just finishing 2 years of research at the Worcester Foundation! Dr. Tom Pokoly and I became friends and eventually published two papers on circulating prostaglandins and the menstrual cycle [10] and during vaginal delivery and caesarian section [11]. I went to dozens of midnight sessions to collect samples with Tom to be analyzed at the Worcester Foundation laboratories. Tom delivered Helen Melissa Yvonne Jordan on April 11, 1973, at the Memorial Hospital, Worcester, Massachusetts.

The voyage to America on the QEII was uneventful, and toward the end of the 5-day "captivity," I was glad to be getting off. However, one activity engaged me daily. The ship provided trap shooting for passengers by hurling traps over the side of the ship. I had never used shotguns, but I had considerable experience with combat shooting with the Army (see Chapter 9). Each day I practiced and found my stride before the competition for a trophy on the day before we docked in New York. However, I had not anticipated the competitive nature on the male sportsmen in their 70s as we all assembled to do battle. I, at the time, was 25 years old. I rapidly discovered that a complaint had been lodged with the ship staff that "it was inappropriate for the ships security officer to be competing with the paying passengers." It was well known that Cunard had increased security on their ships after there had been a bomb threat on the transatlantic voyage of QEII the previous year. The Royal Air

Force sent out a plane and dropped members of the Special Air Service (SAS) and a bomb disposal team. Nothing was found and no one at that time had any idea who the SAS were as it was below the radar in 1972. All that was to change in 1980 when the SAS resolved the Iranian Embassy Hostage situation in London. This was made into an excellent film recently called "5 Days." I recommend the film highly. We will meet the SAS again in Chapter 9.

Yes, I won the trap shooting competition and received a fine QEII beer tankard. As it turns out, Cunard was making a publicity film to entice passengers to take the 5-day cruise option in the age of Concord and jumbo jets. As the winner of the trap shooting competition, I was requested to destroy clays in flight that purportedly had been done on camera by a scantily clad model. "Only too happy to help!"

References

[1] Toft D, Gorski J. A receptor molecule for estrogens: isolation from the rat uterus and preliminary characterization. Proc Natl Acad Sci USA 1966;55:1574−81.

[2] Toft D, Shyamala G, Gorski J. A receptor molecule for estrogens: studies using cell-free system. Proc Natl Acad Sci USA 1967;57:1740−3.

[3] Brzozowski AM, Pike AC, Dauter Z, et al. Molecular basis of agonism and antagonism in the oestrogen receptor. Nature 1997;389:753−8.

[4] Klopper A, Hall M. New synthetic agent for the induction of ovulation: preliminary trials in women. Br Med J 1971;1:152−4.

[5] Williamson JG, Ellis JD. The induction of ovulation by tamoxifen. J Obstet Gynaecol Br Commonw 1973;80:844−7.

[6] Dodds EC, Golberg L, Lawson W, Robinson R. Estrogenic activity of certain synthetic compounds. Nature 1938;141:247−8.

[7] Harper MJ, Walpole AL. Contrasting endocrine activities of cis and trans isomers in a series of substituted triphenylethylenes. Nature 1966;212:87.

[8] Harper MJ, Walpole AL. A new derivative of triphenylethylene: effect on implantation and mode of action in rats. J Reprod Fertil 1967;13:101−19.

[9] Harper MJ, Walpole AL. Mode of action of I.C.I. 46,474 in preventing implantation in rats. J Endocrinol 1967;37:83−92.

[10] Jordan VC, Pokoly TB. Steroid and prostaglandin relations during the menstrual cycle. Obstet Gynecol 1977;49:449−53.

[11] Pokoly TB, Jordan VC. Relation of steroids and prostaglandins at vaginal delivery and caesarian delivery. Obstet Gynecol 1975;46:577−80.

Two antiestrogenic strategies to treat breast cancer at the Worcester Foundation

The Worcester Foundation, founded by Gregory Pincus and Hudson Hoagland in 1944, provided enormous opportunities for me to learn and to develop as a scientist. This was important for both my future career, learning how science should be done in a "team" environment, documenting my "discoveries" and meeting people who "made things happen" in both industry and academia. The Worcester Foundation is not only "home of the oral contraceptives" but also the place where Min Chueh Chang first discovered how to perform in vitro fertilization on laboratory animals that would not normally mate. The mink and the stoat do not like each other very much and, because of their aggression, would not consider breeding. Dr. Chang created the new breed called the STINK using the in vitro fertilization methodology he pioneered in the 1960s. His discoveries heralded the landmark event on my birthday, July 25, 1978, with the birth in England of Louise Brown, the first "test tube baby." My daughter Alexandra (Katherine Louise) was named Louise after Louise Brown.

When I arrived at the Worcester Foundation in September 1972—incidentally, not knowing anything much about prostaglandins—I discovered that Dr. Harper had accepted a job with the World Health Organization in Geneva. I was told I could do anything I liked as long as some of my work included prostaglandins. My wife Marion and I were housed in the Windsor Motor Inn on Route 9 in Shrewsbury, which, basically, was a brothel. I slept with a knife in my hand listening to the doors being broken down and the constant fights. When my new boss Ed Klaiber saw Marion and my living accommodation, he immediately said "My wife and I are off to Austria for 3 weeks. Would you care to look after our home and the children?"—Yes, absolutely! Plus, I got his car! Ed Klaiber was an excellent mentor and lifelong friend (Fig. 4.1). I immediately found myself as an independent investigator with my own laboratory and a technician Suzanne Koerner, and planned my work on prostaglandins. However, my new circumstances would also allow me to explore my passion—to develop a drug for breast cancer.

By 1971, ICI 46,474 had shown modest activity in a preliminary clinical study for the treatment of advanced breast cancer [1]. It was clear, however, that much still remained to be done to develop antiestrogens as acceptable therapeutic agents [2]. ICI did not have a breast cancer research program, but Dr. Walpole agreed to help

Tamoxifen Tales. https://doi.org/10.1016/B978-0-323-85051-3.00004-X

FIGURE 4.1

On the occasion of my award of an honorary Doctor of Science degree from the University of Massachusetts in 2001 based on my translational research work to describe the strategy to use tamoxifen as a preventive and adjuvant treatment of breast cancer started at the University of Massachusetts Medical School in the early 1970s as a visiting scientist at the Worcester Foundation for Experimental Biology. Dr. Ed Klaiber (right) was my boss, and he and his wife Jeanie were exceptional friends during the 2 years as a visiting scientist.

with my request at the Worcester Foundation for assistance to conduct the first systematic laboratory study of the antitumor properties of ICI 46,474. What I did not know at the time was that, in April 1972, ICI scientists had reviewed all the data on ICI 46,474, and by the end of the year, the Research Director had decided to abandon clinical development [2]. The drug was not seen to be financially viable as either a drug to induce ovulation or for the treatment of metastatic breast cancer. Walpole declared he would take early retirement but stay on only if resources could be used to discover an appropriate strategy for the drug to be used optimally in breast cancer. He had met a young Ph.D. candidate, Craig Jordan, who was keen to help, so why not give him funds? As a result, ICI marketed the orphan drug, and I was given the *opportunity* to create the "gold standard" for the antihormone treatment of breast cancer.

However, I had no experience with laboratory models of breast cancer. Fortunately, the Worcester Foundation was a marvelous place to learn, as well as find help in new areas of scientific endeavor. To succeed, you have to find a way to teach yourself how to achieve your scientific goal.

Dr. Elwood Jensen (Fig. 4.2), then Director of the Ben May Laboratory for Cancer Research in Chicago, was a member of the scientific advisory board for the Foundation. He had been appointed to enhance opportunities in endocrinology and cancer following the passing of the National Cancer Act the year before, in 1971. I arrived at the Foundation in September 1972 and spent time with Elwood

FIGURE 4.2

Elwood Jensen and I in my office in the Robert H. Lurie Comprehensive Cancer Center at Northwestern University Medical School in 2002 when we had learned we would be the inaugural recipients of the Dorothy P. Landon/AACR Prize for Translational Research—Elwood for the estrogen receptor target and me for the treatment solution—tamoxifen.

during his 2-day visit, going over my Ph.D. thesis. I told him what I wanted to do and he learned of ICI 46,474 for the first time. Quite generously, he agreed to help me prepare for my studies, and I traveled to Chicago the following May. The short time I spent at the Ben May Institute, with the help of Dr. Gene DeSombre, who taught me about the "Huggins dimethylbenzanthracene (DMBA) rat mammary carcinogen model," and Sylvia Smith, who really taught me how to do sucrose density gradient analysis to identify the ER, were pivotal teachers for my future research career. This time was exceptional and provided me with the skills to evaluate the antitumor actions of ICI 46,474 back in Massachusetts. The lesson to be learned was I had to teach myself the skills I needed to evaluate the receptor binding and anticancer properties of ICI 46,474 in the laboratory.

I also went down to the University of Texas at San Antonio and learned ER assays with Bill McGuire (Fig. 4.3). This was a dream come true. Not only were Bill and I to become close friends and he my mentor before his untimely death in 1993 while diving in Mexico, but also I was to visit New Braunfels where I was born on July 25, 1947. Bill started the San Antonio breast cancer symposium in 1978, but at the end of each of the conferences in the 1980s, we had a special tradition on the Saturday night after the conference was over. He would allow me to pick a "who's who" of breast cancer royalty to travel with us in cars to New Braunfels for dinner and much wine. At the end of the dinner, Bill would play a game and for the prize "can anybody tell me who was born here in New Braunfels?" Nobody ever guessed it was the Englishman, Craig Jordan, sitting at the end of the table! But back to the Worcester Foundation in 1973.

FIGURE 4.3

A dinner in the Prince Solms Inn, New Braunfels, TX, following a San Antonio Breast Cancer Symposium meeting in the late 1980s. Present left to right are Gary Clarke (head of biostatistics in Bill's group in San Antonio), Doug Tormey (then Executive Officer for the Eastern Cooperative Oncology Group—ECOG in Wisconsin), Bill McGuire, Trevor Powles (head of the Breast Program at the Royal Marsden Hospital in London), and Craig Jordan.

To facilitate progress at the Worcester Foundation, Dr. Walpole suggested Ms. Lois Trench, the clinical drug monitor for ICI 46,474 at one of ICI's companies in Wilmington, Delaware (Stuart Pharmaceuticals), contact me for a visit of evaluation. She admitted, however, that no one knew much about the new drug in their clinical department and insisted that I become a consultant to encourage clinical trials with ICI 46,474 at Stuart Pharmaceuticals.

Full of energy and drive (at that time she was just back from representing the United States in the National Women's Rowing team against the Russians), Lois arranged for me to study the interaction of ICI 46,474 with the human tumor ER. One day, a selection of frozen human breast tumors arrived on dry ice at the Foundation. In 1974, she also arranged for me to explain the antitumor effects of ICI 46,474, which was now tamoxifen, at meetings of the Eastern Cooperative Oncology Group (ECOG). Lois introduced me to Doug Tormey who was the Chairman of the ECOG breast committee. He would later be crucial in recruiting me to Wisconsin (Chapter 7 and 8). Thereafter, she invited me to introduce tamoxifen to the National Surgical Adjuvant Breast and Bowel Project (NSABP) at an international symposium she organized in 1976 in Key Biscayne, Florida. Lois and her husband George have remained lifelong friends. Lois is the godmother of my daughter Alexandra.

The work at the Worcester Foundation went exceptionally well. The controversy of whether tamoxifen inhibited the binding of estrogens to the human ER was resolved [3]. However, medical scientists in the United Kingdom did not share this view for a further decade based on, as it turned out, flawed clinical data. The good news was that everyone with breast cancer received tamoxifen in the National Health Service in Britain. Lives were saved for modest costs.

The first laboratory studies of tamoxifen as a breast cancer preventive were also successfully completed in 1974, and Lois sponsored me to present the work at the International Congress of Steroidal Hormones meeting in Mexico City. ICI 46,474 prevented carcinogen-induced rat mammary carcinogenesis, probably by blocking the ER [4]. There was no interest in the concept of prevention at that point (it was 10 years too early!), but at least the first, translation scientific research had commenced. Dr. Trevor Powles (Fig. 4.3) took the initiative to advance the cause of chemoprevention starting in 1985 with an announcement to the media in Britain that he was initiating a feasibility study at the Royal Marsden Hospital to see if tamoxifen could be used as a chemopreventive agent in women at high risk for developing breast cancer. I first learned of this in a transatlantic telephone call from my mother who had read the story in the newspaper. "Somebody is using your drug to prevent breast cancer" was her first statement "do something about it" (this is what mothers do!). We did, by studying the "good, bad, and the ugly of tamoxifen" at the University of Wisconsin Comprehensive Cancer Center throughout the 1980s (Chapter 8). We discovered the drug group selective ER modulators (SERMs) [5], identified and publicized the potential of tamoxifen to encourage an increase in endometrial cancer incidence [6], and discovered the action of SERMs on bones [7]. Trevor and I both miss the years we spent together advocating chemoprevention around the world in back-to-back lectures. Good times with a good friend.

Some of my work at the Worcester Foundation on the ability of ICI 46,474 to control rat mammary carcinoma growth was included in the handbook given to clinicians in America to support their subsequent clinical studies in 1974. My work was also used to support licensing of tamoxifen in Japan and Germany. But I felt no urgency to publish the results since there was still no particular clinical interest in an antiestrogen as a breast cancer drug. Cytotoxic combination chemotherapy was King! This was the way breast cancer was to be cured—declared the clinical community!

No recounting of my 2 years at the Worcester Foundation would be complete without a thank you to Daniel Castracane, a member of the Steroid Training Program. His knowledge of endocrinology was encyclopedic, and his skill in the laboratory was second to none. I had resources but had no expertise in prostaglandin research, i.e., what I was supposed to be doing! Dan had the brains and skill. Dan and I teamed up to complete three refereed publications [8—10], a huge achievement in 12 months.

However, all things come to an end, and Dan was off to a new appointment in Cleveland. I volunteered to help with his move, and we were off on a road trip from Worcester, Massachusetts to Cleveland. All was going to plan until Dan suddenly realized that he was running out of petrol and we glided to a halt off the road; in the middle of nowhere! I realized that over a hill behind us was a small airfield, so I set off to investigate. I discovered that they had no gasoline (petrol), but they would sell me high octane aircraft fuel. Deal, give me 2 gallons! Dan was horrified, but we had little choice at this point. We set off with Dan turning to me to declare: "You must promise never to tell my wife." It transpired that the car was hers. At the first gas station, we filled up with low-grade fuel to dilute out our aircraft fuel. We had no engine problems, thank goodness, as we needed the car to return to Worcester!

Contributing to the clinical development of tamoxifen was my interest and goal. However, my strategic error was ultimately pointed out by Dr. Eliahu Caspi, a rather scary senior scientist at the Worcester Foundation. He called me into his office 1 day and glowered at me from behind his desk saying, "I have been asked to evaluate your *Curriculum Vitae* with a view of offering you a job to stay at the Foundation and not returning to England—but you have not published anything." "We see you collaborating with clinical studies with Dr. Tom Pokoly, a former trainee Fellow at the Foundation, other postdocs (Dan Castracane) on prostaglandins and there is your new work on ICI 46,474. Why not?" After the initial shock, I replied, "But I haven't discovered anything." He taught me his simple adage: "Tell them the story so far." He explained that each paper should take no more than 2 weeks to complete after one has the data. One should create an interlocking theme for your papers. Taking his advice, I have not stopped writing since that day in 1974. My first paper [11] was published with the referees only noting minor typographical errors but that never happens today! I eventually wrote up 11 referred papers for the literature from my 2 years at the Worcester Foundation.

Twenty-eight years after my interview and critical mentoring session with Dr. Caspi, I was honored to be invited to present the Inaugural Dr. Eliahu Caspi Memorial Lecturer at the Worcester Foundation for Biomedical Research in 2002. It was then I discovered from his family that Dr. Caspi had survived Russian prison camps after he was captured as a young man in Poland at the start of World War II. Few know that Hitler and Stalin made a deal at the start of World War II that when Germany invaded Poland from the west, but several days later the Russians would do the same from the east. After the war, he was there for the birth of Israel and joined the Haganah (local Israeli Defense force) before he emigrated to America. He subsequently obtained a Ph.D. in chemistry at Clark University and started his distinguished career in steroid endocrinology at the Foundation.

I now want to comment on one "eye-opening" incident. I was keen to advance my lecturing skills at the university level in America, before I returned to England to start my tenure track job as a lecturer in Pharmacology, at Leeds University. I planned and taught a premed course of Pharmacology for two semesters at Clark University in Worcester. This was a couple of hours twice a week with a couple of exams and a written paper. As we advanced to the climax of the "final exams," in my mind to establish a grade, I was unaware of the US system of continuous assessment. As you recall, in the United Kingdom, the system was a final series of exams and a *viva* to give you a grade—forever. I have always referred to this as "the finals in the Olympics for the gold medal. Winner takes all." It is a lesson of life—be prepared to respond, under stress, at the highest level of competition and win.

When I marked the papers after the exam, I found that one candidate had written nothing on his answer paper so naturally he failed! Then all hell broke loose with visits from faculty—"why do you care whether he passes? He has a place at medical school already and anyway he got good marks on the midterm exam and his paper." I explained how this was not right in my eyes. Then the President of his university wrote to explain "that the student had fallen asleep with exhaustion during the examinations as he had spent long hours overnight studying. A way must be found to allow the young man to go to medical school." Again, I wish I had kept this letter! I gave him an oral exam for an hour and he passed. I often wonder what happened in his career, but he is probably now a dean of a medical school!

Dr. Sam Hellman, a famous radiotherapist and Dean of the University of Chicago Medical School, once summed up becoming a dean, at a dinner in his honor for winning the Karnofsky Award from ASCO. He thanked the assembled guests and commented on the pleasure he had at receiving the award for his research and noted, as an administrator, it was important to observe that DEAN is only one letter away from DEAD!

The clinical application of tamoxifen for the treatment and prevention of breast cancer started with a strategy at the Worcester Foundation that was consolidated later at the University of Leeds (Chapter 5). However, there is a parallel story of initial discovery of a new approach to treat breast cancer starting in the mid-1970s at the Foundation, and subsequently consolidated at the University of Maryland.

The two central figures were Angela M.H. Hartley and Harry Brodie (Fig. 4.4). Angela was born in Oldham, Lancashire, on September 28, 1934, and educated at a Quaker School before obtaining a BSc in Biochemistry (1956) and an MSc (1959) at the University of Sheffield. For her Ph.D. in Clinical Pathology (1961), she attended the University of Manchester (Christie Hospital) after securing a prestigious Medical Research Council Scholarship. It was here she witnessed the mutilating Halstead radical mastectomy and vowed: women deserve better. In her career, she was to do just that. But first, she had to travel to the United States to meet her future husband Harry Brodie, a talented synthetic organic chemist.

Angela won a competitive place on the steroid training program at the Worcester Foundation for Experimental Biology in Shrewsbury, Massachusetts (1962). She stayed on at the Foundation to complete postdoctoral research with the world-famous "Tait Team" (James and Silvia Tait were both Fellow of the Royal Society (FRS) for their discovery of aldosterone). They were only the second married couple to be elected to the Royal Society; Queen Victoria and Prince Albert were the first! At this time, Angela met Harry Brodie who was investigating the possibility of designing specific inhibitors to block the synthesis of estrogen from its precursor androstenedione. Naturally, at the Worcester Foundation, the goal was contraception.

FIGURE 4.4

Harry Brodie (left) and Angela Brodie (right).

Harry and Angela married in 1964. Their two sons Mark and John were born in 1968 and 1969. Angela returned to work in Harry's lab in 1971, but the world of medical sciences had dramatically changed since the 1960s and the development of oral contraceptives. President Richard Nixon signed into law the National Cancer Act and a "war on cancer" was declared.

It is the "crossing of the Rubicon" for the scientist who first receives their own peer-reviewed R01 research grant from the NIH. One is then a principal investigator. Harry Brodie was determined that his wife, and partner in science Angela, should be the principal investigator of their grant and he would be the chemist in a supportive synthetic chemistry role. They were initially invested in discovering new specific aromatase inhibitors as the compounds then available for clinical work were not specific and produced complications with decreases in adrenal hormones.

My work, at the Foundation, on antiestrogen ICI 46,474, a failed contraceptive, also raised the possibility that a specific aromatase inhibitor could be used to treat ER-positive breast cancer. Angela received positive reviews for her grant submission, but the study section raised a concern. The grant would be viewed favorably for funding if the budget could be cut; perhaps the salary of the chemist could be removed? Harry, forever the gentleman, willingly agreed, and Angela was now the PI of her own NIH grant.

Angela was convinced that a specific aromatase inhibitor, to create an estrogen-free woman, would be better to treat ER-positive breast cancer than tamoxifen. She stated that "no estrogen is better than tamoxifen with estrogenic properties of its own." This was now the goal of the Brodie Team. This was Angela's chance to improve women's health.

In September 1974, it was time for me to return to the University of Leeds to take up my position as a lecturer in Pharmacology. I had received my BTA, and I was to begin to climb the academic promotions ladder. But first, I had one more task to complete.

I taught Harry the DMBA model, and he and I gavaged the 50-day-old Sprague—Dawley female rats (20 mg DMBA dissolved in 10 ml of peanut oil) in a laboratory in the attic of the research laboratory building in which he worked. Angela was not permitted to participate, as we both were not taking any chances with her health!

In the following years, the papers on their new suicide inhibitor of the aromatase enzyme 4-hydroxyandrostenedione were published [12—15], but they also concluded it was time to move on from the Worcester Foundation. Harry went to become the program administrator of an NIH study section in Bethesda, MD. Angela was offered a faculty position at the Department of Pharmacology at the Medical School of the University of Maryland in Baltimore. However, Angela was an enthusiastic horsewoman and rode her horse Blue at the end of each work day to unwind. Harry and Angela bought their home in Fulton, Maryland, where they raised their family, in the beautiful Maryland countryside, and commuted each day in opposite directions to focus on their professional careers. Angela had her grants and now a career track trying to develop a new antihormonal treatment for breast cancer.

Repeated investigations and requests for help to the Food and Drug Administration (FDA) were met with the response that there was no need for a new agent, as tamoxifen was now gaining traction (FDA approved on December 29, 1977) for the treatment of ER-positive metastatic breast cancer, clinical trials of 2-year adjuvant therapy had started by the end of the 1970s, and plans were underway to deploy long-term adjuvant tamoxifen therapy.

Throughout the late 1970s/early 1980s, Dr. Richard Santen was rigorously evaluating the clinical endocrinology of an earlier nonspecific aromatase inhibitor aminoglutethimide. However, therapy was usually reserved only for use after tamoxifen failure, as aminoglutethimide had to be administered with a glucocorticoid. This therapeutic complexity creates issues for translation to long-term adjuvant therapy clinical trials.

Breakthrough

Discovery, like all important human advances, requires luck. Angela was away at a scientific meeting where she met Dr. Charles (Charlie) Coombes from the Ludwig Institute for Cancer Research, St. George's Hospital Medical School, London. The plan was conceived that Charlie would organize a "first division team" for the clinical evaluation of 4-hydroxyandrostenedione if Angela could arrange for the upscaling of the chemical synthesis in Baltimore and fly it over for clinical testing. Upscaling and synthesizing the drug 4-hydroxyandrostenedione was not a challenge to their chemical consultant Harry!

I should mention that the clinical testing team (Paul Goss, Mitch Dowsett) that Charlie assembled was to emerge, a decade or so later, as the leaders of investigational research on the new clinical science of aromatase inhibitors. Their career ascent was triggered by the successful results of the first clinical trial published in the Lancet [16].

The principal obstacle for a successful challenge to tamoxifen for primacy and advance to adjuvant therapy was the fact that 4-hydroxyandrostenedione was injectable. Studies were initiated to test 4-hydroxyandrostenedioine orally, but the interest of the pharmaceutical industry had already been triggered to seek new aromatase inhibitors as rapidly as possible. Indeed, Zeneca at Alderley Park in Cheshire had already made the decision to improve upon the performance of tamoxifen in the mid-1980s as the patent was running out in Britain and the rest of the world except for the United States were there had initially been no patent protections until 1985.

The early clinical development of 4-hydroxyandrostenedione, a suicide inhibitor of the aromatase enzyme system, stimulated a long journey by the pharmaceutical industry to find orally active agents with low toxicity. Early candidates to enter clinical trial were rogletimide, and fadrozole but unacceptable side effects stopped further development. By contrast, anastrazole, letrozole, and exemestane all achieved clinical success in clinical trials and followed the clinical strategy established for long-term adjuvant tamoxifen therapy, i.e., 5 or more years.

Postscript

The translational research and successful creation of new therapeutic modalities targeting the ER with the new group of medicines discovered at Wisconsin in the 1980s that became known as selective estrogen receptor modulators (SERMs) and targeting the human CYP19 aromatase enzyme with inhibitors changed medicine. For Angela and I, this resulted in numerous occasions when our work was separately and jointly recognized by the academic community. Separately, we received the Brinker International Award (Jordan 1992, Brodie 2000), Dorothy P. Landon/ AACR Award for Translational Research (Jordan 2002, Brodie 2006), and the Charles F. Kettering Prize of the General Motors Research Foundation (which is considered to be the top clinical award for cancer treatment) (Jordan 2003, Brodie 2005). Award of the Kettering Prize separately and alone for this award for clinical advances is significant as we were the only two Ph.Ds, i.e., not medically qualified recipients, in the history of the clinical Kettering Prize. Angela was the only woman recipient.

Angela Brodie and I were joint recipients of the 24th Gregory Pincus Memorial Award and Medal (June 14, 2007) from the WFEB. Our relationship over 45 years is best summed up by Dr. Thoru Pederson, President of the Worcester Foundation, who stated at our ceremony: "Drs. Brodie and Jordan first met at the Foundation in 1972. Although their subsequent career paths and extraordinary discoveries were totally independent of one another, they have a lifelong spirit of collegiality and open communications, never considering themselves as competitors. We honor them today for their epochal contributions to medical sciences, and we applaud them for their selfless style of science they have practiced, serving not themselves but the World in the tradition of Gregory Pincus."

In 2013, we were both delighted to be inducted into the inaugural class for Fellowship of the AACR Academy (Fig. 4.5). We (Angela, Harry, and I) met at the Academy meetings annually until Angela's untimely death from pancreatic cancer and the complications from Parkinson's disease on June 7, 2017, aged 82. Immediately upon her death, Harry called me to ask me to be the master of ceremonies at her memorial service in Maryland. He was emotionally not up to the task. I was boarding a British Airways flight from Houston to Jeddah in Saudi Arabia and I immediately agreed to accept. This was my honor for a true friend and colleague.

FIGURE 4.5

In 2013, the AACR Academy selected their inaugural class of fellows. Following the award ceremony of a Fellowship medal, there was a dinner and reception. From left to right: Angela (elected for her pioneering studies of aromatase inhibitors) and Harry Brodie, Hiltrud Brauch, a colleague and collaborator from the Fisher—Bosch Institute in Stuttgart and professor at the University of Tubingen and myself.

References

[1] Cole MP, Jones CT, Todd ID. A new anti-oestrogenic agent in late breast cancer. An early clinical appraisal of ICI 46474. Br J Cancer 1971;25:270−5.

[2] Jordan VC. 50th anniversary of the first clinical trial with ICI 46,474 (tamoxifen): then what happened? Endocr Relat Cancer 2021;28:R1−19.

[3] Jordan VC, Koerner S. Tamoxifen (ICI 45,474) and the human carcinoma 8S oestrogen receptor. Eur J Cancer 1975;11:205−6.

[4] Jordan VC. Antitumor activity of the antiestrogen ICI 46,474 (tamoxifen) in the dimethylbenzanthracene (DMBA)-induced rat mammary carcinoma model. J Steroid Biochem 1974;5:354.

[5] Lerner LJ, Jordan VC. Development of antiestrogens and their use in breast cancer: eighth Cain memorial award lecture. Cancer Res 1990;50:4177−89.

[6] Gottardis MM, Robinson SP, Satyaswaroop PG, Jordan VC. Contrasting actions of tamoxifen on endometrial and breast tumor growth in the athymic mice. Cancer Res 1988;48:812−5.

[7] Jordan VC, Phelps E, Lindgren JU. Effects of anti-estrogens on bone in castrated and intact female rats. Breast Cancer Res Treat 1987;10:31−5.

[8] Castracane VD, Jordan VC. The effect of estrogen and progesterone on uterine prostaglandin biosynthesis in the ovulation in the ovariectomized rat. Biol Reprod 1975;13:587−96.

[9] Castracane VD, Jordan VC. Consolidation into the mechanism of estrogen-stimulated uterine prostaglandin synthesis. Prostaglandins 1976;12:243−51.

[10] Jordan VC, Castracane VD. Effect of reported prostaglandin synthesis inhibitors on estradiol-stimulated prostaglandin synthesis in vivo in the ovariectomized rat. Prostaglandins 1976;12:1073−81.

[11] Jordan VC. Prolonged antiestrogenic activity of ICI 46,474 in the ovariectomized mouse. J Reprod Fertil 1975;42:251−8.

[12] Brodie AMH, Schwartzel WC, Shaikh AA, Brodie HJ. The effect of an aromatase inhibitor, 4-hydroxy-4-anrostene-3,17-dione, on estrogen dependent processes in reproduction and breast cancer. Endocrinology 1977;100:1684−95.

[13] Brodie AMH, Garrett WM, Hendrickson JR, et al. Inactivation of aromatase in vitro by 4-hydroxyandrostenedione and 4-acetoxyandrostenedione and sustained effects in vivo. Steroids 1981;38:693−702.

[14] Brodie AMH, Garrett WH, Hendrickson JR, et al. Effects of 4-hydroxyandrostenedione and other compounds in the DMBA breast carcinoma model. Cancer Res 1982;42:3360s−4s.

[15] Brodie AMH, Romanoff LP, Williams KIH. Metabolism of the aromatase inhibitor 4-hydroxyandrostenedione by male rhesis monkeys. J Steroid Biochem 1982;14:693−6.

[16] Coombes RC, Goss P, Dowset JC, et al. 4-Hydroxyandrostenedione treatment of postmenopausal patients with advanced breast cancer. Lancet 1984;2:1237−40.

A new strategy: long-term adjuvant tamoxifen treatment and other discoveries at the University of Leeds

5

Upon my return to the Department of Pharmacology at Leeds University in September of 1974, my principal interest was to understand the pharmacology of tamoxifen and to devise a new strategy for the best clinical application for an anti-estrogenic treatment of breast cancer. The drug had been available for the treatment of advanced breast cancer in Britain since 1973, but similar approval would not occur in the United States until December 1977. Based on my experiences, and new scientific knowledge gained in America working with tamoxifen, I could see a path ahead to develop the drug further. This required separate, but interconnected, lines of research, dependent on an investigation of molecular mechanisms of action of tamoxifen (I was first and foremost a pharmacologist in a pharmacology department) and the exploitation of my new skills with the DMBA-induced rat mammary carcinoma model. This was putting into practice what I considered to be the three cornerstones of pharmacology: the 3M's—models to investigate mechanisms to develop medicines. However, the 3 needs a 4th M—money (with apologies to Paul Ehrlich). Who was Paul Ehrlich? It is important for the young investigator to read and learn about the history and evolution of your chosen discipline. Before I consider the themes of our research strategy at multiple Tamoxifen Teams, I want to identify Professor Paul Erlich as the individual who created the science of translational research to save the lives of patients. This model created the research strategy that is used today in the pharmaceutical industry.

In November 1908, Ehrlich learned he was to receive the Nobel Prize. The citation stated that Ehrlich performed enduring service to medical and biological research, notably in determining the potency of serum preparations. The work to be recognized was the standardization of diphtheria antitoxin. Diphtheria was the "killer of children." However, his lecture was entitled "On Partial Functions of the Cell," a title that gave no clue to the audience. He chose to describe, not his work on standardization of the diphtheria antitoxin but his new work and methods, which essentially continue to be used to this day. However, at the beginning of the 20th century, he was the first. The idea was to emasculate the known poison arsenic by

Tamoxifen Tales. https://doi.org/10.1016/B978-0-323-85051-3.00005-1

creating a carrier molecule based on organic chemistry. His method was to use organic chemistry to synthesize molecules to first be tested in animal models of disease. The animal models resulted from the genius of Sahachiro Hata from Japan. Any promising molecules would be thoroughly tested for toxicities in animals before clinical trials would be considered.

Compound 606, i.e., the six hundredth and sixth compound, synthesized was tested in 1912 and moved successfully to clinical trials for the treatment of syphilis. Before the new synthetic medicine now called Salvarsan was available, patients died horrible deaths with syphilis (most notably Sir Winston Churchill's father). In 1903, Paul Erlich attended the 17th International Congress of Medicine in London. Here he took the opportunity to emphasize the importance of the "four big G's" in research of the new science of experimental chemotherapy. The four big G's (in German) are Geduld, Geshick, Glück, and last, but not the least, Geld. Translated this becomes: patience, skill, luck, and money. In 1914, Paul Erlich was awarded the Cameron Prize at Edinburgh University. He had established a rational method for drug development. This method would result in ICI 46,474 as a putative "morning after pill," just over 60 years later, at Alderley Park. Little did I know that I would receive the Cameron Prize in 1993 for my contributions to the treatment of breast cancer with tamoxifen.

Throughout this period (1974−79), ICI Pharmaceutical Division (ICI/University of Leeds Joint Research Scheme) and the Yorkshire Cancer Research Campaign (YCRC) supported my laboratory at the University of Leeds in England. The YCRC bought invaluable equipment, which allowed me to measure ER by performing state of the art sucrose density gradient analysis using ultracentrifuges (the "Jensen method" this time). The YCRC also provided the salary for a talented technician Graham Prestwich who had previously graduated from the Department of Pharmacology at Leeds. The contribution from ICI Pharmaceuticals Division came in two investments. Dr Roy Cotton, the head of the "tamoxifen clinical program" in 1972 who, incidentally, told me years later, "I was advised not to spend too much time with this project as it was not anticipated to succeed," (1) he provided a PhD scholarship for my first PhD student Clive Dix and a Summer Scholarship for Anna Riegel (née Tate) (Fig. 5.1) who were both very bright, intelligent undergraduates at Leeds University in the Pharmacology Department. Both students were to receive "Firsts" in their BSc (Honors) degrees. Their stories are told in "Case Studies: in their own words" (Chapter 18). (2) Most importantly, Roy Cotton paid for hundreds (perhaps totaling tens of thousands in the 5 year grant) of rats to be chauffeured from Alderley Park to Leeds Medical School each week for the next 4 years. This was from his clinical budget! The inspirational investment changed medicine and propelled tamoxifen forward as a revolutionary new adjuvant therapy and as a potential chemopreventive. Years later, I visited ICI Alderley Park in Cheshire. After landing at Manchester Airport, the designated driver declared "are you the Professor Jordan from Leeds University in the 1970s? If you are, I used to chauffeur rats over to you

FIGURE 5.1

Graduation day for Anna Riegel (then Anna Tate). Leeds University on the occasion of her receiving a first-class Honours Degree in Pharmacology.

every week in this very car (code named—Savlon, after ICI's antiseptic cream)." Real people made things happen in those days.

The time at Leeds University (1974–79) was very exciting, as I introduced all the new techniques learned at the Worcester Foundation for Experimental Biology, into my laboratory. There was a host of keen enthusiastic, undergraduate students in the Department of Pharmacology, all willing to learn and participate in the Leeds University Tamoxifen Team. Once I had secured funding and resources, the initial focus on models and mechanisms resulted in two scientific goals each of which went forward simultaneously. Establishing the DMBA rat mammary carcinoma model evolved into two goals: (1) revisit the issue of tamoxifen preventing carcinogenesis (chemoprevention), i.e., reinvent and publish the data obtained from the Worcester Foundation and (2) investigate the application of tamoxifen as a potential adjuvant therapy for the treatment of breast cancer. At that time in the mid-1970s, both ideas were revolutionary and of only theoretical clinical value. Tamoxifen was used exclusively to treat metastatic breast cancer and was not even approved for that indication in America until December 1977. There was no clinical correlation to link tamoxifen and the tumor ER. Tamoxifen is not mentioned at all in the landmark book resulting from the NCI meeting on estrogen receptors and breast cancer [1]. The first clinical reports of ER and breast cancer response was later, and the authors generously mentioned our laboratory work [2,3]. During the 1970s, I was to learn that in Britain it was not the "done thing" to refer to laboratory work as the genesis of a clinical idea or trial.

I will start our research journey at Leeds in the autumn of 1974 with the immediate objective of establishing the DMBA-induced rat mammary carcinoma model as a new innovation for drug development. The "free" Alderley Park rats were used initially to complete a rigorous series of studies to demonstrate that the responses of the established tumors were dependent upon the presence of the tumor ER. It was well known that the DMBA-induced tumor was also responsive to prolactin for growth, so as the prolactin gene in the pituitary gland is an estrogen responsive gene, then the antiestrogen tamoxifen could be an antitumor agent indirectly. In other words, blocking estrogen-stimulated prolactin production in the rat could be the mechanism of action of tamoxifen in the rat—and therefore the model would be of no clinical relevance. By establishing the DMBA-induced rat mammary carcinoma model at Leeds in 1974, I was tidying up my preliminary data from the Worcester Foundation. With the results collected by 1975, I was ambitious enough to attempt to publish three consecutive papers, back-to-back in a single issue of the *Journal of Endocrinology*. I was putting Dr Caspi's advice into practice with a vengeance, and his words were ringing in my ears, "Tell them the story so far." We had a story and I was determined to bring tamoxifen to a wider clinical audience. I had to make up for lost and wasted time.

I recall, I was attending courses at the Royal Military Academy, Sandhurst (see Chapter 9) in 1975 when I received word that all three of my papers were to be published in the *Journal of Endocrinology*. I regretted that only the first two were to be in the same issue [4,5]. These demonstrated the ability of tamoxifen to block the ER in the DMBA tumors but that prolactin levels were not inhibited efficiently. The third paper would follow in the next issue and demonstrated that responsiveness to tamoxifen was dependent upon tumor ER levels: no ER, no response, i.e., not much tumor regression [6]. Tim Jaspan (Fig. 5.2), a medical student at Leeds, was taking an intercalated BSc in pharmacology and worked on tumor ER predicting tumor response. He went on to qualify in medicine and was assisting Mr. Ronnie MacDonald (Figs. 2.2 and 2.3) for the birth of my daughter Alexandra Katherine Louise on September 24, 1976. Dr Jaspan is one of her godparents; Lois Trench-Hines, the first drug monitor for tamoxifen at ICI Americas, is another. Tamoxifen was becoming a part of my family. Dr Teresa McCarthy (Medean Society, see Figs. 2.2 and 2.3) is one of my daughter Helen's godparents.

Now that we knew we could reproduce my first results with the model and had successfully published the results in the refereed literature, it was time to turn to my three goals: chemoprevention, adjuvant therapy, and the molecular mechanism of action of tamoxifen.

FIGURE 5.2

Me and Tim Jaspan at a Leeds University Research Day for the Public. Tim's excellent research ethic in his one intercalated year for his medical degree was the reason I support intercalating medical students to obtain a science degree at Leeds University. Tim was to be there for the birth of my daughter Alexandra, assisting Mr. MacDonald (Figs. 2.2 and 2.3) at the Leeds Maternity Hospital. Years later in 1985 on the occasion of receiving my DSc degree, I took 1-year old Alexandra back to where she was born only to discover it the building was now the Leeds Drug Rehabilitation Center. Rapid exit from the scene was called for.

Chemoprevention

In 1974, I had published an abstract [7] describing the fact that tamoxifen would prevent the induction of carcinogen-induced rat mammary cancer and that tamoxifen would inhibit the binding of [^{3}H]estradiol to the human ER. These data were presented at the International Congress of Steroid Endocrinology in Mexico City in 1974. The paper was published by 1976 in the *European Journal of Cancer* [8].

These first studies of the effectiveness of tamoxifen to prevent rat mammary carcinogenesis were subsequently to be used by my friend and colleague Dr Trevor Powles (Fig. 5.3) as supporting evidence to initiate a pilot study at the Royal Marsden Hospital. He sought to test the hypothesis of whether tamoxifen could be used to prevent the incidence of breast cancer in women at high risk for the disease [9]. His study after 20 years of follow-up showed efficacy for tamoxifen reducing cancer incidence [10]. Dr Bernard Fisher (Fig. 5.4) and the National Surgical Adjuvant Breast and Bowel Project (NSABP) published the pivotal registration study in 1998 [11] in the United States. Again, they used our laboratory data as supporting evidence to advance the human trial. In 1998, tamoxifen was approved by the US Food and Drug Administration (FDA) for the reduction of risk of breast cancer in high-risk pre- and postmenopausal women. In 2013, the National Institute for Health and Clinical Excellence (NICE) recommended that tamoxifen be made available through the National Health Service (NHS) in the United Kingdom for the prevention of breast cancer in high-risk women. A cheap effective medicine given to many women at risk for breast cancer would benefit the few who will be spared surgery, radiotherapy, and further chemotherapy. However, a better idea would eventually emerge from my Wisconsin Tamoxifen Team. However, that was 10 years in the future.

FIGURE 5.3

Trevor Powles, Paul Carbone, and Louise Rusch. Trevor was presenting the Rusch Memorial Lecture in April 1993, Madison, Wisconsin. Trevor then rushed down to Chicago to attend the celebrations for my marriage to Monica Morrow.

FIGURE 5.4

Craig Jordan left and Bernie Fisher right. This was the occasion of us being awarded the inaugural Brinker International Award from Susan G. Komen for the Cure, Dallas 1992. I received the Basic Science Award and Bernie the Clinical Award.

The move to adjuvant therapy

In 1975, Marc Lippman, who was then the Head of the Breast Cancer Program at NCI, published an important paper to show that tamoxifen could reduce the growth of MCF-7 breast cancer cells in culture and increasing estradiol reversed the block in growth [12]. The same year, we published that tamoxifen could block [^{3}H] estradiol binding to human tumor ER [13] in the refereed literature.

Buried in Marc's paper was the single statement that tamoxifen could actually kill breast cancer cells; today, we know that is true at very high concentrations. I chose, therefore, to devise a model of adjuvant therapy using a 1-month treatment schedule equivalent to 1 year of adjuvant therapy in women with increasing daily doses of tamoxifen. The therapy was administered starting 1 month after the administration of DMBA to the rats, so the test would be to see if microfoci of deranged cells in the mammary glands would be "killed" with increasing doses of daily tamoxifen and animals cured. We found that there were fewer tumors after higher doses of tamoxifen, but, as we followed tumorigenesis over the next several months, eventually all animals had at least one tumor. I knew from the literature in the early 1970s [14,15] that tamoxifen had a very long biological half-life in rats and humans, so I reasoned that tamoxifen was blocking tumorigenesis as long as it remained in the circulation. As an aside, my first publication with tamoxifen in mice was to show the extraordinarily long antiestrogenic action in mice after just a couple of injections [16]. It therefore seemed that longer therapy was going to be the correct strategy if tamoxifen was to be used as an adjuvant after surgery. However, all the first adjuvant clinical trials that were being set up at that time were using only 1 year of adjuvant tamoxifen. To the clinician, this was obvious because tamoxifen is only effective for about 1–2 years for the treatment of metastatic breast cancer [17,18]. Clive Dix, my first PhD student at Leeds, and Karen Allen (a graduate from the Department of Pharmacology who became another excellent technician in my laboratory and later Reader Leeds Institute of Cardiovascular and Metabolic Medicine at the University of Leeds) completed the first studies of short-term (1 month) versus long-term (6 months) tamoxifen versus ovariectomy and long-term tamoxifen won convincingly with a 90% suppression of tumor induction. My ideas were first presented to a clinical audience in mid-1977 at an ICI Pharmaceuticals Division physician education meeting at King College, Cambridge [19]. Michael Baum (Fig. 5.5) was the chair of my session and, after he heard my talk, stated that his clinical trials group the Nolvadex Adjuvant Trials Organization (NATO, for short, to fool the America doctors into reading their paper in the Lancet as the American would think it was their funded study!) had arbitrarily decided on two rather than 1 year of adjuvant tamoxifen. The NATO group quite correctly is credited with the first report that longer adjuvant tamoxifen confers a survival advantage in patients [20]. Nevertheless, the scientific laboratory evidence-based rationale for the new strategy was already published and discussed at meetings (Fig. 5.6). Dr Helen Stewart (Fig. 5.5), who was also at the Cambridge meeting, was eventually to set up and run the Scottish trial [21] of 5 years of adjuvant tamoxifen versus placebo but with tamoxifen treatment upon first recurrence. The results of the Scottish trial were published 10 years after the Cambridge meeting on July 25, 1987. That is my birthday and a fine present with the definitive proof that the use of long-term adjuvant tamoxifen therapy translated from our laboratory in Leeds in the mid-1970s into lives saved. The weekly deliveries of Alderley Park rats to the medical school at Leeds were absolutely essential for my group to turn an orphan drug with no prospects, into the gold standard for the endocrine treatment of breast cancer. After the Cambridge meeting, I set off to Wisconsin for a minisabbatical (Chapter 8) to the Wisconsin Clinical Cancer Center. There I proposed my plan for the clinical development of tamoxifen to the Director Dr Paul Carbone (Fig. 5.3). He was to immediately offer me a job in America, eventually, as the Head of the Breast Cancer Program at the Wisconsin Clinical Cancer Center; long-term adjuvant tamoxifen therapy also changed the rest of my life!

FIGURE 5.5

Participants at a breast cancer symposium in September 1977 at Kings College, Cambridge, England. The concept of extended adjuvant tamoxifen treatment was first proposed by me at this meeting. In the insets (top) Craig Jordan (bottom right), Professor Michael Baum, my session chairman who was planning to launch the Nolvadex Adjuvant Trial Organisation (NATO) 2-year adjuvant tamoxifen trial and (bottom left) Dr Helen Stewart, a participant at the conference who would subsequently guide the Scottish Trial of 5 years of adjuvant tamoxifen treatment versus control in the 1980s. Both trials showed survival advantages for long-term adjuvant tamoxifen treatment.

I also presented my new clinical strategy in America in late 1979 at the Adjuvant Therapy of Cancer meeting in Tucson, Arizona, founded and run by the late Syd Salmon and his colleague Steve Jones [22]. I found I was in the opening session sandwiched between the greats of chemotherapy Dr Vince DeVita, then Director of the NCI and Dr Bernard Fisher, chair of the NSABP (Fig. 5.4). Everyone was

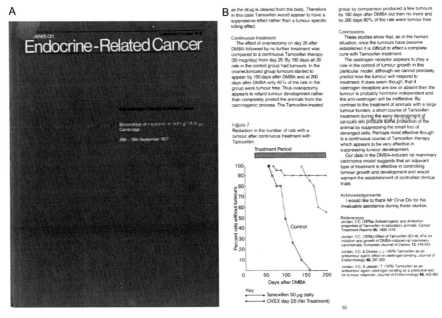

FIGURE 5.6

The first report of the effectiveness of continuous (long-term) tamoxifen treatment to prevent the development of rat mammary carcinoma versus no treatment. In additional experiments (Jordan & Allen 1980), a 1-month treatment equivalent to a 1-year adjuvant therapy in women was not effective in the DMBA-rat mammary carcinoma model. This was published following the Kings College meeting, September 1977 (cited from Endocrine-Related Cancer 28, 1; 10.1530/ERC-20-0335).

talking about cytotoxic chemotherapy combinations as the way forward to cure cancer. I made my case for long-term adjuvant tamoxifen therapy based on my rat data. The important thing for me was I was reaching the right ears. The approach was to prove to be a game changer and, most importantly, documented the concept for this audience who could read about it later. In the audience in Tucson was Lois Trench-Hines who turned to her colleagues from ICI Americas and exclaimed "You have no idea what Dr Jordan has just said about long-term adjuvant tamoxifen, have you? If this strategy works in patients, tamoxifen will be a blockbuster." She was correct for not only the lives saved with the strategy but also the billions of dollars of revenues earned by ICI pharmaceuticals. But all of that was in the future.

At Leeds University, we developed a series of publications [23,24] that demonstrated, in an animal model system with a minute tumor burden of early disease, that long-term tamoxifen therapy was superior to short-term therapy. By the mid-1980s, Richard Peto had proposed a regular process of overview analyses at Oxford to combine the results from the world's adjuvant clinical trials in breast cancer. The plan was to take all the randomized trials, so as to get big numbers and establish what therapy works and which does not. Five years of adjuvant tamoxifen had a dramatic effect when compared with 1 year of adjuvant therapy. Most importantly, the drug is only effective in patients whose tumor was ER positive, and the survival advantage is prolonged after tamoxifen is stopped [25]. Dr Christina Davis, Sir Richard Peto, and the Oxford Team have gone one step further to address the question "if 5 years is excellent and decreases mortality profoundly even after stopping therapy, what will the benefit be after 10 years of adjuvant tamoxifen?" 10 years is better than 5 years of adjuvant tamoxifen—especially in the decade after stopping the 10 years of tamoxifen [26]. I feel this is a remarkable result and of profound benefit for society with a cheap and effective therapy. Again, the investment in free rats in the 1970s to create the original strategy of "longer is better than shorter" or as I would say "Tamoxifen Forever" is a tribute to the scientific process and the good offices of Roy Cotton and the late Arthur Walpole for giving a young scientist the opportunity to contribute new knowledge.

Unanticipated sadness and success of Alderley Park

Arthur Walpole did not see the enormous success of tamoxifen as he died suddenly on July 2, 1977, just before tamoxifen was about to spread its wings and become a long-term adjuvant therapy. A year later, ICI Pharmaceuticals was selected to be presented with the Queens Award for Technological Achievement for tamoxifen at ICI Pharmaceuticals Division Headquarters at Alderley Park. I was honored to be the only invited guest who was not an employee of ICI Pharmaceuticals Division [27]. I sat with my friends and colleagues Drs. Roy Cotton and Sandy Todd (Fig. 5.7). Dr Barry Furr had been promoted to Arthur Walpole's job (he would go on to receive an OBE for Casodex, an antiandrogen for the treatment of prostate cancer) and he sat with Dr Dora Richardson (Fig. 5.8), the guest of honor, who was the talented chemist who created tamoxifen. Lord Leverhulme, the Lord Lieutenant of Cheshire, presented the Queens Award for Technological Achievement, and ICI Pharmaceuticals Division was provided with a flag to fly at their headquarters in recognition of the honor. A truly great day and one I will always remember.

An investigation of the molecular mechanism of action of tamoxifen

The Tamoxifen Team at Leeds initiated a series of studies in rats and mice to understand the molecular mechanism of tamoxifen [28–31] in vivo, but in vitro we conducted the first study with [^{3}H] tamoxifen binding to the rat uterine ER [29]. Here, however, was another scientific lesson. Graham Prestwich, my technician, was absolutely fabulous at precise experimental work. We got perfect data to demonstrate that [^{3}H] estradiol routinely produced the expected 8S ER by sucrose density gradient analysis (Jensen technology, McGuire methodology). The binding of [^{3}H] estradiol

FIGURE 5.7

The Queen's award for industry is an exceptional honor for a company that has excelled. The celebration is only for those considered to have been instrumental in making the award a reality, that is, tamoxifen. A carefully selected group of 230 employees were present and Dr. Jordan was the only one invited from outside of the company. The figure shows the front page of the Alderley Park company newspaper SCAN and Dr. Jordan's personal invitation. The luncheon table photograph shows Dr. Roy Cotton and Dr. Jordan opposite to each other and, unfortunately, Dr. Sandy Todd hidden behind Dr. Jordan (right) (cited from Endocrine-Related Cancer 28, 1; 10.1530/ERC-20-0335).

could be blocked in a concentration-related manner by nonradioactive tamoxifen. But, [^{3}H] tamoxifen **always** produced a 4S peak by sucrose density gradient analyses using a swinging bucket rotor (16 h' spinning) technique—standard at the time! The 4S [^{3}H] tamoxifen peak could again be blocked in a concentration-related manner by nonradioactive estradiol. Since tamoxifen did not increase the growth and replication of rat uterine epithelial cells in vivo, i.e., increase in DNA, but estradiol did, we had "discovered" the mechanism of action of antiestrogens! When the 4S ER bound to estradiol, it could be activated and dimerize (we thought) to 8S units, but tamoxifen prohibited the process. Perfect, and a guaranteed article in Nature. We rapidly wrote up our "Landmark" finding, evaluated it by circulating our manuscript to scientists at ICI Pharmaceuticals Division for feedback. Great result was the reply; submit the manuscript!

FIGURE 5.8

Dr Dora Richardson, the synthetic organic chemist who created tamoxifen and its metabolites at the ICI Pharmaceuticals Ltd laboratories at Alderley Park, Cheshire.

In a few weeks, the reviewers' comments came back from the editor with regrets that the article was not to be published. The referees' comments were not helpful—"I do not believe it." I was absolutely crushed as it was a black and white result. How could our data be wrong? I had used techniques and methodologies I had learned from the world leading scientists Jensen and McGuire in America, who measured ER every day and could not be faulted. We had the best ultracentrifuges money could buy, but just a minute, we also had an alternative approach not available to either Jensen or McGuire. The vertical tube rotator completed the sucrose density gradient analyses in about 2 h (i.e., not 16 h' overnight). We used that technique to analyze the [^{3}H] tamoxifen ER complex from rat uterine extracts and there was the 8S peak! The answer to the binding of [^{3}H] tamoxifen was physical chemistry, because the specifically bound [^{3}H] tamoxifen was falling off the 8S peak and binding to nonspecific proteins in the 4S region during the 16-h overnight run using the conventional technique of sucrose density gradient analysis. The result was right; the interpretation was wrong. We asked a question of Nature (both the journal and the environment), and it did not lie. We just did not decide on the right interpretation.

We reinvented our papers, and it was rapidly published as a "first" in *Molecular and Cellular Endocrinology* [29]. The following year, I met Professor Etienne Baulieu in London and subsequently Dr Paul Robel, his senior staff member in their INSERM unit in Bicêtre, Paris. Etienne was later to become the President of the French National Academy of Sciences. We became friends and Paul later confided that they were the referees and had encountered the same situation with other low affinity compounds that bound weakly to the progesterone receptor. This was the scientific group that gave the world RU486, the abortion pill as a parallel steroid story to the tamoxifen tale. Lessons: The technology of the time can deceive the scientist. The result is not what it may appear to be, as the analysis is artificial in the conversation with Nature and the situation in the test tube is not the cell with the correct set of equilibria for ligand binding to ER.

We subsequently checked our results by conducting binding assays for [³H]estradiol on all fractions of a 16hr centrifugation analysis following tamoxifen binding and there it was—the 8S peak—case closed.

However, our intense investigation of tamoxifen's molecular pharmacology at Leeds was to open yet another door to discovery through the examination of metabolites of tamoxifen. At the Worcester Foundation, I could not understand why tamoxifen was so weak as an antiestrogen at the ER in vitro but so effective and potent in vivo. Was the drug metabolically activated or was the partial estrogenic actions of tamoxifen in the rat a result of estrogenic hydroxylated metabolites? Perhaps, the reported full estrogen-like action of tamoxifen in the mouse was the result of complete metabolism to an estrogen? We should test the metabolites. Dr Dora Richardson at ICI Pharmaceutical Division gave us 4-hydroxytamoxifen and 3,4-dihydroxytamoxifen to test. A surprise was in store!

My group discovered that a metabolite of tamoxifen, 4-hydroxytamoxifen, had very high affinity for the ER, but still retained antiestrogenic activity. This was new territory as all reported antiestrogens until that time, had low potency and weak binding to ER. The evolution of this discovery back in 1975 is interesting and another lesson in the real world of relationships with the pharmaceutical industry. In those days, most interactions were "gentlemen's" agreements, and mine with Roy Cotton and Arthur Walpole was certainly that. It was Clive Dix, during his final year honors project, who discovered that 4-hydroxytamoxifen (I called it monohydroxytamoxifen in those days) bound to the rat uterine ER with the same affinity as estradiol. My response was clear—"Clive, do you know how to make serial dilutions? Do it again. There are no reports of any antiestrogens with high binding affinity for the ER. In fact, it is the low affinity that makes them antiestrogenic—the complex cannot stay together for long enough to produce growth." Well, all of that was rubbish and Clive's result was real. Nature had given us the correct answer—it was a discovery!

More importantly, it was clear that it was the shape of the ligand [32], not the affinity that programmed estrogenic or antiestrogenic activity in estrogen target tissues. We synthesized [33] a series of compounds with a fluorine, chlorine, or methyl group in the 4 position of tamoxifen. Karen found these compounds had low affinity for the ER-like tamoxifen and could not be metabolically activated to 4-hydroxytamoxifen, Karen discovered that these compounds were antiestrogens but had low potency because metabolic activation in vivo was blocked. 4-Hydroxytamoxifen became the standard antiestrogen used by all future laboratory researchers worldwide for studies in vitro. 4-Hydroxytamoxifen was also used to further understand antiestrogen action by crystallization [34] with the ligand-binding domain of the human ER more than 20 years later—but not regrettably by my Tamoxifen Team. I had fortunately moved away from that project in 1969 (Chapter 3)!

At the time of all of our discoveries with tamoxifen metabolites at Leeds in 1975, the response by scientists at ICI Pharmaceuticals Division was not what I expected. I thought this breakthrough in knowledge was fantastic, but the silence was deafening from Alderley Park. A phone call to my home in Leeds secured my honorable promise that I would say nothing of my findings at a forthcoming meeting I was invited to by Lois Trench in Key Biscayne, America. It was there, I was to present the pharmacology of tamoxifen to Dr Bernard Fisher (Fig. 5.4) and clinical investigators from the NSABP who were considering studies with adjuvant tamoxifen in their patients. At the meeting, there was talk about the putative role of metabolites as "estrogens" in vivo, but my lips were sealed! The NSABP went forward to add 2 years of adjuvant tamoxifen to their adjuvant chemotherapy. They started recruitment in 1977.

I had agreed not to discuss the potent activity of the metabolites of tamoxifen for one reason. I believed in tamoxifen as a breast cancer drug, and I wanted to see it go on to be approved for clinical use in America. This would eventually occur on December 31, 1977. In 1976, I agreed not to publish any of our completed studies on tamoxifen's hydroxylated metabolites for a year so that ICI Pharmaceuticals Division could apply for patent protection for the metabolites too. All seemed totally reasonable at the time, but it also now emphasized to me the fact that tamoxifen was an orphan drug with little chance of success. When Walpole insisted on tamoxifen being placed on the market in 1973 and then would not retire but stay on at Alderley Park collaborating with me, this was a longshot for success. However, it worked for ICI Pharmaceutical Division. I was later told that when I had received the metabolites from Alderley Park they had not been patented as per company policy. This was a standard operating procedure for all their drugs going on the market and in clinical use. This patenting of metabolites occurred because the company had been "scooped" earlier when an antimalarial, paludrine, was already marketed but turned out to be a prodrug (i.e., that is converted in the body to the active drug). A competitor found out and marketed the active metabolite as an antimalarial. Additionally, American researchers independently synthesized the same compound but discovered it was an antagonist of folic acid and could be used as an anticancer agent. So you see where all of this was going with tamoxifen. There was no interest or perception of a real market for tamoxifen as a medicine, so why bother patenting the metabolites! Company policy rules for patenting all metabolites were ignored and only rescued at the last minute for the company. In fact, decades into the future, it was discovered that the 4-hydroxy-N-desmethyltamoxifen or endoxifen was an excellent anticancer agent [35], so the tamoxifen maker would have been nibbled away by competitors.

In any event, disaster was avoided retrospectively with patents for the metabolites by 1977 and tamoxifen moved forward in clinical trial—glacially. Karen enthusiastically evaluated 4-hydroxytamoxifen as a long-term adjuvant therapy versus tamoxifen in rats and—tamoxifen was the winner [23]! It became clear that the lipophilic nature of tamoxifen and massive protein binding of the drug result in accumulation in the body that acts as a reservoir for the subsequently slow metabolic activation to 4-hydroxytamoxifen and endoxifen for effective long-term antiestrogen action. The administration of the hydroxylated metabolite is less effective because it is more rapidly conjugated by phase II metabolism and excreted. Simple pharmacology; a lesson that was to be revisited with the poor performance of many hydroxylated antiestrogens tested as antibreast cancer drugs over the next 25 years!

Once we showed that the hydroxylated antiestrogens were not as good as tamoxifen to either treat or prevent DMBA tumors, 4-hydroxytamoxifen disappeared as a candidate for therapeutic applications. Or so I thought! Years later, when I was the director of the Breast Cancer Research and Treatment Program at the Wisconsin Comprehensive Cancer Center in Madison, Wisconsin, I was contacted by a company in New York with a fascinating proposal. "We are planning to develop a new concept for the prevention of breast cancer. We have come to you because of your previously published work on 4-hydroxytamoxifen." French physicians [36] were exploring the possibility of developing a "rub-on" gel containing 4-hydroxytamoxifen that would be applied daily each night to the breasts. I remember my first thought was that only the French would conceive of this strategy at bed time! But upon reflection, the idea is scientifically sound. It can be proven that 4-hydroxytamoxifen will penetrate breast tissue and exert a local antiestrogenic effect, but when the drug entered the peripheral circulation, it would be rapidly excreted, thus keeping systemic effects such as hot flashes, etc. to a minimum. We provided advice, but it was my colleague, Dr Seema Khan [37] who completed initial clinical studies at Northwestern University.

To achieve these scientific advances, I worked very hard, night and day. I wrote every day (7 days a week) and was in the laboratory constantly. There is no other way if you chose to lead and succeed. But I learned that keen enthusiastic young people are often more than willing to be swept up in the excitement of the adventure, even if for only a short time. My publications listed technicians, undergraduate students, and graduate students. As the leader of my Tamoxifen Team, it was I who had my PhD and BTA. You had to know it all to teach it. With my personal adventures in Chapter 9 going on simultaneously in the 1970s, I discovered my personal philosophy, which I put into action in all the institutions that were to continue to "talent spot" me. Just like me in the 1970s, you train yourself to be precise and achieve reproducibility or do something else with your life. However, it is necessary, from time to time, to make a "work or die" speech.

A time of major decisions

The years at Leeds University were exceptionally productive with my young Tamoxifen Team, but the crippling economic situations and reduced investment in university research was ominous in the 1970s. I was fully funded with an independent research grant from ICI Pharmaceuticals Division and the YCRC, I was working each month with the Yorkshire Police at their national training center at Bishopgarth, Wakefield training Drug Squads, and there was my commitment to

23SAS (Chapter 9). All seemed well for my professional career as a pharmacologist, and I was repaying my debt to society with the opportunity of my free education. But university salaries were meagre (I started at £1990 per annum before tax but had been a visiting scientist at $12,000 with no tax at the Worcester Foundation). I was now not able to support my family. It was my wife Marion who insisted we return to America. Opportunity came from Lois Trench in America, who invested in me to visit Wisconsin for 3 months in 1977 to consider a new job.

Unexpected advice came from a group of Professors of Departments at Leeds University Medical School, all honest individuals, who with one voice encouraged me to seek the opportunities in America. Five chairs met with me in secret at the Christmas black tie ball at the Old Medical School in 1978 to sway me to take my chances in America. They had faith in my ability to be even more successful. Mine was an opportunity that they were too old to take; now was my time, but I did not want to go. However, other events made my success more likely. Yes I had been "talent spotted" now by Paul Carbone at the Wisconsin Clinical Cancer Center and ICI Pharmaceuticals Division (Barry Furr chose to invest in my move) provided me with an unrestricted 3-year research support grant. What I could not know was that the American patent for tamoxifen would start for 16 years in 1984 just at the time the National Cancer Institute agreed that long-term adjuvant tamoxifen was recommended as the antihormone standard of care for breast cancer [38]. But how long was long enough? I would be in the right place at the right time. The benefit for society and economic growth was that AstraZeneca would continue to earn billions of dollars from tamoxifen in America to support their emerging position as a major cancer company with anastrozole, Casodex, and fulvestrant.

References

[1] McGuire WL, Carbone PP, Vollmer EP, editors. Estrogen receptors in human breast cancer. New York: Raven press; 1975.

[2] Kiang DT, Kennedy BJ. Tamoxifen (antiestrogen) therapy in advanced breast cancer. Ann Intern Med 1977;87:687−90.

[3] Morgan Jr LR, Schein PS, Woolley PV, et al. Therapeutic use of tamoxifen in advanced breast cancer: correlation with biochemical parameters. Cancer Ther Rep 1976;60: 1437−43.

[4] Jordan VC, Dowse LJ. Tamoxifen as an anti-tumour agent: effect on oestrogen binding. J Endocrinol 1976;68:297−303.

[5] Jordan VC, Koerner S. Tamoxifen as an anti-tumour agent: role of oestradiol and prolactin. J Endocrinol 1976;68:305−11.

[6] Jordan VC, Jaspan T. Tamoxifen as an anti-tumour agent: oestrogen binding as a predictive test for tumour response. J Endocrinol 1976;68:453−60.

[7] Jordan VC. Antitumour activity of the antiestrogen ICI 46,474 (tamoxifen) in the dimethyl benzanthracene (DMBA)-induced rat mammary carcinoma model. J Steroid Biochem 1974;5.

[8] Jordan VC. Effect of tamoxifen (ICI 46,474) on initiation and growth of DMBA-induced rat mammary carcinomata. Eur J Cancer 1976;12:419−24.

[9] Powles TJ, Hardy JR, Ashley SE, et al. A pilot trial to evaluate the acute toxicity and feasibility of tamoxifen for prevention of breast cancer. Br J Cancer 1989;60:126−31.

[10] Powles TJ, Ashley S, Tidy A, et al. Twenty-year follow-up of the Royal Marsden randomized, double-blinded tamoxifen breast cancer prevention trial. J Natl Cancer Inst 2007;99:283−90.

[11] Fisher B, Constantino JP, Wickerham DL, et al. Tamoxifen for prevention of breast cancer: report of the national surgical adjuvant breast and Bowel project P-1 study. J Natl Cancer Inst 1998;90:1371−88.

[12] Lippman ME, Bolan G. Oestrogen-responsive human breast cancer in long term tissue culture. Nature 1975;256:592−3.

[13] Jordan VC, Koerner S. Tamoxifen (ICI 46,474) and the human carcinoma 8S oestrogen receptor. Eur J Cancer 1975;11:205−6.

[14] Fromson JM, Pearson S, Bramah S. The metabolism of tamoxifen (I.C.I. 46,474). I. In laboratory animals. Xenobiotica 1973;3:693−709.

[15] Fromson JM, Pearson S, Bramah S. The metabolism of tamoxifen (I.C.I. 46, 474). II. In female patients. Xenobiotica 1973;3:711−4.

[16] Jordan VC. Prolonged antioestrogenic activity of ICI 46, 474 in the ovariectomized mouse. J Reprod Fertil 1975;42:251−8.

[17] Cole MP, Jones CT, Todd ID. A new anti-oestrogenic agent in late breast cancer. An early clinical appraisal of ICI46,474. Br J Cancer 1971;25:270−5.

[18] Ward HW. Anti-oestrogen therapy for breast cancer: a trial of tamoxifen at two dose levels. Br J Cancer 1973;1:13−4.

[19] Jordan VC. Use of the DMBA-induced rat mammary carcinoma system for the evaluation of tamoxifen as potential adjuvant therapy. Rev Endocrine Relat Cancer; 1978. p. 49−55. October supplement.

[20] Baum M, Brinkey DM, Dossett JA, et al. Improved survival among patients with adjuvant tamoxifen after mastectomy for early breast cancer. Lancet 1983;2:450.

[21] Adjuvant tamoxifen in the management of operable cancer: the Scottish Trial. Report from the Breast Cancer Trials Committee, Scottish Cancer Trails Office (MRC), Edinburgh. Lancet 1987;2:171−5.

[22] Jordan VC, Dix CJ, Allen KE. The effectiveness of long-term tamoxifen treatment in a laboratory model for adjuvant therapy of breast cancer. In: Jones SE, Salmon ES, editors. Adjuvant therapy of cancer II. New York: Grune & Tratton; 1979. p. 19−26.

[23] Jordan VC, Allen KE. Evaluation of the antitumour activity of the non-steroidal antiestrogen monohydroxytamoxifen in the DMBA-induced rat mammary carcinoma model. Eur J Cancer 1980;16:239−51.

[24] Jordan VC, Allen KE, Dix CJ. Pharmacology of tamoxifen in laboratory animals. Cancer Treat Rep 1980;64:745−59.

[25] Davies C, Godwin J, Gray R. Relevance of breast cancer hormone receptors and other factors to the efficacy of adjuvant tamoxifen: patient-level met-analysis of randomized trials. Lancet 2011;378:771−84.

[26] Davies C, Pan H, Godwin J. Long-term effects of continuing adjuvant tamoxifen to 10 years versus stopping at 5 years after diagnosis of oestrogen receptor-positive breast cancer: ATLAS, a randomized trial. Lancet 2013;381:805−16.

[27] Quirke V. Imperial Chemical Industries and Craig Jordan, "the first Tamoxifen Consultant," 1960s−1990s. Ambix 2020;67:1−19.

[28] Jordan VC, Dix CJ, Rowsby L, Prestwich S. Studies on the mechanism of action of the nonsteroidal antiestrogen tamoxifen (I.C.I. 46,474) in the rat. Mol Cell Endocrinol 1977;7:177−92.

[29] Jordan VC, Prestwich G. Binding of [^{3}H]tamoxifen in rat uterine cytosols: a comparison of swinging bucket and vertical tube rotor sucrose density gradient analysis. Mol Cell Endocinol 1977;8:179−88.

[30] Jordan VC, Rowsby L, Dix CJ, Prestwich G. Dose-related effects of non-steroidal antiestrogens and oestrogens on the measurement of cytoplasmic oestrogen receptors in the rat and mouse uterus. J Endocrinol 1978;78:71−81.

[31] Jordan VC, Prestwich G. Effect of non-steroidal anti-oestrogens on the concentration of rat uterine progesterone receptors. J Endocrinol 1978;76:363−4.

[32] Jordan VC, Collins MM, Rowsby L, Prestwich G. A monohydroxylated metabolite of tamoxifen with potent antioestrogenic activity. J Endocrinol 1977;75:305−16.

[33] Allen KE, Clark ER, Jordan VC. Evidence of the metabolic activation of nonsteroidal antiestrogens: a study of structure activity relationships. Br J Pharmacol 1980;71:83−91.

[34] Shiau AK, Barstad D, Loria PM, et al. The structural basis of estrogen receptor/coactivator recognition and the antagonism of this interaction by tamoxifen. Cell 1998;95:927−37.

[35] Goetz MP, Suman VJ, Reid JM, et al. First-in-human phase I study of the tamoxifen metabolite Z-endoxifen in women with endocrine-refractory metastatic breast cancer. J Clin Oncol 2017;35:3391−400.

[36] Pujol H, Girault J, Rouanet P, et al. Phase I study of percutaneous 4-hydroxy-tamoxifen with analyses of 4-hydroxy-tamoxifen concentrations in breast cancer and normal tissue. Cancer Chemother Pharmacol 1995;36:493−8.

[37] Lazzeroni M, Serrano D, Dunn BK, et al. Oral low dose and topical tamoxifen for breast cancer prevention: modern approaches for an old drug. Breast Cancer Res 2012;14:214.

[38] Consensus conference. Adjuvant chemotherapy for breast cancer. J Am Med Assoc 1985;254:3461−3.

Tamoxifen's patenting problems in America, which created a "cancer treatment company"

Before we consider the 1-year interlude in Switzerland to get my permanent resident visa for America, I will set the scene about what was happening with ICI Pharmaceutical Division/Zeneca and AstraZeneca. It is hard to believe today, but when ICI Pharmaceutical Division applied for the worldwide patent for ICI 46,474 in the mid-1960s with the following wording: "The alkene derivatives of the invention are useful for the modification of the endocrine status in man and animals and they may be useful for the control of hormone-dependent tumors or for the management of the sexual cycle and aberrations thereof. They may also have useful hypocholesterolemic activity." They were rejected by the Patent Office of the United States and told that reference to the treatment of cancer was fantastic and must be removed. The Merrell Company, in Cincinnati, where the first nonsteroidal antiestrogen MER25 was discovered in 1958 [1] went on to discover clomiphene [2], a triphenylethylene, a mixture of geometric isomers, but the company chose not to bother separating the isomers initially. It was the Merrell Company that discovered that clomiphene was an excellent postcoital antifertility agent in mice but did the opposite in women during the 1960s (when I started my Ph.D. on failed contraceptives at the University of Leeds!). However, both clomiphene (mixed isomers) and tamoxifen geometric isomers were built on the same triphenylethylene skeleton. Merrell has prepatented all possible substituted derivatives, so the ICI Pharmaceutical Division patent applications failed for a decade or more. Merrell also had evidence that clomiphene (mixed isomers) had activity to treat breast cancer [3].

Simply stated, all the work and effort getting tamoxifen FDA-approved and marketed by Lois Trench and her Team at ICI Americas in the mid 1970s was to approve a medicine without a patent in the United States. This was unprecedented in the pharmaceutical industry, but it was never meant to be successfully marketed in America (or anywhere else), but for Arthur Walpole and his circle of enthusiasts inside and outside ICI Alderley Park!

Arthur Walpole died on July 2, 1977. However, the research momentum continued with vigor with the announcement that ICI pharmaceutical division had been awarded the Queen's Award for Industry for tamoxifen in 1978. Sales of tamoxifen were so high it was hard for the manufacturing section to keep up with demand worldwide.

Tamoxifen Tales. https://doi.org/10.1016/B978-0-323-85051-3.00006-3

The FDA approval for tamoxifen for the treatment of metastatic breast cancer was awarded on December 31, 1977. As a result, half a dozen further applications for the treatment and prevention of breast cancer followed over the next 20 years or so. However, the early development of clinical trials went on before and after FDA approval in the United States without any patent protection! This situation illustrated how unlikely competitors, in the pharmaceutical industry, saw the future success of tamoxifen to be! No one made generic tamoxifen and sold it in the 6 years after FDA approval! Clinical studies with adjuvant tamoxifen were sufficiently advanced in 1984 for the National Cancer Institute to declare that tamoxifen was the adjuvant therapy of choice for ER-positive breast cancer. But this was buried in an article [4] entitled: Adjuvant Chemotherapy for Breast Cancer (remember chemotherapy was King!) but with the statement that the optimal duration of adjuvant tamoxifen had not yet been determined! This clinical trial process would take the next 20 years, but the translation concept from the 1970s as an experimental fact preceded "longer was better than shorter" as a clinical standard of care.

As luck would have it, just as Astra Zeneca was loosing patent protection for tamoxifen in the rest of the world, the patent, originally denied in the United States, was awarded by the court of appeals in 1985. Indeed, the decision granted the company precedence back to 1965 allowing AstraZeneca to start their 17-year patent in America in 1985. However, this did not go uncontested, most notably by Novopharm in Federal Court in Baltimore in 1995. Herein lies a tale.

Lois Trench, the former drug monitor for tamoxifen in the United States in the 1970s, who secured FDA approval for the treatment of metastatic breast cancer, recommended that I be an expert witness for the now Zeneca legal team. A 3-week trial was planed, but before then, multiple meetings were organized for the planning of expert testimony for witnesses and taking depositions by the Novopharm legal team. All was progressing nicely up until the night before the trial in Baltimore, when it was discovered that the allocated judge withdrew as he had a friendship with Zeneca's first star medical witness Dr. Marty Abeloff, the Cancer Center Director at John's Hopkins in Baltimore. It was announced that Judge Smalkin, a no-nonsense Republican appointee, would preside and I was to be second witness for scientific facts in the development of antiestrogens for breast cancer treatment. My encyclopedic knowledge of the history of "failed contraceptives" at the University of Leeds was now of value in the real world! In my case, my expansive CV of firsthand knowledge of the investigators of significance (Walpole) and the international scientists involved of "who did what and when" was critical to be stated publically as were my *bone fides* at the start of my sworn testimony. When Zeneca's first expert witness took the stand, Judge Smalkin abruptly stopped the Zeneca lawyer, stating that he did not wish to hear the qualifications of the Director of the John Hopkins Cancer Center, he accepted them as written. My heart sank! However, I had nothing to fear.

Judge Smalkin became engrossed in scanning my *Curriculum Vitae* (which also documented my military career with the British Intelligence Service and SAS). He focused on my award of the Cameron Prize from the University of Edinburgh in

1993. The award since the end of 19th century has included the greats of medicine e.g., Louis Pasteur, Madam Curie, etc. He pointed out to the council of Zeneca that he was aware that "Dr. Fleming, the Nobel Laureate, who was awarded the Cameron Prize in 1947 had discovered penicillin!" but Judge Smalkin then turned to me and observed that David Sterling (who founded the SAS in World War II) had not been awarded the Cameron Prize, but I was the only one in the SAS who had! The lawyers all became confused having no knowledge in their briefs about who David Sterling was! The Judge's comments to me directly continued, on the same SAS topic, until I was excused. The trial was scheduled to be 3 weeks: first week Zeneca, second week Novopharm, and then a 1 week free for all but then unexpectedly Judge Smalkin brought the proceedings to a halt at the beginning of week 3 declaring he was ready to start his deliberations. I should explain this was not a jury trial but a written decision by a federal judge from the bench.

Zeneca won, but I was thrilled when the written decision was made available. Judge Smalkin was most complementary about the veracity and clarity of my testimony. I also discovered he was a British military history buff and his decision secured $ billions of sales of tamoxifen in America to invest in the research and development of Casodex (for the treatment of prostate cancer), Faslodex (a pure antiestrogen for the treatment of breast cancer by depot injections), Goserilin, an LHRH superagonist (to treat premenopausal breast cancer) and Fulvestrant. AstraZeneca became a world-class player in the treatment of cancer on the strength of the success of tamoxifen, Arthur Walpole's/Lois Trench's investment in an enthusiastic young cancer pharmacologist who would always say "I am the least likely person to be standing before you today, as I am a cancer pharmacologist "self-taught by pictures" illustrated that, at the beginnings of tamoxifen, there were no guarantees of success. Thank you Dr. Roy Cotton, the first drug monitor for tamoxifen at Alderley Park in 1973 who changed the medical world by using his clinical budget to send me hundreds of Alderley Park female rats by ICI pharmaceuticals division executive limousines each week from Alderley Park to the University of Leeds Medical School for 5 years. That resulted in millions of lives saved from breast cancer, over the following decades. The published laboratory results became the clinical standard of care worldwide.

But there is an additional aspect of the University of Leeds/ICI Pharmaceuticals Joint Research scheme that deserves mention. We made an application for ICI Pharmaceutical division to synthesize estradiol derivatives with long 10-member carbon side chain substitutions in the 6 and 7 positions, but the therapeutic activity would be a chemotherapy alkylating group. The plan was to get the ER in the breast tumor to bind our new compound with an estradiol core just like the natural estrogen hormone, but the novel medicine would be transported to the tumor cell DNA and bind to it irreversibly. The breast cancer cells would be killed by a new targeted therapy, and we would have target site specificity against the tumor and kill it. We were unsuccessful in generating much enthusiasm at Alderley Park but Walpole, and I got a publication out of the work [5]. I was surprised when a senior leader at Alderley Park declared: "We liked your "tamoxifen forever," rather than your new idea to target and kill all ER-positive breast cancer cells in a patient's body!" Nevertheless, the idea of substituting estradiol with long side chains triggered a great deal of activity at Alderely Park to study the antiestrogenic properties of these novel compounds. The chemist Jean Bowler and biologist Alan Wakeling discovered an entirely new group of medicines referred to as "pure antiestrogens" [6]. The medicines would subsequently be found to destroy the ER [7]: these pure antiestrogens, unlike tamoxifen, had no estrogenic properties in any animal models. Fulvestrant is today an effective treatment for breast cancer [8].

A year later, a second challenge occurred in court in Boston, but this time, it was a jury trial. I chose not to be an expert witness, and to this day. I am mystified why the legal team of the generic company wanting to make tamoxifen and sell it did not depose me!

Instead, I chose to be an advisor behind the scenes analyzing the responses of the expert witnesses for the generic company. The first day of deliberations did not go well for Zeneca. The nationally famous expert witness for the generic company declared that his hourly sum of reimbursement was only 25% of the Zeneca expert witnesses. This was a shock to all. The tactic of the lawyers would be "so you are being paid to reach this conclusion?" and the response would be "I am only being reimbursed for my time studying the documents." However, the working men and women on the jury were now listening to an hourly sums from the generic company witness that was a small fraction of the sum reimbursing Zeneca expert witness. It was becoming David and Goliath in a courtroom, and the jury was siding with "David." This had to be countered, but how? The witness was witty and throughout the day was successfully neutralizing Zeneca science in their publications with attacks on, in his view, poor statistical work with too few animals per group for Zeneca scientists to claim veracity.

After an evening of mulling over the failing situation and discussing it with my wife, Monica in Chicago, we hit upon an idea: "Ask the expert witness how many hours of work he had claimed for reimbursement from the generic company? It was discovered that the hours of work by the opposition expert witness was more than 10 times that reimbursed for the Zeneca experts." The case was won by Zeneca.

References

[1] Lerner LJ, Holthaus Jr HJ, Thampson CR. A non-steroidal estrogen antagonist 1-(p-2-diethylaminoethoxyphenyl)-1-phenyl-2-p-methoxyphenyl ethanol. Endocrinology 1958;63:295–318.

[2] Holtkamp DE, Greslin JG, Root CA, Lerner LJ. Gonadotropin inhibiting and anti-fecundity effects of chloramiphene. Proc Soc Exp Biol Med 1960;105:197–201.

[3] Herbst AL, Griffiths CT, Kristner RW. Clomiphene citrate (MSC-35770) in disseminated mammary carcinoma. Cancer Chemother Rep 1964;43:39–41.

[4] Consensus Conference. Adjuvant chemotherapy for breast cancer. J Am Med Assoc 1985;254:3461–3.

[5] Jordan VC, Fenuik L, Allen KE, et al. Structural derivatives of tamoxifen and estradiol-3-methyl ether as potential alkylating antiestrogens. Eur J Cancer 1981;17:193—200.

[6] Wakeling AE, Dukes M, Bowler J. A potent specific pure antiestrogen with clinical potential. Cancer Res 1991;51:3867—73.

[7] Parker MG. Action of "pure" antiestrogens in inhibiting estrogen receptor action. Breast Cancer Res Treat 1993;26:131—7.

[8] Nathan MR, Schmidt P. A review of fulvestrant in breast cancer. Oncol Ther 2017;5:17—29.

Two opportunities on different continents

In 1977, I was offered an opportunity to become a faculty member at the Wisconsin Clinical Cancer Center. Paul Carbone MD was the director of the Cancer Center and chairman of the Eastern Cooperative Oncology Group. This was an exceptional opportunity, despite the fact that tamoxifen was not yet FDA-approved in the United States.

Paul Carbone offered me a job as a tenured associate professor at Wisconsin in the Department of Pharmacology, but this opportunity did not amuse my professor back at Leeds. After a difficult 6 months of negotiations with Wisconsin, who **really** wanted me to accept their offer, it was agreed that I would have an associate professor's salary, but be a nontenured assistant professor and reapply for tenure after 1 or 2 years at Wisconsin. It transpired that my professor at Leeds had not supported my tenure appointment at Wisconsin despite the fact he had already recommended and I had received my tenure at Leeds. This was difficult for me and my family because I was now having to leave a tenured faculty job and the security at Leeds for a well-paid opportunity at Wisconsin with only the promise of promotion. I chose the difficult path. Fortunately, and out of the blue, Roger King, a friend from the Imperial Cancer Research Fund in London, rang to tell me he had recommended me to head up a new opportunity in Bern, Switzerland, to create the Ludwig Institute for Cancer Research Laboratories as a "CORE" estrogen receptor (ER) facility for their International Clinical trials group!

My wife and I flew to Switzerland, and I was interviewed by Carl Baker, then the Director of the worldwide Ludwig Organization at its headquarters in Zurich. He was the former director of the National Cancer Institute in Bethesda. The job was to create the laboratories in Bern within a year and establish a worldwide ER quality control system for the clinical trials sites, recruiting patients for adjuvant (only 1 year I regret to say) tamoxifen studies. I accepted with alacrity. This was an opportunity to learn about international clinical trials that were using tamoxifen, live in Bern, Switzerland, design and build a research institute, and again forge lifelong friendships. The latter were Aron Goldhirsch, a wonderful and talented young medical oncologist, who became the medical director of the European Institute of Oncology, with Director Professor Veronesi, "the most famous Doctor in Italy" (Fig. 7.1). Regrettably, both Aron and Professor Veronesi have both died. Aron was also one of the coorganizers of the St. Gallen adjuvant breast cancer meeting. Another colleague is the internationally distinguished biostatistician, Dr. Richard Gelber from Harvard. He has guided the original Ludwig trials (now the

Tamoxifen Tales. https://doi.org/10.1016/B978-0-323-85051-3.00007-5

FIGURE 7.1

The occasion of my award of the third Annual Breast Cancer Award from the European Institute of Oncology in Milan, Italy 2001. The award was presented by Professor Veronesi, who at that time was the Italian Minister of Health and known as "the most famous Doctor in Italy." Left to right Gianni Bonadonna, who initiated combination cytotoxic chemotherapy as an adjuvant for breast cancer, Umberto Veronesi and me. Each of us have won the St. Gallen Breast Cancer Prize and the Karnofsky Award from ASCO.

International Breast Cancer Study Group) for more than three decades. The three of us have enjoyed numerous adventures worldwide, but I recall one heated discussion during the late evening in 1978 on a bridge in Fribourg, Switzerland, about the international merits or demerits of Richard Nixon's presidency. Good times!

My wife Marion deserves the credit for securing our apartment in Switzerland. It was outside Bern in Gümligen a short 20 min train ride to the Main station (Hauptbahnhoff) in Bern followed by a 2 mile walk to the Inselspital. Here is where I would be working and creating a new Ludwig Institute. However, several episodes, unplanned, deserve recounting. These illustrate the spontaneous academic adventures that occurred in the year in Switzerland "waiting for my residency visa to be approved at the US embassy in Bern."

After my family and I had been living for a couple of months in Gümlingen, listening to the BBC world service news each evening, before the Russian radio jamming occurred about 7 p.m., I had a strange encounter at work with the Chief administrator at the Inselspital. He entered our office space and went around the room shaking each person's hand saying "goodbye." A little odd, I thought, but play along. When he got to me, I said "hello" and he stopped. We started a conversation in English, and then he said "have you registered with the Frempt Politzei in Muri (just outside Bern)?" I replied "I had not as I didn't know this was a requirement." He now took a large step back, and the mood changed. He now required me to do this as soon as possible.

I returned home, and Marion agreed to phone the Frempt Polizei and spoke to them in her best French (all Swiss speak at least four languages: French, German, and Romansch [the native regions of Switzerland] and English). The gist of the conversation was I must come the next day to their police station for processing of my passport, which I must surrender. Marion explained I was traveling to Ljubljana in Yugoslavia the next day. We agreed an appointment the day after I returned. I will now recount events in chronological order.

First, was my "adventure" on the way to Ljubljana, Yugoslavia, from Zurich in 1979 (remember we used to say in the Regiment "an adventure is a perfect plan gone horribly wrong"). I had just officially left 23SAS(V) in the United Kingdom and became a Regular Army Reserve Officer (RARO) in the SAS. This status remained active until 50 years of age. One is recalled in the time of war as the situation demands. In 1979, I still had the NATO war plan in my head for Northern Army Group and the role of the British Army of the Rhine, as we had regularly trained and held staff exercises over the ground to be disputed in Western Germany in the event of an invasion by Warsaw Pact forces.

My director in Bern, Switzerland, was a charming, internationally known, radiotherapist called Dr Jan Stjernsward. He had spent much of his earlier career in Africa, and we got along extremely well. He cooked up a plan for me to visit our recruitment site in Ljubljana, ostensibly to inspect their ER assay laboratory, but really I was to smuggle Bacillus Calmette—Guérin (BCG) vaccine taped to my body into the country for the Ludwig lung trials. The injections of BCG were intended to increase nonspecific immune responses and establish whether this would help to stop the progression of lung cancer. Remember that 1979 was well before any of the serious security screening occurred that we see today. However, as an RARO officer in the SAS, I was required to register with the British Military Attaché at the embassy in Bern in the event of a "misunderstanding" in a communist country. Jan took the precautions of giving me a letter of authority that I was carrying medical supplies (all of this palava was because mailing the BCG would guarantee that it would never get through their customs and be stolen—I should point out BCG is used for immunization against tuberculosis). I arranged with the British Military Attaché in Bern—that if I was not on the plane, I planned to leave Yugoslavia; my wife was to call him to "sort out the misunderstanding." In the previous 10 years of my reserve military career, it was not permitted for me to travel to any communist country but now the Ludwig plans were set!

Then things started to go wrong. The plan was I would be met by my hosts in Ljubljana at the airport, but if this did not occur, I did not know who to contact. I had no money. Credit cards had not even been introduced in Europe at this time; cell phones did not exist. It was absolutely clear that the airport meeting in Ljubljana had to be made. The air route on JAT from Zurich to Zagreb started with a passport check by the military and then a change of planes in Belgrade to get my connection back to Ljubljana. The plane was delayed out of Zagreb because of bad weather, but we arrived with 30 min to spare for the connection in Belgrade. Perfect! If this was America or elsewhere in Europe, there was a good chance I could get the connection—but this was Yugoslavia. In Belgrade, I ran up to the gate in the empty departure lounge shouting that "I have made the plane in time with 15 min to spare; where is the plane for boarding to Ljubljana?" I had to get on that plane! The young lady at the counter declared that the plane was taxiing out onto the runway, "look there it is!" In response, I declared "But the convention is that the plane finishes boarding at the departure time—it does not leave when you feel like it!" "I am a guest of your government—get me on that plane NOW!!! If I am not on that plane, things will not go well for you and your family!" Well OK, this was not exactly true and would never work anywhere else. But in a totalitarian regime and Tito lying in hospital in Belgrade after a heart attack, it was worth a try. With BCG taped to your body in a totalitarian regime, anything is worth a try—and it worked.

Soldiers with their AK47s appeared in response to my shouting but were signaled to stop advancing toward us by the gate attendant. I was escorted around security and put in a car with red flags (rather appropriate I thought), and the plane was stopped on the runway and the rear stairs were dropped, and I was shown to my seat much to the consternation of the other passengers. Mission accomplished, Who Dares Wins.

Now for getting out! On the last night, my hosts who were doctors in Ljubljana, drank alcohol like old English ladies drink tea. After countless bottles of wicked types of potent brews and much fun wandering around bars in Ljubljana at night, it was 3 a.m. and I had to find my hotel, get my stuff, and catch my 7 a.m. flight to Belgrade and eventually catch my connection to Zurich. If I did not arrive, the British Military Attaché would receive a call from my anxious and distraught wife and a "missing person" call would go out to Belgrade. Naturally, it now occurred to me the authorities would ask themselves "why does the embassy need to know where Dr. Jordan has got to?" I made the plane and all connections despite a thunderous hangover. Now on to the second adventure, the following week, at the Frempt Politzei headquarters in Muri.

At our appointed arrival time, I noticed palpable tension with one of the waiting policemen. I asked Marion not to speak or get involved and I would sort this out. As the conversation went back and forth and I filled out our forms (the husband represents the whole family in Switzerland; I should point out that women were only allowed to vote in 1971!), I realized tensions were rising with this one policeman. Then it became clear as I was questioned about how long the family had lived at the address in Gumligen.

The nervous policeman was the officer responsible for the area around our apartment block. It was his responsibility to know about any foreigners in his area—we had slipped through and this was serious—for him. Indeed, at that time in Switzerland, it was expected that Swiss nationals would report the presence of foreign nationals in their apartment block. Voices were raised, and I was asked to leave my passport and return for it in a week. I didn't know what happened to the policeman, who had not protected Bern appropriately: this was where all the foreign embassies were so it was essential that they know where every non-Swiss national was in their country.

The story of creating the Ludwig Institute laboratories in Bern from the 18th-century building (Fig. 7.2) is wonderful and was never viewed by me as a challenge. By law, one could not damage the outer façade of the old building, so the laboratories had to be created entirely internally with fake ceilings for 20th-century laboratory standards. Each week, I would have lunch with the Ludwig lawyer Mr. Marty, who would tell me about adventures with Ursula Andress's sister in his class at school. Ursula Andress is the famous Swiss actress who changed cinema forever as she walked out of the sea in her bikini in the Bond film, Dr. No. Now he had my attention! We would dine in a restaurant near the Dome (cathedral) in the center of Bern. All is a beautiful setting, which I can readily recommend, and featured in John leCarre's "Smiley's People." As our meeting progressed each week, he would read the "request," which would always be prefaced by "have another calvados Dr. Jordan." The acceptance of requests ensured completion on time and I started by lifelong love of calvados, a distilled apple brandy from Normandy!

When it came to moving all of our new equipment into the laboratory, this presented a real problem. The ultracentrifuges and scintillation counters were considered to be too heavy to transport up the 18th-century central spiral staircase, so we had to consider an alternate plan. This involved hiring a huge crane to raise

FIGURE 7.2

The Ludwig Institute for Cancer Research in Bern, Switzerland. The big third floor windows we used cranes to get the heavy laboratory equipment into the building are around the side on the left. This picture was taken 15 years after I had created the laboratories in 1979. The space reverted back to the Insetspital Hospital after the decision was made to close many on the Ludwig Units around the world.

the equipment up to the largest windows we could find on the third floor and swing the equipment like a huge pendulum to the open windows where we had erected a large wooden platform to capture the equipment and drag it inside. An exciting days work, but it was also pouring with rain! Again good to have seen real life in the SAS—the impossible just takes a little longer!

During the year, I spent a year in Bern, in 1979 I had established friendships with all of the academic breast cancer doctors in Switzerland. However, one national academic meeting in 1979 will forever remain in my memory. I received a phone call in my office at the Kinderspital in Bern. I was to be invited to be the plenary speaker to present current thinking about the value of tamoxifen therapy! Then, casually, the caller enquired would I present my lecture in French or German? I replied "neither, I will present in English." This was against the regulations for the Society as the country is primarily bilingual and English is not one of them. The lecture invitation was withdrawn. Nevertheless, the meeting organizer was determined to have my attendance in his program. "Will you accept our invitation to be the Chairman of an 1 h discussion panel of "Current Issues in Breast Cancer Therapy?" I pointed out that "I would still be speaking English so how will this work?" "We will have a German speaker translating in your left ear and a French speaker translating in your right ear. You can address the room in English because we all understand and speak English!" The day arrived, and it was quite fun with the to-and-from of languages and opinions about breast cancer.

Naturally, progress in constructing the new Ludwig Unit in Bern had to be monitored by a central board of advisors to the Ludwig Organization. A site visit was arranged for the Bern, Ludwig unit to establish quality control. Jan Stjernsward and I would "perform for a full day." However, there was an unanticipated complication that arose during the site visit proceedings.

Lois Trench-Hines had organized an "all star" symposium in Sorrento, south of Naples. I was to be the opening plenary speaker. The "complication" was that at 2 p.m. that day Alitalia was to go on strike. She phoned me at 10 a.m. that morning in Bern with the command "get on the next flight out of Bern to Sorrento immediately!" I insisted that her plan was not possible as my site visit was underway and would end at 5 p.m. I rapidly formulated plan B and returned to the site visit, after reassuring Lois that I would be there on time.

Bridgette Haldeman was my senior technician who was essential for me to establish the laboratories for the new Ludwig Institute in Bern. I had no car, so I proposed whether she, and her mother as an escort for the return journey, would consider an overnight drive from Bern to Sorrento, to arrive on time for my address. We three set off on our "mission impossible" around 7 p.m. for the 1000 mile round trip journey.

Getting to Sorrento was straightforward, but it was here I discovered a flaw in the citizens of Sorrento to deliver reliable directions to the hotel. I should reemphasize that Swiss citizens spoke multiple languages, so Bridgette was forearmed but to no avail, as we hurtled from one side of Sorrento to another! I discovered that confidence in delivering directions was essential to the citizens of Sorrento; not their veracity. Nevertheless, we arrived with 30 min to spare, to be greeted by Lois who instructed me to shower and change immediately as I was to present, as the first speaker, as soon as possible!

Bridgette had already proved her worth as my senior technician, and she learned quickly from me what would be required of her once I was off to America. "Remember: if it is not published it never happened, so tell them the story so far" (Eliahu Caspi, 1974, Worcester Foundation). Bridgette worked diligently to provide data that was published with Karen Allen back at Leeds University [1]. I was to establish my new career in America so this was my second publication in Endocrinology, the premier journal for the discipline in America. The first had been with my successful PhD student Clive Dix [2]. Lois, in true "Lois fashion" demonstrated her gratitude to Bridgette and her mother upon achieving "mission impossible." I saw Lois empty her pockets of all the money she had in gratitude, and to achieve a safe journey back to Bern. Once I returned to Bern, Bridgette told me how exciting the week for her and her mother had been!

Opportunities occurred during my time in Switzerland. Firstly, if I was to quality control the steroid receptor laboratories within the international Ludwig clinical trials network, I clearly had to visit each site and organize an evaluation of their proficiency using quality control standards. I set off for a 6-week tour of the laboratories flying from Zurich to Johannesburg, down to Cape Town (to visit Ludwig ER laboratories), on to Sydney, Australia, and then Melbourne, Auckland, New Zealand, and Wellington and back to Zurich, Switzerland via Kentucky in the United States.

Small World is an excellent book by David Lodge that captures the life of "Visiting Professors" jetting around the world. It is an extremely funny tale and captures the unlikely meetings in far away places. Imagine my surprise upon boarding my flight from Zurich to South Africa, I literally bumped into Steve Carter from my summer job at Alderley Park. "Small World" indeed.

A stopover in Sydney was important to reconnect with my friend Rob Sutherland (Fig. 7.3). He and I had first met when he visited my Tamoxifen Team in Leeds. He was then a postdoc with Etienne Baulieu in Paris. He was now in charge of a new laboratory within the Sydney Ludwig Unit. We decided to plan an international tamoxifen meeting and publish a book of the proceedings of all that was starting to emerge about the clinical potential of antiestrogens. This we did in between February 4 and 6, 1980, and our proceedings were published by Academic Press [3].

So why did I stop off for a few days in Louisville, Kentucky!? During my 2 years as a visiting scientist at the Worcester Foundation, I had attended numerous national meetings on steroid hormone receptors. Remember, as a young scientist, you need to continuously train yourself to lead your research group effectively. I met Jim Wittliff who was a leader of the emerging applications of steroid hormone receptor assays to predict responsiveness to tamoxifen. He agreed to assist with my goal to quality control the Ludwig Breast Cancer Study Group steroid receptor laboratories worldwide. Our paper was published [4].

All objectives were achieved in Bern. I had established an ER quality control program for our sites in Australia, New Zealand, South Africa, and Yugoslavia, and the institute laboratories were ready to be handed over in 1980 when I left

FIGURE 7.3

Professor Robert L. Sutherland in Sydney at a reception for my visit 20 years ago. The event was to celebrate the anniversary of the establishment of their research institute in Sidney.

Switzerland for Madison, Wisconsin, in February. I was to start a new ascent in science through promotions up the ranks of academia at Wisconsin to become a professor of Human Oncology and Pharmacology in 1985 and director of the Breast Cancer Research & Treatment Program at the UW Comprehensive Cancer Center. Five years after I arrived, tamoxifen had taken off, we discovered selective ER modulators, and chemoprevention became the fashion.

References

[1] Jordan VC, Haldeman B, Allen KE. Geometric isomers of substituted triphenylethylenes and antiestrogen action. Endocrinology 1981;108:1353−61.

[2] Dix CJ, Jordan VC. Modulation of rat steroid hormone receptors by estrogen and antiestrogen. Endocrinology 1980;107:2011−20.

[3] Sutherland RL, Jordan VC. Non-steroidal antiestrogens: molecular pharmacology and antitumour activity. Sydney and New York: Academic Press; 1981.

[4] Jordan VC, Zava DT, Eppenburger U, et al. Reliability of steroid hormone receptor assays: an international study. Eur J Cancer Clin Oncol 1983;19:357−63.

The good, the bad and the ugly of tamoxifen at Wisconsin

When I had secured my future in Wisconsin, one prominent breast cancer medical scientist from Washington enquired "Why on earth go to Wisconsin?" The implication was it is in the Midwest and to those who grow up and live on the east coast of the United States; it is beyond the boundaries of the known world! To me, it was an opportunity. My new laboratories were to be in the brand new University of Wisconsin (UW) Clinical Cancer Center as part of the University of Wisconsin Hospital (Fig. 8.1). This was a spectacular surprise because when I interviewed for the job in 1977; in dingy old buildings on campus, none of the new facilities existed.

During my earlier visits, I had found the whole experience of the UW campus wonderful in the town of Madison, the state capital of just 250,000 inhabitants. It

FIGURE 8.1

The University of Wisconsin Hospital and five-floor comprehensive center (center right). My laboratory occupied half of the fifth floor and there was an excellent mix of clinician and scientist offices. Paul Carbone's office was on the fifth floor with daily access for me. On the right are the state-of-the-art animal facilities used by Marco Gottardis to complete his pioneering studies.

Tamoxifen Tales. https://doi.org/10.1016/B978-0-323-85051-3.00008-7

FIGURE 8.2

The fabulous faculty I joined in Madison, Wisconsin, in 1980. The photograph was taken in 1985 when I had just received my Doctor of Science at Leeds University for my contributions to the pharmacology of antiestrogens, I had been promoted to Professor of Human Oncology and Pharmacology at the University of Wisconsin Comprehensive Cancer Center (UWCCC), and I had just organized a symposium at Madison on "Estrogen and Antiestorgen Action and Breast Cancer Therapy" Jordan VC. Estrogen/Antiestrogen Action and Breast Cancer Therapy. Madison, WI: University of Wisconsin Press; 1986.). Our estrogen/antiestrogen team and participants were, left to right back row, Gerry Mueller, McArdle Laboratory for Cancer Research, Jack Gorski, Dept. of Biochemistry, me, Doug Tormey, Dept of Human Oncology, Wisconsin Cancer Cancer, Head of the Breast Cancer Program. Front row left Harold Rusch, Inaugural Director of McArdle, former inaugural Director of UWCCC right Paul Carbone current Director UWCCC.

was also the perfect place to raise a family. My daughters Helen and Alexandra would both benefit from competitive swimming, and winter sports, becoming accomplished skaters and good skiers. All are advantages for them. That was one reason, why it was wise to seek the opportunity in Wisconsin. Another reason (if I was to survive academically in a new country and support my family with a 1-year deadline for promotion) was the excellence of the University and their facilities. But the University of Wisconsin, at the time, was about the accomplished faculty I was to join (Fig. 8.2).

The quality of the people with whom you work and learn is essential. It is an ill-defined chemistry of enthusiastic compatibility where people share, collaborate, and advance knowledge through mutual respect. This group of stars with whom I would be privileged to work all taught me lessons, and we published together. Well almost. My publication [1] regarding Harold Rusch was written by me about the life of this great leader in cancer research following his death. These colleagues I saw every week were to provide the perfect environment for me, a pharmacologist who wanted to take tamoxifen as far as it could go in clinical applications and a basic drug receptor pharmacologist who always chose to study mechanisms. I required a foot in both camps, and Wisconsin was where it worked for me. Who were the key individuals from whom I was to learn?

Dr Gerald Mueller (Fig. 8.2), a pioneer in estrogen action, was an early recruit to the McArdle Laboratory (after medical school he completed his Ph.D. in McArdle in the 1950s) by the first Director Harold Rusch. He was Dr Jack Gorski's (Fig. 8.2) postdoctoral supervisor at Wisconsin before Jack left for the University of Illinois (Champagne/Urbana). There he did the pioneering work [2] that identified the estrogen receptor protein for the first time and resulted in my initial Ph.D. topic with Ted Clark at Leeds University (Chapter 2). Gerry was instrumental in recruiting Jack Gorski back to the University of Wisconsin Madison into biochemistry, but actually his laboratory was in the Agricultural Sciences building on campus. I was told that Jack's first passion was breeding his herd of cattle in the wilds of Wisconsin. Jack Gorski was subsequently a member of the National Academy of Sciences and President of the Endocrine Society. Both Jack and Gerry were members of my Ph.D. student Anne Riegel's Ph.D. committee in Madison. Most importantly, Jack was on the Ph.D. committee of several of my students in Madison, Marco Gottardis, Doug Wolf, Shun-Yuan Jiang, and Bill Catherino. I was privileged to be mentor to all these students, as well as others. I recruited the best minds of the day for the committees of my students.

Dr Jack Gorski was a friend and a quiet gentleman who wrote a letter of recommendation for me for promotion to associate professor. I was keen for us to publish together when I first went to Madison. I am proud of our three refereed publications because of the contributions we made with our individual laboratories. But he was a gentleman when he made two remarks to me concerning the future careers of his former trainees and my future. He told me he did not want to "compete with his former trainees." They had stellar careers ahead of them in this area. Benita Katzenellenbogen, who remains a leader in estrogen action at the University of Illinois Champagne-Urbana, became President of the Endocrine Society, and with her husband John led the field in basic research in estrogens and antiestrogens for the whole of my career. I continue to admire their lasting contributions and the memories of our meetings, with their growing children, at exotic scientific venues around the world. Jack also gave me professional advice. "If you put my name on your papers of the work you conceived and executed, you will impair your chance for promotion. It will be said, by the promotion or prize committee, that it was really my idea even when it was not." I did not care, as my philosophy was that we could not have done the work without the contributions of his laboratory. He recommended that Mara Lieberman and Wade Welshons join my laboratory at the Cancer Center and both were excellent team members.

Dr Douglas C. Tormey (Fig. 8.2) was director of the Breast Cancer Program at the Wisconsin Clinical Cancer Center. Doug was a Madison native who completed his MD and Ph.D. at the University. Gerry Mueller was his Ph.D. supervisor at the McArdle. He subsequently became the head of the Breast Cancer Program at the National Cancer Center in Bethesda when Paul Carbone was the head of the Medicine branch. Lois introduced me to both Doug and Paul in 1974 when I introduced tamoxifen to the Eastern Cooperative Oncology Group (ECOG). Paul was the chairman of ECOG and Doug was the chair of the Breast committee. Doug, his wife Pat, and I were good friends, and Doug and I took the concept of long-term tamoxifen therapy into clinical trial at Madison first with a series of translational publications [3,4].

I contend that Harold Rusch (Fig. 8.2) is perhaps America's greatest cancer center director who knew what he had to do in Wisconsin, wrestled with grief upon the death of his daughter from breast cancer, chose not to leave to be the president of the MD Anderson Cancer Center, and changed the world of translational cancer research. Our offices were next to each other in his retirement, and I learned much from this truly great quiet man with a will of steel.

Harold advised me to say, when answering my phone "Craig Jordan: how can I help you?" to defuse any hostile caller. He created the McArdle Laboratory for Cancer Research and recruited all the outstanding faculty members in the first wave, starting in the 1950s, who became members of the National Academy of Sciences (Jim and Betty Miller) and Howard Temin (Nobel Prize 1975). He started from nothing but had a vision. He recruited, raised money, and built a revolutionary eye-catching building in the middle of campus that was opened in 1965 but is now abandoned (Nothing stays the same—everything changes). He had his political contacts to make it happen and was an advisor to Presidents! But the death of his young daughter from breast cancer took its toll. He, as an MD and head of the premier cancer research center in the nation, could do nothing, but mourn. He was a catalyst for the National Cancer Act in 1971 in the United States and injected common sense when a senator declared, in writing, that the "War on Cancer" should be won in time for the bicentennial of the United States in 1976. Harold gave us the Clinical (Comprehensive) Cancer Center and was the first director of the Wisconsin Clinical Cancer Center who interviewed me in 1977. Unknown to me then, he was recovering from his daughter's death from breast cancer and recognized I had a realistic plan to change the prognosis for women with breast cancer. That opportunity at Wisconsin turned out to be true. Harold and I enjoyed each other's company and spoke every day. He taught me so much. Harold had seen the essential need to transfer practical knowledge from bench to bedside at McArdle. This is why he saw the need to stimulate further efforts with tamoxifen in Madison. He knew translational research could get results as Dr Charles Heidelberger had rationally synthesized 5-fluorouracil (5FU) at the McArdle in the 1960s, and this had gone straight to the clinic with a clinical trial by Dr Fred Ansfield. By chance, I met the first patient to be treated with 5FU for breast cancer—she was a young librarian at the UW Madison library apparently cured with high doses of 5FU. When Harold was diagnosed with prostate cancer, he planned for me to speak at his memorial service when he died and I read the Presidential Letter of thanks from a grateful nation that I had obtained before he died. He received the document from Donna Shalala, then our Chancellor at UW Madison.

I was asked to write a retrospective of Dr. Harold Rusch's contributions in championing advances in cancer [1], and with the help of his wife Louise Rusch and Paul Carbone, I initiated the Harold Rusch memorial lecture at the Comprehensive Cancer Center. Bernie Fisher, chairman of the NSABP was our inaugural lecturer at a meeting I organized on adjuvant tamoxifen therapy in Orlando, Florida, July 1–3, 1990. Trevor Powles, leader of the Marsden tamoxifen prevention trial, was our second lecturer in April in 1992 (Fig. 5.3), and I was honored to be selected in 1994 to be invited back from Northwestern University to present the third in our series of lectures to memorialize an outstanding leader in cancer research.

Paul Carbone became the next Cancer Center Director after Harold. Paul was chairman of ECOG, and a Lasker Award winner (the American equivalent of the Nobel Prize) for his work on curing Hodgkin's disease. Paul had come from the National Cancer Institute and established a first class center of translational research in a university of excellence in the biological sciences in Madison. Paul Carbone is one of the legendary clinical trialists of the past generation (1970–2000). I recall, when I was still at the University of Leeds Medical School, waiting in line to go down for lunch in the cafeteria, I talked about my impending move to Paul Carbone's Cancer Center. A young faculty member turned around and said to me "Lucky You." I was making the right decision. Paul is appropriately memorialized with the renaming of the Wisconsin Comprehensive Cancer Center as the Paul P. Carbone Comprehensive Cancer Center.

If there is a lesson I have learned from Wisconsin, it is this. Collaborations and scientific advances occur because of friendships and mutual commitment. There is a modern trend, in the panicky response to dwindling resources and harder competing grant renewals, to force faculty to collaborate by trying to mandate and command that oil and water mix. This does not work, but true colleagues make mutual progress for the group good. Discovery is an individual event with flashes of insight to be exploited by individuals. They do that well. A bureaucratic compulsory system akin to the communist system of a managed economy rarely works anywhere. Funds should not be the issue for the scientific survival of talented proven scientists to continue to teach and educate new generations of outstanding young medical scientists. This is an investment for the future of Nations.

The Department was located in the K4 tower in the brand new Wisconsin Clinical Cancer Center attached to the brand new University Hospital (Fig. 8.1). My office and laboratories would be on the fifth floor near to Paul Carbone's offices and all my medical oncology colleagues.

Here was my challenge: I had no laboratory or staff. I had to ensure Anna Tate from the University of Leeds, now a Fulbright Scholar, was settled into the Ph.D. program at the McArdle Laboratory about a mile away from the University Hospital. Publications had to materialize rapidly to justify my application for promotion to associate professor with tenure to be initiated in 18 months and show I could attract funding. Almost as soon as I arrived, I applied and received a UICC traveling scholarship to return to Bern for a 3-week visit back to the University of Bern, Department of Clinical Pharmacology. I was to conduct research on the metabolism of tamoxifen and teach in their 3-week clinical pharmacology course for medical scientists from German-speaking countries. I also could see all my friends at the Ludwig Institute! However, I discovered that the Directorship had become vacant and I was approached to determine whether I would be interested to return for a 5- or 10-year contract. I did not discount the idea!

On my return to Madison, I enrolled in an intermediate German language course over the summer 1981. The German Department at the University of Wisconsin was the best in America, primarily because Wisconsin was initially populated by German immigrants who came to America to seek a better and safer life during the latter half of the 19th century. Their grandchildren and great grandchildren all were keen to learn German, and it was a great summer for me (I also had learned German in my other world). The reason for the need to learn German was that the educational system at the University of Bern required a lecture in German for all new professors. As all of this played out, I was told by Dr Carl Baker that the Ludwig Board had approved another candidate. We will meet Carl Baker again at the end of this Wisconsin chapter.

I had spent weeks preparing my promotion documents and assembling my expanding list of publications. In 1978, when I had been offered my academic opportunity in Wisconsin, I had accumulated refereed research articles and other published articles from meetings or book chapters. I had taken Dr. Caspi's advice seriously, and this aspect of my professional career would not be lacking ever again. The year in Bern created a Ludwig Institute for Cancer Research, and I was now being recognized as an individual who was planning to develop a new medicine for breast cancer that was important. But all success again rested at the letters of recommendations. This time, Dr. Carbone made no missteps. Two internal letters from the Department of Human Oncology were from Drs David Rose and Doug Tormey (both professors) and the world experts of estrogen receptors: Dr. Jack Gorski, Dr. Jim Wittiff, Dr. Elwood Jensen, and Dr. Bill McGuire. I also applied for a joint appointment in the Department of Pharmacology. I was first and foremost a pharmacologist, and remain so to this day. My Ph.D. students all did a minor in Pharmacology.

To satisfy the promotions committee about my record while at Leeds, I now discovered that Professor Barrett had left the Department of Pharmacology, and Dr E. R. Clark, my former Ph.D. supervisor, was the most senior faculty member. He was now the acting Head of Department. He wrote my letter of recommendation. I was awarded tenure with the rank of associate professor in 1983.

The initial focus for my laboratory was the recruitment of Mara Lieberman as a staff scientist in my growing group in 1981. We published our first two papers back to back in the *Journal of Biological Chemistry* [5,6]. I used the preliminary data we generated on the structure−function relationship of tamoxifen analogs to write up and was awarded my first R01 grant as a principal investigator. This grant was renewed two more times during my tenure at Wisconsin. The team who expanded structure—function relationship studies of nonsteroidal antiestrogens were Mara and Rick Koch, a talented technician.

The goal of our quest was to prove, our published hypothesis, that the side chain of 4-hydroxytamoxifen acted as a "stick in the jaws of a crocodile" [5—7]. We also proposed that the dimethylaminoethoxy side chain had to engage with an "antiestrogen region (AER)" in the ER [6]. Productivity was enormous over this period as we classified molecules that were agonists, partial agonists, or antagonists in the "jaws of the crocodile" to regulate prolactin synthesis [8—13].

For Anna (Tate) Riegel Ph.D. thesis, I set her the task of determining whether antibodies to the ER could distinguish differences between the ER binding [3H] estradiol or [3H]4-hydroxytamoxifen (ICI Pharmaceuticals division at Alderley Park had custom synthesized this metabolite for my Tamoxifen Team in Wisconsin). This was an enormous advantage for our team as we could compare and contrast directly estradiol and 4-hydroxytamoxifen ER complexes in vivo and in vitro [14,15]. Anna demonstrated that when the polyclonal antibody, provided by Elwood Jensen and Geoff Greene at the University of Chicago, was preincubated with human breast cancer ER, the ER could not close and the [3H]estradiol "fell out" of the open ER. This did not occur if the "jaws" were already closed. [3H]4-hydroxytamoxifen was unaffected by antibody treatment; it was wedged in the "jaws of the crocodile" [16].

I decided that our Tamoxifen Team focus should be on a progression through normal estrogen response cell model systems, i.e., Mara's immature rat pituitary cell system to determine structure—function relationships of antiestrogens and advance to studies in ER-positive breast cancer cells called MCF-7 and T47D. However, there was a problem with ER-positive breast cancer studies in vitro. Although inoculation of breast cancer cells into special, immune-deficient (athymic) mice and treatment with estrogen caused breast tumors to grow, this experiment could not be replicated in cell culture [17]. Tamoxifen caused ER-positive breast cancer cells to stop growing, but added estrogen caused the growth inhibitions to be reversed. This was a major mystery for years in breast cancer research.

The mystery was solved by the Katzenellenbogens (John and Benita) at the University of Illinois [18]. It turned out that cell culture media contains large amounts of a pH-indicator called phenol red. This is necessary to determine the acidity of media for healthy cell growth. However, John Katzenellenbogen discovered that phenol red contains a contaminant that is estrogenic. This discovery solved the mystery: ER-positive breast cancer cells injected into athymic mice have no phenol red, so administered estrogen causes estrogen-stimulated tumor growth. The breast cancer cells in culture do not grow further with added estrogen because the contaminating phenol red already stimulates growth maximally. The addition of tamoxifen blocks the action of the phenol red contaminant at the breast cancer cell ER and growth is stopped, but added estradiol kicks the tamoxifen off the ER and reactivates growth. Resolution of this technical oddity revolutionized breast cancer research in the laboratory. Now the effects of estrogen deprivation on breast cancer and ER regulation could be established, as this would be essential to understand, eventually in the

1990s, what impact long-term aromatase inhibitor therapy would have as an adjuvant treatment of breast cancer. These studies started at Wisconsin using the T47D breast cancer cell line [19], the MCF-7 breast cancer cell line [20].

However, I am sure you are asking the question: "So how could your Tamoxifen Team determine perfect estrogen-stimulated prolactin synthesis using concentrations of estradiol similar to those that did not work in MCF-7 cells because they both contain phenol-red in the media?" The answer was that in the prolactin assay there was twice as much stripped serum that adsorbed the phenol red **and** protein synthesis requires higher levels of estrogen. The primary pituitary cells do not replicate in cell culture. Cell replication in cancer is very sensitive to even trace levels of estrogen—this is how ER-positive breast cancer survives!

An enormous advantage of the UWCCC in the 1980s was that all patients attending the breast cancer clinics had blood drawn and cataloged on each of the their clinic visits. Sera were stored in dozens of deep freezers organized by Jane Wegenke for Doug Tormey, the clinical director of the Breast Cancer Research and Treatment Program for UWCCC. We knew a lot about the molecular pharmacology of known metabolites of tamoxifen from the prolactin assay, but I wanted to know what was actually circulating in our patients during treatment.

I hired a talented technician, Richard Bain, to ensure we had standard thin-layer chromatography methods to determine tamoxifen and metabolites in sera during treatment. However, Dr. Ray Brown, a faculty colleague in the Department of Human Oncology, accepted the challenge to create a new postcolumn cyclization high-performance liquid chromatography method to measure tamoxifen and its metabolites [21] during breast cancer therapy. Doug Tormey and I were now able to address the translation of my laboratory findings to patient care and monitor circulating levels of tamoxifen and its known metabolites 4-hydroxytamoxifen and N-desmethyl-tamoxifen during long-term treatment. My laboratory was now becoming state of the art. Doug Tormey was also evaluating the effectiveness of high-dose tamoxifen treatment so we had access to the sera from those patients. Richard Bain discovered, to our delight, that increasing the daily dose of tamoxifen resulted in an unknown peak in the sera that increased with dose [22]. We took samples to determine the molecular weight and contacted Dr Sandy Todd at Alderley Park for advice. We had discovered a new metabolite of tamoxifen as an intermediate in the metabolic breakdown of the dimethylaminoethoxy side chain of tamoxifen. Using standards supplied by ICI Pharmaceutical Division, Alderley Park, we identified what is now referred to as metabolite Y. We will revisit the value of these studies for the future development of a new group of medicines called selective estrogen receptor modulators (SERMs), but that was a decade into the future.

In 1982/3, my friend and colleague David Rose decided to accept a new appointment at the American Heart Foundation in Valhalla, New York. He and Doug Tormey had both been investigating a new nonsteroidal antiestrogen, trioxifene, from Eli Lilly in clinical trial. David and I investigated trioxifene in the DMBA-induced rat mammary carcinoma model and the new NMU-rat mammary carcinoma model [23] that reportedly was biologically more similar to human breast cancer than the DMBA model. Trioxifene was not an improvement on tamoxifen. It was then I met Marco Gottardis who was David's technician performing all the animal studies. He was an excellent experimentalist and always very helpful to achieve the goal. His work with the animal experiments was first class.

When David's move to New York was announced, I was called to Paul Carbone's office and informed that I would be the new director of the Steroid Receptor Laboratory, which served the southern counties on Wisconsin. This was based on my previous experience in Switzerland at the Ludwig Institute where I quality-controlled the ER laboratory in the Ludwig Breast Cancer Center (Chapter 7). I would also inherit half a dozen of David's staff members from his laboratory. This doubling of the size of my laboratory, and occupying half the top floor in the Cancer Center, was hard to take in. But, like my other academic experiences at the WFEB in 1972 when my boss, Mike Harper went to Switzerland, or 1978 when my career at the Department of Pharmacology at the University of Leeds evaporated, you either fold or fight.

Within a year, we had integrated both laboratories into a single tamoxifen team. I utilized the databases for a decade of estrogen/progesterone receptor assays in the breast cancer of the patients from Southern Wisconsin to write a review on the topic [24]. This demonstrated our expertise in translational research. I also sat down and wrote a review on all that was known on the nonsteroidal antiestrogens [25]. The antiestrogens was where I was to make my future career and scientific reputation. I would put everything about the pharmacology of nonsteroidal antiestrogens in my manuscript and publish a review in my society's (American Society for Pharmacology and Experimental Therapeutics) journal *Pharmacological Reviews*. I was a pharmacologist first.

Before focusing on translational laboratory research, I will tell two patient's stories and how, through close collaborations between faculty at UWCCC, erroneous results can be deciphered.

One day, Doug Tormey burst into my office and declared: "What is going on in the estrogen receptor laboratory? My breast cancer patient is ER-positive but she is relapsing on tamoxifen!" Now was the time for me to retrieve the patient's blood samples over the past few years of adjuvant tamoxifen treatment. Our established teamwork was excellent. Nancy Fritz had completed all endocrine evaluations on Doug's patient, and Richard Bain confirmed that tamoxifen and metabolite levels were rock solid over the past 5 years. However, a biopsy confirmed she was still ER-positive. Doubling the daily dose of tamoxifen by Doug caused an anticipated rise in circulating tamoxifen and metabolite levels [26]. Poor absorption was not the issue, yet still her blood levels of tamoxifen and metabolites were decreasing. So I asked Doug if I could see the patient in my office to determine her point of view. The reason became clear. She had been recently married and found the side effects of tamoxifen were incompatible with her new life. She had weaned herself off tamoxifen. Regrettably, subsequent chemotherapy and tamoxifen treatments were unable to control the patient's disease.

By contrast, I have recently been contacted by another patient from Wisconsin who wishes to celebrate with me. Dianne Chechnik was a patient of Paul Carbone, who cautioned her to never stop taking her daily tamoxifen tablets. This was in the days before long-term clinical trial results were published. However, Paul was convinced that longer was better based on my animal data. At Wisconsin, Dianne told me she thought of me each night as she swallowed her tamoxifen. She recently generously made a donation to the "UW Carbone Cancer Center Greatest Need Fund" in my name on the occasion of me receiving an honorary doctorate from UW Madison in 2020 for my work completed there in the 1980s.

To my surprise, she tracked me down to MD Anderson Cancer Center this year. She has been on daily tamoxifen for the last 38 years, and for her 40th anniversary, she wants us to celebrate in style! I told her of my current situation (see Prelude) and she told me, as only Dianne could—"you will not die; you have too many discoveries yet to make to keep breast cancer patients alive."

At Wisconsin for the 14 years, we had a remarkable team of enthusiastic Ph.D. students (Anna T. Riegel neé Tate, Ethel Cormier, Marco Gottardis, Stewart Lyman, Cathy Murphy, M.H. Jeng, S.Y. Jiang, John Pink, Doug Wolf, and W.H. Catherino), postdoctoral fellows (Simon Robinson,who completed his Ph.D. at the University of Leeds with Dr. Edward Clark, my Ph.D. supervisor; David Gibson; Michael Fritsch; Peter Ravdin), technicians (Barbara Gosden (Anna's friend also from the University of Leeds), Michael Wolf, Nancy Fritz, Mark Thompson, Delinda Mauel, Chris Parker, Sue Fahey and Richard Bain), and assistant scientists (Mara Lieberman and Wade Welshons).

Animal models—finding the bad about tamoxifen

Once I had assumed the responsibility for the Steroid Receptor Laboratory, I contacted Marco Gottardis because I was very impressed with his interpersonal skills in David Rose's laboratory, but I had bigger plans for him. I invited him for breakfast in the hospital cafeteria and posed the question "I want to take you on as a graduate student (Ph.D.) in Human Oncology on probation, I will support you in my laboratory." Marco agreed, as this was an unexpected opportunity.

About the same time, Stewart Lyman approached me as he was unable to complete his Ph.D. with his current supervisor at the McArdle laboratory. I agreed and set both he and Marco to answer research questions that had to be addressed, as soon as possible, to understand tamoxifen's pharmacology in mice as a safe therapeutic agent in patients.

Stewart addressed the questions of whether there were metabolic differences that resulted in estrogenicity in mice but antiestrogenicity in rats. No, there were not, and several papers resulted [27,28]. With his completed work at McArdle and the four papers from my laboratory, Stewart successfully passed his Ph.D. examination at the McArdle laboratory. Parenthetically, he went on to complete a postdoctoral fellowship at the Fred Hutchinson Cancer Research Center. He discovered that Steel gene encoded a growth factor that binds to c-KIT and the tyrosine kinase receptor encoded by the W gene. This work got a front cover in Cell.

Marco became the key individual to create and utilize animal models in my laboratory. We had superb new facilities to house large numbers of athymic animals. Initially, I planned to address the development of acquired drug resistance to tamoxifen. Following a series of preliminary studies, Marco demonstrated that continuous tamoxifen treatment was not killing implanted MCF-7 tumors, because stopping tamoxifen and reintroducing estrogen again caused remaining MCF-7 cell to grow. This experiment was successful in all cases for up to 6 months of tamoxifen treatment [29].

Kent Osborne in San Antonio with Bill McGuire's group demonstrated the effectiveness of long-term tamoxifen treatment to control MCF-7 tumor growth in athymic mice and additionally demonstrated that continuous, long-term tamoxifen was eventually ineffective in controlling tumor growth despite continuing treatment [30]. Marco took a different approach. He took tumors that had failed tamoxifen therapy and retransplanted them in a new set of athymic mice. The tumor grew **because** of tamoxifen or estrogen therapy **not despite** tamoxifen. For the first time, an anticancer drug was shown to stimulate the growth of human cancer. They were dependent on tamoxifen for growth [31]. Although Stewart Lyman had proved otherwise, we were concerned about metabolism of tamoxifen in mice to estrogens (tamoxifen was an estrogen in the mouse uterus and vagina). Marco retransplanted the tumors from athymic mice into athymic rats (tamoxifen was an antiestrogen in rats). The tumors still grew, so tamoxifen was not being converted to estrogenic metabolites in mice [32]. But it was now realized that tamoxifen had target site-specific estrogenic and antiestrognic actions in animals.

In summary, Marco found ER-positive MCF-7 tumors could grow either with estrogen or tamoxifen and something like a pure antiestrogen or an environment of "no estrogen at all" was required as a second-line therapy in stage IV breast cancer after tamoxifen failure. The new pure antiestrogen discovered at AstraZeneca [33] was tested successfully in Marco's models, and drug development of Faslodex went forward. These basic studies in animal models presaged the clinical trials a decade later that tested Faslodex versus Arimidex (anastrazole), Zeneca's new aromatase inhibitor to establish which was the appropriate second-line therapy following the failure of tamoxifen treatment in stage IV breast cancer. The results demonstrated either drug was equally effective [34]. A double win for AstraZeneca!

As a fact note, Marco's acquired resistance model in vivo of estrogen/tamoxifen-stimulated tumor growth was resolved by Dr. Ping Fan in my laboratory two decades later with her serendipidous discovery on the interconversion of different forms of acquired resistance in vitro to antihormone therapy was dependent upon blocking the oncogene cSrc. This is addressed in Chapter 12.

The animal models that Marco had mastered would now be used to address an unexpected action of tamoxifen: the effect of tamoxifen on endometrial cancer. There were no clinical reports in the 1980s but had anyone looked?

Linking tamoxifen with endometrial cancer

Gynecologists were not usually part of the cancer care team for patients with stage IV breast cancer or adjuvant clinical trials using a couple of years of tamoxifen. However, new trials were extended up to 5 years of adjuvant tamoxifen treatment. This translational research could be important!

Marco bitransplanted athymic mice with an ER-positive breast cancer (MCF-7) and an ER-positive endometrial cancer (EnCa101) obtained from Dr. Satyaswaroop in Hershey, Pennsylvania. Animals were treated daily with either estradiol, tamoxifen of the combination, for 10 weeks. The results were clear [35]. Estradiol stimulated the growth of both the breast and endometrial tumors, as expected; tamoxifen stimulated the growth of only the endometrial tumor; and tamoxifen inhibited the estrogen-stimulated growth of the breast tumor but massively increased endometrial tumor growth (Fig. 8.3).

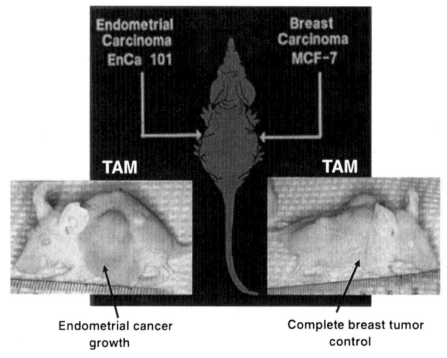

FIGURE 8.3

The pioneering bitransplantation study by Gottardis [Gottardis MM et al. 1988, Cancer Res] with an ER-positive breast tumor (MCF-7) implanted in one axilla and an ER-positive endometrial tumor (EnCa 101) in the other axilla. Tamoxifen blocks estrogen-stimulated growth of the breast tumor, but tamoxifen encourages the growth of the endometrial tumor. With copy right permission from [Gottardis MM et al. 1988, Cancer Res].

I immediately visited Dr. John Patterson, the clinician at ICI America's responsible for tamoxifen in Wilmington, Delaware, to share our concerns about these new data. Marco and I visited Zeneca, at Alderley Park to inform them. Marco did a great job with his formal presentation to a hushed audience!

In that same year 1987, I had been invited to make a presentation to celebrate the 800th anniversary at the University Medical School in Bologna, Italy. I chose to make the case for gynecologists being involved in the care of breast cancer patients prior to long-term adjuvant therapy. The question needed to be asked—was an increase in endometrial cancer observed during tamoxifen treatment?

Imagine my surprise when I discovered, in the Lancet, that Dr L. Hardell from Sweden had heard my talk in Bologna and offered some of his clinical cases he had documented during tamoxifen therapy [36,37]. I replied stressing we needed data from placebo-controlled clinical trials such as the Scottish Trial [38] that was about to be published on July 25, 1987, in the Lancet. None were reported (or had no records been obtained?). However, a report by Fornander and colleagues [39] on the incidence of new primary tumors (breast and endometrial cancers) during 2 or 5 years of adjuvant tamoxifen therapy almost precisely replicated Marco's athymic mouse study. In patients, second primary breast cancers were reduced by tamoxifen, but endometrial cancers were increased by tamoxifen. A gynecological examination is now required before starting adjuvant tamoxifen and patients are warned to report spotting or bleeding to their doctors. Patients can either switch to an aromatase inhibitor or elect to have a hysterectomy.

Doug Wolf took over the athymic mouse models from Marco to investigate mechanisms of tamoxifen-stimulated tumor growth. The strategy had three parts: (1) If tamoxifen-stimulated growth occurs, as a mechanism of acquired drug resistance has the ER mutated to cause the growth with tamoxifen? 2) If tumors that have acquired resistance to tamoxifen but grow with either estradiol or tamoxifen, do the same growth factor pathways become activated? 3) A new theory [40] for the mechanism of tamoxifen-stimulated growth proposed that the 4-hydroxytamoxifen metabolite converted from the antiestrogenic *trans*-isomer to a putative **estrogenic** *cis*-isomer. Is this true, and can it be interrogated as the mechanism of acquired resistance to tamoxifen?

Doug efficiently addressed each topic and made important discoveries that opened the door to resolving Haddow's paradox [41,42]—the original use of high-dose estrogen to treat metastatic breast cancer when applied 5 years after the menopause.

1) A mutation of the ER.

Doug created lines of tamoxifen-stimulated tumors in athymic mice and used the, then state of the art, technique of single-stranded conformational polymorphism to investigate mutations in tamoxifen-stimulated MCF-7 tumors. In one tumor, he identified a significant percent (80%) of an unknown mutation Asp351Tyr ER [43]. However, the position of the mutation was not at either of the activating function sites 1 or 2. Apparently, these two sites controlled all the actions of the ER complex with estradiol and had been investigated by site-directed mutagenesis by others. Doug's discovery in 1992 was to lay dormant until the move to Northwestern.

2) **Growth factors involved in estradiol or tamoxifen-stimulated growth in acquired tamoxifen-resistant MCF-7 tumors.**

The projects seemed simple "what growth factors are involved in estrogen or tamoxifen-stimulated MCF-7 tumors?" Then again so did my Ph.D. "extract the rat estrogen receptor from rat uterus, purify it and crystallize the protein with estradiol or an antiestrogen. Do the X-ray crystallography at the Astbury Department of Biophysics and "Bob's your Uncle!" a successful PhD. Well, that didn't work and neither did it work for Doug! Instead we made a discovery that would preoccupy my laboratory for the next 30 years and sequester $25 million of Federal funding and about $25 million of philanthropy. Herein lies a tale. Doug's task was to establish three sets of animals with acquired resistance to tamoxifen established by Marco and carried by retransplantation for about 5 years now. Small tumors in animals were grown with tamoxifen and divided into three groups. Group A received peanut oil, group B received tamoxifen, and group C received estrogen with the expectation that after about 2 weeks animals would be sacrificed and tumors harvested to measure all known growth factors. The results would be compared and contrasted.

After several weeks, I realized I had not seen Doug around the laboratory. The weeks turned into months, and I even noticed he was avoiding me! I summoned him to my office for a progress report. He started with a most unexpected speech: "I have done exactly as you asked and I repeated it. I get the same answer. The tumors on the animals that received the depot injection of estradiol completely disappeared. We must notify Cancer Research immediately that we are unable to repeat Marco's studies and withdraw his papers." I considered these facts and then declared with glee—"You have made a discovery!"

I immediately realized that we had passaged the tumors in tamoxifen treated mice for more than 5 years. Haddow discovered that estrogen therapy only works effectively as a treatment of breast cancer in postmenopausal women if they are 5 years postmenopause [42]. I immediately assembled all his data and we prepared my presentation I would now give at the St. Gallen Breast Cancer meeting in 1993 [44]. I emphasized that it is not the long-term tamoxifen therapy that enhances the survival advantage. After tamoxifen is stopped at 5 years, it is the woman's own estrogen killing the prepared breast cancer cells with long-term acquired resistance to tamoxifen. Because tamoxifen is a complete inhibitor of estrogen actions, once the tamoxifen is stopped and cleared from the body, estrogen would be expected to cause microscopic tumor recurrences. Instead, patients, for a year or so after tamoxifen was stopped, did not have a rebound of recurrences. But without tamoxifen, these tumors would not—because of estrogen killing the prepared tumor cells.

Thus began our quest to understand the mechanisms of estrogen-induced apoptosis, which would extend over three decades, with confirmatory translational studies and clinical confirmation. The satisfying news was that our search to understand estrogen-induced apoptosis was to be valuable to understand the results of the Women's Health Initiative that had recruited volunteers and was about to start their hormone replacement therapy [45,46].

3) **Isomerization of 4-hydroxytamoxifen to a hypothetically estrogenic *cis*-isomer to cause tamoxifen-stimulated growth.**

   During the years at Wisconsin, we had excellent external chemistry support from colleagues elsewhere in Europe. We already had studies in vitro on the *cis-* and *trans*-isomers of 4-hydroxytamoxifen. These isomers were provided by Dora Richardson (Fig. 5.6) at Alderley Park but with the caution that the *cis*-isomer was unstable in solution and light would convert the molecule to the potent antiestrogenic *trans*-isomer. To solve this problem, my chemical colleague in England Ray McCague synthesized the fixed-ring isomers of 4-hydroxytamoxifen [47].

   Doug's experiments in vivo using transplanted tamoxifen-stimulated MCF-7 tumors demonstrated conclusively that the *cis*-isomer of 4-hydroxytamoxifen was not an estrogen. This is unlike the *cis*-isomer of tamoxifen, ICI 47,699 that is estrogenic. Doug's study, published in the *Journal of the National Cancer Institute* [48], was prima facie evidence that the original published hypothesis was flawed.

   The Tamoxifen Teams in the early 1980s and the late 1980s/early 1990s are shown in Figs. 8.4–8.6.

   Four additional Ph.D. students were essential for the success of the UW Tamoxifen Team in its final years!

1. John Pink provided benchmark publications on the regulations of the ER in T47D and MCF-7 breast cancer cells [49], the identification of a novel and unique, high-molecular weight ER in an LTED MCF-7 cell lines [50,51] and new pure cell lines for T47D breast cancer cells [52] that had lost their ER under LTED conditions.

2. S.Y. Jiang was the first to stably transfect the ER gene into cloned MDA-MB-231 ER-negative breast cancer cells [53]. This opened the door to numerous studies of estrogen action and modulation. She also created the MCF-7:5C- [54] and MCF-7:2A- [50] cloned LTED cell lines that were instrumental in our subsequent deciphering the mechanism of estrogen-induced apoptosis at Northwestern.

3. Mei Huey Jeng discovered that 19-nortestosterone derivatives [55–57], which were clinically used, had estrogen-like activity, and discovered that ER-negative cells were stably transfected with the ER gene-activated transforming growth factor α during estrogen action [58].

4. William Catherino created the stable transfectant of the mutant Asp351Tyr ER in ER-negative breast cancer [59] and established that the progestin gestodene in contraceptives was estrogenic [60].

FIGURE 8.4

The initial Tamoxifen Team at Wisconsin about 1983 following the departure of David Rose, who was in charge of the estrogen receptor laboratory, but now passed on to me. Front row left to right Dr. Ray Brown, myself, and the late Mara Lieberman. Back row left to right Ethel Cormier, Rick Koch, Anna Riegel, the late Barbara Gosden, Richards Bain, Marco Gottardis, Eric Phelps.

FIGURE 8.5

Wisconsin Tamoxifen Team, late 1980s. Front row S.Y. Jiang, M.H. Jeng, myself, Marco Gottardis, Cathy Murphy. Back row unknown, S. Langan-Fahey, Doug Wolf, Yuchi Iino (visiting Professor from Japan), Chris Parker, Mark Thompson, John Pink.

FIGURE 8.6

Farewell dinner for the final Wisconsin Tamoxifen Team in 1992. Front row left to right Monica Morrow, myself, S.Y. Jiang, Mike Fritch. Rear row standing left to right Doug Wolf, M. H. Jeng, John Pink, Chris Parker, Sue Langan-Fahey, Melinda Mauel.

The final laboratory model we studied was a model of rat liver carcinogenesis generated by Dr Henry Pitot and his team in the McArdle laboratory. The laboratory work was organized and led by Yvonne Dragan, a talented postdoctoral fellow in Dr. Pitot's laboratory. Henry suggested that our strategy should be that I, as the "tamoxifen expert", should be the principal investigator for his team at the McArlde laboratory. The strategy was funded immediately with an R01 grant and the papers flowed [61−67]. There was a clinical concern about the report that an animal study comparing an analog of tamoxifen called toremifene did not cause rat liver tumors at high daily doses for a year or more but tamoxifen did! This was an ugly therapeutic situation as now long-term adjuvant therapy had become the standard of care, and the NSABP P-1 study of chemoprevention in high-risk women was moving forward. Added to all this, Zeneca then published its studies of rat liver carcinogenesis confirming the potential problem with tamoxifen that could become a ticking time bomb. At the same time, there was enormous pressure to withdraw tamoxifen for prevention and restart the programs with toremifene. My goal, with the focused research on rat liver carcinogenesis with tamoxifen, was to learn all we could about this unanticipated side effect. However, tamoxifen was not withdrawn in the 1990s, because the Oxford Overview Analysis of all adjuvant clinical trials with tamoxifen provided evidence that human liver carcinogenesis did not occur in patients treated with adjuvant tamoxifen. Case closed.

"Small World" occurred again at Wisconsin. There had been much debate about the veracity of "molecular mechanism of estrogen action," i.e., estradiol binds to cytoplasmic ER to create an activated ER complex that translocates to the nucleus, where it triggers estrogen action.

All that was to change in 1984 with the publications in Nature using either GH3 rat pituitary cells [68] or MCF-7 breast cancer cells [69]. The work by Welshons and Lieberman in Jack Gorski's laboratory [68] employed cytochalasin B (originally discovered by Steven Carter at ICI Pharmaceutical Division in 1967 [70] at the time when I was a summer student) to create nucleoplasts from GH3 rat pituitary cells. The unoccupied ER was in the nucleoplasts of GH3 rat pituitary cells.

The contribution of the Wisconsin Tamoxifen Team was that Wade Welshons conducted his experiments again using cytochalasin B in the ER-positive MCF-7 cells [71]. Additionally, a series of in vivo studies in rats, using an analog of tamoxifen that could not be metabolized, resulted in an estrogen-like increase in growth and uterine progesterone receptors. However, on investigation of the localization of the ER, all was present in the cytosolic fraction and not in the nucleus [72]. It was concluded that the nuclear receptor complex had triggered progesterone receptor synthesis, but upon uterine cell disruption, the weak ER complex fell apart and the artifact of the unoccupied receptor was located in the cytosol [72].

Tamoxifen was attracting much attention academically in pharmacology and therapeutics. However, in closing, I want to revisit my earlier interactions with Dr Carl Baker at the Ludwig Institute in 1981. After one of my lectures, in the late 1980s, Dr. Baker remained behind after the audience had left to speak to me personally. His words were most unexpected. "Craig, when we did not select you to be the Director of the Ludwig Unit in Bern, Switzerland, we made a mistake. You have proved us wrong with your research on tamoxifen."

However, consider the prospect if I had accepted the Directorship of the Ludwig Unit in Bern at age 34 and left Wisconsin. I would not have had the University of Wisconsin Tamoxifen Team with its graduate students keen to contribute to deciphering drug resistance to long-term tamoxifen treatment and the molecular mechanism of action of antiestrogen therapy. We would have no SERMs, which we discovered, by chance at the University of Wisconsin Comprehensive Cancer Center. We would not have deciphered the mechanism of estrogen-induced apoptosis in estrogen-deprived breast cancer. Additionally, there would not have been the close collegial interactions of my Wisconsin Tamoxifen Team with the clinical faculty of the Department of Human Oncology, and scores of young trainees in the Tamoxifen Teams would not have been trained. The world of medicine for women would have been much different.

References

[1] Jordan VC. Harold Rush, MD at the UW Madison- A tale of two cancer centers. Wis Acad Rev 1988:26−32.
[2] Toft D, Gorski J. A receptor molecule for estrogens: isolation from the rat uterus and preliminary characterization. Proc Natl Acad Sci USA 1966;556:1574−81.

[3] Tormey DC, Jordan VC. Long-term tamoxifen adjuvant therapy in node-positive breast cancer: a metabolic and pilot clinical study. Breast Cancer Res Treat 1984;4:297−302.

[4] Tormey DC, Rasmussen P, Jordan VC. Long-term adjuvant tamoxifen study: clinical update. Breast Cancer Res Treat 1987;9:157−8.

[5] Lieberman ME, Jordan VC, Fritsch M, et al. Direct and reversible inhibition of estradiol-stimulated prolactin synthesis by antiestrogens in vitro. J Biol Chem 1983; 258:4734−40.

[6] Lieberman ME, Gorski J, Jordan VC. An estrogen receptor to describe the regulation of prolactin synthesis by antiestrogens in vitro. J Biol Chem 1983;258:4741−5.

[7] Jordan VC. Laboratory models of breast cancer to aid the elucidation of antiestrogen action. J Lab Clin Med 1987;109:267−77.

[8] Jordan VC, Lieberman ME, Cormier E, et al. Structural requirements for the pharmacological activity of non-steroidal antiestrogens in vitro. Mol Pharmacol 1984;26: 272−8.

[9] Jordan VC, Lieberman ME. Estrogen-stimulated classification of agonists, partial agonists and antagonists based on structure. Mol Pharmacol 1984;26:279−85.

[10] Jordan VC, Koch R, Mittal S, Schneider MR. Oestrogenic and antioestrogenic action in a series of triphenylbut-1-enes: modulation of prolactin synthesis in vitro. Br J Pharmacol 1986;87:217−23.

[11] Robinson SP, Kock R, Jordan VC. Estrogenic action in vitro of hydroxylated derivatives of D 16726 9zindoxifene), an agent with known antimammary cancer activity in vivo. Cancer Res 1988;48:784−7.

[12] Jordan VC, Koch R, Langan S, McCague R. Ligand interaction at the estrogen receptor to program antiestrogen action: a study with nonsteroidal compounds in vitro. Endocrinology 1988;122:1449−54.

[13] Jordan VC, Koch R. Regulation of prolactin synthesis in vitro by estrogenic and antiestrogenic derivatives of estradiol and estrone. Endocrinology 1989;124:1717−26.

[14] Jordan VC, Fisher AH, Rose DP. Binding of [^{3}H]monohydroxytamoxifen in human breast carcinoma cytosols. Eur J Cancer 1981;17:121−2.

[15] Jordan VC, Bowser-Finn RA. Binding of [^{3}H]monohydroxytamoxifen by immature rat tissues in vivo. Endocrinology 1982;110:1281−91.

[16] Tate AC, Greene GL, DeSombre ER, et al. Differences between estrogen- and antiestrogen estrogen receptor complexes identified with antibody raised against the estrogen receptor. Cancer Res 1984;44:1012−8.

[17] Shafie SM. Estrogen and the growth of breast cancer: new evidence suggests indirect action. Science 1980;209:701−2.

[18] Berthois Y, Katzenellenbogen JA, Katzenellenbogen BS. Penol red in tissue culture media is a weak estrogen: implications concerning the study of estrogen-responsive cells in culture. Proc Natl Acad Sci USA 1986;83:2496−500.

[19] Murphy CS, Meisner LF, Wu SQ, Jordan VC. Short and long term estrogenic deprivation of T47D human breast cancer cells in culture. Eur J Cancer Clin Oncol 1989;25:1777−88.

[20] Welshons WV, Jordan VC. Adaptation of estrogen-dependent MCF-7 cells to low estrogen (phenol red free) culture. Eur J Cancer 1987;23:1935−9.

[21] Brown RR, Bain R, Jordan VC. Determination of tamoxifen and metabolites in serum in high performance liquid chromatography with post column fluorescence activation. J Chromatogr 1983;272:351−8.

[22] Jordan VC, Bain RR, Brown RR, et al. Determination and pharmacology of a new hydroxylated metabolite of tamoxifen observed in patients during therapy for advanced breast cancer. Cancer Res 1983;43:1446−50.

[23] Rose DP, Fisher AH, Jordan VC. Activity of the antiestrogen trioxifene against N-nitrosomethylurea-induced rat mammary carcinomas. Eur J Cancer 1981;17:893−8.

[24] Jordan VC, Wolf M, Mirecki DM, et al. Hormone receptor assays: clinical usefulness in the management of carcinoma of the breast. CRC Crit Rev Clin Lab Sci 1988;26:97−152.

[25] Jordan VC. Biomedical pharmacology of antiestrogen action. Pharm Rev 1984;36:245−76.

[26] Jordan VC, Fritz NF, Tormey DC. Endocrine effects of adjuvant tamoxifen administration in node-positive patients with breast cancer. Cancer Res 1987;47:624−30.

[27] Lyman SD, Jordan VC. Metabolism of tamoxifen and its uterotrophic activity. Biochem Pharmacol 1984;34:2787−94.

[28] Lyman SD, Jordan VC. Possible mechanisms for the agonist actions of tamoxifen and antagonist actions of MER25 (ethamoxytriphetol) in the mouse uterus. Biochem Pharmacol 1985;34:2795−806.

[29] Gottardis MM, Robinson SP, Jordan VC. Estradiol-stimulated growth of MCF-7 tumors implanted in athymic mice: a model to study the tumoristatic action of tamoxifen. J Steroid Biochem 1988;20:311−4.

[30] Osborne CK, Coronado EB, Robinson JP. Human breast cancer in the athymic nude mouse: cytostatic effects of long-term antiestrogenic therapy. Eur J Cancer Clin Oncol 1987;23:1189−96.

[31] Gottardis MM, Jordan VC. Development of tamoxifen-stimulated growth of MCF-7 tumors in athymic mice after long-term antiestrogen administration. Cancer Res 1988;48:5183−7.

[32] Gottardis MM, Wagner RJ, Borden EC, Jordan VC. Differential ability of antiestrogens to stimulate breast cancer cell (MCF-7) growth in vivo and in vitro. Cancer Res 1989;49:4765−9.

[33] Gottardis MM, Jiang SY, Jeng MH, Jordan VC. Inhibition of tamoxifen stimulated growth of an MCF-7 tumor variant in athymic mice by novel steroidal antiestrogens. Cancer Res 1989;49:4090−3.

[34] Osborne CK, Pippen J, Jones SE, et al. Double-bind, randomized trial comparing the efficacy and tolerability of fulvestrant versus anastrazole in postmenopausal women with advanced breast cancer progressing on prior endocrine endocrine therapy: results of a North American trial. J Clin Oncol 2002;20:3386−95.

[35] Gottardis MM, Robinson SP, Satyaswaroop PG, Jordan VC. Contrasting actions of tamoxifen on endometrial and breast tumor growth in athymic mice. Cancer Res 1988;48:812−5.

[36] Hardell L. Tamoxifen as a risk factor for carcinoma of corpus uteri. Lancet 1988;2:563.

[37] Jordan VC. Tamoxifen and endometrial cancer. Lancet 1988;2:1019.

[38] Edinburgh Scottish Clinical Trials Office. Adjuvant tamoxifen in the management of operable breast cancer: the Scottish trial. Report from the Breast Cancer Trails Committee, Scottish Cancer Trails Office (MRC), Edinburgh. Lancet 1987;2:171−5.

[39] Fornander T, Rutqvist LE, Cedermark B, et al. Adjuvant tamoxifen in early breast cancer: occurrence of new primary cancers. Lancet 1989;1:117−20.

[40] Osborne CK, Coronado E, Alfred DC, et al. Acquired tumor resistance: correlation with reduced breast tumor levels of tamoxifen and isomerization of trans-4-hydroxytamoxifen. J Natl Cancer Inst 1991;83:1427—82.

[41] Haddow A, Watkinson JM, Paterson E, Koller PC. Influence of synthetic oestrogens on advanced malignant disease. Br Med J 1944;2:393—8.

[42] Haddow A. David A. Karnofsky memorial award. Thought on chemical therapy. Cancer 1970;23:737—54.

[43] Wolf DM, Jordan VC. The estrogen receptor from a tamoxifen stimulated MCF-7 variant contains a point mutation in the ligand-binding domain. Breast Cancer Res Treat 1994;31:129—38.

[44] Wolf DM, Jordan VC. A laboratory model to explain the survival advantage observed in patients taking adjuvant tamoxifen therapy. Recent Results Cancer Res 1993;127:23—33.

[45] Hays J, Hunt JR, Hubbell FA, et al. The Women's Health Initiative recruitment methods and results. Ann Epidemiol 2003;13(9 Suppl. l):S18—77.

[46] Stefanick ML, Cochrane BB, Hsia J, et al. The women's health initiative postmenopausal hormone trials: overview and baseline characteristics of participants. Ann Epidemiol 2003;13(9 Suppl. l):S78—86.

[47] McCague R, LeClerq G, Jordan VC. Nonisomerizable analogues of (Z) and (E) 4-hydroxytamoxifen. Synthesis and endocrinological properties of substituted diphenylbenzocyclophtenes. J Med Chem 1988;31:1285—90.

[48] Wolf DM, Langan-Fahey SM, Parker CJ, et al. Investigation of the mechanism of tamoxifen-stimulated breast tumor growth with nonisomerizable analogues of tamoxifen and metabolites. J Natl Cancer Inst 1993;85:806—12.

[49] Pink JJ, Jordan VC. Models of estrogen receptor regulation by estrogen and antiestrogens in breast cancer cell lines. Cancer Res 1996;56:2321—30.

[50] Pink JJ, Jiang SY, Fritsch M, Jordan VC. An estrogen-independent MCF-7 breast cancer cell line which contains a novel 80 kilodalton estrogen receptor-related protein. Cancer Res 1995;55:2583—90.

[51] Pink JJ, Wu SQ, Wolf DM, et al. A novel 80 kildalton human estrogen receptor containing a duplication of exon band 7. Nucleic Acids Res 1996;24:962—9.

[52] Pink JJ, Bilimoria MM, Assikis VJ, Jordan VC. Irreversible loss of the estrogen receptor in T47D breast cancer cells following prolonged estrogen deprivation. Br J Cancer 1996;74:1227—36.

[53] Jiang SY, Jordan VC. Growth regulation of estrogen receptor negative breast cancer cells transfected with cDNA for estrogen receptor. J Natl Cancer Inst 1992;84:580—91.

[54] Jiang SY, Wolf DM, Yingling JM, et al. An estrogen receptor positive MCF-7 clone that is resistant to antiestrogens and estradiol. Mol Cell Endocrinol 1992;90:77—80.

[55] Jeng MH, Jordan VC. Growth stimulation and differential regulation of $TGF\beta_1$, β_2, β_3 mRNA levels by norethindrone in MCF-7 human breast cancer cells. Mol Endocrinol 1991;5:1120—8.

[56] Jeng MH, Parker CJ, Jordan VC. Estrogenic potential of progestins in oral contraceptives to stimulate human breast cancer proliferation. Cancer Res 1992;52:6539—46.

[57] Jeng MH, Langan-Fahey SM, Jordan VC. Estrogen action of RU486 in hormone-responsive MCF-7 breast cancer cells. Endocrinology 1993;132:2622—30.

[58] Jeng MH, Jiang SY, Jordan VC. Paradoxical regulation of estrogen-dependent growth factor gene expression in estrogen receptor (ER)-negative human breast cancer cell stably expressing ER. Cancer Lett 1994;82:123—8.

[59] Catherino WH, Wolf DM, Jordan VC. A naturally occurring estrogen receptor mutation results in increased estrogenicity of a tamoxifen analog. Mol Endocrinol 1995;9: 1053−63.

[60] Catherino WH, Jeng MH, Jordan VC. Norgestrel and gestodene stimulate breast cancer cell growth through an oestrogen receptor mediated mechanism. Br J Cancer 1993;68: 945−52.

[61] Dragan YP, Fahey S, Street K, et al. Studies of tamoxifen as a promoter of hepatocarcinogenesis in female Fisher F 344 rats. Breast Cancer Res Treat 1994;31:11−26.

[62] Nuwaysir EF, Dragan YP, Jefcoat CR, et al. Effect of tamoxifen administration on the expression of xenobiotic metabolizing enzymes in rat liver. Cancer Res 1995;55: 1780−6.

[63] Dragan YP, Vaughn J, Jordan VC, Pitot AC. Comparison of the effects of tamoxifen and toremifene on liver and kidney tumor promotion in female rats. Carcinogenesis 1996; 16:2733−41.

[64] Dragan YP, Nuwaysir EF, Fahey S, et al. Effects of tamoxifen and two fixed-ring analogs on rat hepatocarcinogenesis. Carcinogenesis 1996;17:585−94.

[65] Sargent LM, Dragan YP, Sattler C, et al. Induction of hepatic aneuploidy in vivo by tamoxifen, toremifene and idoxifene in female Sprague-Dawley rats. Carcinogenesis 1996;17:1051−6.

[66] Nuwaysir EF, Daggett DA, Jordan VC, Pitot HC. Phase II enzyme expression in rat liver in response to the antiestrogen tamoxifen. Cancer Res 1996;56:3704−10.

[67] Li D, Dragan YP, Jordan VC, Wang M. Effect of chronic administration of tamoxifen and toremifene on DNA adducts in rat liver, kidney and uterus. Cancer Res 1997;57: 1438−41.

[68] Welshons WV, Lieberman ME, Gorski J. Nuclear translocation of unoccupied estrogen receptors. Nature 1984;307:747−9.

[69] King WJ, Greene GL. Monoclonal antibodies localize oestrogen receptor in the nuclei of target cells. Nature 1984;307:745−7.

[70] Carter SB. Effect of cytochalasins on mammalian cells. Nature 1967;213:261−4.

[71] Welshons WV, Cormier EM, Wolf MF, et al. Estrogen receptor distribution in breast cancer cell lines using enucleation. Endocrinology 1988;122:2379−86.

[72] Jordan VC, Tate AC, Lyman SD, et al. Rat uterine growth and induction of progesterone receptor without estrogen receptor translocation. Endocrinology 1985;116:1845−57.

"Sliding Doors" and serendipity

"Sliding Doors" starring Gwyneth Paltrow and John Hannah is an excellent film based on the premise that by just missing or catching a tube train in London, a life can be altered forever. The film then portrays two parallel lives to the conclusion. In this chapter, I would like to go back to the beginning of the story you have just read and consider my alternate lives. Like "Sliding Doors," things could have been very different.

"Tamoxifen Tales" recounts a journey from my first faltering steps and failures in my teens to seek out my path to a career in cancer therapeutics. The story then gallops through decades of discovery that changed women's health. The story is linear, one-dimensional and appears too focused to be true despite what you will read about my focus as the testimony of others in Chapter 18. The story is not exactly true, because life is not one dimensional and cannot be predicted. What you have read is the result, not the random reality of the journey. It is not possible to have a goal "to develop the gold standard for the endocrine treatment of breast cancer"; no one can do that or plan that far ahead. What you have read is what worked for me and what lessons I learned from those I met, who helped or hindered me in my quest for a career. It was how I responded to failure and prejudice by drawing on resources I found I had, which were to make the difference. It all boils down to a skill set that you have or skills you can learn: enthusiasm, ability to organize, ability to lead, developing hidden talents, accepting failure or responding to failure, discipline, focus, commitment, loyalty to others, embracing an opportunity, having a sense of right and wrong, and addressing injustice. I am reminded of "We are all better than we know. If only we can be brought to realize this, we may never be prepared to settle for anything less" attributed to Kurt Hahn in 1933. He was a German refugee who created the revolutionary and tough Gordonston School in Scotland. The school trains leaders by encouraging physical achievement. The late Duke of Edinburgh and Prince Charles, the future Charles III, were attendees. Serendipity is defined as "the faculty of finding interesting things not sought," and these moments will be your "Sliding Door." Opportunities come and go for us all as we weigh the advantages or disadvantages for the life we want. I constantly say to my Tamoxifen Team members "I will not stop giving you opportunities; only you can stop accepting them."

The Mottrams and their lands originated from the small Cheshire Village of Mottram St. Andrew established in their name in 1086. They held their lands until 1360 when they ran out of boy babies and Agnes Mottram was married to David Calverly, brother of the famous knight Sir Hugh Calverly of Bunbery. The lands of the

105

Mottrams were dowry to the Calverly's. By all accounts Sir Hugh was a fearsome warrior during the Hundred Years War against the French and gained a dubious reputation as a mercenary during peaceful periods. But what of the Mottram men? Edward the Black Prince held Cheshire as his private property. Wars waged with the Welsh and Scots by his great grandfather Edward I. He had honed the most powerful weapon of the age: the English (Cheshire) bowmen. Bowmen were trained in their profession from their early teens, and their skill would win battles by raining death from the sky at a range of 250 yards. The archer could fire accurately every 4 s so a thousand archers could place 15,000 arrows a minute in the midst of an advancing enemy. It was the machine gun of 1356 at the Battle of Poitiers in Aquitaine.

There are three classic battles won by the English in the Hundred Years War against the French: Crécy (1346) won by Edward III and where the youthful Black Prince won his spurs, Agincourt (1415) where Henry V won against overwhelming odds of 4−1 against, and sandwiched in between, Poitiers (1356) where the Black Prince won perhaps the greatest battle of the three. All were won by archers against the odds. At Poitiers, an army of 35,000 French led by the King of France, John II, had stalked the retreating English army. The Black Prince had a meagre 6000 soldiers but with 2000 archers. They were exhausted, hungry, and hunted. But, at the end of the day on September 19, 1356, there were 3000 French dead (200 English) and the flower of the French nobility was captive including King John II who remained a prisoner in London until his death in 1364 (incidentally with the captive Scottish King—the English were good at this game of chess).

History records in 1356 that Hugh and Adam Mottram were present at Poitiers. Roger Mottram was also present and was commended, with a pension, for his actions that day. The Black Prince is known to have recruited 100 horse archers as his personal bodyguard from the Macclesfield Hundred, which contains Mottram St. Andrew. Thus was born the tradition that the Mottrams were natural expert marksmen. The Mottram coat of arms is ancient and as such does not record a motto. These came later. But the arms record a goose feather on the helm. Goose feathers were used as flights on the arrows to steer them to their target. These men were horse archers.

In the front of this book, you will note my personal coat of arms, provided for me by the Royal College of Arms in London. This was on the occasion of my OBE from Her Majesty Queen Elizabeth II for services to international breast cancer research. The creation of a coat of arms takes about a year when all facts about your qualifications for the patent are verified as true. My coat of arms was based on the Mottram coat of arms but when I requested that the three roses on the arms were white, like the rose of the coat of arms for the University of Leeds, I was informed that I was not of a royal blood line so this was not possible! We decided upon quartered red and white roses, but now for my motto. The Mottram coat of arms has none as it was established prior to this tradition in early times. This was to identify men in battle. The motto cannot have been used by anyone else in the centuries old tradition of coats of arms.

I came up with *per scientiam vires*—strength through knowledge, which was declared unique by the College of Arms and now available only for myself and my heirs. The device is born from the early tradition, in battle, of carrying a pendant to identify your family line based on achievement and connections. The pendant, half man and half horse represents "horse archers" as do the goose feathers (for arrow flights) in the helm. The scallop depicts the connection with the Spencer family, with the Diana, Princess of Wales, Professorship.

Grandfather had his own "Sliding Doors" experience where the alternate life would have resulted in no "Tamoxifen Tales" and perhaps a very different world of women's health. Grandfather had just been commissioned into the Cheshire Regiment and arrived at their Headquarters at Chester Castle. A mounted senior officer rode by him on the parade ground, and then exclaimed, "You're James Mottram's son of Wilmslow. I know your father, an excellent shot. I have a job for you and our Regiment." Colonel Greg (incidentally owner of Greg's Mill in Styal, Cheshire some 5 miles walking distance from Wilmslow) ordered that my grandfather was ideal to train musketry instructors, as Colonel Greg had already seen his range scores with a rifle.

Grandfather was a crack shot, and in World War I (Fig. 9.1), he trained the NCO musketry instructors for the Cheshire Regiment prior to deployment for the final push into Germany in 1918 (Fig. 9.2). He survived the war probably because of

FIGURE 9.1

My grandfather, James Frederick Mottram, as a newly commissioned officer in the Cheshire Regiment, 1918.

FIGURE 9.2

My grandfather seated as the officer in the front on the right (without the raincoat) following a training session on marksmanship with his musketry instructors, 1918. I wore his Sam Browne and carried his bamboo swagger stick when I was commissioned as an infantry officer.

Colonel Greg. Colonel Greg was less fortunate. His two sons were killed in World War I, and they are memorialized in St. Bartholomew's Church in Wilmslow (Fig. 2 in the Prelude section of the Front Matter). This is the Mottram family church. My grandfather was educated at the Church of England school next door and carried the cross at services. My mother was christened here, as were my daughter Helen and I. My mother was first married here on November 1st, 1944 and she secretly buried my grandfather's ashes there in sight of the clock tower, when he died in 1972. He is with other Mottrams who came before.

When I was growing up, my grandfather would say to me "Have nothing to do with the Army. I have been in two World Wars" and then he would say "But when it comes, you had better be ready." This I took as a challenge. As a schoolboy growing up with air rifles, I found I could hit anything at 40 yards, I knocked down all the lupins in the back garden from my bedroom window. I remember my mother remarking to my father one evening, how strange it was that some large insect had bitten a chunk out of the lupin stems! Another cross my mother had to bear.

Each of my skills, in chemistry and marksmanship, now came together, as I went off to the Department of Pharmacology at Leeds University in October 1965. My first stop was to the Leeds University Officers' Training Corps (LUOTC). I filled out the forms, signed the Official Secrets Act, and swore allegiance to the Queen. The training sessions were great over the next 12 weeks, stripping Bren guns, target shooting, and planning platoon attacks.

However, early in 1966, the Commanding Officer called me into his office and declared: "You were born in Texas in the United States of an American father, and as such, you are not eligible to be an officer in the British Army. It is not a

Commonwealth country. I am sorry but there it is. Your resignation is accepted immediately." I was devastated. But, after thinking about the situation for a month, I decided, without telling my father, to visit our family solicitor for advice. He was delighted to help. He would act pro bono and write to the Home Office for a ruling.

Yes, I was born in the United States in New Braunfels, Texas, of an American father from Dallas, but following my parents' divorce, my English mother returned to Wilmslow, Cheshire, with me in 1950 and remarried. My English stepfather, Geoffrey Webster Jordan, from Bramhall, Cheshire, adopted me as his son. I had a British birth certificate; I was British. The letter, from the Home Office, which I keep to this day, states that I have all rights offered to any British subject. There are no exceptions. I rejoined the LUOTC.

As an introduction to the real world of battle, I spent two weeks of intense training in a place called Culty Braggan near Thetford with Leeds University Officers Training Corps. VERY stressful. I nearly killed someone on an attack exercise. All live ammunition. I was the Bren gunner tasked with keeping the heads down of the fictitious enemy about 100 yards away ahead. Meanwhile, 10 soldiers would advance left of the position, and then 15 yards from the enemy, charge the position and kill the fictitious enemy.

I was told to stop firing when instructed—but I didn't hear the order! The next I saw was the attacking officer cadets in my sights but no deaths as the magazine was empty

The visiting General gave an enthusiastic speech as this was the most realistic and well-timed attack he had ever witnessed. He went on to explain that in WW2 against the Japanese soldiers when he was commanding a Gurkha regiment, the enemy was so ferocious that any slackening of fire by the Bren would result in failure of the attack as the Japanese would pop up and kill the attackers. As a result, usually one or two attackers were killed by their own Bren gun!

I also nearly got killed. On the final day, with us all exhausted, we had an escape and evasion exercise all day with jeeps contains the directing staff hunting us as we tried to reach the safe haven.

Our three man team heard a hunter jeep coming down the road. We were walking behind a bushy hedge at the side of the road and we scattered. I hit the ground but sensed the others ran. Unfortunately, the jeep driver chose to leave the road and drive at speed behind the hedge. I found myself alone and looked up to see only a jeep wheel coming towards me. I was about to die but fortunately rolled my body the correct way and the jeep missed me by inches.

I have recounted above my unusual entry into the British Army. The only other unusual story like this I know of in the Army is Lt. Colonel Herbert (H) Jones of the second Parachute Regiment who won the Victoria Cross posthumously at the Battle of Goose Green during the Falklands War in 1982. His father was an American millionaire who loved Britain and moved there during World War I. Then just before World War II, he returned to America, divorced, and married a Welsh girl in New York. They moved back to Britain just before World War II and H was born in 1940. But he was officially an American. His father subsequently chose to take out British citizenship and on June 22, 1947, 33 days before my birth in Texas, H became a British citizen. As a result, his selfless actions at Goose Green became legend. But what happened that required H at a moment in history.

Following the hazardous but successful landings on East Falkland from San Carlos water, where large numbers of British ships had been damaged or sunk by the brave pilots of the Argentinean air force, a sharp, victorious land action was required to demonstrate the ruthless efficiency of the professional British Army. The 690 men of 2 Para marched south some 16 miles to liberate the settlement at Goose Green. The task ahead was not easy as the Falkland Islanders in Goose Green were "jailed" in the community hall; the center of the future battle! There were, as it turned out, also Pucará ground attack aircraft equipped with napalm bombs and a garrison of 1002 military personnel dug in strong defensive positions. Standard British military doctrine dictates that attacking forces must have a superiority of 4−1 to win an attack against a defended position, but the true strength of the Argentinean forces was unknown when 2 Para prepared to attack! Fortunately, these were the men whose forebears in 2 Para (740) had held the bridge at Arnhem against overwhelming odds in World War II not for the planned 2−3 days but for 4 days and the remnants of first Airborne Division for 9 days until overwhelmed by Obergruppenfuhrer Wilhelm Brittrich II SS Panzer Korps of 16,000 battle hardened soldiers. Watch a "Bridge Too Far" as the best depiction of these events. I tell my Tamoxifen Teams to do the same.

Over the years, because of my other life, I have "parachuted" into universities in Wisconsin, Chicago, Philadelphia, Washington DC, and Houston with my Team to make a world class laboratory from nothing—we have only ourselves to depend upon to succeed and we do—but only as long as we are supported. We have never surrendered yet but it was close at Fox Chase. I am pleased to say the evil was eventually vanquished, and the Team was withdrawn to Georgetown safely. The British professional army had taken Goose Green. This also delivered Prime Minister Margaret Thatcher her first land battle victory on the Falkland Islands. H died during the retaking of Goose Green and received the Victoria Cross for his valor. But what if H had not been in the Army and not been at Goose Green with 2 Para? Would the Falklands War have had a different ending? We will never know, but it is "Sliding Door."

For reasons you will learn later in this chapter, I chose to visit the Falkland Islands just following the 25th Anniversary of the Falklands War (Fig. 9.3). I can tell you it is very hard to get to even today with only one flight in and out per week from Santiago, Chile. You get a sense of the enormous effort required to send a self-sufficient Task Force, 8000 miles away by sea from the United Kingdom to the end of the earth. If it was not on the ship, you had to do without whatever it was. For my visit, I had chosen to retrain myself physically and walk the battlefields of the war in which I may have participated. Men of my Regiment were everywhere behind enemy lines, raiding and dying but that story has been told by others [1−3].

Back at Leeds University in 1969, I was commissioned as a Second Lieutenant in the Infantry, and armed with a First-Class Honours Degree and a Medical Research Council Scholarship at Leeds University. I started my PhD in Pharmacology with

FIGURE 9.3

At the grave of Colonel "H" Jones 2 Para on the Falkland Islands, January 2008.

Dr Edward Clark in our quest to crystallize the ER with an estrogen and an antiestrogen (Chapter 3). Then, things really started to happen in my alternate life as a reserve army officer.

During my commissioning interview, at Imphal Barracks in York, I was disheartened to overhear from the interview room the committee talking negatively about my chances of a commission because I had not completed my 2-week obligatory summer training camp for that year. The words "Well we had better interview him anyway" rang in my ears. It clearly did not matter to them that I had planned on marrying on July 29 and you could not be in two places at once. I had made my choice, but now I had to respond within the next 30 min in the face of failure. During my interview, I spontaneously volunteered to complete the Regular Army Nuclear, Biological and Chemical (NBC) warfare course at Winterborne Gunner near Porton Down, the UK Chemical Warfare Defence Research establishment (Today we call these "weapons of mass destruction"). This bold approach was successful; I was commissioned, and much to my PhD supervisor's annoyance, I was off to the Regular Army 3 week NBC Officer's course in January 1970 just 4 months into my Ph.D., studies (Fig. 9.4). I had also come to the growing realization that my Ph.D. topic was a Herculean task (the project to crystallize the whole ER has not yet been accomplished by anyone in the scientific community). I had, however, used my scientific knowledge on drug abuse gained at Leeds University to participate in Society with lectures to parent—teachers association and students, as well as army units around Northern Command.

I had prepared myself to assist in the defense of the realm in the event that Soviet Forces invaded Europe. This may seem very remote now, but I was living in a different time. The events in my lifetime spoke a different language, all of it not good. The Berlin airlift in 1947 established that America would not desert the people of Berlin. The brutally suppressed uprisings in East Germany (1953), Hungary

FIGURE 9.4

A 3-week NBC officer's course at Winterbourne Gunner near Porton Down. I am located top right. The course, my second, containing a sprinkling of NATO officers. My first course was when I was a newly commissioned second lieutenant in 1970.

(1956), and then Czechoslovakia (1968) had set an uncompromising tone by communism. This list fails to mention the Cuban Missile Crisis of 1962 with the world on the brink of nuclear war. One could not just ignore what was happening in the world around. There was also the Vietnam War, which for me became real in 1965/67 with the visiting American students demanding that we all watch reports on the War in our TV room at Woodsley House, of Leeds University's Boddington Hall. That is where they were going when they finished their studies at Leeds.

For me, the Prague Spring of 1968 was the wakeup call in Europe. I had just returned a month earlier from my LUOTC summer camp training in Norfolk when my mother shouted upstairs to me at our home in Bramhall, Cheshire "the Russians have invaded Czechoslovakia." I was not out of bed yet and I thought to myself—this is it, grandfather was right. Please remember that World War II was all about freedom in Czechoslovakia and severe miscalculations by the incompetent British politicians. Freedom was lost when the Germans invaded. It was the lighting rod and eventual wake-up call. This led to a realization that war was the only way to stop Hitler. This occurred on September 3, 1939, when Germany invaded Poland. In 1968, I was an officer cadet and there was no war, but now 2 years later in 1970, I was commissioned and I was training myself to play my part with my regular Army NBC Officer's course. But life was dull at LUOTC. I decided I would explore the possibility of becoming a Reserve Officer in the Intelligence Corps.

I told my commanding officer my plan and he arranged for me to travel to Templar Barracks, the Headquarters of the Intelligence Corps in Ashford, Kent. This complex is now gone as a concession to the end of the Cold War, replaced by the opening of the Channel Tunnel! My invitation to Templar Barracks was a 3-day event with many potential recruits and at the cocktail party on the evening of the first day, I was asked, "Why do you want to join the Regular Army as an Officer in the Intelligence Corps?" I replied that this was absolutely not why I was there, as I was only interested in transferring my commission to the Intelligence Corps (V). I had a

First-Class Honours degree, and I had been selected to do a Ph.D. in Pharmacology at Leeds University with a Medical Research Council Scholarship. I was a trained Regular Army NBC Officer.

The next day, I found myself at the Ministry of Defense in Whitehall being interviewed by the Deputy Chief Scientist for the Army, for a vacant slot in an Army Reserve Unit of 12 Senior University Faculty who were the academic advisors for all aspects of science, medicine, and engineering, relevant to the Ministry of Defense. All were Majors and Colonels. I was to be the NBC expert for the group if I passed my Positive Vetting (PV, security clearance by MI5 to Top Secret) and I would be transferred to the Intelligence Corps with the rank of Captain. For a while at least, I would be the youngest Captain in the British Army but a lowly graduate student in the Pharmacology Department at Leeds University. Exciting stuff as I had only been commissioned 9 months earlier!

My PV went well with my interview by an MI5 officer at home. I did, however, make a small political wave by phoning the Ministry of Defense to check up on the chap who was coming to my house. Was he really MI5 or Russian? When he arrived at my home in Adel, Leeds, he declared that no one had ever done that! The whole process took about 6 months, and there were robust examinations of bank accounts, family members, and school friends. I was told by Dr Kaye in the Department of Pharmacology that the security services were particularly interested in my sexual preferences!

When all was complete, I was debriefed and informed that from time to time, I would be "tested." In this way, I would not know whether the beautiful woman was our side as a test or the Russians for the real thing. This certainly kept me on the straight and narrow but in retrospect, regrettably there was neither a test nor the real thing! Then we might be telling a really interesting story (and a film?)!

Once I was gazetted and rebadged as a captain in the Intelligence Corps, I found myself attending numerous courses on Security and Foreign Armies Studies at Ashford. There was also the obligatory range courses with 9 mm pistol and submachine gun. I liked the complex at Templar Barracks and the museum of the Intelligence Corps. I was at the center of national activities and was exposed to visiting delegations from armies from around the noncommunist world. I reflected that in 1965 I was declared a potential enemy of the state by the Ministry of Defense but now I was one of a select few defending the "Holy Grail." My combat kit was from 4th Para (V) in Pudsey outside Leeds and I was parachute-trained. My role in the British Army of the Rhine in North Army Group took me to the HQ in Bielefeld routinely for attachments on exercises. On one occasion, at a Staff Officer meeting one day in Germany with German NATO officers, I was met with a stage whisper as I walked into the briefing room. "Fallschirmjäger" (paratrooper). I felt great! Additionally, I would routinely disappear for 2 weeks at a time, during my Ph.D. student training, and be unable to tell anyone, including my family where I was in Europe. However, this was an acute problem for my wife when my father died of a heart attack. This was spring 1972, and I was "somewhere in Europe." In fact, I was assigned as the G NBC officer for the headquarters of I BR Corps of the British Army of the Rhine, briefing the General each day of the week on the potential or actual NBC play in the exercise. But this was not all for that month. As luck would have it, I had also been selected by the Medical Research Council to be the British student representative at the Nobel Prize Winners meeting in Lindau in Bodensee! A strange combination for the month of defending West Germany from attack by the Warsaw Pact forces in the north and then cocktails with Chancellor Willy Brandt and an array of Nobel Laureates on Bodensee in the South.

On learning of the death of my father, my wife immediately went to Leeds Medical School to seek advice from Professor Barrett. How do we find Craig? NOW!

The solution was like something out of a spy novel. Professor Barrett realized that if I had communicated with anyone in the Intelligence Corps, I would have used the general access phone in the Pharmacology Department (no cell phones in 1972!). The unbelievable, but true, system was the caller would talk to the Medical School operator who would record the number for payment and connect the call. Professor Barrett scanned the call book and found I had called a number in Kent several times. He was connected to "my handler" Colonel Dick Armlott MBE who agreed to find me "immediately" wherever I was in Europe!

I was found in Bellenberg Wood in 1 BR Corp headquarters after I had survived 4 days of constantly moving our headquarters around Germany with virtually no sleep. We had to stay "one step ahead of Soviet Forces." In Bellenberg Wood, as we fell back in our prepared plan westwards from the border, a Major came to my tent at 4 in morning, stating he wanted a word (we British are so polite!). However, only after repeated visits did I agree to accompany him on a dawn walk together in what now appeared to me to be a surreal scene in a misty wood. "I regret to inform you your father has died and we will now get you back home as quickly as possible for the funeral." I was driven out immediately by a 1 BR Corps security detachment to Gütersloh, Gorings old squadron headquarters. I retain my "destroy after use" map of 1 BR Corps HQ unit dispositions from Bellenberg Wood and I promised I would return one day. This I did in July 2015. I then was the honorary Colonel of Leeds University Officer's Training Corps. I was met by my German scientific colleague Dr Hiltrud Brauch, after my annual camp in Sennelager, who took me to Bellenberg wood in her car. I took my map and found exactly the spot I was in 1972. For me this was very important, but then disaster struck upon exiting Bellenberg wood. The brake on Hiltrud's car had failed, and her car was now in the middle of a field! Our adventure would be resolved over the next few days!

In 1970, when I was recruited into the Intelligence Corps as a pharmacologist at Leeds University, naturally I was aware of the disastrous potential for drug abuse in our Army. The 1960s was the time of "make love and not war." It was clear to everyone that the conscript American Army had been greatly weakened by drug use in Vietnam so, as an Intelligence Corps Staff Officer, I took the initiative to plan an education program for British Regular Army Units in Northern Command in the United Kingdom. I was still only a Ph.D. student at this point (1969–72), but I was already giving drug abuse lectures in the Pharmacology Department and to parent–teacher organizations around Leeds. I had made it my business to connect with Officers of Leeds Drug Squad, and I was a regular visitor at their events. The sergeant in charge was a regular visitor at my home in Alwoodley, Leeds, and I could have as many "samples" as I needed for my lectures. In my mind, I was bringing my pharmacological knowledge to the aid of society through lectures and information transfer. But to me it was more than this. My Ph.D. was less than inspiring with a study of "failed contraceptives," but drug abuse was on the rise.

When Professor Barrett "talent spotted" me in early 1971 to be a prospective lecturer on his new departmental staff, this was an exceptional opportunity—but now for the job interview. The competition of nationally selected candidates was daunting with a single chance for success. I was one of six candidates to be interviewed—all but me had their Ph.D. and publications, so all I could play was the enthusiasm card. When I was interviewed, I was immediately informed by the committee members I should not put down summer jobs as research experience (remember I had worked in the summer of 1966 at the Yorkshire Cancer Research Campaign laboratories with David Clayson's Ph.D. students and at ICI Pharmaceuticals Division, Alderley Park with Steven Carter, Chapter 2). What the committee required was real research resulting in publications. I had none—so I told them all about antiestrogens and my view of their potential in cancer but in my enthusiasm, I stated I was "obsessed with discovering how antiestrogens worked at the estrogen receptor." In his debrief, Professor Barrett cautioned me to never use the word "obsessed" in an interview as I sounded unbalanced, and by the way, congratulations—you got the job. I have, however, remained obsessively focused in my desire to discover how antiestrogens work in target cells for the past 40 years. Molecular mechanisms in pharmacology continue to give me immense pleasure.

Oh! And then Professor Barrett mentioned as he was walking away "First, you have to get your "Been to America" (BTA). Now we have to organize how this can be sponsored for a couple of years. The plan is that you learn new ideas and techniques and bring them back to the Department in Leeds."

I had a very tight deadline and only 6 months to do everything. I had to write up my Ph.D., get it examined (Leeds had to find an examiner, see Chapter 2), fulfill my obligation as a Reserve Army Officer, secure a scholarship to sponsor me in America, book my travel to wherever, and consider who was going to look after our home for the next 2 years (we will say nothing more about the house-full of Iranian law students and their parties with the heating turned up full!).

Securing a scholarship or obtaining sponsorship to go to America was a challenge. At that time, it was considered unwise to continue your Ph.D. studies with a postdoctoral training program in the same area. Learn new science was the dictum. Anyway, I was not inclined to continue my study of "failed contraceptives." Nobody cared. By contrast, I saw great potential in learning more about drug abuse in America. I was giving lectures to the undergraduate students already, each week I would present lectures to army units in Northern Command, go to parent—teachers organizations or discuss with Leeds Police what was "the drug of choice this month" for fringe students in the University Union. Yes, I would formulate a plan to study clinical pharmacology research in drug abuse in Lexington, Kentucky, and apply for sponsorship from the prestigious Commonwealth Fund. Their selection committee, I was to discover, was formidable with three vice chancellors including my very own Lord Boyle, the US Ambassador, and a scattering of Professors of American History from Oxford and other universities. Armed with letters of recommendation for my study plan from my Ph.D. supervisor Dr. Clark, my head of Department, Professor Barrett, and the Deputy Chief Scientist (Army), I was as ready as I could ever be at such short notice. The interview was a challenge and very intimidating. After an invitation to make an opening statement to the question "Why should we select you?" I decided it was best to focus on my leadership experience and steer away from failed contraceptives. I had a First-Class Honours Degree, an Akroyd scholarship, and an MRC Scholarship, and created and led the Medean Society in the Pharmacology Department, and I had a Captain's Commission in the Intelligence Corps. Why not—a leader in pharmacology and a good representative for Britain in the United States. I was stopped short by the Chairman of Shell who interrupted stating. "It is we who are here to decide whether you have leadership qualities." Apparently, I did not and neither did I get the scholarship. Later Lord Boyle asked me to visit him in his office in Leeds and told me that I would have received the scholarship if only I had not chosen to study America's struggle with drug abuse. If you had wanted to go to study, say the estrogen receptor, somewhere in America then you would have been successful. OK, I GOT IT, so Professor Barrett and Arthur Walpole (Fig. 2.2) sent me to the Worcester Foundation to study "once a month contraceptives" with their former colleague and friend Mike Harper (Fig. 3.1). When I got to Worcester, I found he had gone to a job with the World Health Organization in Geneva, Switzerland, and I was alone to work on my remaining passion, "developing a drug to treat cancer." If Mike had not gone to Geneva—"Sliding Door"—I would not have worked on the anticancer properties of ICI 46,474. It was my lifeline to a career. Again, this story would have been very different if I had been successful with my Commonwealth Scholarship and studied Drug Abuse in Kentucky. No book. No trainee careers in Chapter 18.

I squeezed my military obligation into the middle of May 1972, but my father's death following two heart attacks was a terrible blow to our family. He had just retired from his job as a bank manager at Barclays, my mother was facing being completely alone (her father James Fredrick Mottram had died 3 months earlier from colon cancer), and her only son and daughter-in-law were off to America in September. At this point, I had not finished writing my thesis, and at the last minute, I discovered a potentially fatal flaw in my methodologies. I had to go back to the laboratory. At the same time, the Ministry of Defense was insistent that I should complete my annual training to comply with the law and receive my annual bounty (a financial incentive to complete your training). They also required that I complete my annual marksmanship range course.

Fortunately, my experiments in the laboratory were successful, but I now had to go to Porton Down, our chemical defense establishment, "to chat" with the scientists about chemical weapons defense. Each evening, I wrote up the appendices to my thesis, but to my surprise, one evening I was approached by a lady in the bar who felt the need to confess that she had taken home classified documents from work and she was sorry. Was this a test? I found there was an aura of mystery about a young intelligence officer suddenly appearing unannounced sent by the Ministry of Defense. Our security services should use this technique as it was clearly viewed by the staff that there must be a security problem! As a Ph.D. student, this situation was all exciting and an uncharted territory for me!

So after a successful examination for my Ph.D., we were off to the Worcester Foundation for Experimental Biology in Shrewsbury, MA. I elected to spend all my money saved from my Army commitment, to book two first-class tickets on the QEII, but 2 months before sailing, my wife discovered she was pregnant (with Helen). The prospect of leaving the security of the National Health Service and moving into "sort it out yourself—how much money do you have to pay for this," was daunting. Now serendipity took charge.

By sheer coincidence, a friend of my mother's in Bramhall was traveling first class on the QEII on the same voyage from Southampton (what are the chances of that!?). She planned to visit her daughter Libby in Boston who was married to an American doctor. We enjoyed the company on the voyage and thought nothing more about it. For entertainment for the 5-day voyage, I could shoot with shotguns trapshooting each day. Therein lies a tale. I have never spent much time with shotguns, but I was very good with military firearms and I had just ended up some months earlier as the winner of a small arms competition at the Scots Guards barracks at Purbright, outside London. Like grandfather, I was a good shot. Anyway, there was a commotion with other passengers during the build-up to the trapshooting final, after a week of practice every day. Apparently, an official objection had been lodged by other passengers/competitors that it was unfair that the "security officer" for the ship should be allowed to compete with the "paying passengers." To place this in context, the year before there had been a bomb threat to the QEII in mid-Atlantic and an SAS team with a bomb disposal expert had been parachuted into the sea near to the ship to deal with the problem. False alarm, but lots of publicity and new heightened security awareness. In 1972, no one knew about the SAS in the general public, other than World War II adventures in the desert of North Africa; but I did. To the passengers who were in their 70s, I, at the age of 26, clearly fit and able to use firearms, I must be the onboard "protection." Anyway, I did win!

The first few days in Shrewsbury were daunting in America especially since the pregnancy issue had not "gone away," and my wife and I were housed in a "brothel" on Route 9 called the Windsor Motor Inn. I slept with a knife within easy reach as the screams, banging on the doors, and drunken revelry went on around us throughout the night. What were we doing here?! We were rescued by my new boss, Ed Klaiber, and his wife Jeannie. Ed was going to Austria for 2 weeks so he insisted that we stay at his home in Princeton, MA and use his car to find an apartment. Now we were settling in. A week later, out of the blue, I received a phone call from a Gert Pokoly that found me in the library at the Foundation. She invited my wife and I to dinner. Her husband was a former fellow at the Foundation—and a qualified obstetrician/gynecologist. Tom Pokoly and I became fast friends, subsequently publishing together our 2 years of clinical studies. Problem solved. Helen Melissa Yvonne Jordan was born on April 10, 1973, at Worcester Memorial Hospital. By coincidence, a dual national like her father had been earlier in his life.

You have already read about what I did in my academic world for the 2 years at the Worcester Foundation (Chapter 7), but my other passion of service to the nation was set to mold the value of the rest of my other life.

I had taken the precaution of securing a letter of introduction from the Ministry of Defense. You never know when you need one on official stationary. The letter had three lines. This Intelligence Officer is on the staff of the Deputy Chief Scientist (Army). He is security cleared for Top Secret. He is an expert on Nuclear, Biological and Chemical Warfare. With my letter, I chose to take the initiative with two approaches: (1) reach out to introduce myself to the State Director of the Civil Defense headquarters in Framingham, MA, and (2) go to the Federal Building in Boston to introduce myself to the local Head of the Drug Enforcement Administration, Special Agent Joe Catalli.

Director Lewis Saba of the Massachusetts Civil Defense Agency and Office of Civil Preparedness liked the idea of having a "Brit Officer" around so he invited me to be an international observer on a state-wide weekend disaster preparedness exercise called LABMATE I. I spent the weekend being flown around by Huey helicopter inspecting sites around the state but, more importantly, I met Allen R. Zenowitz Director Region I, Federal Civil Preparedness Agency (Fig. 9.5). I was just what he needed, a trained NBC (Chemical, Biological, and Radiological [CBR] in America) Officer for his Federal Bunker in Maynard, Massachusetts, in the event of war. Rapid clearance between Washington and London through the Defense Intelligence Agency got me appointed to the Mobilization Designee group of colonels who would take over the facilities in the event of war. I was cleared to visit NORAD in Colorado, the Naval War College and exercises in Maynard, MA, where we trained to survive Armageddon (Figs. 9.6 and 9.7). I also threw in some lectures on drug abuse. My role was to get the bunker staff up to speed in CBR, and my role, in time of war, was to communicate with Air Force One and give the overall picture of devastation in the states in Region 1 (New England, New York, Puerto Rico, and the American Virgin Islands).

I visited DEA Special Agent Catalli in Boston, and during our long chat, I pointed to the certificate hanging on his wall, "Bureau of Narcotics and Dangerous Drugs, Narcotic Agents Training Certificate." "How do I get one of those?" "You don't, you're neither a Federal Agent nor a police officer in a drug squad," he replied. Well, to cut a long story short I got the Deputy Chief Scientist (Army) at the Ministry of Defense to write to Perry Rivkind, Joe Catalli's boss in Washington, I started my course in Meridan State Police Barracks in July 1974. This was total emersion for 21 days of international narcotics trafficking, kits to field test drugs, following suspects and planning and executing drug raids. Outstanding! In parallel, I was introduced to Captain Bill Gross of the Massachusetts State Police who was also the President of the Massachusetts Narcotics Officers Association. He insisted I speak at their regular meetings, and I was thrilled to be elected a member of the

FIGURE 9.5

Presentation of an Intelligence Corps Shield to Director Allen Zenowitz and Colonel Robert Davenport Officer Commanding Mobilisation Designee Region One, 1974. Colonel Robert Davenport wrote a final annual report and assessment of me to Dr. E.R.R. Holmberg, Deputy Chief Scientist (Ministry of Defence): "Aside from the fact he is the only British Officer assigned to this particular Agency, and perhaps the only British Officer in a reserve training capacity with any American Reserve Group, these are some notable aspects to Captain Jordan's association with us. Captain Jordan has not received from us any training as he has contributed to us in specific experiences in his profession areas of Drug Abuse Law Enforcement and Nuclear Chemical and Biological Warfare. He undertook an expansive program of training on his own initiative without any possibility of personal gain other than the training and exposure it will give him. Were I to have a military command in an active war activity, I would be most comforted having a man like Captain Jordan working with me." Dr. Holmberg forwarded my evaluation to me stating: "I have received a most interesting and complimentary letter from Colonel Davenport. There is no doubt you created an extremely good impression with the Americans and you have done much to benefit Anglo-American relations. It is most refreshing to read of your initiative and keeness and I congratulate you on your achievement. I look forward to seeing you soon and hearing more of your exploits."

Massachusetts Narcotics Enforcement Officers Association. All of these experiences would help with my alternate life in the future when our family returned to Leeds in September 1974.

During my time in America, all I did with the Army and Federal Narcotics personnel for 2 years was voluntary. I waived any liability and chose to return to England at my own expense to complete my annual military training between1972 and 1974.

FIGURE 9.6

On attachment to the American Army in 1974. This weekend exercise was to practice the survivability of the North-Eastern United States of America in the event of nuclear war. I was a Captain in the Intelligence Corps, parachute regiment-trained (hence the "parasmock") and we were "entombed" in the Federal bunker in Maynard, Massachusetts, for the duration of the exercise.

Back at the Department of Pharmacology at the University of Leeds, I put together my first Tamoxifen Team between 1974 and 1979 (Chapter 5). In my alternate life, I resumed my Reserve Army Service with the "Pool of Technical Intelligence Staff Officer" advising the Deputy Chief Scientist (Army). I had gained unique qualifications with the Americans as the CBR officer for Region I and also completed as many of their chemical weapons courses as possible. Back in Britain, I was fast-tracked to complete additional training in Security and Foreign Armies studies as an Intelligence Staff Officers, and I was sent to Sandhurst for a "complete emersion" experience on Soviet Studies for the summer in 1975. This was also the time I had access to train with all the firearms available in the armory at Sandhurst. The British Army officer is supposed to be able to excel with the weapons of any nation but as the photograph betrays, the Intelligence Officer does it in his suit

FIGURE 9.7

Me lecturing about Chemical, Biological and Nuclear Defense at the many training exercise weekends with the Defense Civil Preparedness Agency bunker in Maynard, Massachusetts.

(Fig. 9.8)! It was at Sandhurst, I had my first experience with the Gurkhas. A company (80) of these amazing soldiers from the mountains of Nepal were the "resident" enemy for the fledging officers in training. The rationale is that if you can survive against the Gurkhas, you can survive against anyone. I, on the other hand, had a fateful experience in the officers' mess when I enquired of the mess sergeant what was for lunch and he pointed to the buffet. I was delighted to be able to focus on the curry. I love curry! After struggling through this "food on fire" experience, with pints of water to wash it down, I explained to the mess sergeant that this was the most vicious curry I had ever eaten. "Sorry, Sir, that was only intended for the Gurkha Officers." The curry did not remain with me for very long!

I also had the opportunity to attend a supercourse on the East German Army at Sandhurst. Opposite us in 1Br Corps (3 Divisions), in Northern Army Group in West Germany, were 20 Soviet Divisions and 3 Divisions of East Germans. The Russian strategy was to destroy 1Br Corps of professional soldiers and then the two other

FIGURE 9.8

Firearms training at the Royal Military Academy, Sandhurst, 1975.

NATO Corps, who were composed of conscript armies, would fold after the professional army was gone. The course was most memorable because of the time I spent with the son of Colonel Claus von Stauffenberg, then a West German Army Officer. Colonel Claus von Stauffenberg was the Wehrmacht officer who planted the bomb in the July 1944 plot to kill Hitler. Eerie to be able to touch human history.

On another occasion, I was to spend the summer in London at the Old War Office in Operational Intelligence to understand how my job, in time of war, would play out. I recall asking a Brigadier how the plan would be formulated for me to identify, capture, and send back for assessment any advances in Soviet NBC pertinent to the survival of 1Br Corps in the face of overwhelming Warsaw Pact forces coming over the border. "That's for you to work out" was the concise reply. Fortunately, there was no need.

One day in the spring of 1975, there was a knock at my front door at 9 Barfield Grove, Alwoodley, Leeds. The gentleman stated: "I need your help. You have 30 seconds to answer my question-will you accept the challenges of the SAS Regiment and rebadge to 23 SAS immediately after security clearance and other details?" I was informed by this Colonel in civilian clothes that I was just what he was looking for and would I transfer to the Special Air Service (SAS) as my skills were necessary to keep his Sabre Squadrons alive behind the advancing Russian front on the NBC battleground in the area of Northern Army Group in Germany. I would be with 23 SAS attached to 1Br Corps headquarters and train up the Regiment in NBC (and other stuff!). I had worked with the Americans and that was good to pass on combat intelligence to them in time of war. I was parachute-trained, PV'd, and well known for my skills with firearms in the Intelligence Corps (Fig. 9.8). "Do what we do—no questions asked," the Colonel said. Now it was another advanced NBC course at Winterbourne Gunner (Fig. 9.4) and another visit by MI5 for another 5 year Positive Vetting for Top Secret Clearance. I was required to volunteer an individual who had known me all my life. I nominated Peter Sidwell. We had been to primary school at Neville Road and Moseley Hall Grammar School together, and we had been friends ever since. Peter was a solicitor and toyed with the MI5 investigator when he visited him at work. Peter's boss was most impressed and volunteered his office for Peter's interview. Apparently, following a brief introduction by the MI5 officer, who described why he was interviewing him, Peter later told me that he jumped in right away challenging the information he had just learned about me: "So you have just informed me that Dr. Jordan is being security vetted prior to recruitment to the SAS Regiment. Isn't what he is doing for the country supposed to be a secret?" Stunned silence from "the man from the Ministry." I was rebadged and gazetted into the SAS. An exciting time of just getting on planes and showing my identity card and intense sleep depriving exercises called Summer Sales and Reforger with the Americans.

My final report from Colonel Amlot at the Intelligence Corp headquarters in Ashford, Kent: "He carried over last years training to this year—one period at the Royal Military Academy Sandhurst and another in London at the Directorate of Intelligence. A great enthusiast and regrettably has now transferred to 23SAS. Their gain!"

The adjutant of 23SAS responded:

1. "Your transfer has now been authorized from December 27, 1975."
2. You have been taken onto unit strength and posted to Ops/Int Troop HQ Squadron (Detached to B Squadron for training and administration).
3. You should rebadge yourself immediately.
4. The occurrence will be published in the London Gazette supplement on April 13, 1976.

Welcome Aboard. Bob Reid".

I was to have many adventures with Bob! My annual report from Colonel Roy Walker following the first year read:

A highly intelligent scientist who was initially recruited to coordinate and direct the NBC training in the Regiment. This he has continued to do and has taken an interest in the normal working of the Ops/Int Troop, where his considerable analytical powers are of great value. His expertise is well appreciated throughout the Regiment. An excellent find for 1976.

When I returned to Leeds in September 1974, I told Sergeant Derek Bolderson, Head of the Leeds Metropolitan Police drugs squad, about my DEA training and he got me in touch with Chief Superintendent Roy Smith of the West Riding Police. Roy guided me toward the National Police training school in Bishopgarth in Wakefield. "Would you consider coming to Bishopgarth once a month to give a series of four lectures in the morning, on International Narcotics Trafficking and Law Enforcement? We train 60% of UK police forces at the Criminal Investigation Division (CID) and also drug squad officers." This started a wonderful relationship between me and the West Yorkshire police. Well, actually not always wonderful, as I got into a significant disagreement with the Chief Constable when, at a cocktail party. He discovered I was from Leeds University, so he decided I must be a communist! I am a thin-skinned Cheshire man and I was an SAS officer so I did take offense easily. I wrote and told him so, and the situation required an apology. My poor friend Roy Smith had to sort that one out delicately, but we reconciled years later when the Chief Constable presented me with gold Bishopgarth Police Officers cufflinks in gratitude for my years of service to his police force.

He was a tough man who did not compromise. He was the first to insist on firearms training of specialists units in his force well ahead of all others in Great Britain. He saw the problems with violent crime increasing so he acted. It was also the era of the IRA; I was checking the car every day for bombs before I drove to the Medical School. The IRA did not care whether you are a Regular or Reserve member of the SAS. None of us in the Reserves were allowed to travel to Northern Ireland.

My monthly visits to Bishopgarth were fantastic. I was training the nation's police forces, an officer in the Intelligence Corps and then the SAS, and tamoxifen was starting to twitch into life (Chapter 3). ICI Pharmaceutical Division and the Yorkshire Cancer Research Campaign was funding my research and by the middle of the 1970s, publications were pouring out and I was lecturing around the world—care of ICI. I then decided on a bold plan to use my transatlantic training with the DEA to bring one of their teams over to Bishopgarth to give their whole Narcotics Officers course to our police force. This would be my service to the Nation. What could be the harm in that?

I often went down to London for work with the Army at the Ministry of Defense, so I boldly strode into the US Embassy in Grosvenor Square. It was all bullet proof glass in the lobby with armed US Marines as the obligatory rapid reaction force. Outside in Grosvenor Square had been the scene of major riots and street fighting against mounted police on March 17, 1967, in protests against the Vietnam War so there was no reason to relax security. The 1970s was also the era of Palestinian terrorists.

I politely announced myself and asked for a meeting with the resident DEA agent. Much to my surprise and great pleasure I was greeted by a middle-aged man in a gray suit. I proceeded to explain my credentials, connections to the DEA and my plan. They knew already I was born in New Braunfels, Texas! He was sympathetic and supportive, promising to pass my request for an official training team to present their course at Bishopgarth. This all happened to plan and I was thrilled to have pulled this off on behalf of the West Yorkshire police. Only years later did I discover that questions were asked around Whitehall and the House of Commons about how a "foreign police force was permitted to come to our country and train our police." Knowing the Chief Constable of West Yorkshire, he probably did not care about any government repercussions as long as his police had the best training.

After service with the Regiment for 4 exciting years as a reserve Captain in operational intelligence and as the Regimental NBC Officer, it was time to go to Switzerland and then America (Chapter 4). I transferred to the Regular Army

Reserve Officer (RARO) list, and I remained an RARO until I was 50. I moved to Switzerland in 1979 and then to Wisconsin in early 1980.

Roy Walker had moved on from 23SAS and was replaced by Lt. Colonel Tony Hunter Choat. He had an earlier, extremely colorful career in the French Foreign Legion, and had the distinction of fighting on both sides in the Algerian uprising! Tony wrote my final annual report:

He has just transferred to the Regular Army Reserve of Officers (RARO). I am most grateful to this Officer who despite an extremely demanding civilian employment, which frequently took him out of the country. We look forward to his eventual return.

As a RARO, one is expected to report to the British Embassy in time of War. I did that on April 1, 1982. It was the first day of Falklands War and I was given daily briefings by one of the military attaché staff at the Embassy in Washington, DC, by phone to my office in the Wisconsin Comprehensive Cancer Center. I remember the fateful call telling me that the British ship Sheffield had been hit and I breached security rushing out of my office in the Cancer Center to tell Anna (Tate). I was invited to consider TV interviews once the land battle started. Anna counseled me not to go on the TV at the request of the Embassy after the Belgrano was sunk—"I need a live Ph.D. supervisor" she insisted. Common sense trumps a patriot.

I was told by the Military Attaché at the Embassy to get fit as there was a possibility of mobilization if the conflict was protracted. There are many stories of me being sighted around Madison in my Para smock and combat kit (Fig. 9.9), but when things started to get serious and men from the Regiment were dying, I approached my Chairman, and Cancer Center Director, Paul Carbone for help. I realized that this could be my war, but I had to consider the security of my wife and two children. Paul was understanding as I described how it would be a challenge financially on a Captain's pay in the British Army to pay the bills in Wisconsin, even if the paperwork ever went through. "How many vacation days do you have?" "About 21," I replied. "Well that gets you 'til May, how about sick days?" Was he suggesting a slight wound in mid-May? We will never know as the war ended quickly on June 14, 1982.

At the University of Wisconsin, I was invited to join the Officers Education Committee. Our role was to act as evaluators of students who had military scholarships in return for service following graduation. I gravitated with a close relationship with the Naval Regular Officers Training Corps (Naval ROTC) because this was the domain of the Marines. I was invited to present the address at the annual dinner of the Naval ROTC at the Madison Club. I chose as my theme "The choice between your life and your duty to your Country and Comrades." I received a standing ovation. The reality for me a year earlier was the Falklands War.

The after dinner party was forever remembered by the Marine Corps permanent staff. As it was well known, I was a RARO in the SAS, a Marine instructor presented me with a Fairbain & Sykes Commando knife stating: "Let's see if you can throw this with accuracy." Mission accomplished as it struck in the wall across the

FIGURE 9.9

Full combat kit at the time of the Falkland War April 1982. In Wisconsin, I was instructed by the British Embassy to "get fit" and "find out everything you can about the Falkland Islands. We know next to nothing!"

room. A year later, after the Naval ROTC dinner, a group of uniformed Marines greeted me outside the restaurant and stated: "We are part of the training staff at University Naval ROTC units in Chicago. We had to come to meet the SAS Officer who threw the knife across a crowded room to stick it in the wall. You are a legend."

The Falkland Islands is contentious to this day, but I felt the need to travel there in January 2008 to see for myself. This could have been my war and I had studied all the battles, so I wanted to walk the ground. I still believe in supporting those who serve our nations (United States and United Kingdom) and following an exchange with General Sir Michael Rose concerning his book "Washington's War," he generously recommended me for membership to the SAS Regimental Association with this citation. "This officer has saved more lives than any soldier in the SAS Territorial or Regular." Who is Mike Rose? He was the commanding officer of 22 SAS for the successful storming of the Princess Gate Iranian Embassy in London in 1980 to conclude the siege and incidentally making members of the Regiment superheroes and safely liberating the hostages. Watch the film "5 Days."

The Falklands War could have been my "Sliding Door" if more men were needed in 1982 and Michael Rose would have been my commanding officer down there. In any event, I learned a huge amount about the Falklands just in case. It is a place of fascination for me to this day. My commitment to service and defense of the Realm might have been fatal. Nevertheless, the legacy of tamoxifen would have been safe. The principles of taking tamoxifen forward to long-term adjuvant therapy were starting in clinical trial, and Trevor Powles would still have moved forward with chemoprevention with tamoxifen. Only Wisconsin would have been different. All students and Tamoxifen Teams after 1982 would not exist; we would have no selective ER modulation and no raloxifene. But that version of "Sliding Door" did not occur and I strongly believe that the excellent advances in medicine and women's health that you read about are something for which we can all be very proud in the Tamoxifen Team. "We are in it for life" is our official motto.

That may have been the end of the story, except for the unanticipated tragedy of 9/11 on September 11, 2001. I watched on the TV the two hijacked airliners slam into the twin towers in New York. We were under attack. Until there was more information, I chose to go to work at the Robert H. Lurie Comprehensive Cancer Center. A film crew was waiting to film my Tamoxifen Team, but I was aware that Chicago possessed two ideal targets for an aerial terrorist: the Hancock building, a block away from the Cancer Center and the Sears Tower across town. All went well filming, and all staff were sent home at 4 p.m. However, the attacks became real for me as I passed the Hancock building. A Chicago fireman, in full operational protective kit, walked toward me extending two enormous leather boots. "Please, give to aid the families of the dead firemen in New York: those protecting New York are all dead, and our units will drive overnight to protect New York." Those in my Tamoxifen Teams know I carried a lot of cash in my pockets as a self-defense tactic when I traveled the world: if attacked, I would throw the money one way and run the other. The mugger would follow the money! The "boots" got all I had.

As the country went into "siege modality" with no flights, Mayor Daly's wife Mary contacted me to ask whether I was willing to help the city defend itself. I knew Mrs Daly from numerous meetings concerning the care of patients with breast cancer. I made numerous suggestions during meetings with the senior leadership with the Chicago Police.

The personal result for me of this was that the US and British authorities were now allies in the "Hunt for Osama bin Laden" and the invasion of Afghanistan. My US citizenship that I "deswore" in 1972 to keep my Captain's commission in the British Army before I would go to the Worcester Foundation for Experimental Biology as Visiting Scientist was returned with the words "We are all on the same side now. Welcome back."

One evening, on one of my many visits to work on tamoxifen studies with Professor Hiltrud Brauch at the Fisher-Bosch research institute, I received a phone call from the Secretary at the University of Leeds. Professor Roberts would be officiating

FIGURE 9.10

My surprise presentation by General Sir Richard Dannatt, Chief of Defense Staff to recognize my continued service to Leeds University Officers' Training Corps at a dinner and lecture event at Leeds University Officers Training Corps.

and it would be an opportunity to meet and listen to a lecture by the Chief of General Staff General Sir Richard Dannett (Fig. 9.10), I declined as this would be "mission impossible" to travel to Leeds from Stuttgart and back to Stuttgart in 48 h. Then on reflection I thought" "Who Dares Wins." I got there for a surprise. General Dannett was to make a presentation to me of a bronze caste, Griffon, the emblem of Leeds University OTC made by Colonel Roberts. Colonel Roberts made my introduction with the usual former Leeds Graduate, OTC member Captain in the Intelligence Corps/SAS. But then stated: "He is known as the "Father of tamoxifen." Two dozen women in the room took my photograph, and one (Fig. 9.10) was sent to me. "Father of tamoxifen beats the SAS!"

During my tenure at MD Anderson, I made regular training visits back to Leeds. But it was on an American Airline's Flight, when I was wearing my SAS lapel wings, that I was approached by flight attendant Christiana Cruz about a project called "Honor our Heroes."

On Memorial Day 2017, the project placed flags near the reflecting pool in Washington, DC, in honor of every American who fell during the Iraq and Afghanistan wars. I saw the opportunity to sponsor the display of a Union Flag for each of the British Fallen as American Allies (Fig. 9.11). I sought authorization through the Military Attaché at the British Embassy in Washington, DC, who attended the ceremony.

When asked why I continued my national service while enjoying a successful career in research and investing in prizes and scholarships for young students, I answer: "I am a participant. This was my way of paying back the free education I received in Britain. That sense of service is very, very strong in me."

FIGURE 9.11

American and British Union Flags were displayed on Memorial Day 2017 near the reflecting pool in Washington, DC, to represent soldiers from both nations who fell during the Iraq and Afghanistan wars. I am a citizen of both countries and secured the British Flag's representation.

References

[1] Freedman L. Vol I & II the official history of the Falklands campaign. Oxford: Routledge; 2005.

[2] McKay F, Cooksey J. Special Air Service Pebble Island. The Falklands War 1982. Barnsley, South Yorkshire: Pen and Sword Book Ltd.; 2007.

[3] Delves C. Across an angry sea: the SAS in the Falklands War. London: Hurst & Co, Ltd.; 2018.

South to Northwestern in Chicago

10

In 1991, Paul Carbone, the Director of the UWCCC, was a member of the Scientific Advisory Board of the Robert H. Lurie Cancer Center in Chicago. Dr Steven Rosen was the new director with the mission to build a nationally recognized Cancer Center with support from the Federal Government and the Lynn Sage Breast Cancer Foundation.

Dr Carbone was well aware of what I had achieved at Wisconsin as director of the Breast Cancer Research and Treatment Program for the Cancer Center. He recommended that, given Steve's support, I could create a program of national prominence at Northwestern University.

I was already applying for a position at the University of Chicago, as deputy director of the Ben May Institute for Cancer Research, but this did not come to pass. As it turned out, this played to Steve's advantage. He immediately organized a dual recruitment: I was offered the immediate construction of custom-built laboratories at the Robert H. Lurie Cancer Center with a philanthropic stream of $1 million annually from the Lynn Sage Breast Cancer Foundation to build a new program. Steve's opportunity was dependent on the fact that the University of Chicago had failed to recruit me, so by accepted recruitment protocols at hospitals in Chicago, Steve could now recruit the Head of their Breast Cancer Treatment Program; Dr Monica Morrow. She would have the immediate construction of the Lynn Sage Breast Cancer Center and she would be the inaugural Director.

The research plan to build a new Tamoxifen team at the Robert H. Lurie Cancer Center

I left two of my three R01 grants back in Wisconsin. My grant on rat liver carcinogenesis with tamoxifen was passed on to Dr Henry Pitot, Director of the McArdle Laboratory for Cancer Research. He was the real expert in rat liver carcinogenesis and with his team, especially Dr Yvonne Dragan created a steady stream of peer-reviewed publications [1—7]. My R01 grants to study the impact of stable transfection of the ER gene into ER-negative breast cancer cells and the study of structure—function relationships of ligands that bind to the ER remained at Wisconsin for the next 2 years to allow John Pink and William (Bill) Catherino (a medical student doing a 4-year intercalated Ph.D. with my Tamoxifen Team) to complete their PhDs

Tamoxifen Tales. https://doi.org/10.1016/B978-0-323-85051-3.00010-5

under my continuing supervision for the next 2 years as a visiting professor at the UWCCC (Fig. 10.1).

During this period, a few of my recollections about Bill deserve mention. My first impression of Bill, when he went to a meeting in New York, was, whatever the topic, he was the first to be on his feet to ask a provocative question! He was not shy! In the laboratory, he also was not reserved. He learned the necessary skills of molecular biology and created numerous excellent peer-reviewed publications to be worthy of his Ph.D. [8–12].

Years later, when Bill was completing his residency in Vanderbilt, I was invited to speak at a "Think Tank" on breast cancer at Cambridge. There would be the breast cancer experts, accomplished faculty in other disciplines (mathematics, philosophy, etc.), and the "best trainee" (protégé) the breast cancer experts had produced. The idea was to fertilize and enthuse a new generation with potential new research directions previously not considered. Bill was my immediate choice to survive in this academic environment. We were on our way to Cambridge!

After having lunch at the Eagle pub in Cambridge, where Jim Watson (Fig. 1 in the Front Matter) and Francis Crick had famously announced their discovery of structure for DNA, we prepared for our meeting. The three categories of participants had color-coded name badges, but then I discovered that Bill had upgraded to breast cancer expert. He wisely obtained the appropriate badge as my protégé.

During the write-up of his papers, Bill would ensure I was reading his work, and I was not just saying "OK, let's publish." He was well aware I traveled internationally

FIGURE 10.1

Bill Catherino and John Pink two Ph.D. students supported by my R01 grants left behind at Wisconsin. Also shown are the lab technicians working with Bill and John.

on a continuous basis. Each year, a faculty member in the Department of Human Oncology at the UWCCC, was selected as the most traveled. I was the "TWA Visiting Professor" on more than one occasion. An award was presented at our annual Faculty dinner at the Madison Club.

As I read Bill's paper, I though to myself, "excellent work." Then I got to the last page of his Discussions! "In summary, with these data we have demonstrated that we have cured cancer and this will now be applied to patient care." Bill had a sense of humor!

He later told me that, what he found remarkable was that John Pink and he saw me more often at UWCCC when I moved to Chicago (4 h away by car), than when I lived in Madison! To me it was incredibly important that I should ensure their future careers would get a good start. What each of my 17 Ph.D. students achieved is explained later in this memoir. Today, William Catherino, MD, Ph.D., is Professor and Chair of the Research Division, Department of Obstetrics and Gynecology at the Unformed Services University of Health, Bethesda, Maryland.

We had a firm foundation of a $1 million annually from the Lynn Sage Breast Cancer Research Foundation. Overall, they raised a total of $13 million at their annual fund raising Gala. With this incredible investment in Research, staff could be hired and laboratories filled with postdoctoral fellows, Ph.D. students, and technicians.

The Tamoxifen Team at the R.H. Lurie Cancer Center of Northwestern University was built from nothing in 1993. However, the program got off to an unanticipated stellar start with rapid recognition by the professional pharmacology community on both sides of the Atlantic and recognition for contributions to breast cancer research in the United States.

Three prizes for my translational research on tamoxifen.

As soon as I joined the American Society for Pharmacology and Experimental Therapeutics (ASPET; 1981), I published a series of papers in Molecular Pharmacology on the structure−function relationships of compounds related to tamoxifen to regulate prolactin in Mara Liebermans's immature rat pituitary prolactin assay [13]. Tamoxifen was taking off clinically as a long-term adjuvant therapy, and there was increasing interest in using tamoxifen to prevent breast cancer. Unknown to me, Dr Paula Stern, Professor in the Department of Pharmacology at Northwestern, had successfully nominated me to be the 1993 recipient of the ASPET Award for Therapeutics to be presented at the ASPET annual meeting in New Orleans.

I had been invited to travel to the University of Cambridge annual meeting of the British Pharmacological Society to receive the Gaddum Memorial Award and present the Award lecture. I realized that the Lecture at Cambridge was to be held on the same date as a symposium in honor of the life and work of the late Bill McGuire who had died tragically in a diving accident in Mexico. Doug Wolf would take my place and present our work on the discovery of an Asp351Tyr mutation in the ER from a tamoxifen-stimulated MCF-7 breast tumor that had developed acquired resistance to tamoxifen [14]. On the strength of his presentation and expertise, Doug received an offer of a postdoctoral fellowship down in San Antonio.

My lecture at Cambridge went well, but when I and the audience were leaving, I overheard "the great and the good" of the British Pharmacological Society discussing my work and presentation with the words: "That is the best translational research lecture I have ever heard." Yes, I was thrilled.

A few months later, back in Chicago, I received a letter from the Principal of the University of Edinburgh which stated. "You have been selected to present the Cameron Prize lecture before the Faculty and students of the Medical School. We note you are the recipient of a DSc degree from the University of Leeds, and you will be required to present your lecture in full academic dress. We will reimburse your coach class air fare and cover the cost of 3 days lodging at the University hotel."

I had never heard of the Cameron Prize, but replied in the affirmative, as Monica and I would have a holiday in Edinburgh and tour the countryside. Then in their reply letter, they enclosed a list of prior Cameron Prize winners that took my breath away. The Prize was first awarded in 1879. The names of Nobel laureates and "famous medical researchers" leapt off page. The award cannot be applied for but is given "biannually to a person who, in the course of the 5 years immediately preceding, has made any highly important and valuable additions to practical therapeutics." I present but a few names that leapt off the page: Pasteur (1889), Ross (1902), Ehrlich (1914), Dale (1926), Curie (1931), Fleming (1945), Huggins (1958), Pincus (1966), and Black (1980) my mentor.

I suspect that the Chair of Pharmacology at Edinburgh was one of the "Great and the Good" who was discussing the merits of my Gaddum Memorial lecture at Cambridge, and he had nominated me. A lesson learned, always teach yourself to present first-class lectures of your work so that you can be talent-spotted!

Educational outreach and research priorities at the Robert H. Lurie Comprehensive Cancer Center

Monica Morrow, Bill Gradishar and I initiated the start of the Lynn Sage Breast Cancer Symposium not only to be an educational outreach program for physicians in the Midwest, but also to act as a fundraising mechanism for our breast cancer program. We initiated the annual Lynn Sage Distinguished Lectureship, which would become the highlight of the Lynn Sage Symposium (Fig. 10.2).

Our breast cancer program had to grow and innovate to secure Federal funding. The formula for my successful career development so far had required me to have the organization and determination and resolve to move repeatedly; as opportunities emerged, I led, organized, and innovated.

The Tamoxifen Team laboratory at the Robert H. Lurie Comprehensive Cancer Center (Steve Rosen achieved that milestone) expanded with technicians, Ph.D. students, postdoctoral fellows, but most importantly there was a steady stream of surgical and medical oncology residents who came to work in the laboratory, at no cost

FIGURE 10.2

Dr. Marc Lippman (center), then the Cancer Center Director at Georgetown as our inaugural Lynn Sage lecturer. He is flanked Dr. Monica Morrow and I during his Award ceremony.

to me. They were in the laboratory to gain experience in medical research. Additionally, there were visitors (for years!) from overseas sent by Dr. Iino in Japan, as well as South Korea and Ireland. All produced a wonderful and vibrant mix in the science of medicine for our breast cancer program.

I chose these priorities to establish research continuity with Wisconsin: train a new generation of innovators and leaders in academic medicine, obtain Federal Funding for our program, and solve translational research questions of relevance to patient care.

The major shift in therapeutics in the first 20 years of my career was the demonstration of the merit of translational research with tamoxifen (at the Worcester Foundation for Experimental Biology, the University of Leeds, and the Ludwig Institute for Cancer research in Bern, Switzerland) and ascent of aromatase inhibitors as treatments from the landmark research by Angela and Harry Brodie for ER-positive breast cancer. Lives were being extended dramatically, and far beyond initial expectations. But then what? When the antiestrogenic strategies for primary treatment fail, there must be an emphasis on antiestrogenic drug resistance. The question was simple: can we map out the evolution of antihormone resistance, identify vulnerabilities, and discover mechanisms to apply to clinical care. Our trainees at the Lurie Cancer Canter of Northwestern University would be the next generation of leaders and innovators of breast cancer therapy (Figs. 10.3, 10.4).

FIGURE 10.3

The final "Tamoxifen Team" at the Robert H. Lurie Comprehensive Cancer Center 2004: left to right Bin Chen, Jennifer McGregor, unknown, Sandra Pierce, Dawn Chen (lab manager), Betty (my program manager), Joan Lewis, unknown, Eric Ariazi, myself, Clodia Osipo, Hong Liu, Sherry Lim, Katherine Meeke (lab tech).

Deciphering the molecular mechanism of antiestrogen action and the new science of estrogen-induced apoptosis

The gold standard for the physical chemist to illustrate structure in matter is X-ray crystallography. It seemed like a good idea in 1969 for my thesis, but this was impossible at that time. Little did I know, or anyone else, that one needed pure protein and high-affinity antiestrogens. High-affinity antiestrogens were born [15] and then became part of standard laboratory studies of the mechanism of action of antiestrogens in 1977 at Leeds University with 4-hydroxytamoxifen, a trace metabolite noted in all species including humans. However, a process to crystallize the ER following purification and sequencing was 20 years into the future. "We didn't care; been there, tried that, move on!" "My Tamoxifen Teams would use laboratory models, to define mechanisms, to create medicines to treat breast cancer." We would develop new models to define a mechanism, despite our ignorance about ER structure.

Bill Catherino at UWCCC (Fig. 10.1) (University of Wisconsin Comprehensive Cancer Center) and Ana Levenson (as my first Tamoxifen Team member I hired at the Robert H. Lurie Cancer Center) were to define a molecular model to modulate the wild-type ER receptor and Doug Wolf's unexplained mutant ER Asp351Tyr.

FIGURE 10.4

With the work conduced during her training in the Robert H. Lurie Comprehensive cancer Center "Tamoxifen Team" Ruth O'Reagan graduated with her MD research degree at the University College, Dublin. The photograph shows myself as an Honorary Fellow of University College, Dublin and on the right Ruth and Professor Eamon O'Regan at the University College Dublin. At this event the surprise for me was to discover that the other honorary faculty Fellow was Patrick Hillary, former President of Ireland and a graduate of the University College, Dublin.

They further deployed our pioneering advance of stably transfecting the two ER genes (wild type and Asp351Tyr) into cloned MDA-MB-231 ER-negative breast cancer cells as models to ask a simple question with a yes/no answer. "Can the human ER regain control of the ER-negative breast cancer cell?"

Ana compared and contrasted two nonsteroidal antiestrogens: 4-hydroxytamoxifen and a new arrival, a failed breast cancer medicine keoxifene. The latter compound was later to be reinvented (i.e.,: renamed) as the first SERM raloxifene.

4-Hydroxytamoxifen was estrogen-like, i.e.,: stopped cell replication of the ER-negative breast cancer cells stably transfected with the wild-type ER gene. The same was true for ER-negative breast cancer cells stably transfected with Asp351Tyr ER gene. By contrast, the nonsteroidal antiestrogen raloxifene, which at the time was being tested in clinical trial as a SERM for the treatment of osteoporosis, was an antiestrogen in ER-negative breast cancer cells transfected with wild-type ER gene, i.e., raloxifene did not stop cell replication. By contrast, raloxifene caused ER-negative cells transfected with the Asp351Tyr mutant ER, to stop replicating. We concluded that antiestrogenic properties of the raloxifene molecule required the antiestrogen side chain to block Asp351 to stop the "jaws of the crocodile (ER) from closing." By contrast, the natural mutation Asp351Tyr now promoted the "jaws" of the ER to close [16].

The same year that we published our first refereed paper, the X-ray crystallography of the ligand-binding domain of the ER was published [17] bound to either estradiol, which is planar and raloxifene with angular structure with a "stick in the jaws of the crocodile." The end of the antiestrogenic side chain of raloxifene bound directly to Asp351 in the ER ligand-binding domain.

We subsequently published a larger paper on the topic in Cancer Research [18].

Extensive animal models of estrogen-induced apoptosis to decipher pathways and clinical utility

All our successful expertise in discovery at the University of Wisconsin on estrogen-induced apoptosis, stemmed from the skill of two Ph.D. students: Marco Gottardis and Doug Wolf. To this point, we had been unsuccessful creating models in vitro, so with our "money mountain" at the Robert H. Lurie Cancer Center, and numerous fellows from the Department of Surgery and Medical Oncology, we chose to reestablish and investigate apoptotic mechanisms in vivo. However, as a prelude, we needed to repeat validation experiments of tumor viability and estrogen action.

The project went well and we submitted our, as we thought, final experiments for publication in 2000 to Clinical Cancer Research. However, the referees suggested numerous experiments that needed to be done before publication would be approved. Disaster! The members of the original experimental team had either returned to their country of origin or returned to their clinical studies in either Medical Oncology or Surgery. The savior of the day was Dr. David Bentrem, a new member of my team at Northwestern who, without any prior experience with animal experimentation, completed all experiments required by the reviewers, and it was immediately accepted [19]. David is currently professor of Surgery at Northwestern University Hospital, Chicago. But then the unexpected happened!

Dick Santen's group at the University of Virginia published their studies on the induction of estrogen-induced apoptosis in vitro with long-term estrogen-deprived (LTED) MCF-7 breast cancer cells in vitro [20]. They proposed, what is called, an extrinsic mechanism of action for estrogen to kill LTED breast cancer cells. What this meant was that estradiol:ER complexes create a stress situation in LTED cells, which secretes proteins that attach back on the LTED cells, to orchestrate cell death.

Clodia Osipo [21] and Hong Liu [22], two superb postdoctoral fellows, had followed up with our studies in vivo in immune-deficient animals that examined the biology of either estrogen-induced apoptosis in tamoxifen-resistant LTED breast cancer or Hong Liu's new model of raloxifene-resistant breast cancer. After the publications in the *Journal of National Cancer Institute*, it was clear that we and Dick Santen's group were all on the same page about the final consequences of LTED breast cancer and estrogen therapy. However, the big problem was an actual mechanism of action at the molecular level. What we knew was (1) estrogen binds to the ER, (2) a week later, something happens, and (3) the extrinsic mechanism occurs to feed back to the prepared breast cancer cell to trigger death! Not exactly a molecular mechanism!

Our models in vivo could not address the precise time-related actions in vivo because of pharmacokinetic complications. We needed our own in vitro models to settle a mechanism story. Enter Joan Lewis, a new postdoctoral fellow who was tasked by me to resurrect our in vitro models (MCF-7:5C and 2A), waiting for a decade in our deep freeze for the time that aromatase inhibitor treatment would replace tamoxifen for the treatment of breast cancer. Now was that time!

To my surprise, when Joan showed me her MCF-7:5C data demonstrating estrogen-induced cell death, whereas a decade earlier S.Y. Jiang saw **none** in our refereed publications [23]. I enquired whether Joan had repeated exactly what my Ph.D. student S.Y. Jiang had done to culture the cells. Joan's reply was "No. I used the culture media that I had used previously for MCF-7 cells throughout my Ph.D." [24]. After recovering from this revelation, I told Joan never to take this approach in science again! Followed by: "Thank you, you have made a discovery!"

With this new model, Joan fully documented the mitochondrial intrinsic pathway of the early stages of estrogen-induced apoptosis [25].

Consolidating the financial flow with federal grants

Steve's vision to create a "Cancer Center" evolved to a "Comprehensive Cancer Center." This required not only our "money mountain" but also required Federal peer-reviewed funding. He solved each requirement sequentially. He ticked the "education box" with his grants administrator Dr Robin Leikin, marshalling our NIH Ph.D. and postdoctoral training grant and our Department of Defense postdoctoral training grant with me as their principal investigator. Each went through successful renewals at 5 years.

Dr. Morrow became the principal investigator on a Department of Defense Center of Excellence Grant focused on addressing "Healthcare Disparities for the Detection and Treatment of Breast Cancer in Chicago." I was not involved in the grant, but said I would "tweak" the abstract to stress that the model presented could be translated to any major city in the United States. She was awarded this prestigious clinical research grant.

A Specialized Program of Research Excellence (SPORE) in Breast Cancer is the jewel in the crown of any aspiring breast cancer program with national aspirations. Steve set his sights on that! I was selected to be the principal investigator. This was primarily because tamoxifen was front page news—still, but this time as the first medicine to be tested as a chemopreventive in women at high risk. Monica was the clinical breast cancer co-PI already funded by the DoD. Anne Thor, MD was also a co-PI as a pathologist of national standing within the national clinical trialist community. I was unsure that our proposal was going to be competitive but Anne was adamant—we would be successful. She was correct. Additionally, raloxifene, the first SERM had successfully been evaluated for the prevention of osteoporosis for postmenopausal women at risk and I was the chairperson of the breast cancer evaluation panel (Morrow, Powles, Lippman, Costa, Norton) for the Eli Lilly placebo-controlled clinical trial (Multiple Outcomes Relative to Evista [MORE]) [26].

Monica and I had been at the Robert H. Lurie Comprehensive Cancer Center since 1993 when there was nothing of significance in breast cancer. Now, at the dawn of a new millennium we had gone from nothing to world class in 7 years. But why do I say world class?

An improbable series of events occurred that shone a spotlight on the activities of our breast program at the Robert H. Lurie Cancer Center: This started with a 3-day event organized around the visit of Diana, Princess of Wales in 1996 (Fig. 10.5) and then the tragedy of her death on August 31, 1997, that resulted in Anne Lurie, the benefactor of the Robert H. Lurie Comprehensive Cancer Center creating, with the approval of Diana's blood family the Spencers, the Diana, Princess of Wales Professor of Cancer Research to be presented to me, at a 3-day event in Chicago in 1997. Additionally, an unanticipated flood of international awards was of huge benefit for the Robert H. Lurie Comprehensive Cancer Center and validated what had been achieved by translational research at the Worcester Foundation for Experimental Biology (1972–74), Department of Pharmacology of the University of Leeds (1974–78), Ludwig Institute for Cancer Research, Bern, Switzerland (1979–80), University of Wisconsin Comprehensive Cancer Center (1980–93), Robert H. Lurie Comprehensive Cancer Center (1993–2005).

Celebrations around the Diana, Princess of Wales Professorship in Cancer Research

The event surrounding the award of my personal chair at Northwestern the "Diana, Princess of Wales Professor of Cancer Research" was to take place over 2 days in Chicago. During the day on Day 1, there was a symposium in my honor (Fig. 10.6). Lois Trench-Hines, the original clinical monitor of tamoxifen in the 1970s, was present with her husband George. She specifically recorded Dr. Morrow's

FIGURE 10.5

Diana, the Princess of Wales, and I at the reception at President Biden's home in honor of Diana's spending these days at Northwestern. She was my keynote speaker at the symposium I organized and spoke at on breast cancer.

talk on the value of tamoxifen to prevent breast cancer. The other participants in the symposium were Clive Dix, then Research Director of Glaxo, Marco Gottardis, then at Bristol Myers Squibb, Elwood Jensen an emeritus Professor at the University of Cincinnati (who had received the Lasker Award), Geoffrey Greene, from the University of Chicago, and Anait Levenson representing my Tamoxifen Team at Northwestern.

On day 2, during early brunch at the Ritz Carlton, President Biden, of Northwestern University, presided over the ceremony to invest me as the inaugural Diana, Princess of Wales, Professor of Cancer Research. Naturally, Anne Lurie did the honors.

During the evening, there was a gala dinner on the roof top suite of rooms for residents of our home at 1000 Plaza on Oak Street overlooking the Drake Hotel on Michigan Avenue. The hosts were AstraZeneca, and the evening was spent with my Tamoxifen Teams and their spouses, the President of Northwestern University, the Governor of Illinois and staff from the British Consulate in Chicago.

FIGURE 10.6

Symposium in my honor the day before my inauguration as the Diana, Princess of Wales Professor of Cancer Research. Right to left Steven Rosen, the Cancer Center Director, Ana Levenson, Northwestern Tamoxifen Team Geoff Greene, University of Chicago, Barry Furr, AstraZeneca Chief Scientist, Clive Dix, Glaxo Research Director, Marco Gottardis, Bristol-Myers-Squibb, Elwood Jensen, Monica Morrow (hidden).

The highlight of the evening was the call from Clive Dix for all my Ph.D. students present to assemble on stage for a presentation. Marco had arranged for a British Army Officer's sword from Wilkinson Sword to be engraved, on the chrome scabbard, with the names and dates of their PhDs of the (then) dozen Ph.D. students (Fig. 10.7). Marco discovered that never before had anyone engraved the chrome scabbard. Wilkinson Sword offered to do the engraving for free, if they could use the engraved sword in their catalogs as publicity for future projects!

A surprise honor

Early one morning in Chicago, I was woken up by the phone, but it was only the high pitched whistle of a fax machine. That's odd, I thought, but I calculated that 3 a.m. in Chicago would be 9 a.m. in London. When I got to work at the Robert H. Lurie Cancer Center, there was a message on my voice answering machine "to call this number and it will connect you directly to the British Consul." When I called, their voice-answering machine told me that the Consul was away and try again on a date in the future.

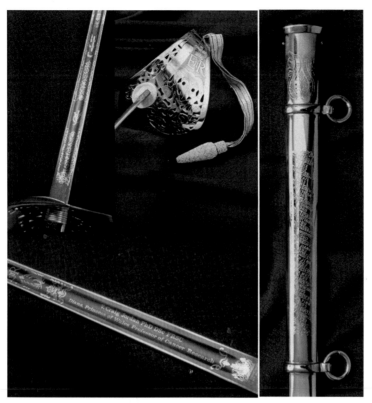

FIGURE 10.7

The British Army officer's sword presented to me on the occasion of my induction as the Diana Princess of Wales Professor of Cancer Research. The scabbard is engraved with the names of my then one dozen Ph.D. students C.J. Dix (1982). A.C. Tate (1983), S.D. Lyman (1984), E.M. Cormier (1988), M.M. Gottardis (1989), C.S. Murphy (1990), S.Y. Jiang (1992), M.H. Jeng (1992), D.W. Wolf (1993), W.H. Catherino (1995), J.J. Pink (1995), and J.M. McGregor (1999).

When the date arrived, the British Consul requested my absolute secrecy about what he was to ask. The question was: "If you were to be offered an honor in the next years Birthday Honours list would you accept it?" I replied affirmatively and the Consul then revealed that at the appropriate time I was to be named as an Officer of the Most Excellent Order of the British Empire for my services to international breast cancer research. Monica and I were off to Buckingham Palace!

However, many arrangements had to be made beforehand. The invitations to the Palace could not leave the county, for the threats of the passes getting into the wrong hands were real. I asked Clive Dix to be my contact person and, when the time for my ceremony arrived, we met up at the Savoy, where my mother, Jack Baker, Monica, and I were off to Buckingham Palace for my ceremony. Subsequently, Monica,

Helen, and Alexandra went to Westminster Abbey for the photograph of myself, Helen, and Alexandra (Fig. 1.10).

The actual ceremony went well and was well orchestrated and excellent. Only one minor incident occurred with Monica and Jack on the way to the presentation hall. Jack became so engaged with the art collection (perhaps the finest in the world) hanging on the walls of the Palace everywhere that they only managed to get to the ceremony at the last minute. They were at the back of the hall. However, once Her Majesty made an entry, she passed right in front of our family group.

I had been separated from the family group and educated first in a separate suite of rooms of what to do as the ceremony progressed: one lines up, in batches, in alphabetical order within the award that one is to receive. One is informed that Her Majesty will present one's honor, in my case pinning it on my chest, and then answer her question. I was prepared for every eventuality except the question I was given (protocol dictates one never discloses what Her Majesty says to you). My mind went blank as I struggled to find a coherent answer to present. I chose to throw caution to the wind and inject enthusiasm. Her Majesty then shook my hand and pressed on the back with her thumb to indicate the audience is over. Never to be forgotten, and the photographs were delivered to anywhere in Great Britain the morning of the next day (Fig. 10.8).

Before we left London, on the evening after the events at Buckingham Palace, Monica and I had arranged to host a dinner at our favorite boutique restaurant in London owned by two delightful Italian brothers. They had arranged our family celebration dinner as a long table with the family (Monica, myself, Alexandra, Andy Noel, Helen, Tom Turner, my Mother and Jack). I was in charge of choosing the wine, but for the main meat course, I decided to order a secret bottle of my favorite Italian wine Tignanello, then about £150 a bottle but a lesser red wine for the table in the £70 range. As the wine waiter served Monica and I the Tignanello, it was then Alexandra's turn. When asked which wine, she would like X or Y she replied: "I will have what my Father is drinking!" As a blood family, Helen, Alexandra, and I are three Mottrams when it comes to wine!

Monica and I next went to Prestbury, Cheshire, as Barry Furr had organized a celebration of my recognition by the Team at ICI Pharmaceuticals who worked in the new cancer therapeutics area. I thank them all for their friendship over the years. At the evening dinner, I was presented with an antique map of Cheshire that hangs proudly in my collection of antique maps displayed on my staircase at home in Houston.

The glamor of the "Big Three of Cancer Research": Bristol Myers Squibb Award (2001), American Cancer Society Medal of Honor (2002), and the Charles F. Kettering Prize (clinical) from General Motors (2003): a triumph for the Robert H. Lurie Comprehensive Cancer Center at its zenith

The Award ceremonies for the "Big Three": Bristol Myers Squibb Award and Medal for Distinguished Achievement in Cancer Research (2001), the American Cancer

FIGURE 10.8

The award of my officer of the most excellent Order of the British Empire (OBE) for Services for International Breast Cancer Research occurred in 2002 at the Buckingham Palace by the Majesty Queen Elizabeth II.

Society Medal of Honor (2002), and the Charles F. Kettering Prize for the most outstanding recent contributions to cancer treatment (2003) were unique events, amazing, and never to be repeated, because for the Bristol Myers Squibb Award and the Charles F. Kettering Prize, it was the end of an era and the economic realities of philanthropic investment clashed with the Assault on New York and America on 9/11.

The event for the Bristol Myers Squibb Award started with a celebration dinner at the home of the President of Princeton. The event was hosted by Dr Susan Horwitz (Fig. 10.9), Chair of the Selection Committee, and distinguished in her own right for researching and advocating cisplatinum as a successful anticancer agent to be used in clinical care. The house is famous because it had been Woodrow Wilson's home prior to him being elected the President of the United States as America entered World War I. The aftermath, with the Versailles Treaty that restructured Europe,

FIGURE 10.9

Photograph of myself with the Bristol-Myers-Squibb Selection Committee that was chaired by Dr. Susan Horwitz (center).

unintentionally set in motion preparation for part 2 with World War II! The following day was a symposium and Marco Gottardis, who had at the time a leadership role at Bristol Myers Squibb, delivered a masterful introduction for my Award presentation.

All too soon, it was time to leave Princeton for New York City and the evening festivities and awards ceremony at the Pierre Hotel. The surprise for Monica and I was this was to be by helicopter, which hugged the river into the city. A memorable entrance!

The black-tie event, planned for the evening, was hosted by Dr John Mendelson (Fig. 10.10), who chaired the Selection Committee, but the actual medal/award presentation was by the Chairman of Bristol Myers Squibb (BMS). The celebration was spectacular with guests invited by BMS from all eras of my life in biomedical research in the United States from Dr Thoru Peterson, President of the Worcester Foundation for Biomedical Research up to my then cancer center Director Dr Steven Rosen and Mrs Anne Lurie (Fig. 10.11), the benefactor of the Robert. H. Lurie Cancer Center. An evening never to be forgotten but unknown to me only the beginning.

The world changed for us all on September 11, 2001, when the hijacked civilian airplanes slammed into the twin towers of the World Trade Center in New York (Fig. 10.12). There were additional fatalities as a hijacked passenger airliner hit the Pentagon in Washington, DC. During this attack, Anna Riegel, who was at Georgetown University on the faculty of the Lombardi Cancer Center, phoned me to tell

FIGURE 10.10

Dr John Mendelson and I at the Bristol-Myers-Squibb celebrations at the Pierre Hotel in New York. John was the chair of the Selections Committee for the award. As you have read, he was very well aware of my career development over the decades since we first met at the external advisory committee annual meetings at the Wisconsin Comprehensive Cancer Center in the 1980s.

me she could see the smoke from her home; can you arrange us for move to Chicago?! A fourth aircraft had been hijacked, but the brave passengers decided on their own to retake the plane! It crashed with no survivors in the fields of Pennsylvania.

The following year, America recovered and chose to demonstrate defiance. The American Cancer Society planned to move their annual Medal of Honor Ceremony from New York to Washington but invite donors to ensure that this was to be a demonstration of American resurgence in the face of adversity.

For this premier event, they chose the Reagan Center as the cavernous venue for the ceremonies and subsequent performance by Cirque Du Solei. I was selected to receive the basic award for my work on tamoxifen and Brian Drucker, the clinical award for Gleevec. Both were shown to be breakthrough drugs with lives saved: the story the American Cancer Society wanted to tell. President George W. Bush

FIGURE 10.11

A memorable moment at the Bristol-Myers-Squibb Award with Anne Lurie, the benefactor of the Robert H. Lurie Cancer Center and Steve Rosen, my cancer center Director (the best boss I have had).

was the President of the United States, but his father former President George H. W. Bush was a major supporter of cancer research with the George and Barbara Bush Foundation for Cancer Research (indeed now I have moved to the MD Anderson Cancer Center I am supported by their Foundation). They would receive the award for philanthropy through their support for cancer research.

The family (myself, my daughters Helen and Alexandra and their husbands Tom Turner and Andy Noel, respectively) all attended. Monica could not attend as she was receiving an award from Penn State and she would be there with her parents. I planned to join them the next day. Again, this was an opportunity to invite Luther and Loraine Trammel from Houston. Steve Rosen, my cancer center director, and Tim Volpe, our cancer center chief administrator, were my guests.

I took all day perfecting and practicing my acceptance speech to be perfect, to tell a story, and keep the audience surprised and engaged. Then it was time! I rose to my feet, ascending the steps to the stage to receive my certificate and medal

FIGURE 10.12

Brystol-Myers-Squibb Award at the Pierre Hotel in the New York City. Marco Gottardis, myself and Monica Morrow.

and have photographs. I moved to the podium and began. My plan was to thank all family members, and my Director Steve Rosen and my Tamoxifen Teams (Anna Riegel and her husband Anton Wellstein were my guests), but I chose to focus upon my birthplace in Texas. I turned to President Bush and declared: "Mr. President, you will have noticed I have an accent and I am not from around these parts; you are correct (long pause), I was born in New Braunfels, Texas in 1947." This caused an uproar from the audience, and I continued by telling the story of my mother and I leaving Houston following my parents divorce—"helped and supported by Luther and Loraine Trammel who are with us tonight." The audience exploded with applause and cheers as Luther and Loraine stood. All went as planned, but only practice will make it look spontaneous (Fig. 10.13).

President Bush rose to his feet to address the room: "Ladies and Gentlemen, long pause—"Tex" he turned to look at me as he said Tex. The room exploded with laughter and applause.

After the ceremony, the award recipients formed a "receiving line," and President Bush insisted that each member of the audience should leave their seats and meet each of the Medal of Honor winners. I was positioned between the Bushes at the end of the line. However, two other delightful and flattering events happened in the "receiving line."

Mrs Bush continued to try and persuade me to accompany them on their private jet to Kennebunkport in New England for a few days (Fig. 10.14). I had previously told her that my wife Monica was receiving an alumna award the following day and I had to be there. This did not deter Barbara Bush! But it was a distinguished guest,

FIGURE 10.13

American Cancer Society Medal of Honor. Left to right Ms. Bush, Luther Trammel, former president George H.W. Bush, Lorraine Trammel and myself.

Dr Everett Koop, the Surgeon General of the United States, who shook my hand saying "that is the best acceptance speech I have ever heard." Naturally, I was thrilled to accomplish my goal to tell the story.

Nancy Brinker, the inspiration behind Susan G. Komen For the Cure, was able to organize with the First Lady Laura Bush a luncheon and tour of the White House for a select group of Komen contributors (Fig. 10.15).

The General Motors Charles F Kettering Prize is awarded for the most outstanding recent contribution to cancer treatment. It was considered to be the top award in the world for cancer clinicians. Imagine my delight when I learned, via telephone, that I was to be the winner for 2003. The "deliverer of good news" went on to apologize by saying that I should have really received the award years earlier, but the good news was that the amount of the award had been increased!

FIGURE 10.14

Mrs. Barbara Bush and I chatting together on the stage during the ceremony during our award of the American Cancer Society Medal of Honor.

FIGURE 10.15

With the First Lady of the United States Laura Bush at the White House.

The General Motors Prize Awards were to be held in Washington, DC. I was required to present a lecture on my prize winning work at the National Institutes of Health (Anna Riegel and Bill Catherino both attended as Tamoxifen Team members) (Fig. 10.16). My ceremony was held, as a magnificent evening at the State Department (this was to be the last time). The event was spectacular, followed by a grand banquet. In my party, Monica and my two daughters Helen and Alexandra with their husbands Tom and Andy attended. Even now I can recall how stunned I was hearing the director of the NIH introducing me as a winner to the few hundred guests at the meal. "How can we create more Craig Jordans." My blood runs cold on reflection of my early faltering steps at Moseley Hall Grammar School in Cheshire. Thank you Mr Armishaw (headmaster), Mr Bescoby, Mr Anderson, and Mr Radford. It is their commitment to me, at the right time that made my future happen.

This period of my academic career brings me to a story about checks for hundreds of thousands of dollars "magically" and "mysteriously" arriving in my bank saving account. The Federal Tax authorities contacted me for an audit and an explanation where was this "mystery money" was from! Naturally, I was suspected of being an international drug smuggler especially if they examined my flight record with American Airlines to present lectures all over the globe! My tax lawyer in New York was (and still is) Larry Lorusso asked me to transfer my audit from Chicago to New York. This was completed and Larry attended the appointment at the "Federal

FIGURE 10.16

My lecture at the National Institutes of Health as part of the celebration of my award of the Charles F. Kettering Prize from General Motors Foundation in 2003. Anna Riegel and Bill Catherino attended.

Building" well armed. His defense was I was a famous medical scientist who had saved the lives of millions of breast cancer patients worldwide. These sums of money going to his bank account are medical prizes. To support his position, he took books I had written on tamoxifen, photographs with Royalty and Presidents of the United States. His final statement was "Here is the evidence and he has paid taxes on it." After his tour-de-force, the only words spoken were "You can leave now!"

Conclusion

In this section, I have summarized the benefits to Society of a focused examination of the good, the bad, and the ugly of a single orphan drug tamoxifen that gave birth to a whole new group of medicines for women's health the SERMs. The company who discovered and developed tamoxifen for patient benefit worldwide created a different strategy (no hormonal activity is better than an "estrogen tickle" with tamoxifen) with an instant portfolio of breast cancer medicines (Anastrazole, Faslo-dex, and Zoladex) and one medicine for prostate cancer (Casodex). Overall, patients benefited for two decades from the success of tamoxifen and the "offspring" from Alderley Park as the true legacy of my friend and mentor Dr Arthur Walpole.

References

[1] Xu YD, Dragan YP, Young T, Pitot HC. The effect of the format of administration and the total dose of phenobarbital on altered hepatic foci following initiation in female rats with diethylnitrosamine. Carcinogenesis 1991;12:1009–16.
[2] Dragan YP, Pitot HC. Multistate hepatocarcinogenesis in the rat: insights into risk estimation. Prog Clin Biol Res 1992;374:261–79.
[3] Dragan YP, Fahey S, Street K, et al. Studies of tamoxifen as a promoter of hepatocarcinogenesis in female Fischer F344 rats. Breast Cancer Res Treat 1994;31:11–25.
[4] Sargent LM, Dragan YP, Bahnub N, et al. Tamoxifen induces hepatic aneuploidy and mitotic spindle disruption after a single in vivo administration to female Sprague-Dawley rats. Cancer Res 1994;54:3357–60.
[5] Dragan YP, Hully JR, Nakamura J, et al. Biochemical events during initiation of rat hepatocarcinogenesis. Carcinogenesis 1994;15:1451–8.
[6] Dragan YP, Fahey S, Nuwaysir E, et al. The effect of tamoxifen and two of its non-isomerizable fixed-ring analogs on multistage rat hepatocarcinogenesis. Carcinogenesis 1996;17:585–94.
[7] Sargent LM, Dragan YP, Sattler C, et al. Induction of hepatic aneuploidy in vivo by tamoxifen, toremifene and idoxifene in female Sprague-Dawley rats. Carcinogenesis 1996;17:1051–6.
[8] Jordan VC, Jeng MH, Catherino WH, Parker CJ. The estrogenic activity of synthetic progestins used in oral contraceptives. Cancer 1993;71:1501–5.

[9] Catherino WH, Jeng MH, Jordan VC. Norgestrel and gestogene stimulate breast cancer cell growth through an oestrogen-receptor mediated mechanism. Br J Cancer 1993;67: 945—52.

[10] Catherino WH, Jordan VC. The biological action of cDNAs from mutated estrogen receptor transfected into breast cancer cells. Cancer Lett 1995;90:35—42.

[11] Jordan VC, Catherino WH, Wolf DM. A mutant receptor as a mechanism of drug resistance to tamoxifen treatment. Ann NY Acad Sci 1995;761:138—47.

[12] Catherino WH, Wolf DM, Jordan VC. A naturally occurring estrogen receptor mutation results in increased estrogenicity of a tamoxifen analog. Mol Endocrinol 1995;9: 1053—63.

[13] Lieberman ME, Gorski J, Jordan VC. An estrogen receptor model to describe the regulation of prolactin synthesis by antiestrogens in vitro. J Biol Chem 1983;258: 4741—5.

[14] Wolf DM, Jordan VC. The estrogen receptor from a tamoxifen stimulated MCF-7 tumor variant contains a point mutation in the ligand binding domain. Breast Cancer Res Treat 1994;31:129—38.

[15] Jordan VC, Collins MM, Rowsby L, Prestwich G. A monohydroxylated metabolite of tamoxifen with potent antiestrogenic activity. J Endocrinol 1977;75:305—16.

[16] Levenson AS, Catherino WH, Jordan VC. Estrogenic activity is increased for an antiestrogen by a natural mutation of the estrogen receptor. J Steroid Biochem Mol Biol 1997;60:261—8.

[17] Brzozowski AM, Pike AC, Dauter Z, et al. Molecular basis of agonism and antagonism in the oestrogen receptor. Nature 1997;389:753—8.

[18] Levenson AS, Jordan VC. The key to the antiestrogenic mechanism of raloxifene is amino acid 351 (aspartate) in the estrogen receptor. Cancer Res 1998;58:1872—5.

[19] Yao K, Lee ES, Bentrem DJ, et al. Antitumor action of physiological estradiol on tamoxifen-stimulated breast tumors grown in athymic mice. Clin Cancer Res 2000;6: 2028—36.

[20] Song RX, Mor G, Naftolin F, et al. Effect of long-term estrogen deprivation on apoptotic responses of breast cancer cell to 17beta-estradiol. J Natl Cancer Inst 2001;93: 1714—23.

[21] Osipo C, Gajdos C, Liu H, Chen B, Jordan VC. Paradoxical action of Fulvestrant in estradiol-induced regression of tamoxifen-stimulated breast cancer. J Natl Cancer Inst 2003;95:1597—608.

[22] Liu H, Lee ES, Gajdos C, et al. Apoptotic action of 17beta-estradiol in raloxifene-resistant MCF-7 cells in vitro and in vivo. J Natl Cancer Inst 2003;95:1586—97.

[23] Jiang SY, Wolf DM, Yingling C, et al. An estrogen receptor positive MCF-7 clone that is resistant to antiestrogens and estradiol. Mol Cell Endocrinol 1992;90:77—86.

[24] Lewis JS, Osipo C, Meeke K, Jordan VC. Estrogen-induced apoptosis in a breast cancer model resistant to aromatase inhibitors. J Steroid Biochem Mol Biol 2005;94:131—41.

[25] Lewis JS, Meeke K, Osipo C, et al. Intrinsic mechanism of estradiol-induced apoptosis in breast cancer cells resistant to estrogen deprivation. J Natl Cancer Inst 2005;97: 1746—59.

[26] Cummings SR, Eckert S, Krueger KA, et al. The effect of raloxifene on risk of breast cancer in postmenopausal women: results from the MORE randomized trial. Multiple outcomes of raloxifene evaluation. J Am Med Assoc 1999;281:2189—97.

Forward to the Fox Chase Cancer Center in Philadelphia

11

Nothing lasts forever, and the political environment at Northwestern University was changing in the early 2000s: Deans came and went, the hospital proposed a new priorities for the Lynn Sage organization (they were to build a new women's hospital and the clinical breast program would move into that building), Monica had been promoted to Professor of Surgery and then the unlikely happened. After the creation of the Diana, Princess of Wales Professor of Cancer Research, there was an assumption that Monica and I would not leave Northwestern University. Everything that had been gained in academic recognition had happened at Northwestern. However, Northwestern became an unstable environment and others saw opportunity.

I remember it well. It was at a reception during the annual meeting of American Society of Clinical Oncology (ASCO). Over a buffet dinner, Bob Young, President of the Fox Chase Cancer Center, and the Deputy Director Bob Ozols approached Monica to consider becoming the new Chair of Surgery at the Fox Chase Cancer Center. Frankly, I was not enthusiastic as Fox Chase was not integrated into a university environment like all the others. It would mean I would step away from my academic environment "comfort zone" with its faculty rights, tenure commitments, etc. A job was offered to me to become Vice President and Research Director of Medical Sciences. Money had been raised to create an Endowed Chair for me: the Alfred G. Knudson Chair in Basic Sciences, I would receive a substantial recruitment package and have an interconnecting suite of new laboratories. My executive office suite would be opposite from Dr. Morrow's, Chair of Surgery suite. Prospects at Northwestern were turning grim. We had no choice but to say farewell and I bid Steve Rosen (the best Boss I have ever had- SAS terminology for "the leader") farewell. He subsequently moved to be the Provost and Chief Scientific Officer of the City of Hope National Medical Center in Duarte, California. From this experience, and from future experiences at Fox Chase and Georgetown where the Greats of the "War on Cancer Generation" were being replaced by administrators whose eyes were on saving money changed the goal: the idea of a nimble Cancer Center in each state, conducting clinical/basic research in the service of the patients was no longer a priority. The excitement of Wisconsin with enthusiastic students and pioneering basic and clinical researchers charting new territory with tamoxifen and the adventure of the Robert H. Lurie Comprehensive Cancer Center with tamoxifen and SERMs becoming front-page news were receding in the rear view mirror of life.

Tamoxifen Tales. https://doi.org/10.1016/B978-0-323-85051-3.00011-7

Now cancer science became dominated by "the faceless ones" who wield power on behalf of their master above in the chain of command.

Once we settled in the Fox Chase Cancer Center, Monica and I led the "Good Life": not in the sense of the British TV series "The Good Life" based on recycling everything and growing one's own food, but a palatial home in a few acres of woodland. We wanted to entertain on a grand scale (as we had with our legendary Christmas parties at Northwestern) but our tastes in homes differed. Monica preferred modern designs, whereas I preferred a traditional design in the colonial style. My aspirations were dashed once I discovered that the traditional Pennsylvania house room sizes in my plan for a house were too small and replaced by multiple interconnected small rooms. Monica tried one last time to get me into her camp. We drove into the driveway, and I was confronted with a gloomy single story half-moon fortress in a modern style. It was snowing, and with only my everyday shoes, I declined to take a look at it; I would sit in the car! After a while, Monica shouted for me to come and have a look; I begrudgingly agreed.

Going through the front door, I was met with a cavernous living area with a 20 ft ceiling, perfect for our legendary Christmas parties in Chicago! Bedrooms and the dining room and adjoining kitchen were left and right of the central living room in a semicircle. Perfect! But where was my library of 5000 books to go and my ever-expanding antique weapons collection; the product of my prize money. Simple answer: we would build out and rebuild a double garage (we had dueling Jaguar cars, I had a gold XJ6 sedan [for my 50th birthday], and she had an XK8 Jaguar sport car for going to Fox Chase). We were ready for business!

The Fox Chase Cancer Center Tamoxifen Team

Although Fox Chase was small for a hospital/Cancer Center/basic research center, it is quality and not quantity that is the key to academic excellence. The Director, Bob Young, and Deputy Director Bob Ozols forged their reputations at the National Cancer Institute. Additionally, Bob was the President of the American Cancer Society (ACS). He had chaired the selection committee for my ACS Medal of Honor Award and introduced my career at the ACS award ceremony. They had connections. More importantly for my future, there were members of the National Academy of Sciences "sprinkled around": Barry Bloomberg (Nobel Laureate) for the discovery of the hepatitis B virus, Alfred G. Knudson Jr. for the two-hit theory of retinoblastoma and tumor suppressor genes, Beatrice Mintz, a pioneer in genetic engineering techniques who generated both chimeric and transgenic mammals. I was fortunate to have gained such a prestigious circle of new academic colleagues.

The new environment at Fox Chase and the immediate creation of outstanding interconnected laboratories by the "command" of Bob Ozols, allowed me to set out my plan to build the Fox Chase Tamoxifen Team. Eric Ariazi and Joan Lewis both accepted invitations to join and aid my transition from Chicago. They both knew the research theme of our Tamoxifen Teams, but it was now essential to build a critical mass of trained scientists and technicians. Most notably, Surojeet Sengupta brought expertise from Benita Katzenellenbogen's laboratory and Ping Fan expertise from Dick Santen's laboratory, Gregor Balaburski, another postdoctoral fellow was to publish our 10-year data on the ebb and flow of our raloxifene-resistant breast cancers treated with or without estrogen [1]. As you will recall, this new model was created by Hong Liu at Northwestern, Myles Brown's trainee from Harvard. We had retransplanted it for a decade, primarily because raloxifene treatment to prevent breast cancer in the Study of Tamoxifen and Raloxifene (STAR trial) was now recommending indefinite raloxifene treatment to maintain the chemoprevention of breast cancer. Our studies would be valuable if or when acquired drug resistance to raloxifene occurred and treatment options were necessary.

At the Fox Chase Cancer Center, I transferred my project from my SPORE grant at Northwestern. Monica and I assembled a new SPORE grant for the Fox Chase Cancer Center and the University of Pennsylvania Comprehensive Cancer Center where I had a joint appointment. Additionally, I decided upon constructing a translational research project to be supported by the whole of a Department of Defense Center of Excellence grant. My topic would be the antitumor mechanism and clinical utility of low-dose estrogen therapy, following LTED in breast cancer. The results of my labors came in 1 day and within 2 h of each other: SPORE grant unfunded, Center of Excellence grant funded, as the only grant funded that year!

Eric Ariazi took the lead to focus all our efforts on developing a roadmap of estrogen-induced apoptosis by documenting the first 90 h of estrogen treatment in MCF-7:WS8 clones, MCF-7:5C, and MCF-7:2A cells. The two cell lines MCF-7:5C and MCF-7:2A were LTED and cloned out by Wisconsin Ph.D. student S.Y. Jiang [2,3]. Joan Lewis had resurrected the cells at Northwestern in 2004. The MCF-7:2A cells underwent apoptosis in the second week of treatment and the MCF-7:5C after 3 days of physiologic estrogen treatment [4]. Our roadmap for apoptosis was published in the Proceedings of the National Academy of Sciences [5].

Unlike the University of Wisconsin, there were no Ph.D. students at FCCC, or so I thought. In my attempt to build my FCCC Tamoxifen Team, I advertised in the journal *Science* for postdoctoral fellows. Marge, my outstanding executive secretary, was the listed contact person. She informed me that she had been contacted by a Russian MD who was on a training program from his medical school in Moscow to obtain a master's degree in cancer research at Fox Chase. She had booked an appointment for him to be interviewed by me that afternoon. At the meeting, Philipp Maximov explained that his Medical School was the top medical school in the country and he was very keen to do a Ph.D. in my laboratory. He would do the same work as a postdoctoral fellow I was advertising for, but cheaper! Welcome to the Fox Chase Tamoxifen Team, Philipp!

Joan Lewis would be Philipp's day-to-day laboratory supervisor, and I selected a project to study the molecular modulation of estrogen-induced apoptosis in MCF-7:5C cells. This would be a start of studies that would, for he and I, extend for the next

10 years at two further institutions, but at that time our plan was to complete his PhD. Another individual I brought to the project was Ramona Curpan from Timisoara, Romania. I had met her when I was visiting a colleague Eric Prossnitz at the University of New Mexico. Ramona remained our outstanding "molecular modeler" for the next dozen years, collaborating from Romania.

Fox Chase had excellent chemistry, and Cynthia Myers did us a great service by synthesizing large quantity of triphenylethylene derivatives [6] that would create a steady stream of publications for the next decade. The focus on deciphering the precise structure−function relationship of the ligand-binding domain of the ER could now be solved to discover the molecular mechanism of estrogen-induced apoptosis at the ligand-binding domain (see Chapter 14).

Philipp completed his Ph.D., despite the fact that one day everyone in my Tamoxifen Team was lined up in my laboratory and was handed a "you are terminated" letter. Herein lies a tale!

A change of the leadership occurred with Drs Bob Young and Bob Ozols choosing to step down as the leaders of the Fox Chase Cancer Center. A search for a new director was initiated and several internal candidates (including Monica and myself) applied. Not a good plan for any of us. Once the inexperienced new director arrived, it was "the night of long knives" for about 15 senior faculty, including Monica and I. I advised Monice to save herself and explore opportunities at Memorial Sloan-Kettering in New York where they were seeking a Chief of Breast Surgery. She was selected and moved away from Fox Chase. I was stripped of my scientific position at the Fox Chase Cancer Center, and my salary was reduced accordingly. I was told "you will chair the search committee to select a new Scientific Director who will decide what to do with you."

The date was set for my departure from the Fox Chase Cancer Center. However, a week prior to that, the new Chief Scientist required all my Team to gather in my laboratory space and each was handed a severance letter to take effect 1 week prior to my move. Put simply, none of my staff would be available to assist in my move. I protested to the Fox Chase board. This was walked back as a secretarial error with the date! Another example of collateral damage from the "day of the long knives" was Joan Lewis-Wambi. As you recall, she was one of my postdoctoral fellows at the Robert H. Lurie Comprehensive Cancer Center. She was now an independent researcher at the Fox Chase Cancer Center with independent NIH funding for outstanding minorities. I am sure there were a few eyebrows raised at the NIH at the bizarre turn of events at the Fox Chase Cancer Center! The closure of my laboratories was also changed to allow Philipp's Ph.D. to be completed and examined in Moscow and my staff to leave in an orderly manner! I am reminded of the words of Henry Kissinger: "why are the members of the academic community so unpleasant to each other; because the stakes are so low!"

Peer recognition at Fox Chase Cancer Center for the accomplishments of the Tamoxifen Teams

The top clinical award at ASCO is the Karnofsky Award. The recipients are those clinicians who have changed medicine. So I was stunned to receive a phone call from my long-time friend Gabriel Hortobagyi, who introduced the conversation by stating he was the Chairman of the Karnofsky Committee and I had been selected as the winner for 2008. I realized this was an award for clinical care and I expressed my concern that the rules were for improvements in patient care. Our conversation went back and forth for a few minutes and in frustration he said "Is this a 'yes' or a 'no'?" Yes. I was proud to be the only Ph.D. translational laboratory scientist to win a Karnofsky!

For my topic, I chose a title that reflected my work on blocking estrogen action in breast cancer and our discovery of the mechanisms of estrogen to kill estrogen-starved breast cancers 5 years following menopause. I dedicated the 38th David A. Karnofsky lecture: the paradoxical actions of estrogen in breast cancer—survival or death? [7]—to Sir Alexander Haddow who was the inaugural recipient of the Karnofsky Award for his translational research of the first chemical therapy to treat cancer [8]. It was synthetic estrogen that produced 30% response rates in metastatic breast cancer but only if used 5 years after the menopause high-dose estrogen became the standard of care in the 30 years prior to the introduction of tamoxifen. But ASCO had another surprise for me. For their 50th anniversary celebration, ASCO identified 50 oncology luminaries who had changed cancer care. Tamoxifen and my contributions was on that list (2014). This recognition in the history of medicine had its reward with becoming embedded in medical progress globally.

International prizes identify significant scientific discovery of an individual leader. However, election to the "National Academies" of a Nation is a mark of distinction second to none. World-class scientists are selected, over a period of years, by their academic peers for the future, and so it was at the Fox Chase Cancer Center during the "troubles."

Barry Bloomberg and Alfred Knudson were most gracious when I won, the Karnoffsky Award, especially during the "troubles." Barry wrote me a letter of congratulations, which ended with this prophetic sentence: "It was a good way to start 2008 and a sign that even better things are to come." He was correct as I was informed that I had been elected to the National Academy of Sciences. In celebration of both accolades, Al Knudson took me out to breakfast and presented me with a red card that depicted a bullfighter slaying a bull. He had written in my card "You slayed the bull." Simultaneously, I also learned that I had been elected as a fellow of the Academy of Medical Sciences (equivalent of the National Academy of Medicine in the United States) in the United Kingdom, on the first ballot.

My priority was to save the careers of my trainees and staff from the venom of the "troubles" at Fox Chase Cancer Center. The Tamoxifen Team was academically recognized at the highest level and papers flowed.

As has been my practice with Rita Dardes from Brazil, when Philipp returned to Russia for his examination of his thesis (once he recovered from initially being fired), I joined him. This turned out to be a wonderful 5 days in Moscow with Philipp's family, but the focus was to be Philipp's public defense at his Medical School.

Philipp had to present a synopsis, and then the adversal event began in front of an audience of about 100 guests; 30 of whom were the faculty voters on the thesis committee. The adversary was none other than the Chair of Pharmacology from Philipp's University. He addressed the room (obviously in Russian) with the following sentence: "This thesis cannot be examined as the work is too revolutionary." This was a show stopper! After a moment of uncertainty, the Chairman of the proceedings asked the 30 person committee to vote—Philipp had passed.

Before he had gone to the podium, I had expressly instructed Philipp not to tell the assembled throng that I was present. The first words out of Philipp's mouth were: "Thank you. I would like to thank my supervisor who is with us here today and I would like to invite him to the podium to say a few words; Professor V. Craig Jordan, Member of the National Academy of Sciences." I thanked them "for their wisdom with their decision!"

I was invited to visit Russia several times and made presentations at their international meetings, at their nascent pharmaceutical industry, and then I came up with a plan to pilot a massive program in St. Petersburg to sequence and classify the genome of thousands of cancer patients (treated or who were not because of the limitations of the healthcare system). The Russians are skilled in computer technology, and my goal was to seek patterns so we could decipher trends and pick new targets after a decade of observation. Once the first site was up and running, we would create a few more. Disease would be deciphered by massive recruitment, sequencing, and longitudinal follow-up. A massive first for Russia.

I assembled my team to provide expert counsel: Dr. Gary Clark originally from the late Bill McGuire's group (he was the mastermind behind their original tissue bank in San Antonio), Jane Wegenke who organized all the frozen tissues and sera at the Wisconsin Comprehensive Cancer Center when I was there in the 1980s, and Professor Alan Roberts who oversaw the huge regional tissue and serum bank in Yorkshire. I was primed and ready to go. Unfortunately, Russia chose to liberate Crimea instead. We will meet Philipp Maximov MD, Ph.D., again!

The lesson from Fox Chase is clear: if you are selected by a leader at an institution and he/she has an agenda and you are in it, then all is well. But if the leader has interpersonal issues and is intimidated by the success of his employees, then this situation does not bode well for your future career development. It is also important for the leader of a research team, not to abandon your team members and save yourself. As the leader, it is your responsibility to fight for the career survival of your team members.

References

[1] Balaburski GM, Dardes RC, Johnson M, et al. Raloxifene-stimulated experimental breast cancer with the paradoxical actions of estrogen to promote or prevent tumor growth: a unifying concept in antihormone resistance. Int J Oncol 2010;37:387−98.

[2] Jiang SY, Wolf DM, Yingling JM, et al. An estrogen receptor positive MCF-7 clone that is resistant to antiestrogens and estradiol. Mol Cell Endocrinol 1992;90:77−86.

[3] Pink JJ, Jiang SY, Fritsch M, Jordan VC. An estrogen-independent MCF-7 breast cancer cell line which contains a novel 80-kilodalton estrogen receptor-related protein. Cancer Res 1995;55:2583−90.

[4] Lewis JS, Osipo C, Meeke K, Jordan VC. Estrogen-induced apoptosis in a breast cancer model resistant to long-term estrogen withdrawal. J Steroid Biochem Mol Biol 2005;94: 131−41.

[5] Ariazi EA, Cunlifee HE, Lewis-Wambi JS, et al. Estrogen induces apoptosis in estrogen deprivation-resistant breast cancer through stress responses as identified by global gene expression across time. Proc Natl Acad Sci USA 2011;108:18879−86.

[6] Maximov PY, Myers CB, Curpan RF, et al. Structure-function relationships of estrogenic triphenylethylenes relayed to endoxifen and 4-hydroxytamoxifen. J Med Chem 2010;57: 4569−83.

[7] Jordan VC. The 38th David A. Karnofski lecture: the paradoxical actions of estrogen in breast cancer—survival or death? J Clin Oncol 2008;26:3073−82.

[8] Haddow A. David A. Karnofsky memorial lecture. Thoughts on chemical therapy. Cancer 1970;26:737−54.

Get out and go to Georgetown

I had been offered the position of research director for the Vincent T. Lombardi Cancer Center and to resurrect first class breast cancer research. Originally in the 1970s, Georgetown University had a cancer center with modest accomplishments. That all changed when Marc Lippman, Head of the Breast Cancer Program at the National Cancer Institute (NCI), was seduced to Georgetown to create a world-class cancer center. He brought with him a dozen new faculty from the NCI, all of whom were high achievers and used to working as a team under Marc's direction. He was a master at fund raising, and very quickly, new buildings housing new laboratories, were cropping up. Robert Clark was an early recruit, as was Anna Riegel. This would be a good place to build a new Tamoxifen Team, despite the fact that Marc had moved on to new pastures, first at the University of Michigan and then the University of Miami. Interestingly, he has now returned to Georgetown; an area he loves.

I arrived in 2010, and again the new director Louis Wiener, who had also fled Fox Chase where he was the chair of Medical Oncology, ensured I had a wonderful suite of interconnected laboratories. Lou, wisely, had seen the writing on the wall at Fox Chase and left. I was also awarded the title Vincent T. Lombardi Chair of Translational Research. Now for my new Tamoxifen Team.

Building my Tamoxifen Team at Georgetown

Ping Fan and Surojeet Sengupta both accepted positions at Georgetown. The Susan G. Komen breast cancer organization appointed me as a scholar with a handsome annual sum for research; in return, I was committed to annual grant review sessions to select the best projects by the brightest midlevel career scientists. With this boost, I invited Philipp Maximov back from Russia to be a Susan G. Komen International Fellow.

The hot topic of that time was the relevance of tamoxifen metabolite endoxifen (4-hydroxy-N-desmethyltamoxifen) in the treatment of breast cancer. The hypothesis contended that patients with a mutation in the CYP2D6 enzyme could not produce endoxifen, so they would be less likely to respond during breast cancer therapy [1,2]. The whole field was filled with positive and negative trials, so Philipp created two therapeutic scenarios in vitro under premenopausal and postmenopausal situations: not surprisingly antiestrogenic results for the control of breast cancer cells in vitro were dependent on estrogen concentrations [3,4]. To recreate these

Tamoxifen Tales. https://doi.org/10.1016/B978-0-323-85051-3.00012-9

two scenarios, we collaborated with my friend and colleague Dr Hiltrud Brauch, who at the time was the deputy director of the Fischer-Bosch Institute for Clinical Pharmacology in Stuttgart, Germany, and was involved in the clinical studies of the relevance of endoxifen in tamoxifen-treated breast cancer patients [5–7] and provided us with the indispensable information about metabolite concentrations of tamoxifen in patient with different CYP2D6 genotypes. Philipp also wrote our definitive review on the discovery and clinical usefulness of the selective estrogen receptor modulators [8]. Our discoveries at the Wisconsin Comprehensive Cancer Center were catching on worldwide with raloxifene alone being a $1 billion medicine annually. Five SERMs were now FDA-approved: tamoxifen, raloxifene, bazedoxifene, toremifene, and ospemiphene, and all had origins to discoveries made by my Tamoxifen Teams [8].

Our strengths continued to be the models we created to decipher mechanisms. Our examination of those models would now be used to decipher the modulation of estrogen-induced apoptosis not only to map out the steps that triggered cell death, under the correct LTED conditions in breast cancer, but also to start to decipher the results of the Women's Health Initiative trial that was designed to establish the value of either estrogen replacement therapy (ERT) alone in hysterectomized women or hormone replacement therapy (HRT; estrogen plus medroxyprogesterone acetate [MPA]) in women with an intact uterus. The MPA was used to prevent endometrial cancer. In my case, the excitement (and shock by the rest of the clinical community) with the release of the WHI study results was that in the ERT trial the estrogen-treated patients had a decrease in breast cancer compared with placebo.

To the modern generations of clinicians educated since the 1980s, the "mantra" is estrogen is bad for women with breast cancer and tamoxifen, an antiestrogen is proven to be beneficial for the treatment and prevention of breast cancer [9–13]. But to those aware of the evolution of breast cancer treatment, they would know of the paradox that high-dose synthetic estrogen treatment administered 5 years after menopause was the first chemical therapy, based on translational research, used to treat breast cancer [14,15]. Dr Alexander Haddow, later knighted, established the rules for breast cancer treatment, based on the first multisite clinical trials. For our Tamoxifen Teams at Northwestern University, at the Fox Chase Cancer Center, and then at Georgetown, the apoptotic action of estrogen was the explanation for the decrease in breast cancer incidence and survival in the estrogen-alone placebo-controlled WHI clinical trial. The trial design: to test the efficacy of estrogen alone, required a 5–10 year gap since menopause so that the level of cardiac events would be high enough in placebo to show a significant decrease in events and/or deaths with hormone replacement. However, what was the reason for an increase in breast cancer in the HRT CEE plus MPA? The naïve view would be "well, that's what sex steroid hormones do, stimulate the growth of breast cancer!" However, looked at another way: if estrogen causes a decrease in breast cancer incidence and death, why does the synthetic progestin MPA reverse that?

The clue for progress came from our roadmap of biological steps that occur in LTED breast cancer cells that undergo apoptosis and those that do not. Most noticeably, prior to apoptosis, there was an increase in intracellular stress and a profound inflammatory response [16]. However, it was the closing sentence of Eric Ariazi's PNAS paper [16] that stuck in my mind. "Furthermore, these findings lead to the hypothesis that antiinflammatory agents prescribed for clinical problems should not be used during antitumor estrogen therapy." But how did the synthetic progestin MPA block estrogen-induced apoptosis to increase the initiation and growth of breast cancer. The answer came to me on one of my long walks beside the Potomac River in Alexandria. I suddenly remembered my lessons in medicinal chemistry at Leeds University. A known side effect of MPA, used to treat breast cancer in the pretamoxifen era, was an increase in weight gain. The synthetic progestin had glucocorticoid activity. Now to prove it!

The Peacock Café, Georgetown

Building our new team at Georgetown required long working hours. I would routinely travel from my home in Alexandria before the morning rush-hour, which started around 6:30 am; I would also avoid the rush-hour going home by walking into Georgetown to discover new dining experiences. It was then I had discovered the Peacock Café on Prospect Street and the owners Maziar and Shahab became wonderful hosts to my dining experiences and their wide range of after-dinner drinks! On these occasions, I would take a cab home. The Peacock Café became the center point for my entertainment of my Tamoxifen Team members when we all were attending a meeting in Washington, DC. Fig. 12.1 documents a recent reunion with Dr. Surojeet Sengupta and the wonderful hosts, who I was delighted to discover had survived an economic calamity of the coronavirus pandemic (Fig. 12.1).

FIGURE 12.1

A return to the Peacock Café with Balkees Abderrahman and Surojeet Sengupta, 2021 Thanksgiving. Left to right: El Houssine — Ouben Adidi (floor manager), Surojeet Sengupta, myself, Balkees Abderrahman, Shahab Faribar (proprietor), and missing is Maziar Farivar (chef proprietor).

Graduate students at Georgetown

Elizabeth Sweeny and Ifeyinwa (Ify) Obiorah both declared they had no interest in doing the mandatory rotation of laboratories for them to find the "right fit." Their decision was right for all three of us!

Elizabeth Sweeney, working with Ping Fan, designed and executed experiments that demonstrated that MPA acted as a glucocorticoid to prevent apoptosis in LTED breast cancer cells MCF-7:5C [17]. An examination of the WHI protocol revealed that there was a gap of at least 5 years following menopause before the women received either CEE or MPA plus CEE. Sir Alexander Haddow was speaking to us again!

The MPA was shown to activate a glucocorticoid reporter inserted into the MCF-7:5C cells. That was the explanation to prevent estrogen-induced apoptosis and cause breast cancer cell growth. The paper in Cancer Research [17] attracted considerable attention in academic circles by being selected for Faculty 1000 Prime. However, we still did not understand how estrogen actually triggered apoptosis as an event triggered by the estrogen:ER complex. That would have to wait.

Ify focused on the molecular pharmacology of ligands that bound to the ER, which in turn modulated apoptosis in LTED cells. Ify was an MD with an additional master's degree. She was particularly fortunate to have Angela Brodie (the Mother of aromatase inhibitors) and Anna Riegel, my former Ph.D. student from Wisconsin, who was now Professor of Oncology and Pharmacology at Lombardi, on her committee. The required annual review sessions of data showed the strength of the Ph.D. system in the United States. I remember at Ify's first annual review, Anna noted "these effects you are documenting on estrogen-induced apoptosis are very odd. Why does this process with estrogen take so long when chemotherapy kills cells in 24 h. Estrogen triggers all its actions for replication within 24 h, but your data shows that estrogen eventually kills after 5 days. Why?"

This input refocused work on time to apoptosis for CEE, and our collection of analogs of triphenylethylenes to study [18,19]. Analysis of the constituents of CEE present in the mix of estrogen metabolites in the preparation prescribed to postmenopausal women with a uterus to understand the potential to trigger estrogen-induced apoptosis [20], thereby reducing the risk of breast cancer. Her work quantifying and categorizing the time course of different triphenylethylenes provided a firm foundation for our knowledge of the structure—function relationships of triphenylethylenes [21] that modulate estrogen-induced apoptosis.

Surojeet Sengupta provided exemplary service to move forward with, not only invaluable assistance with advancing our understanding of the mechanism of estrogen-induced apoptosis [19,21,22—25], which aided graduate student and postdoctoral fellow Philipp Maximov, careers but also novel topics of interest [26—30]. He is currently an associate professor with Professor Robert Clark, executive director of the Hormel Institute, and I.J. Holton Chair in Cancer Research at the University of Minnesota.

A highlight of Surojeet's time in my laboratory at Georgetown was our visit to India in 2013. I was delighted to discover that I had been selected to present the 38th Sir Edward Mellanby Oration, at the Central Research Institute, Lucknow, India. The visit started with a flight to New Delhi and then to Lucknow. The original research institute was where Surojeet had obtained his PhD, but now they had built and were opening a new research institute, and I was to present the Sir Edward Mellanby Oration to commemorate the event. I was also honored to be part of the ceremony to replant a tree from the old Institution in the grounds of the new University; continuity was established.

I was delighted to meet Surojeet's family and former teachers during our visit. However, as an amateur student of British military history, I was interested to be able to tour the ruins of the Residency of the local Governor in Lucknow, which is preserved to this day as a historical memorial. The Residency was besieged but was rescued by a strong force of British soldiers in November 1857, which then became trapped itself! The city of Lucknow was not restored to British control until March 1858.

Most importantly, with Lizzie's and Ify's Ph.D. complete, and Philipp completing his postdoc, all trainees were successful and published. Ping completing her "tour de force" investigation of her MCF-7:PF cells, which recapitulated in cells culture, Marco Gottardis's model in vivo of acquired resistance to tamoxifen, i.e., the tumor had learned to be dependent upon either tamoxifen or estrogen for growth after 5 years of tamoxifen with an inhibitor of cSrc. Now we had mechanisms for Marco's models [31−33].

In my personal life, I was making plans to retire.

References

[1] Regan MM, Leyland-Jones B, Bousyk M, et al. CYP2D6 genotype and tamoxifen response in postmenopausal women with endocrine-responsive breast cancer: the breast international group 1-98 trial. J Natl Cancer Inst 2012;104:441−51.

[2] Rae JM, Drury S, Hayes DF, et al. CYP2D6 and UGT2B7 genotype and risk of recurrence in tamoxifen-treated breast cancer patients. J Natl Cancer Inst 2012;104:452−60.

[3] Maximov PY, McDaniel RE, Fernandes DJ. Pharmacological relevance of endoxifen in a laboratory simulation of breast cancer in postmenopausal patients. J Natl Cancer Inst 2014;106:dju283.

[4] Maximov PY, McDaniel RE, Fernandes DJ. Simulation with cells in vitro of tamoxifen treatment in premenopausal breast cancer patients with different CYP2D6 genotypes. Br J Pharmacol 2014;171:5624−35.

[5] Schroth W, Antoniadou L, Fritz P, et al. Breast cancer treatment outcome with adjuvant tamoxifen relative to patient CYP2D6 and CYP2C19 genotypes. J Clin Oncol 2007;25: 5187−93.

[6] Schroth W, Goetz MP, Hamann U, et al. Association between CYP2D6 polymorphisms and outcomes among women with early stage breast cancer treated with tamoxifen. J Am Med Assoc 2009;302:1429−36.

[7] Mürdter TE, Schroth W, Bacchus-Gerybadze L, et al. Activity levels of tamoxifen metabolites at the estrogen receptor and the impact of genetic polymorphisms of phase I and II enzymes on their concentration levels in plasma. Clin Pharmacol Ther 2011;89:708–17.

[8] Maximov PY, Lee TM, Jordan VC. The discovery and development of selective estrogen receptor modulators (SERMs) for clinical practice. Curr Clin Pharmacol 2013;8:135–55.

[9] Powles T, Eeles R, Ashley S, et al. Interim analysis of the incidence of breast cancer in the Royal Marsden Hospital tamoxifen randomized chemoprevention trial. Lancet 1998;352:98–101.

[10] Fisher B, Constantino JP, Wickerham DL, et al. Tamoxifen prevention of breast cancer: report of the National Surgical Adjuvant Breast and Bowel Project P-1 Study. J Natl Cancer Inst 1998;90:1371–88.

[11] Veronesi U, Maisonneuve P, Costa A, et al. Prevention of breast cancer with tamoxifen: preliminary findings from the Italian randomized trial among hysterectomized women. Italian Tamoxifen Prevention Study. Lancet 1998;352:93–7.

[12] Cuzick J, Forbes J, Edwards R, et al. First results from the International Breast Cancer Intervention Study (IBIS-I): a randomized prevention trial. Lancet 2002;360:817–24.

[13] Fisher B, Constantino JP, Wickerham DL, et al. Tamoxifen for the prevention of breast cancer: current status of the National Surgical Adjuvant Breast and Bowel Project P-1 study. J Natl Cancer Inst 2005;97:1652–62.

[14] Haddow A, Watkinson JM, Paterson E, Koller PC. Influence of synthetic oestrogens on advanced malignant disease. Br Med J 1944;2:393–8.

[15] Haddow A. David A. Karnofsky memorial lecture. Thoughts on chemical therapy. Cancer 1970;26:737–54.

[16] Ariazi EA, Cunlifee HE, Lewis-Wambi JS, et al. Estrogen induces apoptosis in estrogen deprivation-resistant breast cancer through stress responses as identified by global gene expression across time. Proc Natl Acad Sci USA 2011;108:18879–86.

[17] Sweeney EE, Fan P, Jordan VC. Molecular modulation of estrogen-induced apoptosis by synthetic progestins in hormone replacement therapy: an insight into the women's health initiative study. Cancer Res 2014;74:7060–8.

[18] Obiorah I, Jordan VC. Differences in the rate of oestrogen-induced apoptosis in breast cancer by oestradiol and the triphenylethylene bisphenol. Br J Pharmacol 2014;171:4062–72.

[19] Obiorah I, Sengupta S, Fan P, Jordan VC. Delayed triggering of oestrogen induced apoptosis that contrasts with rapid paclitaxel-induced breast cancer cell death. Br J Cancer 2014;110:1488–96.

[20] Obiorah I, Jordan VC. Scientific rationale for postmenopause delay in the use of conjugated equine estrogens among postmenopausal women that causes reduction in breast cancer incidence and mortality. North American Menopause Society/Pfizer-Wulf H. Utian Endowed Lecture. Menopause 2013;20:372–82.

[21] Obiorah IE, Sengupta S, Curpan R, Jordan VC. Defining the conformation of the estrogen receptor complex that controls estrogen-induced apoptosis in breast cancer. Mol Pharmacol 2014;85:789–99.

[22] Peng J, Sengupta S, Jordan VC. Potential of selective estrogen receptor modulators as treatments and preventives of breast cancer. Anticancer Med Chem 2009;9:481–99.

[23] Patel RR, Sengupta S, Kim HK, et al. Experimental treatment of oestrogen receptor (ER) positive breast cancer with tamoxifen and brivanib alaninate, a VEGFR-2/

FGFR-1 kinase inhibitor: a potential clinical application of angiogenesis inhibitors. Eur J Cancer 2010;46:1537—53.

[24] Maximov P, Sengupta S, Lewis-Wambi JS, et al. The conformation of the estrogen receptor directs estrogen-induced apoptosis in breast cancer; a hypothesis. Horm Mol Biol Clin Invest 2011;5:27—34.

[25] Sengupta S, Obiorah IO, Maximov PY, Jordan VC. Molecular mechanisms of action of bisphenol and bisphenol-a medicated by estrogen receptor alpha in growth and apoptosis of breast cancer. Brit J Pharmacol 2013;169:167—78.

[26] Sengupta SS, Sharma CGN, Jordan VC. Estrogen regulation of X-box binding protein 1 and its role in estrogen-induced growth of breast and endometrial cancer. Horm Mol Biol Clin Invest 2010;2:235—43.

[27] Balaburski G, Dardes RC, Johnson M, et al. Raloxifene-stimulated breast cancer with the paradoxical actions of estrogen to promote or prevent tumor growth: a unifying concept in antihormone resistance. Int J Oncol 2010;37:387—98.

[28] Sengupta S, Biarnes MC, Jordan VC. Cyclin-dependent kinase-9 mediated transcription deregulation of c-Myc as a critical determinant of endocrine therapy resistance in breast cancer. Breast Cancer Res Treat 2014;143:113—24.

[29] Sengupta S, Biarnes MC, Clark R, Jordan VC. Inhibition of BET proteins impairs estrogen-mediated growth and transcription in breast cancer by passing RNA-polymerase advancement. Breast Cancer Res Treat 2015;150:265—78.

[30] Sengupta S, Sevigny CM, Bhattacharaya P, et al. Estrogen-induced apoptosis in breast cancers is phenocopied by blocking dephosphorylation of eukaryotic initiation factor 2 alpha (eIF2α) protein. Mol Cancer Res 2019;17:918—28.

[31] Fan P, McDaniel RE, Kim HR, et al. Modulating therapeutic effects of the c-Src inhibitor via oestrogen receptor and human epidermal growth factor receptor 2 in breast cancer cell lines. Eur J Cancer 2012;48:3488—98.

[32] Fan P, Griffith OL, Agboke FA, et al. c-Src modulates estrogen-induced stress and apoptosis in estrogen-deprived breast cancer cells. Cancer Res 2013;73:4510—20.

[33] Fan P, Agboke FA, McDaniel RE, et al. Inhibition of c-Src blocks oestrogen-induced apoptosis and restores oestrogen-stimulated growth in long-term oestrogen-deprived breast cancer cells. Eur J Cancer 2014;50:457—68.

Closing the circle on Tamoxifen Tales

13

"Now this is not the end. It is not even the beginning of the end. But it is, perhaps, the end of the beginning" (Winston Spencer Churchill in a speech, November 10, 1942, The Lord Mayors luncheon, Mansion House, London in response to the decisive victory at the second Battle of El Alamein, North Africa). The creation of a logical translational strategy of the failed "morning after pill" ICI46,474 by my Tamoxifen Team at Leeds University, to become the gold standard for the treatment and prevention of breast cancer, was a decisive victory for pharmacology and a major advance for women's health. Tamoxifen is unique as a therapy because it is deployed effectively at every stage of the disease and as a preventive. No other cancer therapy has that distinction, and as a result, millions of women continue to benefit worldwide. The medicine was precise and remarkably trouble free when compared with the aggressive life-threatening use of high-dose cytotoxic combination chemotherapy during the 1970s and 1980s. Tamoxifen was the successful start of targeted therapy because it was directed to block estrogen binding to the tumor ER to prevent estrogen stimulated growth. This concept was not embraced by the clinical community in the early 1970s, as there was a need to cure cancer with a knockout blow with new combinations of cytotoxic chemotherapy. It was known from early clinical trials of late stage breast cancer that "hormone therapy" could not perform to save lives; it was a palliative therapy for a few but only for a year or two. That conclusion was to prove to be incorrect based on translational research from our Tamoxifen Teams on our new adjuvant strategy for the treatment of breast cancer. You have already read of the clinical advances in the pages before, and the personal stories of some of the Tamoxifen Team participants can be read in Chapter 18. But it was not the target that was the only critical factor. It was the deployment of long-term adjuvant tamoxifen therapy that saved the lives of millions of women with breast cancer. The studies in the laboratory by my Tamoxifen Team at Leeds changed breast cancer treatment forever. As it turned out, there was something unusual about micrometastatic spread that was different from those well-established metastases in advanced breast cancer. The micrometastases were vulnerable to long-term tamoxifen treatment. The inspirational leadership of Sir Richard Peto and his Oxford Team, validated, through analysis of clinical trials, that long-term adjuvant therapy as the strategy of choice [1,2]. But it is the continuing action of tamoxifen after stopping long-term adjuvant tamoxifen that continues to save lives [2]. The benefit was in health care and decreased mortality for mothers and grandmothers to maintain family integrity and cohesiveness. We contend it is the phenomenon we discovered of

Tamoxifen Tales. https://doi.org/10.1016/B978-0-323-85051-3.00013-0

171

estrogen-induced apoptosis that kills vulnerable micrometastases around a woman's body. The long-term tamoxifen therapy holds microscopic tumor growth until new populations form tamoxifen-stimulated microtumor cells slowly appear. These are destroyed once the tamoxifen is stopped and the woman's own estrogen protects her from death by triggering estrogen-induced tumor cell apoptosis. A self-defense mechanism that was unappreciated until this discovery. This is also an explanation for the decrease in breast cancer and mortality as women who take estrogen alone as a replacement therapy in their 60s [3].

Tamoxifen taught the clinical community many lessons but it, perhaps, taught me the most. The 1970s for me was a time of self-education. I was not shackled by pre-conception; I just wanted to learn the model or technique and to do the experiment. Early in my career, I saw many investigators invent many reasons for not doing the experiment. Charles Huggins, who gave us the carcinogen-induced rat mammary carcinoma model, which became the work horse of endocrine-related tumor growth in the 1960s, used to say "just follow your instincts and do the experiment, don't go to the library and find out what others did." He won the Nobel Prize in 1966 for his work on hormones and prostate cancer. The carcinogen-induced rat mammary carcinoma model, I would always hear from my clinical colleagues, was not like human breast cancer. But as it turns out, the control of microscopic tumor growth and prevention with tamoxifen proved in practice to be a valid strategy for the treatment and prevention of breast cancer. I like what Bob Weinburg once stated, "Just because it's a model, doesn't mean it's wrong."

However, it was Trevor Powles (Fig. 13.1) who reminded me, about three decades ago, that the ER was not a tumor-specific target. We were very lucky that the toxicology of tamoxifen was not more unforgiving as the ER is all over a woman's body in bones, liver, brain, uterus, vagina, colon, and breast. You name the tissue and the ER, in one form or another, has a function. But that is what we learned in the 1980s at the Wisconsin Comprehensive Cancer Center. Our Tamoxifen Team members could selectively modulate the ER in different tissues and a new group of medicines was born [4,5]—the selective ER modulators or SERMs as they became known in the pharmaceutical industry in the 1990s. Let us linger here a moment and settle on the science of current SERMs.

As I am a pharmacologist who always wanted to understand the receptor mechanism of drug action at the ER, one could not preplan this journey in molecular pharmacology but it did happen. The end is not revealed in the beginning. The formula for success in science is young talented scientists who energize each other and create synergy as a Team. We discovered the pharmacology of the new antiestrogens 4-hydroxytamoxifen and dihydroxytamoxifen as the first antiestrogens with high affinity for the ER [6] that gave the research community the start of new molecules to study and crystallize with the ER and ultimately gave us SERMs [5,6]. It was the chance visit to Wisconsin in the late 1970s and Mara Lieberman's immature rat pituitary cell system in vitro [7–9] that opened up a host of opportunities at Wisconsin to develop a basic model to describe mechanisms of estrogen-regulated gene targets [7]. The skilled hands of Rich Koch, a great technician who wanted to be an actor but

FIGURE 13.1

Trevor Powles at a celebration of my 50th birthday (July 25th, 1997) at the Barclay Hotel, London, organized by Monica Marrow.

found his career in teaching, worked wonders in cell culture and the papers flowed. We could modulate the SERM:ER complex and could predictably describe the mechanics of estrogenic and antiestrogenic ligands at the ER for 4-hydroxytamoxifen [10], raloxifene, and the pure antiestrogen ICI164,384 (in the 1970s, we pointed ICI in the right direction to discover that too) [11] a decade before the X-ray crystallography was published. But once the ligand-binding domain of the ER was cloned and sequenced in the laboratories of Pierre Chambon and Geoff Greene [12,13], could we find evidence for the precise molecular modulation of the ER at a cancer relevant gene target? Serendipity led Doug Wolf to discover Asp351Tyr in a tamoxifen-stimulated tumor line he had created in athymic mice [14]. He was following in the footsteps of Marco Gottardis who created tamoxifen resistant breast cancer grown in athymic mouse models—then cutting edge breast cancer research [15]. Doug discovered the mutant ER, but the location of the mutation was apparently buried in the ligand-binding domain of the ER, so the molecular biologists in our academic community all said it was irrelevant and anyway, the mutation is not in human tamoxifen-resistant breast cancers from patients! No one has actually looked but that is not the point. I thought "there is a lot of this in the tamoxifen stimulated MCF-7 tumor cells, so nature is telling us something"—but what was it telling us and how do we find out? Shun-Yuan Jiang was the first to stably transfect the cDNA for ER into an ER-negative breast cancer cell and gave us S30 clone [16]. Bill Catherino repeated the magic with Asp351Tyr and gave us BC2 [17]. Mei Hucy Jeng discovered that ER transfected ER negative cells activated the estrogen-regulated transforming growth factor (TGFα) gene so we had a model to discover a mechanism [18]. Ana Levenson did just that. She discovered that 4-hydroxytamoxifen was promiscuous and estrogen-like (as it is in patients) to turn on the TGFα gene just like estradiol. Raloxifene, the less estrogen-like SERM, did not. The discovery was that the BC2 cells with Asp351Tyr had estrogen-activated TGFα synthesis further stimulated by the 4-hydroxytamoxifen ER complex, but raloxifene was now estrogen-like [19]. This is the first natural mutation that altered the pharmacology of an antiestrogen to an estrogen, and it was a line of research to follow up but how? The X-ray crystallography was significant progress in understanding the mechanics of antiestrogen action [20] but produced no clues about modulation of the complex with different SERMs. Asp351Tyr was in the wrong place to be important—or so it seemed!

"Chance favors the prepared mind" (Louis Pasteur). I had been invited to Signal Pharmaceuticals in California as a consultant to advise on my opinion of the potential of a new nonsteroidal antiestrogen. After a long day, I was told to go to one of the rear entrances of the company, and a taxi would soon come to take me back to my hotel. Well this was California and their *soon* and mine was now drastically diverging! Never one to lose heart, I decided to explore my new surroundings and found a man in a room at a computer, so I inquired—"what do you do?" He said he was responsible for molecular modeling of the ER ligand receptor interactions so I thought "OK, let's see what you can do?" "Can you show me the outside of the human ER liganded with estradiol?" Nobody had looked at that in papers—it was all from the inside of the ligand-binding pocket and I did not care. The outside was where the action was to interact with the new group of bioreactive molecules called coactivators discovered by my friend and colleague Bert O'Malley [21]. "OK, Jim (we were now on first name terms), where is helix 12—can you color that in for me?" "No problem—there it is," replied Jim. "OK, where is Asp351?" I said. "Well, it's here just under helix 12—it is not involved in anything, it's masked by helix 12." It was then I realized Asp351 was on the surface of the estrogen ER complex—not inside the ligand-binding pocket! "OK, Jim can you do the same for raloxifene?" In a flash, there it was, helix 12 pushed back exposing Asp351 that was neutralizing and shielding Asp351 with its pyrrolidine ring sticking out. This "eureka moment," as Jim called it, started a string of publications between my Tamoxifen Team and Jim Zapf from Signal Pharmaceuticals [22—25] as well as a front cover of Cancer Research when I received the Bristol Myers Award for SERMs [26] and again for the reanalysis of the STAR trial with a front cover in Cancer Prevention Research [27] (Figs. 13.2 and 13.3). We were able to visualize

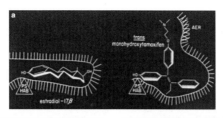

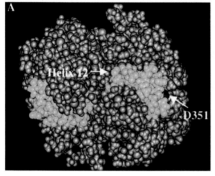 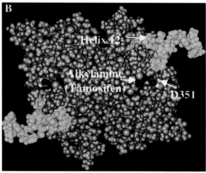

FIGURE 13.2

Top: The "crocodile model" of antiestrogen action of 4-hydroxytamoxifen [7, 34] and the side antiestrogenic chain interaction with the antiestrogenic region (AER) of the ER. Early work by Lednicer in the 1960s [35] concluded "that the presence of a basic group at *a given position in space* is required to obtain a molecule, which will antagonize the effects of concurrent estrogen administration." The finding that the oxygen in the basic side chain can be replaced by a methylene group created compounds, which show the same potency as both antifertility agents and estrogen antagonists bolster the hypothesis. However, the introduction of ring methyl groups into triphenylethylene and triphenylethane antiestrogens *ortho* to the alkylaminoethoxy side chain is disadvantageous. This suggests that the side chain cannot be inhibited from rotation [36]. A From Lieberman ME, Gorski J and Jordan VC. An estrogen receptor model to describe the regulation of prolactin synthesis by antiestrogens in vitro. J Biol Chem 1983;258: 4741–4745 and A, B from Liu H, Lee ES, De Los Reyes A, et al. Silencing and reactivation of the selective estrogen receptor modulator-estrogen receptor alpha complex. Cancer Res 2001;61:3632–3639 with copy right permission.

the external surfaces of the estrogen receptor complex with estradiol, 4-hydroxyta-moxifen and raloxifene.

Credit must now go to members of my Tamoxifen Team at the Robert H. Lurie Comprehensive Cancer Center of Northwestern University Medical School, Chicago: Jennifer MacGregor Schafer, Sandra Pearce, Hong Liu, Anait Levenson, and Dave Bentrem who created a wonderful mosaic of modulation for the SERM:ER complex in vitro at the TGFα target. This work in molecular pharmacology led us to reclassify estrogens [28] and created a novel approach for our Team at Georgetown and MD Anderson to decipher the shape of the estrogen:ER complex that triggers apoptosis

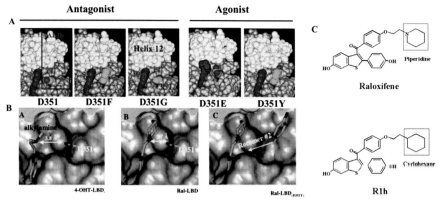

FIGURE 13.3

Prior to the resolution of the ligand-binding domain of the ER with either raloxifene [37] or 4-hydroxytamoxifen [38], we had identified amino acid Asp351 in the ER as the AER, i.e., the amino acid that interacts with the antiestrogenic side chain of raloxifene [39]. This was followed by structure—function analyses of the ER complexes with mutations substituted at Asp351 (panels A). These were classified as retaining antiestrogenic properties or changing their actions to be estrogens (agonists). Panel 3A: Surface structures around amino acid 351 of raloxifene-bound LBDs of ERα. A structural model of dimeric human ERα bound to raloxifene was derived from the Protein Data Bank (code 1ERR) by removing all water molecules with the exception of the ordered water-forming H-bond with the O_3 of raloxifene, adding hydrogens and minimizing in the consistent valence force field (CVFF) using Discover (Accelrys, San Diego, CA). Mutant receptors were constructed using Biopolymer (Accelrys) to replace Asp351 with Gly, Glu, Phe, or Tyr and to obtain a minimum energy rotamer for the mutant side chain. The results were visualized using Insight II (Accelrys). Panel 3B: Molecular modeling of the surface structures of 4-hydroxytamoxifen-LBD (wild type) (A) or raloxifene-LBD (wild type) (B) and raloxifene-LBD (Asp351Tyr) (C). Asp351 replaced with Tyr351 in raloxifene-bound ERα LBD. To avoid steric clashes, Tyr351 is placed in a rotamer that projects the side chain upward. The side chain of Tyr351 is out of reach of the raloxifene side chain. Tyrosine residues typically lay down on the surface of proteins. In the ERR.pdb structure, small rearrangements in structure around Tyr351 are required to sterically accommodate the side chain. If this happens, the phenolic side chain would be oriented in rotamer #2. It is important to point out that the antiestrogenic N-containing side chain of tamoxifen (Fig. 3B) is further away from Asp351 than the N of raloxifene. This observation is consistent with the more estrogen-like actions of tamoxifen that results in higher blood clots and endometrial cancer than raloxifene [1,40]; B, the piperidine side chain of raloxifene, shields the charge of Asp351 and disturbs the local charge available for binding coactivators. As a result, AF1 and AF2 cannot collaborate properly, and TGF-α is silenced. C, the tyrosine at amino acid 351, changed the local charge available for coactivator binding because the piperidine can no longer shield the charge. Conformation of raloxifene-Asp351Tyr ERα to be 4-hydroxytamoxifen-ERα-like and TGFα gene is switched on. Panel 3C: Structures of raloxifene and the derivative R1h used in structure—function studies. Compound R1h is a raloxifene derivative that has a cyclohexane ring instead of a piperidine ring with no antiestrogenic actions. 3A From Liu H, Park WC, Bentrem DJ, et al. Structure-function relationships of the raloxifeneestrogen receptor alpha complex for regulating transforming growth factor-alpha expression in breast cancer cells. J Biol Chem 2002;277:9189—9198 and 3B from Liu H, Lee ES, De Los Reyes A, et al. Silencing and reactivation of the selective estrogen receptor modulator-estrogen receptor alpha complex. Cancer Res 2001;61:3632—3639 with copyright permission.

in estrogen-deprived cells. What a wonderful group of young scientists who all contributed to the connection between the shape of the ER complex with the modulation of a target gene and then the modulation of estrogen-induced apoptosis.

All these receptor models of the molecular pharmacology and modulation for SERMs were to lie dormant until the discovery of mutations in metastases from breast cancer patient who received aromatase inhibitor treatment [29–31]. The pleasant surprise was that the unoccupied ER became closed and activated through mutations of the amino acids 537 and 538 that close helix 12 by using (wait for it!) Asp351 as the universal anchor. We were now able to publish a unifying theory of SERM and AI resistance [32].

I now want to tie up our Tamoxifen Tales with some final examples of discovery and insight that have occurred because of the unusual mixture of experiences I have had in my life's journey. Lois Trench (now Lois Trench-Hines) was the right person who was in the right place at the right time. A different person with a closed mind or rigid values would not have succeeded to catalyze the commercialization of tamoxifen in America. She was the conduit to "make it happen" and then say sorry to her bosses at the company later. This approach worked with the clinical community (Doug Tormey and Paul Carbone at Wisconsin, and Bernie Fisher at Pittsburgh), and her energy and drive changed my life. She is the Godmother of my daughter Alexandra, and I was thrilled that Lois and her husband George could attend the celebration (Fig. 13.4) arranged by the Swiss Ambassador Manuel Sager at his

FIGURE 13.4

George Hines and Lois Trench Hines at the celebration at the Swiss Ambassador's, Manuel Sager, Residence, Washington DC, on May 11, 2011, to celebrate my winning the St. Gallen Prize for advancing breast cancer therapy. This is considered to be the most prestigious prize in clinical breast cancer research, and the event also recognizes my 20-year "love affair" with Switzerland (Chapter 7). George and Lois remain lifelong friends. Professor Senn, my corecipient, as a young doctor, traveled to America to learn the latest advances and established the St. Gallen breas cancer meeting to inform doctors (initially in Switzerland) the latest techniques to save lives (Fig. 13.6).

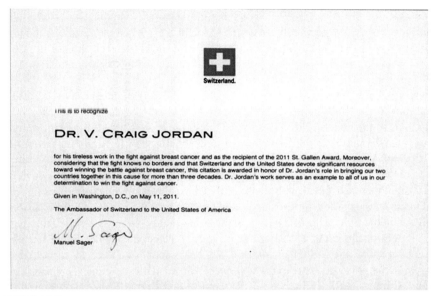

FIGURE 13.5

The certificates presented to Dr. V. Craig Jordan one to Professor Hans-Joerg Senn to celebrate the advances in breast cancer clinical research and the enhanced friendship by the clinical communities of Switzerland and the United States.

residence in Washington DC (Fig. 13.5) when I was awarded the St.Gallen Prize for Breast Cancer Research in 2011 (Fig. 10.2) [33]. This clinical award recognizes advances in the adjuvant therapy for breast cancer.

As an endocrine pharmacologist, I initially found myself drawn to contraception for my Ph.D. and the mechanism of action of "morning after pills." The oral contraceptive remains one of the most successful advances in the medical chemistry of women's health. As a result, I was sent by chance to the "home" of the oral contraceptive, the Worcester Foundation for Experimental Biology in Shrewsbury, MA for 2 years as a visiting scientist (Chapter 4). There I taught myself cancer research and ICI46,474 became the focus of my life's work. I was introduced to Lois Trench by Arthur Walpole when I was at the Worcester Foundation and she introduced me to the Eastern Cooperative Oncology Group, Paul Carbone, and Doug Tormey. But it was more than 30 years later that I saw another side of the contraception debate from the Catholic Church that had so troubled. Dr John Rock, the Catholic Boston clinician who with Gregory Pincus, then head of the Worcester Foundation, conducted the first clinical trial.

This was a moment of insight that only resulted from me being in my two worlds and was a cause for pause. In 2007, I had the good fortune to meet Dr Elias Castanas, a medical scientist from the University of Crete in Heraklion. For me, Crete has

FIGURE 13.6

The St. Gallen Prize for Clinical Breast Cancer Research Lecture at the 12th St. Gallen International Breast Cancer Conference, St. Gallen, Switzerland, March 16, 2011. The St. Gallen Breast Cancer Award is given every 2 years to a scientist who has made exceptional contributions to the field of breast cancer research and is considered to be the most prestigious Award in breast cancer. Professor Hans-Joerg Senn, the founder of the St. Gallen Oncology Conferences, presented Dr. Jordan with this prestigious Award, and then he delivered his Prize Lecture: "Evolution of long-term adjuvant anti-hormone therapy: Consequences and Opportunities." [33].

always been mythical and a place I always wanted to visit and explore. This was not only because it was famous for the archeology conducted by Sir Arthur Evans and his discovery (and reconstruction) of the palaces at Knossos as a marvelous example of the Minoan culture, but also because of the epic battle named Operation Mercury starting on May 20, 1941, when waves of German Fallschirmjäger (paratroopers) descended on Crete winning a pyrrhic victory. The Fallschirmjäger were never committed to a major airborne assault again. During the time Elias and I spent together during our first meeting—actually in Cyprus, we became instant friends as Elias was a former member of the Greek parachute Regiment, so you can see where our mutual respect has its foundation. I will be forever grateful to Elias for proposing and fighting for me to receive an honorary Doctor of Medicine degree from the University of Crete in Heraklion in 2009 and a most memorable visit with a wonderful introductory lecture from my lifelong friend Dr Guy LeClercq, from the Institute Jules Bordet in Brussels. It was, however, on this visit to Crete that I heard another interpretation of our medical success story of the reinvention of a "failed contraceptive" to become the "gold standard" for the treatment of breast cancer in a Greek Orthodox country.

Elias and I were invited to be interviewed live on a Greek radio station and discuss the reasons for my honorary Doctor of Medicine degree at their medical school. After telling the story of the birth of tamoxifen to treat breast cancer and its original conception as a "failed morning after pill," the interviewer stated, "so something very good for Society came out of the failure of something bad." Food for thought. The only similar heart-stopping statement was made by Dr. Bill Wood, a world-class surgeon, friend and gentleman from Emory University in Atlanta for whom I have the greatest respect. He stated one evening at a faculty Lynn Sage Breast Cancer Symposium dinner in Chicago that "each person on this earth is here for a purpose and Craig's was tamoxifen." During my recent personal "War on Cancer," Bill remained a loyal friend with his support through prayer. I have never been a religious person. However, all of that was to change for me 1 day while having a breakfast in a remote area of the hospital at MD Anderson in Houston. I was dressed respectably in shirt, jacket, and trousers, when I noticed a man emptying bins around the room. When he got to my area he advanced toward me and said "Can I lay my hand on you and we can pray together?" There was no indication I was a patient, nor could he see my MD Anderson ID badge under my coat. I replied "You may not put your hands on me (coronavirus had now struck in 2020), but I will pray with you." He then walked off to continue his tasks emptying waste bins, and I headed to the MD Anderson Chapel to pray! I told Bill Wood and he was delighted saying "You have been hit. When the Lord receives prayer for the sick he sends a messenger to say the prayers have been received." I saw the man on only one other occasion. He came into the room to empty bins but payed no attention to me. When he finished he walked away, but 30 yards from me, he turned and said "Good to see you again, Doctor." I had never told him my name or that I was on the Faculty as Professor of Breast Medical Oncology, at the MD Anderson. These two interactions changed my life and religion convictions.

There were, however, other instances of chance playing a leading role to be "talent spotted" when one least expects it. I was the recipient of the American Cancer Society Award for Chemoprevention from the American Society of Clinical Oncology (ASCO) at their annual meeting in 2006. I was both thrilled and honored to be able to present a lecture that recounted the conceptual leaders and clinical trialists who created a true advance in health care for women. During my talk, I noticed that waves of women were running up to the front of the cavernous lecture hall to occupy the front seats. This perplexed me but in a very flattering way—silly me!

After my talk, I was leaving the stage when all became clear. Lance Armstrong was in front of me as he was to receive an award for advancing cancer research through his Foundation. I explained how honored I was to meet him, but he retorted "No Craig—you're the man!" And he invited my wife Monica and I to the reception he was hosting that evening. I gladly accepted but when we arrived, there was no Lance so we walked around the guests until one prominent oncologist greeted us and exclaimed: "That was a magnificent lecture and review of chemoprevention— why aren't you a member of the National Academy of Sciences?" As it turned out, he was and I was at the Fox Chase Cancer Center with three other Members of the National Academy (Chapter 11).

FIGURE 13.7

Signing the Great Book of Members of the National Academy of Sciences (2009). The Academy was founded by President Lincoln, at the start of the American Civil War. The goal was to apply emerging knowledge in the sciences to aid the Northern States to win, by harnessing the best minds available to ensure that happened.

There is actually no answer to that as it is not an organization that encourages self-promotion. Sometime later, when I was in a hotel in Moscow visiting Philipp Maximov, I received an email that asked "Tell me you're an American." I replied "I am looking at my passport. If Texas is still in the Union, then I am an American by birth." Few know my birthplace, but all knew of my British roots. The first requirement for election to the National Academy of Sciences is to be an American citizen so clearly someone had said "but he is so British!" Sometime later, my friend Carlo Crocce phoned to congratulate me upon my election, and a year later, I was signing the "Great Book" of members (Fig. 13.7).

My continuing need to reinvest in the future generation of scientists reminds me of another Tamoxifen tale. The Jordan Prize in Medicinal Chemistry at Leeds University has been established for as long as the LUOTC Jordan Prize, i.e., 20+ years. The late Professor Ron Grigg awarded the prize annually to the best chemistry graduate at Leeds University. Again, much to my pleasant surprise and out of the blue, I was contacted by a Ph.D. student at the Institute for Cancer Research. The Royal Marsden Hospital was to invite me to present the 2012 LINK lecture in translational cancer research. The graduate student, Jamie Mallinson at the Institute for Cancer Research, had been awarded the Jordan Prize in Medicinal Chemistry at Leeds and now in London, the student body annually selected the LINK lecturer. I was Jamie's first choice for nomination based on "my inspirational story of research success." I presented the 18th annual LINK lecture on March 15, 2012, and we all had a wonderful 2 days of interactions and discussions. I had great fun with Jamie and the other graduate students, but an usual adventure also occurred! (remember in the SAS that is—a perfect plan gone horribly wrong!) Trevor Powles was charged with looking after me in London and after a great evening watching a critical local football match on TV and, after liberal quantities of Sambuca, I returned to my hotel. Sleep was not a problem after international travel and a long evening, but when I got up in the dark at 2 a.m. to go to the bathroom, located through the door on the left of my bed, I exited by the door on the right into the corridor, with the door slamming behind me. I was naked!

Striding boldly down to the lobby, the gentlemen at the front desk appropriately averted his eyes and handed me a spare key. Mission accomplished no one around. But by the next day, I thought again about this bizarre experience so I asked at the front desk whether I could get a copy of the CCTV tape, only to learn that the police have exclusive access to the tape in hotels, but only with a warrant! This incident was an amusing topic of conversation for everyone the following day at the Marsden and I found it fun and potentially unique—or so I thought! At the San Antonio breast cancer symposium that year, my friend Dr Sandy Patterson from Canada stopped me to tell me that he had heard all about my adventure over in London earlier that year but that the same thing had happened to him recently on his visit to the Marsden! We are starting a select club of hotel victims (or is it a setup from the Marsden?).

What of my other life and investments in the next generation of soldiers or scientists at Leeds University? Colonel Alan Roberts, OBE (Fig. 13.8), and I had reconnected since my early days at Leeds University Officers Training Corps (LUOTC),

FIGURE 13.8

Colonel Professor Alan Roberts OBE (center) at an evening event with the guest of honor the late Duke of Edinburgh. Colonel Roberts was appointed as Deputy Lord Lieutenant for West Yorkshire and one time as an Aide-de-Camp to Her Majesty Queen Elizabeth II (1980—84).

FIGURE 13.9

Colonel Alan Roberts, OBE presenting the first Jordan Trophy to officer cadet J.E.N. Butcher in 1996 as the top officer cadet of that year at Leeds University Officers Training Corps.

and he was a Major in the Royal Artillery. He had subsequently been a professor at Leeds University and the Pro Chancellor. I had approached him in the mid 1990s about establishing an award annually for the top cadet and this became the Jordan Trophy, and Medal (Fig. 13.9).

The world came full circle in the Army when I learned that Her Majesty Queen Elizabeth II had approved my appointment to be the honorary Colonel of Leeds University Officer's Training Corps in 2014. This is a singular honor. For any serving officer, it is the mark of distinction for career service. For me, it is more than that as this is the same Leeds University Officer's Training Corps that in 1966 asked me to leave as I was not eligible for a commission in the British Army as I was born in Texas of a Texan father from Dallas. But you fold or fight. At 18 years old, I chose to fight and was successful against the Ministry of Defense!

With that closure, all seemed complete except a surprise was in store!

References

[1] EBCTCG. Tamoxifen for early breast cancer: an overview of the randomized trials. Lancet 1993;351:1451—67.

[2] EBCTCG. Effects of chemotherapy and hormonal therapy for early breast cancer on recurrence and 15-year survival: an overview of the randomized trials. Lancet 2005; 365:1687—717.

[3] Chlebowski RT, Anderson GL, Aragaki AK, et al. Association of menopausal hormone therapy with breast cancer incidence and mortality during long-term follow-up of the women's health initiative randomized clinical trials. J Am Med Assoc 2020;324: 369—80.

[4] Jordan VC, Phelps E, Lindgren JU. Effects of anti-estrogens on bone in castrated and intact female rats. Breast Cancer Res Treat 1987;10:31—5.

[5] Lerner LJ, Jordan VC. Development of antiestrogens and their use in breast cancer: eighth Cain memorial award lecture. Cancer Res 1990;50:4177—89.

[6] Jordan VC, Collins MM, Rowsby L, Prestwich G. A monohydroxylated metabolite of tamoxifen with potent antiestrogenic activity. J Endocrinol 1977;75:305—16.

[7] Lieberman ME, Gorski J, Jordan VC. An estrogen receptor model to describe the regulation of prolactin synthesis by antiestrogens in vitro. J Biol Chem 1983;258:4741—5.

[8] Lieberman ME, Jordan VC, Fritsch M, et al. Direct and reversible inhibition of estradiol-stimulated prolactin synthesis by antiestrogens in vitro. J Biol Chem 1983; 258:4734—40.

[9] Jordan VC, Lieberman ME, Cormier E, et al. Structural requirements for the pharmacological activity of nonsteroidal antiestrogens in vitro. Mol Pharmacol 1984;26:272—8.

[10] Jordan VC, Koch R, Mittal S, Schneider MR. Oestrogenic and antioestrogenic actions in a series of triphenylbut-1-enes: modulation of prolactin synthesis in vitro. Br J Pharmacol 1986;87:217—23.

[11] Jordan VC, Fenuik L, Allen KE, et al. Structural derivatives of tamoxifen and oestradiol 3-methyl ether as potential alkylating antioestrogens. Eur J Cancer 1981;17:193—200.

[12] Green S, Walter P, Greene G, et al. Cloning of the human oestrogen receptor cDNA. J Steroid Biochem 1986;24:77—83.

[13] Greene GL, Gilna P, Waterfield M, et al. Sequence and expression of human estrogen receptor complimentary DNA. Science 1986;231:1150—4.

[14] Wolf DM, Jordan VC. The estrogen receptor from a tamoxifen stimulated MCF-7 tumor variant contains a point mutation in the ligand binding domain. Breast Cancer Res Treat 1994;31:129—38.

[15] Gottardis MM, Jordan VC. Development of tamoxifen-stimulated growth of MCF-7 tumors in athymic mice after long-term antiestrogen administration. Cancer Res 1988;48:5183—7.

[16] Jiang SY, Jordan VC. Growth regulation of estrogen receptor-negative breast cancer cells transfected with complimentary DNAs for estrogen receptor. J Natl Cancer Inst 1992;84:580—91.

[17] Catherino WH, Wolf DM, Jordan VC. A naturally occurring estrogen receptor mutation results in increased estrogenicity of a tamoxifen analog. Mol Endocrinol 1995;9: 1053—63.

[18] Jeng MH, Jiang SY, Jordan VC. Paradoxical regulation of estrogen-dependent growth factor gene expression in estrogen receptor (ER)-negative human breast cancer cells stably expressing ER. Cancer Lett 1994;82:123—8.

[19] Levenson AS, Catherino WH, Jordan VC. Estrogenic activity is increased for an anti-estrogen by a natural mutation of the estrogen receptor. J Steroid Biochem Mol Biol 1997;60:261—8.

[20] Brzozowski AM, Pike AC, Dauter Z, et al. Molecular basis of agonism and antagonism in the oestrogen receptor. Nature 1997;389:753—8.

[21] Oñate SA, Tsai SY, Tsai MJ, O'Malley BW. Sequence and characterization of a coactivator for the steroid hormone receptor superfamily. Science 1995;270:1354—7.

[22] MacGregor-Schafer J, Liu H, Bentrem DJ, et al. Allosteric silencing of activating function 1 in the 4-hydroxytamoxifen estrogen receptor complex is induced by substituting glycine for aspartate at amino acid 351. Cancer Res 2000;60:5097—105.

[23] Liu H, Lee ES, De Los Reyes A, et al. Silencing and reactivation of the selective estrogen receptor modulator-estrogen receptor alpha complex. Cancer Res 2001;61:3632—9.

[24] Liu H, Park WC, Bentrem DJ, et al. Structure-function relationships of the raloxifene-estrogen receptor alpha complex for regulating transforming growth factor-alpha expression in breast cancer cells. J Biol Chem 2002;277:9189—98.

[25] Bentrem D, Fox JE, Pearce ST, et al. Distinct molecular conformations of the estrogen receptor alpha complex exploited by environmental estrogens. Cancer Res 2003;63:7490—6.

[26] Jordan VC. Selective estrogen receptor modulation: a personal perspective. Cancer Res 2001;61:5683—7.

[27] Vogel VG, Constantino JP, Wickerman L, et al. Update of the National Surgical Adjuvant Breast and Bowel Project study of tamoxifen and raloxifene (STAR) P-2 trial: preventing breast cancer. Cancer Prev Res 2010;3:696—706.

[28] Jordan VC, Schafer JM, Levenson AS, et al. Molecular classification of estrogens. Cancer Res 2001;61:6619—23.

[29] Li S, Shen D, Shao J, et al. Endocrine-therapy-resistant ESR1 variants revealed by genomic characterization of breast cancer-derived xenografts. Cell Rep 2013;4:1116—30.

[30] Marenbakh-Lamin K, Ben-Baruch N, Yeheskel A, et al. D538G mutation in estrogen receptor-alpha: a novel mechanism for acquired endocrine resistance in breast cancer. Cancer Res 2013;73:6856—64.

[31] Toy W, Shen Y, Won H, et al. ESR1 ligand-binding domain mutations in hormone-resistant breast cancer. Nat Genet 2013;45:1439—45.

[32] Jordan VC, Curpan R, Maximov PY. Estrogen receptor mutations found in breast cancer metastases integrated with the molecular pharmacology of selective ER modulators. J Natl Cancer Inst 2015;107:djv075.

[33] Jordan VC, Obiorah I, Fan P, et al. The St. Gallen prize lecture 2011: evolution of long-term adjuvant anti-hormone therapy: consequences and opportunities. Breast 2011;(Suppl. 3):S1—11.

[34] Jordan VC. Laboratory models of breast cancer to aid the elucidation of antiestrogen action. J Lab Clin Med 1987;109:267—77.

[35] Lednicer D, Lyster SC, Duncan GW. Mammalian antifertility agents. IV. Basic 3,4-dihydronaphtalenes and 1,2,3,4-tetrahydro-1-naphtols. J Med Chem 1967;10:78—84.

[36] Clark ER, Jordan VC. Oestrogenic, anti-oestrogenic and fertility effects of some triphenylethanes and triphenylethylenes related to ethamoxytriphetol (MER25). Br J Pharmacol 1976;57:487—93.

[37] Brzozowsi AM, Pike AC, Dauter Z, et al. Molecular basis of agonism and antagonism in the oestrogen receptor. Nature 1997;389:753—8.

[38] Shiau AK, Barstad D, Loria PM, et al. The structural basis of oestrogen receptor/coactivator recognition and the antagonism of this interaction by tamoxifen. Cell 1998;95: 927−37.

[39] Levenson AS, Jordan VC. The key to the antiestrogenic mechanism of raloxifene is amino acid 351 (aspartate) in the estrogen receptor. Cancer Res 1998;58:1872−5.

[40] Cummings SR, Eckert S, Krueger KA, et al. The effect of raloxifene on risk of breast cancer in postmenopausal women: results from the MORE randomized trial. Multiple Outcomes of Raloxifene Evaluation. J Amer Med Assoc 1999;281:2189−97.

"If I wanted to buy your brain, what would that cost?": rebirth at M.D. Anderson Cancer Center

At Georgetown, I had decided to return to Europe to be closer to my mother in England who was in her early 90s in a care home. I had visited her regularly for the previous 8 years; every other month for a week. However, I would now move to Munich where I found great joy in the mountains around Lofer in the Austrian Tyrol. However, fate was to take a hand and transport me to Texas. I can say a force greater than I know brought me back to Houston, Texas, a town we had both left in 1950 once my mother's divorce was finalized. The world top cancer care hospital was the facility waiting for me to arrive.

I had been invited to an MD Anderson Cancer Center reunion party at the AACR, hosted by Ethan Dimitrovsky, MD, the Provost. I escorted Hiltrud Brauch, our collaborator from the Fischer-Bosch Institute in Stuttgart, where she was the deputy director. We had published numerous papers together, and she was actively involved in the CYP2D6 mutation story and cancer patient response to tamoxifen.

At the MD Anderson reception, Ethan, in the presence of John Mendelson (my long-term supporter since Wisconsin and now former Director at the MD Anderson Cancer Center) approached me and Ethan spoke: "If I wanted to buy your brain to come to MD Anderson, how much would that cost?" After having had a "few drinks," I restated the standard multimillion sum I had received from Fox Chase and Georgetown. "Deal!" said Ethan. John was ecstatic. I was coming out of pending retirement, with a return to Europe. Change of plan. I was returning to the State of my birth to create my final Tamoxifen Team! Ethan stated that my recruitment was based on my past and future "prize worthiness" and the fact that I was a member of the National Academy of Sciences. These attributes were of value for the MD Anderson Cancer Center as the top cancer care facility in the United States.

Who could have predicted the impending series of events, in quick succession, that would have been catastrophic for me in Germany: my mother died at 94 years old, the United Kingdom left the European Union for me as a dual British/US citizen, the residency options would have been limited: return to the United Kingdom, a country I had not lived in for 35 years, uncertain rights to UK healthcare but no legal rights of abode in Germany. You know my diagnosis at the beginning in this book, so I would almost certainly have been dead as I would not had paid any attention to the signs and symptoms of my fatal disease.

Tamoxifen Tales. https://doi.org/10.1016/B978-0-323-85051-3.00014-2

Drs Ping Fan and Philipp Maximov were up for the challenge of coming to Houston. They were both experienced in conducting our Tamoxifen Team moves around America; however, this move proved to be more complex.

When we arrived, we discovered we had only temporary space on the other side of campus from where my office was in the Department of Breast Medical Oncology. Visiting my nascent laboratory daily involved a 1-h period to be reserved for bus rides. Recruiting able staff also became a major problem, but fortunately, Dr Ping Fan preferred to conduct all her own experiments, so high-quality data production was controlled despite changing institutions.

Philipp could rapidly resurrect his mechanistic studies to explain the delay in apoptosis documented first by Ify at Georgetown [1]. Now was the time to solve the paradox and define the molecular mechanism of action of the delay in apoptosis caused by bisphenol.

As luck would have it, Dr. Balkees Abderrahman was on a 1-month medical education visit to MD Anderson, and she impressed me with her writing and analytical skills, which let to many publications in the refereed literature—several as sole author as a contributing editor for the Pharmaceutical Journal in Great Britain! She was hired as a postdoctoral fellow because of her recent MD degree, but it was clear she had talent, grasping complex scientific problems in estrogen-induced apoptosis. There was no possibility that she could return to student life as a Ph.D. student in Houston—that would take over 5 years. However, the University of Leeds (or rather Jayne Glennon!) came to the rescue. Balkees entered a "split-site" program "for applicants of very high quality" between Leeds, the degree granting institution, and MD Anderson where she completed her thesis work in less than 3 years, as a member of my MD Anderson Tamoxifen Team. Dr John Ladbury was to be her Ph.D. supervisor at the University of Leeds. At the time, he was the Dean of Science at Leeds, but he had previously been on the faculty at MD Anderson. His goal was to enhance complimentary research activities between Leeds and MD Anderson. This new Ph.D. program was a start.

Ping Fan completes our molecular mechanism to explain the increase in breast cancers in the CEE/MPA treated women 10 years after menopause in the WHI

Over the previous 15 years, we had assembled the mosaic of laboratory models that mimic LTED breast cancer in vivo and in vitro. NF-κB was depleted during estrogen-induced breast cancer regression in vivo [2,3]. Models in vitro indicated that estrogen-induced apoptosis was heralded by a massive increase in subcellular inflammation [4]. Ping and graduate student Lizzie Sweeny, at Georgetown, had demonstrated that the glucocorticoid properties of MPA blocked estrogen-induced apoptosis [5].

Ping's study at MD Anderson identified the molecular link with the activation of NF-κB [6], and the suppression of apoptosis with glucocorticoids and MPA [7]. The resulting publications at MD Anderson created a scientific solution for the breast cancer results of the WHI based on experimental evidence [8].

Philipp Maximov, Balkees Abderrahman, and Ramona Curpan define the molecular mechanism of action of the partial estrogen agonist bisphenol to delay apoptosis

We were fortunate to have published structure—function relationship studies of triphenylethylenes that we were custom synthesized at the Fox Chase Cancer Center [9]. Philipp Maximov, Balkees Abderrahman, and our molecular modeler Ramona Curpan in Romania worked as a team to solve the molecular mechanism of how bisphenol delays apoptosis for a week [10,11].

Ramona Curpan used molecular dynamics computer simulations to demonstrate that not only does the phenolic hydroxyl of bisphenol in the stilbene structure bind in the position in the ER that is naturally occupied by the 3 phenolic hydroxyl of estradiol, but also the second phenolic hydroxyl of the triphenylethylene of bisphenol, now interacted with Thr347 to displace Asp351. This key Asp351 must be precisely positioned as it is essential to bind amino acids in helix 12 to seal over a planar estrogen-like estradiol and activate the ER complex [10,11]. It is the side chains of 4-hydroxytamoxifen and raloxifene that shield Asp351 to prevent this closure like a "stick in the jaws of a crocodile" [12,13]. It is also important to note that raloxifene shields [14] Asp351 more effectively than 4-hydroxytamoxifen. This explains why raloxifene is the more complete antiestrogen in the uterus of mammals, whereas 4-hydroxytamoxifen has more estrogen-like activity in the uterus. This is reflected by more endometrial cancer with tamoxifen [15,16] but none with raloxifene [17].

The bisphenol ER complex prevents an initial response to E_2 to trigger apoptosis. The bisphenol complex is, in fact, an antiestrogenic influence initially [1], by displacing the Asp351 to prevent the initial full activation of the ER complex. Nevertheless, the bisphenol ER complex eventually generates enough UPR to trigger delayed apoptosis. The experimental proof for this mechanism was the structure—function relationships of a series of triphenylethylenes with or without the phenolic hydroxyl of bisphenol [10] and the comparison of the estrogen mimic TTC-352 that is a weak full agonist at the tumor cell ER to induce apoptosis rapidly when compared with bisphenol, a true partial agonist with a delay in apoptosis [11].

Balkees Abderrahman and Ramona Curpan define the molecular mechanism of action of the clinically relevant estrogen mimic TTC-352

The answer to the third question has its roots in an independent research effort by former members of the Northwestern Tamoxifen Team. Dr Debra Tonetti initially, an assistant professor in my Chicago Tamoxifen Team, went to the University of Illinois campus in Chicago. She and Dr Greg Thatcher created a novel group of medicine called selective estrogen mMimics—that evolved into ShERPAs (selective human estrogen receptor partial agonists).

Compounds were synthesized [18] and a few selected for further study. Former Tamoxifen Team member, Ruth O'Regan, was then at the University of Wisconsin, Carbone Comprehensive Cancer Center and Division Chief Hematology, Oncology Palliative Care, Department of Medicine, where she headed the clinical team to test TTC-352, as a new promising estrogen-like treatment for endocrine-resistant MBC [19]. It is important to note that Ruth was a coauthor on the breakthrough article by Yao et al. 2000 [20] on the potential clinical application of low-dose estrogen therapy. The body of laboratory work from the Northwestern Tamoxifen Team was confirmed in patients, half a decade later, by Dr Mat Ellis [21] using high- and low-dose estrogen to provide clinical benefit for breast cancer patients who recurred during aromatase inhibitor treatment.

We were initially unable to obtain TTC-352 for Balkees to conduct experiments, but we did obtain a related analog: BMI-135. That paper was published [22] comparing and contrasting its actions with estetrol, a fetal metabolite of estradiol also being tested in clinical trial for the treatment of antihormone-resistant breast cancer [23].

With the release of information about TTC-352 and a clinical paper in Breast Cancer Research and Treatment [19], we tested the ShERPA against the benchmark partial agonist bisphenol, which has been well studied in laboratory models [24,25]. Both BMI-135 and TTC-352 were weak full agonists, whereas bisphenol was a true partial agonist. The journey from the laboratory to successful clinical testing with mechanisms deciphered was complete.

Battle with the "enemy within" 4 years later

Dr Tannir, along with the staff at the MD Anderson, continued to make major progress with reducing the size of my chest and sacral metastases. However, unexpectedly, Dr Andrea Califano from Columbia University, New York, stepped forward to declare: "Craig Jordan has saved the lives of tens of millions of women with breast cancer. I volunteer to save the life of Craig Jordan." His technique takes biopsies from cancer patients, prepares cell cultures, and, using mouse models, determines what combinations of therapeutic agents will cure the disease. His published results are remarkable [26–28]. I traveled the New York for a biopsy, but again, just as happened at MD Anderson, I had a pneumothorax and was required to delay my return to Houston until I was safe to travel. Dr Abderrahman was the required escort.

Dr. Califano's analysis of therapies to deploy in Houston takes many weeks in a pandemic, and this is where we are now. I am extremely grateful for the Herculean efforts of my doctors and colleagues at MD Anderson Cancer Center in Houston and Dr Caliphano at Cornell in New York.

Nevertheless, I was recruited to MD Anderson Cancer Center based on my "prize worthiness." Was their investment wise?

Recognition from national academies and major international awards that acknowledge a change in medicine while at the MD Anderson Cancer Center

2014 Selected by ASCO as one of the 50 Oncology luminaries. These individuals, living or deceased, changed practice of oncology during the past 50 years. http://cancerprogress.net/role/2086.

2015 Elected to the Academy of Medicine, Engineering and Science of Texas (rcscrvcd for National Academy of Sciences and Medicine members and Nobel Laureates).

2016 German Society of Gynaecology and Obstetrics. Identified as one of the "Big 4 of the Millennium" who in the 20th century changed the practice of women's health in the 21st century. Professors zur Haussen (Nobel Laureate), Veronessi, Senn, and Jordan.

2017 Elected to the National Academy of Medicine.

2017 "Professor V. Craig Jordan OBE, FMedSci" recognized on the "Wall of Honour" at the Royal Society of Medicine, London, United Kingdom.

2019 Appointed Companion of the Most Distinguished Order of St. Michael and St. George (CMG) *for services to women's health* by Her Majesty, Queen Elizabeth II.

2021 In recognition of the 50th anniversary of the signing of the National Cancer Act with the goal to cure cancer the National Cancer Institute selected individuals who had successfully achieved that goal in their discipline. Jordan was recognized for advances in the treatment and prevention of breast cancer with Selective Estrogen Receptor Modulators (particularly tamoxifen).

Recognition from professional academic societies

2015 Sir James Black Award for Contributions to drug discovery from the British Pharmacological Society.

2018 Laureate: Gerald D. Aurbach Award for Outstanding Translational Research. For the discovery and development of SERMs as a new group of medicines for women's health from the Endocrine Society.

2018 Elected to the Giants of Cancer Care Oncolive for Tamoxifen and SERMs. Invited to contribute the inaugural podcast of eminent electees.

2019 The Reynold Spector Award in Clinical Pharmacology from the American Society for Pharmacology and Experimental Therapeutics.

2019 The American Cancer Society Award and Lecture for Basic Science in Medicine, Society for Surgical Oncology.

2021 The American Association for the Advancement of Science "Golden Goose" Award. To recognize an individual who, proposed unlikely ideas that resulted in major advances in new knowledge and economic prosperity through competitive funding from Federal Grants ($30+ million with $35 million of philanthropy) (Fig. 14.1).

FIGURE 14.1

With my Golden Goose Award from the AAAS for changing medicine through competitive Federal Research grant support. I am standing in the entrance hall of my home - "Golden Goose meets a BIG Eagle."

Recognition, honorary appointments or honorary degrees, etc

2016	Elected Honorary Fellow of the German Society of Gynaecology and Obstetrics for SERMs.
2016	Elected the inaugural Honorary International member from the German Society for Senology for SERMs.
2020/21	Honorary Doctor of Science for the discovery and development of SERMs. University of Wisconsin.

At my 5-year point, "tenured professors" are required to be independently evaluated to continue their academic trajectory. Fifteen referees at the professorial rank and above are required to evaluate academic progress. This process was successfully completed, so the Team continues and the fight continues.

References

[1] Obiorah I, Jordan VC. Differences in the rate of oestrogen-induced apoptosis in breast cancer by oestradiol and the triphenylethylene bisphenol. Br J Pharmacol 2014;171: 4062—72.

[2] Osipo C, Gajdos C, Liu H, et al. Paradoxical action of fulvestrant in estradiol-induced regression of tamoxifen-stimulated breast cancer. J Natl Cancer Inst 2003;95: 1597—608.

[3] Liu H, Lee ES, Gajdos C, et al. Apoptotic action of 17beta-estradiol in raloxifene-resistant MCF-7 cells in vitro and in vivo. J Natl Cancer Inst 2003;95:1586—97.

[4] Ariazi EA, Cunliff HE, Lewis-Wambi JS, et al. Estrogen induces apoptosis in estrogen deprivation-resistant breast cancer through stress responses as identified by global gene expression across time. Proc Natl Acad Sci USA 2011;108:18879—86.

[5] Sweeney EE, Fan P, Jordan VC. Molecular modulation of estrogen-induced apoptosis by synthetic progestins in hormone replacement therapy: an insight into the women's health initiative study. Cancer Res 2014;74:7060—8.

[6] Fan P, Tyagi AK, Agboke FA, et al. Modulation of nuclear factor-kappa B activation by the endoplasmic reticulum stress sensor PERK to mediate estrogen-induced apoptosis in breast cancer cells. Cell Death Dis 2018;4:15.

[7] Fan P, Siwak DR, Abderrahman B, et al. Suppression of nuclear factor-κB by glucocorticoid receptor blocks estrogen-induced apoptosis in estrogen-deprived breast cancer cells. Mol Cancer Therapeut 2019;18:1684—95.

[8] Jordan VC. Molecular mechanism for breast cancer incidence in the women's health initiative. Cancer Prev Res 2020;13:807—16.

[9] Maximov PY, Meyers CB, Curpan RF, et al. Structure-function relationship of estrogenic triphenylethylenes related to endoxifen and 4-hydroxitamoxifen. J Med Chem 2010;53:3273—83.

[10] Maximov PY, Abderrahman B, Hawsawi YM, et al. The structure-function relationship of angular estrogens and estrogen receptor alpha to initiate estrogen-induced apoptosis in breast cancer cells. Mol Pharmacol 2020;98:24—37.

[11] Abderrahman B, Maximov PY, Curpan RF, et al. Rapid induction of the unfolded protein response and apoptosis by estrogen mimic TTC-352 for the treatment of endocrine-resistant breast cancer. Mol Cancer Therapeut 2021;20:11−25.

[12] Lieberman ME, Gorski, Jordan VC. An estrogen receptor model to describe the regulation of prolactin synthesis by antiestrogen in vitro. J Biol Chem 1983;258:4741−5.

[13] Jordan VC. Laboratory models of breast cancer to aid the elucidation of antiestrogen action. J Lab Clin Med 1987;109:267−77.

[14] Jordan VC. Turning scientific serendipity into discoveries in breast cancer research and treatment: a tale of PhD students and a 50-year roaming tamoxifen team. Breast Cancer Res Treat 2021. https://doi.org/10.1007/s10549-021-06356-8 (online ahead of print).

[15] EBCTCG. Tamoxifen for early breast cancer: an overview of the randomized trials. Lancet 1998;354:1451−67.

[16] Fisher B, Costantino JP, Wickerham DL, et al. Tamoxifen for prevention of breast cancer: report of the National Surgical Adjuvant Breast and Bowel Project P-1 Study. J Natl Cancer Inst 1998;90:1371−88.

[17] Cummings SR, Eckert S, Krueger KA, et al. The effect of raloxifene on risk of breast cancer in postmenopausal women: results from the MORE randomized trial. Multiple Outcomes of Raloxifene Evaluation. J Am Med Assoc 1999;281:2189−97.

[18] Xiong R, Patel, Gutgesell LM, et al. Selective human estrogen receptor partial agonists (ShERPAs) for tamoxifen-resistant breast cancer. J Med Chem 2016;59:219−37.

[19] Dudek AZ, Liu LC, Fischer JH, et al. Phase 1 study of TTC-352 in patients with metastatic breast cancer progressing on endocrine and CDK4/6 inhibitor therapy. Breast Cancer Res Treat 2020;183:617−27.

[20] Yao K, Lee ES, Bentrem DJ, et al. Antitumor action of physiological estradiol on tamoxifen-stimulated breast tumors grown in athymic mice. Clin Cancer Res 2000;6:2028−36.

[21] Ellis MJ, Gao F, Dehdashti F, et al. Lower-dose vs high-dose oral estradiol therapy of hormone receptor-positive, aromatase inhibitor-resistant advanced breast cancer: a phase 2 randomized study. J Am Med Assoc 2009;302:774−80.

[22] Abderrahman B, Maximov PY, Curpan RF, et al. Pharmacology and molecular mechanisms of clinically relevant estrogen estetrol and estrogen mimic BMI-135 for the treatment of endocrine-resistant breast cancer. Mol Pharmacol 2020;98:364−81.

[23] Schmidt M, Lenhard H, Hoenig A, et al. Tumor suppression, dose-limiting toxicity and wellbeing with the fetal estrogen estetrol in patients with advanced breast cancer. J Cancer Res Clin Oncol 2020;147:1833−42.

[24] Jordan VC, Lieberman ME. Estrogen stimulated in vitro: classification of agonist, partial agonist and anti-agonist based on structure. Mol Pharmacol 1984;26:279−85.

[25] Obiorah I, Sengupta S, Curpan R, Jordan VC. Defining the conformation of the estrogen receptor complex that controls estrogen-induced apoptosis in breast cancer. Mol Pharmacol 2014;85:789−99.

[26] Alvarez MJ, Subramaniam PS, Tang LH, et al. A precision oncology approach to the pharmacological targeting of mechanistic dependencies in neuroendocrine tumors. Nat Genet 2018;50:979−89.

[27] Paull EO, Aytes A, Jones SJ, et al. A modular master regulator landscape controls cancer transcriptional identity. Cell 2021;184:334−51.

[28] Obradovic A, Chowdhury N, Haake SM, et al. Single-cell protein activity analysis identifies recurrence-associated renal tumor macrophages. Cell 2021;184:2988−3005.

"Invest in the young"

15

Sir James Black, Nobel Laureate

Throughout the pages of this book, I have described and documented my journey through the education system in the United Kingdom (1952–65). This system was to prepare the individual for a future career by national examinations that would decide your life's path. In my case, the goal was to pass the 11+ examination, and the county education authority would decide which grammar schools you would attend.

The next hurdle was the National Ordinary ("O")-level examinations which one was required to obtain at least five passes to remain at the Grammar school. The alternative was to go into the 16 year old workforce. I did not, and obtained only 3 "O" levels, but the intervention of my mother and the offer of a job at ICI Pharmaceutical Division as a synthetic chemistry technician (if I stayed in school and took "O"-level physics and "A"-level chemistry) did the trick with a stay of execution by Mr Armishaw. This allowed a path in academia.

My parents were approached by Mr Bescoby to consider whether I should apply to university. I received one interview at one university based on the words of my headmaster, Mr Armishaw (actually Mr Bescoby) in his letter of evaluation and support: "Craig Jordan is an unusual man; a VERY UNUSUAL YOUNG MAN." I passed the required A-level examinations and an "O" level in physics. I was off to the Department of Pharmacology at the University of Leeds.

This unconventional beginning, to some, who would describe mine as an exemplary academic career, was the result of school masters, and the University faculty being supportive, when instead they could have remained indifferent and not encouraged and advanced my horizons. At Moseley Hall Grammar School, it was chemistry teachers Mr Anderson and Mr Radford who sparked and developed my unusual interest in chemistry. Indeed, I spent a considerable amount of time in detention after school (I was not responsive to school rules!), or standing in the corridor in the Main building of Moseley Hall as punishment at lunchtimes. I used the time wisely memorizing chemistry text books. Mr Bescoby allowed me to teach younger boys voluntarily, university-level biochemistry in a laboratory unsupervized by staff! Without their commitment and professionalism as teachers who "went the extra mile," I would not have progressed. However, it was winning the zoology prize at Moseley Hall Grammar School that ignited a chain of events, taught at the school "obtain as many pieces of paper that demonstrate what you have achieved." It is not what you say or claim, it is the written opinion of others, that is the only benchmark. "If it is not written down, it never happened."

It was Drs Kaye and Clark who offered me a place at the University of Leeds based on an interview and an academic "line in the sand" of grades to enter university. But it is the "secret supporter" of immense integrity exemplified by Dr George Mogey, who, having declared "I was not good enough" to transfer from a Pharmacy to a Pharmacology degree, personified academic integrity. It was he who supported me with a confidential letter to be a faculty member in the Department of Pharmacology and ensured I would be an Ackroyd Scholar at Leeds. I now had two pieces of paper where it was written down, by others, what I had achieved so far.

The transition to graduate student from undergraduate required honest faculty members in the Cancer Research Department and the Chemistry Department not "to poach me" from my path to a Ph.D. with the last MRC scholarship (because someone returned theirs at the last moment), and the failure of my project to crystallize the ER with an estrogen and an antiestrogen. This changed my destiny by studying the pharmacology of "failed contraceptives" that resulted in my examination by Dr Arthur Walpole from ICI Pharmaceuticals Division, Alderley Park, as the only personal willing to do so in Great Britain! Our meeting now resulted in his support and collaboration to advance my career in America (1972–74) and Leeds (1974–78) that resulted in the tamoxifen we have today.

So how do we invest in the young? I have chosen to emulate those who, without personal gain, chose to provide me with opportunities. In your careers, you can do the same. Give support to all who want to advance their education and achieve. The chapter of "In Their Own Words" are but a few of the scores of enthusiastic young minds I have been honored and committed to assist. I, however, in the spirit of "it's not written down—it never happened" have chosen to advance the commitment to others, one step further.

I have described my career ascent, based on published academic research, to be documented by the evaluation by my academic superiors with the award of prizes by professional societies or at the international prize level. As a result, more than 20 years ago, I chose to invest in the young at the University of Leeds. This came in three instalments: prizes for "the best," paying the fees for students of exceptional merit and establishing an annual lectureship with invited academic superstars "to create excitement in a future of translational medicine."

My initial focus was both, at the Department of Chemistry at the University of Leeds (where I achieved an unheard of mark of 87/100, when a First is 70 in 3E Organic Chemistry) with the Jordan Prize for Medicinal Chemistry for the top student annually. My friend, colleague and coauthor, the late Professor Ron Grigg FRS administered the award. Another surprise in 2021 from out of the blue was Lewis Turner who was the winner of the 2014 "Craig Jordan" prize for the top medicinal chemistry student. Lewis went on to secure his Ph.D. at Leeds. Following a postdoctoral position at the Scripps Research Institute, he has now been offered a job in the pharmaceutical industry in America and asked for a letter of evaluation. I was happy to do so, and he has now secured his work visa in America.

As a second award, I chose Leeds University Officers Training Corps for the Jordan Trophy that recognizes, annually, the top Officer Cadet. This was administered by my friend, the former Provost at Leeds University OTC, Colonel Alan Roberts OBE, PhD. Leeds University OTC challenged me and was the mechanism whereby I was talent spotted by the Intelligence Corps and recruited as the NBC advisor to the Deputy Chief Scientist (Army). I volunteered with the US Army when I went to the Worcester Foundation for Experimental Biology for 2 years and became the only nonlaw enforcement individual to be trained as a Drug Squad Officer by the DEA. This service was very important to me as I was privileged to receive a grant from Cheshire County Council and later the Medical Research Council to complete my education at the University of Leeds. My education was free based on merit. I invested in the OTC to identify the top student cadets to receive the Jordan Trophy and a cash award for more than 20 years. Regrettably, the Ministry of Defense has recently chosen to sever links with universities and administer OTCs directly from Sandhurst.

Medical students have the potential to create enormous advances in health care and therapeutics. At the University of Leeds, Timothy Jaspan (Fig. 5.2) was an intercalating 1-year pharmacology student who excelled in my University of Leeds Tamoxifen Team. He published two papers in 9 months. Based on his model, I created scholarships for medical students to complete a 1-year intercalating BSc in pharmacology. Unfortunately, the pharmacology department evaporated at Leeds, so I agreed to sponsor degrees of the medical student's choice. These scholarships continue to this day at the University of Leeds Medical School.

I received an invitation by Professor Terence (Terry) Rabbitts FRS (2008–11) to chair his external advisory board at the Leeds Institute for Molecular Medicine. As a result, I chose to sponsor a short (3 year) lecture program to invite external cancer researchers to address the students at the Leeds Cancer Center. We will follow Terry to the Weatherall Institute at Oxford University, but first I will recount an improbable story of the past meeting the present day!

On one of my numerous return visits to the University of Leeds, I felt the need to visit the Astbury Department of Biophysics. This, as you recall, was where I planned to crystallize the purified ER both with an estrogen and an antiestrogen in 1969. I looked up whom I should contact as the Director. It was Professor Sheena Radford, FRS. At the appointed time, late on a Friday afternoon, I arrived at Astbury only to discover that access was only possible by a coded card. This situation resolved itself, and I was shown into Professor Radford's office where she was rapidly printing out the CV and bibliography I had sent to introduce myself. Then the unexpected occurred; "I see you attended Moseley Hall Grammar School (1958–65). Did you get taught chemistry by P.R. Radford?" It immediately dawned on me that I was sitting across the desk from his daughter! This is the genesis of the V. Craig Jordan/PR Radford Prize (https://astbury.leeds.ac.uk/about/the-vc-jordan-pr-radford-prize/) for the best Ph.D. student thesis for a given year. Small World but perhaps other forces beyond our control are moving the chess pieces of our lives around.

Terrance Rabbitts was recruited to the University of Oxford. That move enhanced his research interactions. Once he was established at Oxford, he enquired whether I would consider endowing a lecture series at Weatherall to invite cutting edge leaders in biomedical research to address the faculty and students annually. It is called the Craig Jordan Translational Medical Research Lecture, and I was invited to inaugurate the lecture series. The stated goal of the lecture series is to ignite a future generation of medical scientists to advance health care through innovative research. This was established in 2017 and remains an excellent asset at Weatherall (https://www.imm.ox.ac.uk/about/seminars/jordan-translational-medicine-lecture).

My final commitment to "invest in the young" was at the MD Anderson Cancer Center. My chance meeting with Dr Balkees Abderrahman (she had obtained her MD degree at the University of Jordan [British system]) started an educational journey for her that was unanticipated by either of us. She had not planned on working with me, but she did her homework of the faculty in Breast Medical Oncology.

One morning, I found myself in my temporary office in the Department of Breast Medical Oncology, waiting for things to happen with my move down the corridor to my larger office nearer my new Chairman Dr Debu Tripathy. Balkees was pacing the corridor waiting for the allocated faculty mentor to arrive. Upon passing my office, she exclaimed "You are the Father of Tamoxifen!" Naturally, we all like this sort of recognition from those we have never met, but there was a lesson here that is worthy of emphasis to the young. By reading the faculty listing for Breast Medical Oncology and her other rotation in leukemia, she was informed and that knowledge changed her future.

It was immediately clear that she could synthesize complex issues in medical science into published articles. Indeed, she became sole author on many opinion articles for journals in the United Kingdom. I saw an opportunity for her to advance her career, but starting an American 5-year Ph.D. was out of the question. I reached out to my trusted Leeds University contact Jayne Glennon. Despite early resistance by the Faculty committee, at my proposed innovation of me as an accomplished Leeds Graduate supervising her in my laboratory at the MD Anderson Cancer Center, and her being examined for her Ph.D. to be awarded at the University of Leeds, an administrative mechanism was discovered called Model C for "Applicants of Very High Quality." As I was not a faculty member at Leeds University, I was not permitted to be her official supervisor. Fortunately, Professor John Ladbury, the then Dean of Science, stepped forward with indispensable assistance and support. He had come from the MD Anderson to the University of Leeds with a plan to create collaborative links between MD Anderson and Leeds. This Ph.D. was a start! I chose to pay the (substantial) fees required for the 3-year course as I strongly believed it was unreasonable to require Balkees to obtain loans to attempt to complete her Ph.D. as "the inaugural candidate." What if further obstacles occurred and the project failed?

She transferred to my Tamoxifen Team at MD Anderson as a Dallas/Ft. Worth Living Legend Fellow of Breast Medical Oncology; successfully completed a split-site Ph.D. at Leeds University in 3 years; and became the first person at MD Anderson to be selected as a Forbes 30 under 30 for Science and selected as an attendee at the gathering of Nobel Laureates at Lindau, in Germany in 2020. Balkees could not attend because the event was canceled due to the coronavirus pandemic, but a surprise was in store for her. Balkees was selected to be a panelist with Nobel Laureates Brian P. Schmidt, Carl-Henrik Heldin, and Hans-Jörg Rheinberger chaired by Adam Smith, President of the Nobel Foundation. Her 90-minute Zoom "tour-de-force" is available at https://www.mediatheque.lindau-nobel.org/videos/39161/why-trust-science/meeting-2021, and she was invited to publish a paper https://www.lindau-nobel.org/blog-6-tools-to-supercharge-your-science-communication. "If it is not written down, it never happened." In 2020 during the coronavirus pandemic, she successfully completed her 4-h video viva with the examination committee having met the requirements of the number of high-quality manuscripts published. Mission accomplished Balkees Abderrahman MD, PhD. In my 50-year run of graduate students from my Tamoxifen Teams, mine was the first from the University of Leeds (1973), Clive Dix my first student (1982), and, finally, Balkees Abderrahman (2020).

I recommend that any future successful medical scientist reading this product of my life's work commit to providing opportunities for excellent students that follow, so that the momentum in therapeutics can continue apace. It is people who make discoveries and those people can change the world of medicine for the better.

Everyone is guilty of all the good they did not do.

Voltaire

Scientific survival suggestions

16

I have but one lamp by which my feet are guided and that is the lamp of experience. I have no way of judging of the future but by the past.
Patrick Henry, the First Elected Governor of Virginia, 1775.

This book represents an ongoing evolution of interconnected and complementary research areas that I have experienced over the past five decades, during my scientific training and as the leader of my "Tamoxifen Teams" throughout Europe (Leeds University, UK and Bern, Switzerland) and the United States (Worcester Foundation for Experimental Biology, University of Wisconsin—Madison, Northwestern University—Chicago, the Fox Chase Cancer Center—Philadelphia, at the Lombardi Comprehensive Cancer Center—Georgetown University, Washington, DC and currenlty at the University of Texas MD Anderson Cancer Center-Houston). In the 1970s, I used to say "have brain, will travel …" (With apologies to Paladin and "Have Gun Will Travel" in the United States television series in the late 1950s).

This has been an exciting and sometimes challenging career with excellent staff and students, but the 50 years have provided me with some useful personal lessons that some have said deserve to be passed on to the next generation:

A Dozen Scientific Survival Suggestions:

1. Carefully decide on your mentor or supervisor for your doctorate or fellowship.
2. Train yourself to ascend in science.
3. Know the literature of your chosen topic: who did what.
4. Ensure your Director or Chair has an agenda and you are in it.
5. Get documentation that says what you achieved.
6. Experiments are a conversation with Nature.
7. Follow your instincts about what you want to achieve: have a goal.
8. Know an opportunity when you are presented with change.
9. Give opportunities to allow your team members to excel.
10. Understand it is your responsibility to obtain support for your science.
11. Science can be distracting, but publish or perish.
12. When you publish, your colleagues and competitors will often ignore your landmark work!

1. Carefully decide on your mentor or supervisor for your doctorate. Choosing a Ph.D. supervisor is critical. This individual will be your mentor and guide, maybe for life. Several qualifications for the mentor and supervisor are

Tamoxifen Tales. https://doi.org/10.1016/B978-0-323-85051-3.00016-6

201

required for success, and you should ask yourself important questions: Has this individual done this before or will his/her efforts with me end in failure? Has this mentor already earned tenure? If your mentor is caste out, then you are also gone with nothing. If the faculty member has not yet achieved tenure, ask yourself whether they have the adequate funds, experience and vision to run a laboratory for 5 years (or at least demonstrate they have that potential)? Are there skilled individuals in the laboratory who can teach you new laboratory skills rapidly? Trial and error is a poor path to progress especially today with few resources and accelerated deadlines. Can you ever see your mentor? Once a month is fine but the phantom supervisor can turn into the phantom Ph.D.! Be cautious of the faculty member who will tell you their plan for you to finish in a couple of years. No project is what it seems on paper. That is just talk. Experiments are a conversation with Nature. The answers are reality. Nature does not lie. The Ph.D. path I chose in the Department of Pharmacology was to crystallize the ER. Well, that did not work, but great on paper (see Chapter 3)! The good news was that my Ph.D. supervisor, Dr Edward Clark, a senior tenured faculty member, was a wonderful teacher of pharmaceutical chemistry, had encyclopedic knowledge and a long row of bound Ph.D. theses in his office. I had a scholarship from the Medical Research Council, so all was well (except no one cared initially what I had learned). For my own trainees—each is a special individual who excelled at what they chose to do. What we achieved together is in Chapter 17 and as individuals in Chapter 18.

2. Train yourself to ascend in science. Your personality, dedication, achievements, and experience will determine whether you have trained yourself to be ready and are talent-spotted. In my own case, career risks were essential to profit from opportunities. This was, in fact, training to ascend. Change is good for scientific development, which, in turn, provides academic and personal security. New environments and challenges provide invaluable experience to apply in the next stage of your career development.

3. Know everything you can about your chosen topic. Do not become too broad and do not flit from topic to topic because it is fun or interesting at that moment. Do not dilute your theme by being too willing to collaborate. Become an expert in your small area and learn all the literature written by those who came before. By knowing "who did what," you already have a database when introduced to the leaders in your broader area. Once you have an expanding publication record in your chosen field, write a refereed review for a strategic professional journal. Surprise the competition, and get your ideas written down. "If it isn't written down it never happened."

4. As a young scientist, I wanted the University to provide help and security. It was obvious to me at least that I should be talent-spotted. My Chairman replied, "You keep talking about the University—there is no such thing. It is a group of men with an agenda and you are not in it." I have carried this philosophy with me ever since. At the Robert H. Lurie Comprehensive Cancer Center later in my career, my Director Steve Rosen saw the opportunity for a world-class

breast program. He had "an agenda and I was in it!" He was right. Monica Morrow and I had $58 million invested in our Breast Cancer Research and Treatment Program alone in a decade. At the Fox Chase Cancer Center, the Director Robert Young had an agenda and we were in it. A change in Directors and life becomes unbearable, unstable, hostile, and support in research is impossible. A move is necessary to survive and achieve your promise.

5. Get documentation that says what you have achieved. At my grammar school in Cheshire, where I first learned the harsh realities of competitive academic success or failure, a teacher once told our class "Get as many pieces of paper that say what you did, what you can do and how good you are." Invaluable advice to be talent-spotted. It tells the story of what you did and not what you will do in the future. It does, however, provide a greater security and promise for further investment in your laboratory. The more professional awards you receive, these reflect the opinions of your professional colleagues about the value of your professional contribution to medical science.

6. Experiments are a conversation with nature. You define a question and, based on the selection of an appropriate model to answer your question in humans, you isolate the parameter of interest as a single variable with appropriate controls. The controls are critical to prove you can do what others before you have done. If the answer to your question does not give you what you antici- ipate, then your premise may be wrong, but only if all the controls are perfect. Nature does not lie. Several of my students, over the years, presented me with data that did not comply with my "mental model" of what should happen. By way of example, Clive Dix (1976) first showed me the high-affinity binding of 4-hydroxytamoxifen to the ER. I told him to go away and do it again, as no antiestrogen has the same binding affinity to the ER as estradiol. He was right! It was a discovery. Doug Wolf (1991) first showed me that physiologic estradiol induces tumor regression in tamoxifen-resistant breast cancer. He tried everything to explain why he could not reproduce a previous students (Marco Gottardis) work. What had occurred was that the tumor had changed with years of retransplantation and it was a discovery. The new biology of estrogen-induced apoptosis was born in 1992, but, like a child, took 10 years to mature. It is said that new knowledge only becomes accepted once the ardent detractors die. Change in science takes time and must be sustained with determination.

7. Follow your instincts about what you want to achieve: have a goal. I have never followed the fashion in medical science. I only wanted to participate in developing medicines to help people. That is pharmacology. Pharmacology and chemistry were always my passion, and my goal was to advocate for change in medical practice. Through molecules, models, and mechanism, drugs were reinvented (tamoxifen—a failed contraceptive and raloxifene, formerly keoxifene a failed breast cancer drug) and became pioneering medicines. Eat, sleep, and work at your passion. It is a privilege to participate, not a right.

8. Know an opportunity when you are presented with change. Opportunities occur rarely, but when they occur, they must be seized with alacrity. It is the only way forward. The opportunities to learn at the Worcester Foundation in American (1972—74) and the Ludwig Institute for Cancer Research, Switzerland (1979—80) were both career changing experiences second to none. But both were a gamble and not easy decisions to embrace with a young family, overseas for a year or two. However, I did not truly understand the process in identifying opportunity until Wisconsin. It was decided that I would inherit the space, staff, and directorship of the Steroid Receptor Laboratory of a departing senior faculty member. At the time, the prospect was overwhelming as my laboratory space would become half the floor of the sixth floor of the Comprehensive Cancer Center. I would double my staff overnight and the Clinical Steroid Receptor Laboratory required absolute quality control and focus on tracking all clinical samples and reports for Southern Wisconsin. I phoned my mentor Bill McGuire in San Antonio to explain to him my circumstances and to explain that I did not feel equal to the task. He told me "… You are looking at the task incorrectly—this is an opportunity …" Now I understood. Wisconsin was where we discovered SERMs and estrogen-induced apoptosis. I was "talent-spotted" and advanced from Assistant Professor through Associate Professor (selected as an H.I. Romnes Faculty Fellow) to become Professor of Human Oncology and Pharmacology in 5 years. I was 38 years old. I became director of the Breast Cancer Research and Treatment Program for the WCCC. Mine was their flagship program in the Cancer Center. Very good decision to go to Wisconsin.

9. Give opportunities to allow your team members to excel. I had the good fortune to have dedicated teachers whose job description they stated "as helping pupils (or later at University, students), to attain their full potential" (www. 175heroes.org.uk/ronnie_kaye). Theirs was a system of a "gut feeling" and giving people a chance to excel. Give opportunities without self-interest. This means you must ensure a team member leaves better than when they joined. This means not only your graduate students and postdoctoral fellows, but also your technical staff. Their inclusion on publications is essential to enhance their career prospects. For them, remember #3.

10. Understand it is your responsibility to obtain support for your science. My desire as a teenager to develop medicines to treat cancer naturally drew me to the astonishing contributions of Professor Paul Ehrlich and his creation of synthetic chemical therapies (chemotherapy) to treat disease successfully. Erhlich gave us one more lesson of science as true today as it was in 1890: the 4-G's—Glück, Geduld, Geschick, and Geld. Medical science requires luck (Glück), but patience (Geduld) is critical. Recognition of the discovery through luck must also be consolidated during the skilled (Geschick) conversation with nature. But all of this process requires money (Geld). Ehrlich was perhaps the first to create a mosaic of funding sources from the government, private philanthropy (the Speyer Stiftung), and the pharmaceutical

industry (Hoechst). In the same way, each young scientist must become expert at "selling" the project by writing grants and advocating opportunities to philanthropic organizations or the pharmaceutical industry.

11. Science can be distracting, but publish or perish. Experiments are fun and can be exciting as your conversation with nature develops. Unfortunately, some scientists only see experiments as the goal and their attention keeps wandering from experiment to experiment. They become distressed once they realize that they have not cured cancer and keep trying more experiments. However, the profession of science is about communication so that you can participate and contribute to the web of knowledge. Unless you have the discipline to write every day, create a balanced manuscript, and publish your results in an appropriate, refereed journal, it is as if you never did your experiments. No one knows! Some young scientists delude themselves that abstracts at meetings are science. This is only true if a refereed paper is hot on the heels of the abstract after the meeting! Only refereed papers are relevant for jobs, promotions, and grants. Remember Dr Caspi at the Worcester Foundation for Experimental Biology, "Tell them the story so far."

12. When you publish, your colleagues and competitors will often ignore your landmark work! Publications are the record of scientific ideas and progress. Nevertheless, you should realize that others need to create their careers and will not feel it necessary to refer to your laboratory research or ideas. It is a truism that you will experience: "Not practical; won't work" followed by "Even if it does work, not relevant" followed by "OK it works, but not important" and finally, "Fantastic! You've cured cancer. I thought of it first!" If you choose to be a translational scientist, you should understand at the outset that the clinical publication is the "discovery" and will be heralded as a breakthrough, and your contribution may not be included as the justification for the transition from the laboratory to the clinical trial. However, your contribution, over time, with discipline and enthusiasm will be documented in the literature and provide retrospective evidence to propel your career forward. This and your talent and flexibility to adapt to new environments and opportunities will ensure your recognition but only if you (or if someone else ascribes it to you) wrote it down.

An account of students obtaining a Ph.D. degree (or an MD for physicians in the British System) while in the Tamoxifen Team over the last 50 years

Should we ask anybody who is undertaking a major project in sciences in the heat of the fight, what drives and pushes him so relentlessly, he will never think of an external goal; it is the passion of the hunter and soldier. The stimulus of the fight with its setbacks.

Freidrich Miessner, Discoverer of DNA

Each student came to read for a Ph.D. with only a general outline of the area of research to be addressed. I have never subscribed to the predictable, logical, methodical, stepwise approach to science demanded by granting agencies. "Year three we will!" I subscribe to the words of Meissner above. I believe the process is a conversation with Nature and a "battle" to be won, with all its setbacks. Battles can never be predicted after the first clash; it is the response you make to the replies of Nature that predicts success or failure in science. The Duke of Wellington was asked by his second-in-command, the Earl of Uxbridge, before the Battle of Waterloo: What was the plan to be continued should he be killed? "To defeat the French…" was the simple reply from the Duke. The tactical and strategic brilliance of the Duke was to prepare the disposition of his forces, and respond to the answer from the enemy. He never lost a battle.

As a mentor and supervisor, you have essential responsibilities to prepare the prospective scientist for the conversation (battle) ahead with Nature. Here is my approach. Each student must learn the practical side of science from the experts in the laboratory. These are usually skilled technicians who perform experiments in cell culture or maintain the cell culture facility all day, every day. Senior postdoctoral fellows or junior faculty in the team must teach the more complex techniques.

There is no conversation in science if the student does not know the language, so it is critical at the outset that they complete a published review or two (no more) in either a book or a journal (preferably the latter). This is the best way to learn about the scope of the literature and its translation to practical benefit for society. Cathy

Tamoxifen Tales. https://doi.org/10.1016/B978-0-323-85051-3.00017-8

207

Murphy and Jennifer MacGregor-Schafer each completed "heroic" reviews in the refereed literature. However, their outstanding efforts have been cited 494 and 666 times, respectively. I usually set two or three practical tasks for each Ph.D. project, with the anticipation that at least one will be fruitful. Remarkably, almost always the student produces data that are worthy of publication from each task. The student develops unique findings on new mechanisms or provides valuable new tools for future generations of students to exploit.

To illustrate these points, I have chosen to describe the accomplishments of my students over the decades with what was found, and what was the publication.

Clive J. Dix, Department of Pharmacology, University of Leeds, 1976—79; ICI Pharmaceuticals Division Research Scholar

- Jordan et al. [1]
- Dix and Jordan [2]
- Dix and Jordan [3]

Defined the pharmacology of the potent tamoxifen metabolite 4-hydroxytamoxifen, which became the "standard" antiestrogen and laboratory reagent for the next 30 years and was used by others to crystallize the antiestrogenic complex with the ligand-binding domain of the ER. Defined the benefits of long-term tamoxifen therapy as a potential adjuvant therapy to treat breast cancer. A very important paper at a meeting that defined the future direction of adjuvant tamoxifen therapy as a long-term treatment (I presented the paper at the meeting in Tuscon, Arizona so by tradition in the publication I was the first author).

Anna T. Riegel (Neé Tate), McArdle Laboratory for Cancer Research, University of Wisconsin, 1980—83; Fulbright Hays Scholar

- Tate et al. [4]
- Tate and Jordan [5]
- Jordan et al. [6]

Used both polyclonal and monoclonal antibodies generated by Geoffrey Greene at the Ben May Laboratory, University of Chicago, in a collaborative study with Dr Elwood V Jensen to compare and contrast the properties of the estradiol and antiestrogen ER complex. These data supported our proposed model for estrogen and antiestrogen action using ER structure—function relationships at a target gene. The model was correct. The pharmacology of tamoxifen analogs (with very low affinity for ER) that could not be metabolically activated was used to investigate the growth and progesterone receptor synthesis in the immature rat uterus in vivo. The standard cell disruption techniques showed that the ER was not present in the nuclear compartment; only an unoccupied ER was present in the cytosol. This was evidence that the technology to demonstrate ER localization was always faulty or suspect. Work by others (e.g., Greene) using the first monoclonal antibodies established that the ER was a nuclear protein that "fell out of the nucleus" once cells were disrupted. The tamoxifen analogs that weakly bind to the nuclear ER would turn on growth and progesterone receptor synthesis, but when the tissue was disrupted the ligand fell off the ER in the nucleus and the unoccupied receptor fell out of the nucleus into the cytosol. This paper is a wonderful example of the Heisenberg "uncertainty" principle, which declares that the technique used to determine location in and of itself alters the structure and location of the target being observed in Nature.

Stewart D. Lyman, McArdle Laboratory, University of Wisconsin, 1982–84

- Lyman and Jordan [7]
- Lyman and Jordan [8]

Conducted a wonderful systematic study of the actions of nonsteroidal antiestrogens through the ER in mouse uterine models. This really created an extensive database for the subsequent understanding of the selective estrogenic and antiestrogenic actions of nonsteroidal antiestrogens that became selective ER modulation!

Ethel M. Cormier, Molecular and Cellular Biology Graduate Program, University of Wisconsin, 1982–88

- Cormier and Jordan [9]
- Cormier et al. [10]

In the early 1980s, growth factor signaling became a "hot" topic. She compared and contrasted the efficacy of antiestrogens to inhibit estrogen or epidermal growth factor (EGF)–stimulated growth. Antiestrogens did not block EGF-stimulated growth and EGF reduced estrogen-stimulated induction of the progesterone receptor. Highlighted resistance mechanisms for antiestrogens that were subsequently confirmed.

Marco M. Gottardis, Department of Human Oncology, University of Wisconsin, 1983–89

- Gottardis and Jordan [11]
- Gottardis et al. [12]

- Gottardis and Jordan [13]
- Gottardis et al. [14]

Contributed four major findings for translation into medical practice. Was the first to show that raloxifene can prevent rat mammary carcinogenesis, a drug that is now FDA-approved for breast cancer risk reduction in postmenopausal women. Was the first to illustrate that patients using adjuvant tamoxifen may have an increased incidence of endometrial cancer; subsequently demonstrated in clinical trial. Was the first to develop a transplantable model in vivo of acquired resistance to tamoxifen and showed that tumors grew in response to either tamoxifen or estrogen (a unique finding supporting the use of aromatase inhibitors as a treatment after tamoxifen failure), and was the first to use a pure antiestrogen to illustrate the potential advantage for the treatment of tamoxifen resistance (subsequently proven in clinical trial).

Catherine S. Murphy, Department of Human Oncology, University of Wisconsin, 1984–90

- Murphy et al. [15]
- Murphy et al. [16]
- Murphy et al. [17]

Was the first to demonstrate that ER-positive breast cancer cell line T47D, had the potential to lose the ER during estrogen deprivation (see John J. Pink). Used structure–function relationships and medicinal chemistry to prove that both geometric isomers of hydroxylated tamoxifen derivative 4-hydroxytamoxifen were antiestrogens. Before this definitive study, it was assumed that the cis isomer of 4-OH tamoxifen was fully estrogenic, and this hypothesis was used to create a putative mechanism of resistance. Mapped out the structure–function relationships of antiestrogens to regulate breast cancer cell proliferation prior to X-ray crystallography, subsequently refining and defining the conclusions.

Meei-Huey Jeng, Department of Human Oncology, University of Wisconsin, 1987–92

- Jeng and Jordan [18]
- Jeng et al. [19]
- Jeng et al. [20]
- Jeng et al. [21]

Growth factors again! This time the regulation of the TGFα family. Insisted (constantly!) on conducting a study of progestins, which eventually broke my resolve (and, I thought, my better judgment), so I gave her a synthetic panel of progestins to test in her cells. She discovered the estrogen-like qualities of the progestins that are 19 nor-testosterone derivatives and the estrogen-like properties of the antiprogestin RU486. Discovered the "paradoxical" growth factor gene control by estrogens in ER cells, stably transfected with the ER. The growth inhibitor TGFβ went down and the growth stimulator TGFα went up—growth stopped! No idea why this stops transfectants from growing. However, we have used estradiol-stimulated TGFα induction as a gene marker ever since.

Shun-Yuan Jiang, Department of Human Oncology, University of Wisconsin, 1987—92; Scholarship from the Taiwanese Ministry of Defense

- Jiang and Jordan [22]
- Jiang et al. [23]
- Pink et al. [24]

Was the first to stably transfect the ER gene into ER-negative breast cancer cells. Other molecular biology groups had failed. I presented the first results at a symposium organized by the late Bill McGuire at the Endocrine Society meeting in Washington, DC, June 19—22, 1991. A prominent member of the cancer endocrinology scientific community congratulated me with the following words: "You are the least likely person in the world anyone would predict to do this!" Created two cloned MCF-7 derivative cell lines, MCF-7:5C and MCF-7:2A, in response to estrogen withdrawal. This advance was to position us subsequently to study acquired resistance to aromatase inhibitors 10 years later. But, at the time, nothing too exciting was found. We put them in the liquid nitrogen tank until Joan Lewis-Wambi, as a postdoctoral fellow, changed all our previous understanding of the biology of the cells by changing the serum in which the cells grow. Gave us tools to understand E_2-induced apoptosis.

Doug M. Wolf, Department of Human Oncology, University of Wisconsin, 1988—93; Susan G. Komen graduate student

- Wolf et al. [25]
- Wolf and Jordan [26]
- Wolf and Jordan [27]

Used medicinal chemistry to demonstrate that tamoxifen was not converted to estrogenic metabolites by isomerization that caused acquired resistance, as had been suggested previously in the literature. Discovered the first natural mutation of the ER (D351Y) in an experimental tamoxifen-stimulated breast tumor, which was stably transfected into an ER-negative cell line in the laboratory and subsequently shown to be the first mutation to change the pharmacology of the anti-estrogen raloxifene to become estrogen-like by Anait Levenson. Based on subsequent X-ray crystallography, D35l was discovered (working with Jim Zapf) to be a critical surface amino acid for modulating the antiestrogenic side chain of both tamoxifen and raloxifene as estrogens/antiestrogens. Was the first to discover that long-term tamoxifen treatment creates a vulnerability to physiologic estrogen in breast cancer that causes apoptosis and tumor regression. The "Tamoxifen Team" kept the project going with philanthropy, but it took me 15 years to get competitive funding. Now medicine has changed again, with new potential for treatment and prevention. Thank goodness for Susan G Komen for the Cure Grant SAC100009 (2010−14) and the Department of Defense Center of Excellence Grant W81XWH-06-1-0590 (2006−14).

John J. Pink, Department of Human Oncology, University of Wisconsin, 1990−95

- Murphy et al. [28]
- Pink et al. [29]
- Pink et al. [30]
- Pink and Jordan [31]
- Pink et al. [32]
- Pink et al. [33]

Recruited to my laboratory at the Wisconsin Comprehensive Cancer Center to introduce new techniques in molecular biology into the lab and enhance the productivity of C Murphy, SY Jiang, and M H Jeng. Did just that, but cloned and confirmed the first ER-negative breast cancer cells from ER-positive cells by estrogen deprivation in breast cancer cells, described the biology of the MCF-7:2A cells, described the different mechanisms for ER regulation, and cloned and characterized the first high molecular weight ER protein in breast cancer; as a Ph.D. student!

William H. Catherino, Department of Human Oncology, University of Wisconsin, MD/Ph.D. program, 1991−95

- Catherino et al. [34]
- Catherino and Jordan [35]
- Catherino et al. [36]

With great self-confidence, created the BC-2 (Bill Catherino, of course) cell line by stably transfecting the asp351tyr ER into ER-negative MDA-MB-231 breast cancer cells. This created another essential cell model for all subsequent work on the predictable modulation of the estrogenic and antiestrogenic actions of the selective estrogen receptor modulator (SERM)−estrogen (ER) complex. Continued work on progestins and breast cancer growth with the new progestin, gestodene, a third-generation oral contraceptive. Most importantly, created an ERE luciferase construct widely distributed and used in the research community for a decade.

Jennifer I. MacGregor-Schafer, Northwestern University, Department of Defense Graduate Student Training Program, Chicago, IL, 1995—2001

- MacGregor et al. [37]
- MacGregor et al. [38]
- MacGregor et al. [39]

Advanced the understanding of SERM-ER complex relationships, proving that a new nonsteroidal "pure antiestrogen" EM-652 was actually a raloxifene look-a-like binding in the ER. The hypothesis for Jennifer to test was the result of Dr Hiro Takei (an associate professor of surgery visiting from Japan), making me a slide of the published orientation of raloxifene in the ligand-binding domain of the ER in 1998. During the presentation of my lecture, I turned to look at the slide on the screen and realized that EM-652, which had previously always been classified as a "pure antiestrogen"; was actually raloxifene-like when redrawn upside-down and backward. Later, EM-800 was confirmed to be a SERM that maintained bone density in rats. No surprises in the conversation with Nature here! Created the JM-6 (Jennifer MacGregor, naturally) stably transfected cell line with Asp351Gly ER in MDA-MB-231 cells. Proved that the surface of the ligand-binding domain can communicate with AF-1 (previously this had not been thought to happen) and provided a tool for enabling subclassification of planar estrogens (class I) and bulky nonplanar estrogens (class II). In our lab-speak of the original crocodile model, jaws (helix 12) closed and jaws opened, respectively. Simultaneously created the first tamoxifen-resistant cell line with ER-positiveT47D cells in athymic mice. Three projects all successful!

Ruth M. O'Regan, University College, Dublin, Ireland, 1996—2000 (Faculty in Medical Oncology, Northwestern University, Chicago, IL)

- O'Regan et al. [40]
- O'Regan et al. [41]
- O'Regan et al. [42]

A medical oncologist who chose to complete a Doctor of Medicine degree at University College in Dublin through research published from work completed in my laboratory. Three clinically relevant publications; each had practical applications in therapeutics and health care for cancer patients. The use of raloxifene after adjuvant tamoxifen was controversial, but she demonstrated that it was an unwise clinical intervention.

Rita C. Dardes, Department of Obstetrics and Gynecology, University of Sao Paulo, Brazil, 1998–2001

- Dardes et al. [43]
- Dardes et al. [44]

A gynecologist from the University of Sao Paulo, Brazil, who completed her Ph.D. as the first-ever Avon International Scholar. The day I was phoned by Dr Joe Bertino (the Chair of the Landon Prize Committee) that I was to share the inaugural Dorothy P. Landon/AACR Prize with Elwood Jensen, I was in Florida, invited to attend a global meeting of Avon managers and have dinner with their CEO, Andrea Jung (Fig. 17.1). During the dinner in the evening, I was introduced as "the father of tamoxifen" and asked to suggest to the audience how cancer research

FIGURE 17.1

A photograph of Dr. Rita Dardes (left) and CEO of Avon Andrea Jung (right) celebrating at an Avon event in Brazil.

could be advanced by Avon. You have to be able to think on your feet as you walk to the podium! I stated that they should sponsor young researchers coming to America for research who would return to their countries, where they could be supported and enhance progress in cancer treatment in their countries. I spoke to the Avon audience of Rita, not knowing that Brazil was Avon's second-largest market in the world. She became the first success as an official Avon Scholar. I traveled to Sao Paulo to witness her public Ph.D. examination. Her successful translational research identified her as a talented medical scientist back in Brazil, where she became the Medical Director for Women's Health at the Avon Institute, as well as a successful clinician and adjunct Professor and Vice Chair at the Federal University of Sao Paulo. Others, subsequently, advanced the idea to the AACR to establish a major formal program of travel to America for scientific training and return to their country of origin.

Philipp Y. Maximov, N.I. Pirogov Russian National Medical Research University, Russia, 2006–10

- Maximov et al. [45]
- Maximov et al. [46]

The first creation of ER-negative cell lines containing the transfected wild-type ER gene (S. Y. Jiang), the discovery of the natural mutant ER Asp351 Tyr (D. Wolf), the transfection of this gene into ER-negative cell lines (W.C. Catherino), and adaptation to be an Asp351Gly ER transfected into an ER-negative cell line (J. MacGregor-Schafer) all ultimately resulted in the creation of a new classification of natural and synthetic estrogens based on planarity. These advances with laboratory models converged to discover that the shape of the estrogen-ER complex is the controlling factor in E2-induced apoptosis. I traveled to Moscow to witness his public Ph.D. examination. He survived an onslaught from a chairman of pharmacology, who felt that it was all too advanced and outside the scope of their expertise to be examined. He responded magnificently (all of this was being conducted in Russian to a filled lecture hall), and the 20-member committee voted overwhelmingly in Philipp's favor, with only one dissent. He continued his research at the Lombardi Comprehensive Cancer Center as a Susan G Komen for the Cure Foundation International Postdoctoral Fellow and as an assistant professor (research) of Breast Medical Oncology Department at the MD Anderson Cancer Center. His research theme was advanced by two subsequent graduate student, Ifeyinwa Obiorah and Elizabeth Sweeney, both supported by scholarships from the Susan G Komen for the Cure Foundation. He is currently a research assistant professor, Department of Breast Medical Oncology at the MD Anderson Cancer Center, Houston, TX.

Ifeyinwa Obiorah, Department of Oncology, V.T. Lombardi Comprehensive Cancer Center, Georgetown University, Washington, DC 2010 14

- Obiorah et al. [47]
- Obiorah et al. [48]

- Obiorah and Jordan [49]
- Obiorah et al. [50]

Ifeyinwa Obiorah graduated from the top medical school in Nigeria (British System) and, following further education in the United Kingdom, where she obtained a master's degree, she successfully applied to the graduate program at the Lombardi Comprehensive Cancer Center at Georgetown University, Washington, DC. She was the first to document the time courses of estradiol and bisphenol, and contrast these data with cytotoxic chemotherapy in LTED ER-positive breast cancer. She is currently an Assistant Professor, Attending Physician, Department of Pathology, University of Virginia School of Medicine.

Elizabeth Sweeney, Department of Oncology, V.T. Lombardi Comprehensive Cancer Center, Georgetown University, Washington, DC 2011—14

- Sweeney et al. [51]
- Sweeney et al. [52]
- Sweeney et al. [53]

Focused on an interrogation of models and mechanisms of antihormone resistance in breast cancer following long-term estrogen deprivation. The work provided the first evidence that estrogen-induced apoptosis in breast cancer could be reversed by the glucocorticoid action of medroxyprogesterone acetate used as HRT in the Women's Health Initiative.

Balkees Abderrahman, Department of Breast Medical Oncology, University of Texas, MD, Anderson Cancer Center/ University of Leeds, split site model C applicants of very high quality (inaugural candidate) 2017—20

- Abderrahman and Jordan [54]
- Abderrahman and Jordan [55]
- Abderrahman et al. [56]
- Abderrahman et al. [57]

Aside from her Ph.D. requirements above, she published a further 30 contributions to the scientific and medical literature. She had the distinction of being the first at MD Anderson to be named as a Forbes 30 under 30. She was selected for attendance at the Nobel Laureates congregation at Lindau, Germany, 2021, and was selected as a panelist with Nobel Laureates and members of Nobel Organization. She was invited to submit a paper for publication by the Nobel Foundation.

References

[1] Jordan VC, Dix CJ, Allen KE. The effectiveness of long term tamoxifen treatment in a laboratory model for adjuvant hormone therapy of breast cancer. In: Salmon SE, Jones SE, editors. Adjuvant therapy of cancer II. Philadelphia: Grune & Stratton; 1979. p. 19−26.

[2] Dix CJ, Jordan VC. Subcellular effects of mono-hydroxy-tamoxifen in the rat uterus: steroid receptors and mitosis. J Endocrinol 1980;85:393−404.

[3] Dix CJ, Jordan VC. Modulation of rat uterine steroid hormone receptors by estrogen and antiestrogen. Endocrinology 1980;107:2011−20.

[4] Tate AC, Greene GL, DeSombre ER, Jensen E, Jordan VC. Differences between estrogen- and antiestrogen-estrogen receptor complexes identified with an antibody raised against the estrogen receptor. Cancer Res 1984;44:1012−8.

[5] Tate AC, Jordan VC. Nuclear [^{3}H]4-hydroxytamoxifen (4-OHTAM) and [^{3}H] estradiol (E$_2$)-estrogen receptor complexes in the MCF-7 breast cancer and GH3 pituitary tumor cell lines. Mol Cell Endocrinol 1984;36:211−9.

[6] Jordan VC, Tate AC, Lyman SD, Gosden B, Wolf M, Bain RR, Welshons WV. Rat uterine growth and induction of progesterone receptor without estrogen receptor translocation. Endocrinology 1985;116:1845−57.

[7] Lyman SD, Jordan VC. Metabolism of tamoxifen and its uterotrophic activity. Biochem Pharmacol 1985;34:2787−94.

[8] Lyman SD, Jordan VC. Possible mechanisms for the agonist actions of tamoxifen and the antagonist actions of MER-25 (ethamoxytriphetol) in the mouse uterus. Biochem Pharmacol 1985;34:2795−806.

[9] Cormier EM, Jordan VC. Contrasting ability of antiestrogens to inhibit MCF-7 growth stimulated by estradiol or epidermal growth factor. Eur J Cancer Clin Oncol 1989;25: 57−63.

[10] Cormier EM, Wolf MF, Jordan VC. Decrease in estradiol-stimulated progesterone receptor production in MCF-7 cells by epidermal growth factor and possible clinical implication for paracrine-regulated breast cancer growth. Cancer Res 1989;49:576−80.

[11] Gottardis MM, Jordan VC. The antitumor actions of keoxifene (raloxifene) and tamoxifen in the N-nitrosomethylurea-induced rat mammary carcinoma model. Cancer Res 1987;47:4020−4.

[12] Gottardis MM, Robinson SP, Satyaswaroop PG, Jordan VC. Contrasting actions of tamoxifen on endometrial and breast tumor growth in the athymic mouse. Cancer Res 1988;48:812−5.

[13] Gottardis MM, Jordan VC. Development of tamoxifen-stimulated growth of MCF-7 tumors in athymic mice after long-term antiestrogen administration. Cancer Res 1988;48: 5183−7.

[14] Gottardis MM, Jiang SY, Jeng MH, Jordan VC. Inhibition of tamoxifen-stimulated growth of an MCF-7 tumor variant in athymic mice by novel steroidal antiestrogens. Cancer Res 1989;49:4090−3.

[15] Murphy CS, Meisner LF, Wu SQ, Jordan VC. Short-and long-term estrogen deprivation of T47D human breast cancer cells in culture. Eur J Cancer Clin Oncot 1989;25: 1777−88.

[16] Murphy CS, Langan-Fahey SM, Mccague R, Jordan VC. Structure-function relationships of hydroxylated metabolites of tamoxifen that control the proliferation of estrogen-responsive T47D breast cancer cells in vitro. Mol Pharmacol 1990;38:737−43.

[17] Murphy CS, Parker CJ, McCague R, Jordan VC. Structure/activity relationships of non-isomerizable derivatives of tamoxifen: importance of hydroxyl group and side chain positioning for biological activity. Mol Pharmacol 1991;39:421—8.

[18] Jeng MH, Jordan VC. Growth stimulation and differential regulation ofTGFβl,TGFβ2 andTGFβ3 mRNA levels by norethindrone in MCF-7 human breast cancer cells. Mol Endocrinol 1991;5:1120—8.

[19] Jeng MH, Parker CJ, Jordan VC. Estrogenic potential of progestins in oral contraceptives to stimulate human breast cancer cell proliferation. Cancer Res 1992;52:6539—46.

[20] Jeng MH, Langan-Fahey SM, Jordan VC. Estrogenic actions of RU486 in hormone-responsive MCF-7 human breast cancer cells. Endocrinology 1993;132:2622—30.

[21] Jeng MH, Jiang SY, Jordan VC. Paradoxical regulation of estrogen-dependent growth factor gene expression in estrogen receptor (ER)-negative human breast cancer cells stably express-ing ER. Cancer Lett 1994;82:123—8.

[22] Jiang SY, Jordan VC. Growth regulation of estrogen receptor-negative breast cancer cells transfected with cDNA's for estrogen receptor. J Natl Cancer Inst 1992;84:580—91.

[23] Jiang SY, Wolf DM, Yingling JM, Chang C, Jordan VC. An estrogen receptor-positive MCF-7 clone that is resistant to antiestrogens and estradiol. Mot Cell Endocrinol 1992;90:77—80.

[24] Pink JJ, Jiang SY, Fritsch M, Jordan VC. An estrogen-independent MCF-7 breast cancer cell line which contains a novel 80-kilodalton estrogen receptor-related protein. Cancer Res 1995;55:2583—90.

[25] Wolf DM, Langan-Fahey SM, Parker CJ, McCague R, Jordan VC. Investigation of the mechanism of tamoxifen-stimulated breast tumor growth with non-isomerizable analogs of tamoxifen and metabolites. J Natl Cancer Inst 1993;85:806—12.

[26] Wolf DM, Jordan VC. The estrogen receptor from a tamoxifen-stimulated MCF-7 tumor variant contains a point mutation in the ligand-binding domain. Breast Cancer Res Treat 1994;31:129—38.

[27] Wolf DM, Jordan VC. A laboratory model to explain the survival advantage observed in patients taking adjuvant tamoxifen therapy. Recent Results Cancer Res 1993;127:23—33.

[28] Murphy C, Pink JJ, Jordan VC. Characterization of a receptor-negative, hormone-nonresponsive clone derived from T47D human breast cancer cell line kept under estrogen-free conditions. Cancer Res 1990;50:7285—92.

[29] Pink JJ, Jiang SY, Fritsch M, Jordan VC. An estrogen-independent MCF-7 breast cancer cell line which contains a novel 80-kilodalton estrogen receptor-related protein. Cancer Res 1995;55:2583—90.

[30] Pink JJ, Wu SQ, Wolf DM, Bilimoria MM, Jordan VC. A novel 80-kilodalton human estrogen receptor containing a duplication of exons 6 and 7. Nucleic Acids Res 1996;24:962—9.

[31] Pink JJ, Jordan VC. Models of estrogen receptor regulation by estrogens and antiestrogens in breast cancer cell lines. Cancer Res 1996;56:2321—30.

[32] Pink JJ, Bilimoria MM, Assikis VJ, Jordan VC. Irreversible loss of the estrogen receptor in T47D breast cancer cells following prolonged estrogen deprivation. Br J Cancer 1996;74:1227—36.

[33] Pink JJ, Fritsch M, Bilimoria MM, Assikis VJ, Jordan VC. Cloning and characterization of a 77-kilodalton estrogen receptor isolated from a human breast cancer cell line. Br J Cancer 1997;75:17—27.

[34] Catherino WH, Jeng MH, Jordan VC. Norgestrel and gestodene stimulate breast cancer cell growth through an estrogen receptor-mediated mechanism. Br J Cancer 1993;67: 945−52.

[35] Catherino WH, Jordan VC. Increasing the number of tandem estrogen response elements increases the estrogenic activity of a tamoxifen analogue. Cancer Lett 1995; 92:39−47.

[36] Catherino WH, Wolf DM, Jordan VC. A naturally occurring estrogen receptor mutation results in increased estrogenicity of a tamoxifen analog. Mol Endocrinol 1995;9: 1053−63.

[37] MacGregor JI, Liu H, Tonetti DA, Jordan VC. The interaction of raloxifene and the active metabolite of the antiestrogen EM-800 with the human estrogen receptor (ER). Cancer Res 1999;59:4308−13.

[38] MacGregor-Schafer JI, Liu H, Bentrem D, Zapf J, Jordan VC. Allosteric silencing of activating function 1 in the 4-hydroxytamoxifen-estrogen receptor complex by substituting glycine for aspartate at amino acid 351. Cancer Res 2000;60:5097−105.

[39] MacGregor-Schafer JI, Lee E-S, O'Regan RM, Yao K, Jordan VC. Rapid development of tamoxifen-stimulated mutant p53 breast tumors (T47D) in athymic mice. Clin Cancer Res 2000;6:4373−80.

[40] O'Regan R, Cisneros A, England GM, MacGregor JI, Muenzer HD, Assikis VJ, Bilimoria MM, Piette M, Dragan YP, Pitot HC, Chatterton R, Jordan VC. Effects of the antiestrogens, tamoxifen, toremifene and ICI 182,780, on endometrial cancer growth in vivo. J Natl Cancer Inst 1998;90:1552−8.

[41] O'Regan RM, Gajdos C, Dardes RC, De Los Reyes A, Park W, Rademaker AW, Jordan VC. Effects of raloxifene after tamoxifen on breast and endometrial tumor growth in athymic mice. J Natl Cancer Inst 2002;94:274−83.

[42] O'Regan RM, Osipo C, Ariazi E, Lee ES, Meeke K, Morris C, Bertucci A, Sarker MAB, Grigg R, Jordan VC. Development and therapeutic options for the treatment of raloxifene-stimulated breast cancer in athymic mice. Clin Cancer Res 2006;12: 2255−63.

[43] Dardes RC, Bentrem D, O'Regan RM, MacGregor-Schafer J, Jordan VC. Effects of the new selective estrogen receptor modulator LY353381.HCl (arzoxifene) on human endometrial cancer growth in athymic mice. Clin Cancer Res 2001;7:4149−55.

[44] Dardes RC, O'Regan R, Gajdos C, Robinson SP, Bentrem D, de los Reyes A, Jordan VC. Effects of a new clinically relvant anti-estrogen (GW 5638) related to tamoxifen on breast and endometrial cancer growth in vivo. Clin Cancer Res 2002;8: 1995−2001.

[45] Maximov PY, Myers CB, Curpan RF, Lewis-Wambi JS, Jordan VC. Structure-function relationships of estrogenic triphenylethylenes related to endoxifen and 4-hydroxytamoxifen. J Med Chem 2010;53:3273−83.

[46] Maximov P, Sengupta S, Lewis-Wambi JS, Kim HR, Curpan RF, Jordan VC. The conformation of the estrogen receptor directs estrogen- induced apoptosis in breast cancer: a hypothesis. Horm Mol Biol Clin Invest 2011;5:27−34.

[47] Obiorah IO, Sengupta S, Fan P, Jordan VC. Delayed triggering of oestrogen-induced apoptosis that contrasts with rapid paclitaxel-induced breast cancer cell death. Br J Cancer 2014;110:1488−96.

[48] Obiorah IO, Sengupta S, Curpan R, Jordan VC. Defining the conformation of the estrogen receptor complex that controls estrogen-induced apoptosis in breast cancer. Mol Pharmacol 2014;85:789−99.

[49] Obiorah IO, Jordan VC. Differences in the rate of oestrogen-induced apoptosis by oestradiol and the triphenylethylene bisphenol. Br J Pharmacol 2014;171:4062−72.

[50] Obiorah IO, Fan P, Jordan VC. Breast cancer cell apoptosis with phytoestrogens is dependent on an oestrogen-deprived state. Cancer Prev Res 2014;7:939−49.

[51] Sweeney EE, McDaniel RE, Maximov PY, Fan P, Jordan VC. Models and mechanisms of acquired antihormone resistance in breast cancer: significant clinical progress despite limitations. Horm Mol Biol Clin Invest 2012;9:143−63.

[52] Sweeney EE, Fan P, Jordan VC. Mechanisms underlying differential response to estrogen-induced apoptosis in long-term estrogen-deprived breast cancer cells. Int J Oncol 2014;44:1529−37.

[53] Sweeney EE, Fan P, Jordan VC. Molecular modulation of estrogen-induced apoptosis by synthetic progestins in hormone replacement therapy: an insight into the Women's Health Initiative study. Cancer Res 2014;74:7060−8.

[54] Abderrahman B, Jordan VC. Successful targeted therapies for breast cancer: the Worcester Foundation and future opportunities in women's health. Endocrinology 2018;159:2980−90.

[55] Abderrahman B, Jordan VC. Hormones and cancer, textbook of cancer biology (Pezzella, Tauccodi, and Kerr). Oxford University Press; 2019. p. 123−35.

[56] Abderrahman B, Maximov PY, Curpan RF, Hanspal JS, Fan P, Xiong R, Tonetti DA, Thatcher GRJ, Jordan VC. Pharmacology and molecular mechanisms in clinically-relevant estrogen estetrol and selective estrogen mimic BMI-135 for the treatment of endocrine-resistant breast cancer. Mol Pharmacol 2020;98:354−81.

[57] Abderrahman B, Maximov PY, Curpan RF, Fanning SW, Hanspal JS, Fan P, Foulds CE, Chen Y, Malovannaya A, Jain A, Xiong R, Greene GL, Tonetti DA, Thatcher GRJ, Jordan VC. Rapid induction of the unfolded protein response and apoptosis by estrogen mimic TTC-352 for the treatment of endocrine-resistant breast cancer. Mol Cancer Therapeut 2021;20:11−25.

Case studies: in their own words

Here I have invited several of my past members of my Tamoxifen Teams, over the past 50 years, to express their personal views of their experiences as a trainee, balanced with what they now know of the "outside world" in academia or the pharmaceutical industry. Their experience is the living testimony of what can be achieved by the investment of Federal competitive research funding and philanthropic organizations at the national or local levels. The goal of our research endeavors is the benefit to Society of lives saved, and families not being fractured by the death of a parent or grandparent. The other fundamental benefit from successful work on cancer treatments is the economic benefits to Society with thriving businesses and employment for hundreds of thousands of citizens. This research benefits our Society and creates economic security!

For my own laboratory, over 50 years, we competed successfully for $30 million-worth of Federal funding and attracted $35 million in philanthropic funding. However, a special thanks is necessary for Dr. Roy Cotton of ICI Pharmaceuticals Division in the 1970s for 6 years of free rats from ICI to create the translational research strategies of long-term adjuvant tamoxifen therapy and chemoprevention. He also provided a Scholarship for Clive Dix and Anna Riegel at Leeds University.

The success of our translational research in the United States, based on Federal funding, resulted in the American Association for the Advancement of Science to identify my contribution to the Nation with an award announced on the September 22, 2021. This award called "the Golden Goose Award" (that lays Golden Eggs) recognizes those, who are federally funded for an "improbable idea" that ultimately benefits Society. In my case, the study of "failed contraceptives" to be reinvented as applied to a lifesaving strategy came in two instalments: (1) long-term adjuvant tamoxifen treatment for patients with an ER-positive primary breast cancer and the direct use of tamoxifen to reduce the risk of breast cancer in high-risk women and (2) the discovery of selective ER modulators (SERMs) in my laboratory with a published plan of how SERMs could prevent multiple diseases in a single pill (breast cancer, osteoporosis, coronary heart disease, endometrial cancer) [Lerner L and Jordan VC (1980) Cancer Res]. All this came to pass by the translational research clinical trials conducted by others [Maximov PY et al. (2013), Curr Clin Pharmacol].

Tamoxifen Tales. https://doi.org/10.1016/B978-0-323-85051-3.00018-X

Clive James Dix, Ph.D.

I was fortunate to be Craig Jordan's first Ph.D. student. While I was an undergraduate in the Department of Pharmacology at Leeds University, I chose one of Craig's undergraduate projects and therefore experienced the excitement of working in a laboratory where the research was both cutting edge and applied to solving an important health problem, breast cancer.

Craig persuaded me to stay at Leeds to do my Ph.D. At the start of this journey, Craig gave me a rousing lecture on his philosophy with regard to research and mentoring. My initial thought, being young and carefree, was this might have been a mistake this guy is a — (unpublishable word). How wrong could I have been. Craig's philosophy was that every student should excel and achieve more than he does. A hard act to follow and one most of us probably won't achieve but certainly a philosophy that has also held me in good stead.

This philosophy and Craig's attention to scientific rigor has been a real foundation for my career. I took these teachings into my postdoctoral years as a researcher at the bench. After 6 years, I chose to join industry, and by applying my learnings in what seemed no time at all, I was appointed Director of Research at Glaxo Wellcome. I then moved into the biotech sector as Senior VP of R&D at Powder Ject plc where I started understanding how smaller companies worked and how I could apply my experience and philosophy to good effect.

This encouraged me to stretch myself, and in 2004, I entered the world of Venture Capital—funded startups and raised £20m to form PowderMed, a company developing DNA vaccines to help some of the world's problems with infectious diseases. In 2006, Pfizer acquired this company. I am now considered a serial entrepreneur having started or help run five startup companies and giving them my experience to help them to success. In this age of coronavirus, biotechnology has become the key strategy to create novel vaccines—in fact, more rapidly than ever before. I was honored to be invited to be the Chair of the Coronavirus Vaccines Committee providing advice for the British Government at this dangerous time throughout the world.

Importantly throughout my career to date, I have made the success of others central to my philosophy and therefore my success. This I believe stems from my time under the tutelage of Craig Jordan to whom I and many other people owe an enormous debt of gratitude, especially those who have benefitted from tamoxifen.

Anna Riegel, Ph.D.

I met Craig when I was an undergraduate at Leeds University, United Kingdom, in the 1970s. I had several outstanding lectures from him in pharmacology and found his research on antiestrogens and their potential use in breast cancer very interesting. I was extremely lucky to undertake my senior year thesis with him, since there was a lot of competition to work in his lab, and this turned out to be a choice that changed my life. It was in those weeks in Craig's lab in Leeds, studying how antiestrogens bound to the estrogen receptor, which I found my passion for research and a new and enduring direction for my life. I recall Craig's massive enthusiasm and inspira-

tional speeches and his larger-than-life energy that was at odds with the somewhat laconic atmosphere of the rest of the department. I was not surprised when Craig announced that he was taking a position in the United States at the University of Wisconsin Madison. However, I was surprised and incredibly honored when he asked me to join him as a graduate student. With Craig's help, I had successfully applied for a Fulbright-Hays scholarship, so I was off to America!

It was with trepidation that I embarked on the Ph.D. program in Oncology run by the McArdle Laboratories. This was the flagship Oncology program in the US boasting researchers such as Howard Temin and James and Betty Miller. It was an intimidating and inspiring environment. In hindsight, I realize that I wouldn't have survived the Ph.D. experience without Craig's mentorship and his steadfast belief that I could make it. I recall many moments when I hit bumps in the road and Craig was always there with guidance and advice. I published five papers from my Ph.D. work with Craig and more importantly gained from him the skills and the most solid foundation for a future academic scientific career. I have always tried to emulate his mentoring example when training my own graduate students.

I left Wisconsin and went to postdoctoral fellowships at NIH and then onto a faculty position at Georgetown University. I am currently the Cecilia Rudman Fisher Endowed Professor in Breast Cancer Research and Education, Director of Cancer Research Education in Lombardi Cancer Center, and Senior Associate Dean of Biomedical Graduate Education. My research is in the regulation of nuclear receptor coactivators in breast cancer. Craig became a colleague at the Lombardi Cancer Center, and we were once again working together on projects related to estrogen effects in breast cancer. In recognition of his work on antiestrogens and their impact on the lives of thousands of women, Craig is now a member of the National Academy of Sciences. Despite the many demands on his time, it is gratifying to observe that Craig is still training and inspiring graduate students with an undiminished energy and enthusiasm.

Marco Gottardis, Ph.D.
Survival for the scientist in Big Pharma, biotech, and beyond
Introduction

When Craig Jordan asked me to write about my experiences for survival in science, as I thought through the history of my career over the past 25 years, it became instantly clear the events and messages that I wanted to impart to the reader. As practice, I have had literally over a hundred students and trainees ask me: "What does it take to succeed in science, specifically, in industry?" My answers to folks have frankly evolved over the years, as the landscape of science and the pharmaceutical industry have changed and continued to change quite rapidly. So I will focus for you the observations I have made that I believe are standards in the face of changes within industry as part of the narrative of my career progression.

Beginnings

Back in the 1980s at Columbia College, I was sure that I wanted to be in science. I was always the lab rat, even in those early days, setting up Biology course experiments at the University as part of my work study program scholarship. I enjoyed being in the lab night and day, and my advisor gave me a job in her yeast genetics lab at Columbia with a project of investigating the various subforms of the maltase enzyme in yeast. Here I first learned the scientific method, and she shocked me one day by saying she wanted to sign over the whole lab to me. I was puzzled but then she explained that being an orthodox Jew she could not own or possess yeast or leavened products during Passover. I was so pleased that she chose me as the resident Gentile to entrust with this duty. My project went very well, and although I did not get my first authorship, I was mentioned in the acknowledgments.

My second brush with the realities of science was in my Inorganic Chemistry Course during my laboratory practical. My professor was an odd quirky duck who had an abnormal fear of people cheating on his exams. When you took his course, you had to sign a contract that you would not cheat on his exams. In one instance, he chased a student, who had come to complain about his grade onto a window ledge outside his office. Our practical exam involved mixing salts solutions that were blinded to us. We mixed them and matched the precipitates to our exam list. Two of the unknowns on the list were identified as water and hydrogen peroxide. I quickly went through my analysis, and I had correctly identified all of these in the lab practical exam (as I later found out). As I waited at my lab bench for the final to complete, I got bored and had the bright idea that another way you could distinguish the H_2O_2 from H_2O was by putting it on a scab and seeing which one would fizz. I showed my examination preceptor this observation, but I did not see the professor lurking in the background. After the exam, the preceptor said that the professor wanted to see me. I went to his office, and he dropped a bombshell on me telling me he was deciding whether to have me expelled or fail the course because I had cheated on my exam. He would think about my fate over the weekend and tell me on Monday.

This was one of the worst weekends I spent in my life. I told my parents and my father said he wanted to come with me to talk to the professor. We got there on Monday, and after some initial conversation, my father asked if he could speak to the Professor alone. Just to describe my dad to you, he had forearms like the cartoon character Popeye. He was actually a gentle man but an imposing physical specimen which came from years of being a brick mason. Surprisingly, at my dad's insistence, they compromised and he reduced me one grade step from A− to B+. My dad told me that the professor thought it was quite clever that I had thought this "test" up, but in his opinion it was not in the "spirit" of the exam. I learned the next year that he had told his students how he had expelled a student (me) for cheating on his exam the previous year. He amended the cheating contract to forbid the students from using any body parts or fluids during his exams!

After I completed University, I did not know exactly what kind of career I wanted in science. The whole thing was still very glamorous to me as I took a technical position at Columbia Presbyterian Medical School in the Department of Reproductive Endocrinology. In vitro fertilization was the new big thing, and people were flocking to the Department for fertility treatments as it was one of the big centers in the world with many star faculty. I met, drew blood, and performed hormonal assays for movie stars, celebrities, and even queens of nations. There was one instance that, as a favor, I ran some clinical samples for a well-known actress over a holiday while she was in London. In gratitude, she brought me a Burburry raincoat as a gift for my efforts. It was totally unexpected, but it was something that put a smile on my face for weeks. I thought to myself, "This science business is really exciting!"

More importantly, it was at Columbia where I learned animal pharmacology, a skill set, that would set me apart from many others throughout my career. I was responsible for pharmacology experiments and testing the effects of various fertility treatments in primates. Part of my role was performing a new test measuring peptide and steroidal hormones called a radioimmunoassay. It sounds quite primitive now, and it has largely been replaced by ELISAs and other nonradioactive methods, but it was at the cutting edge at the time. It is an important lesson to learn that techniques come and go, but actual disciplines such as pharmacology, computational statistics, immunology, and cancer biology are important. Techniques are just a method or a stepping stone to the next experiment and should only be regarded as part of one's tool kit. During my time at Columbia, it was the first time that I worked with a compound called tamoxifen, and it would not be the last time.

Into the great white open …. (apologies to Tom Petty)

After my 1-year stint at Columbia, for personal reasons, my future wife and I decided to go to the University of Wisconsin, Madison, to continue my career in Science and her career in Law and Economics. I applied for another technical position at the University of Wisconsin Clinical Cancer Center (UWCCC) working in the laboratory of David Rose on the Endocrinology of Breast Cancer. The UWCCC was one of the premier cancer centers at that time with a number of established and rising stars (one in particular will be mentioned soon). UWCCC was a perfect fit for me from the experience I had at Columbia. I was grateful for the techniques I had learned that got me my first lab job at Wisconsin under Dr. David Rose, and for the first time, I obtained authorship on several papers. I still did not know what I really wanted to do with my career. Did I want to stay as a technician, go to grad school, or take another path in the field of research? It was a crossroad and a defining moment for me from both a professional and a personal side. I was getting a divorce and David Rose was moving his laboratory to New York City. It was then Dr. Craig Jordan came into my life. He was a rising professor at UWCCC and already a noted leader in the field of antiestrogens such as tamoxifen. He was 34. There was something about Craig that was different from a lot of the scientists I met. He was outgoing and carried himself with much purpose and determination. Most importantly, folks were very happy to work in his group, and there was electricity in the air that important things were happening in his lab. I saw he was highly demonstrative in motivating folks, and at the same time, he deeply cared about them. He assimilated David's Lab, during this time, and sat down with me in the Cafeteria of the Cancer Center to talk to me about what my options were in his lab. I will never forget this conversation as long as I live. He asked me point blank: "Was I prepared to take the next step in my life?" I replied by asking him what he meant by that statement. He stated to me that he knew I had the scientific talent and makeup to enter the doctorate program. He understood that I was going through a hard time but was I ready to show what I could do. He had the confidence in me that I would succeed. Here began a long mentoring friendship that survives to this day.

Graduate school discovery

I began my course work at the Cancer Center and continued in the laboratory on a new project that Craig had set out for me that would form the basis of my thesis. I found out that I had an advantage over most of the other students that my experience as a technician allowed me to dive right into my project. As a graduate student, I learned to bear down on my work more than I ever had in my life. Craig instilled in me a very strong work ethic which I have carried throughout my career. His "work or die" speech was something that I always remember and his metaphors taken from history really spoke to me. It was probably the only lab that had the complete set of Winston Churchill's A History of the English Speaking Peoples.

Craig taught me that being a successful scientist involved collaborations across labs, advocacy groups, and industry. At first, I did not grasp why he wanted me to meet this Professor or work with this lab, but I came to understand that success in science revolved around putting yourself out there and networking. With all his students, he fostered these collaborations and taught us the art of presenting our work. His methodologies I have used throughout my career to this day, whether I am giving a talk to 10 or to 1000 people. I finally started to understand for the first time what it meant to work in medical science and how important it was for people.

Working one day on the weekend at the Cancer Center as I usually did, a frail grandmotherly woman peered into my lab as I was working. I looked at her in her hospital bed clothes and noticed for the first time the IV pole that she was shepherding alongside her. We started a series of conversations over the next few months each weekend. She told me she was a late-stage breast cancer patient and was ready to go through bone marrow transplantation, a now discontinued practice in breast cancer treatment. She was very inquisitive of my work, and we spoke at length of my project and her family of grandchildren. It was then it hit home that what we do in the lab can change people's lives, and it is a great responsibility we hold to do our best to succeed in our work. My friend would tell me about her treatment and her hopes for the future, and she would cajole me every visit to work hard because people needed us to succeed. After a while, the visits stopped, but her memory still burns in my mind. Thereafter, in my leadership roles, I told folks on my team that I only wanted those working with me that understood this was more than a job. The total amount of academic and industry research dollars is always finite, and it is a great responsibility we all bear in our work in translational research in that it affects lives.

Toward the end of my graduate studies, I was completing a large study for Craig looking at tumor stasis with tamoxifen in animal models. I had spent the last year setting up the athymic mouse facility which was also cutting-edge technology at the time. Craig and I expected the experiment to show that you could keep these breast tumors in check with tamoxifen and then reactivate them when you took away the drug. This was Craig's dogma at the time based on his experiments with carcinogen-induced rat mammary cancer in the 1970s. To my surprise, the tamoxifen-treated animals started to breakthrough and grow. Craig at the time thought I had cocked up an expensive experiment and he laid into me that I had mixed up the groups. He ordered me to repeat the experiment. While this was going on, we noticed that a competitor had done a similar experiment and reported the tamoxifen-induced growth despite treatment resistance. We repeated the result and established in subsequent experiments that the growth was actually tamoxifen driven, not resistance. This opened up a large new area of research for the lab and taught me not to force conclusions but to realize where they are taking you. Years later, another graduate student, Doug Wolf, found that these tamoxifen-stimulated tumors could be paradoxically inhibited by estrogen, the major hormonal driver of breast cancer. Goes to show you that one must follow the science where you least expect it, to be the most successful scientist you can be.

Postdoctoral blues

After I graduated at the University of Wisconsin, I got an appointment at Georgetown University in Washington, DC, under the leadership of Marc Lipmann. I spent

4 years at the Lombardi Cancer Center at Georgetown University, where I was immersed in a group that was filled with breast cancer research stars that had moved with Marc from the NIH. The laboratory was large, and the competition was fierce. I worked with Mary Beth Martin on the estrogen receptor and first felt the pain of how experiments and projects do not always go as planned. I was lucky that everything went so smoothly when I was in graduate school and I realized then this was not the norm. I did enjoy the environment, and I kept to most of the doctrine of how to succeed in science from my experiences in grad school. I still have many close friends from that postdoctoral period and came to understand that establishing one's self from the security of grad school was a difficult thing. I plodded through publishing several papers and was nearing the end of my third year when I received a job offer in San Diego at a biotech. I went to tell Marc that I was leaving, and he asked me if I was sure I was making the right decision. Marc was very supportive of all his people, and he had a notable history of both developing their careers and keeping them in his group. I will never forget what he told me which on that day. "Go and be a leader." It was never my goal to be a manager of a large group of researchers, but he predicted correctly my path. As I prepared for our relocation to San Diego at LIGAND Pharmaceuticals, I reflected on my postdoctoral experience. I came to realize more and more that my interests in science were drawn to the translational side of research and that industry was the right choice for me.

The wild wild west of biotech

When I arrived at LIGAND, the company was buzzing with excitement because it has just gone public. It was heralded as one of the premier biotech companies in San Diego both from the promise of its nuclear receptor research platform and from the fact that it had hired wisely a mixture of veteran academic leaders and experienced Big Pharma functional area leaders. David Robinson was touted as one of the best biotech CEOs, and the underlying science derived from the founder Ron Evans from the Salk Institute was cutting edge. All the seeds were there for this company to become, we all hoped, the next Genentech.

It was an exciting time for me, I was asked to manage a small group of scientists and also manage the animal facility. At the time, we were in the midst of several alliances with major Pharma, and we also were filing several INDs for our lead drug candidates. In the first couple of years, I became immersed in the drug discovery process and learned a lot about what it took to put a drug into development. I had several mentors during my time at LIGAND Scott Hayes, my supervisor, and Dave Robertson, my CSO, whom I thank for mentoring me during this time and becoming lifelong friends. I mention those individuals because it is important in industry to maintain a network of mentors and people you can rely on for advice. These folks and others had a wealth of information for me because they had been through all the battles and victories during long and successful careers at LILLY. I learned from them the importance of mentoring my people in industry and the duty I had to them in developing their careers.

LIGAND was a frantic place, and we were rushing to beat the timelines of funding in accordance with the expectations of the financial community on our progress. In 5 years, I went through many scientific projects from ER, AR, RAR, PR, and RXR. I came to understand that success was not based on focusing on one small area of science, but you were expected to quickly move on to the next project that was more promising at the pleasure of the company. After being a part of some successful drug registrations at LIGAND, I came to realize that in biotech there is a constant change in a company and a natural evolution that occurs from a focus on research to one of development of the drugs on which you are working. For a basic researcher, it can mean that research will be drastically cut or stay static over time as money is being poured in the company's clinical trials. So, in biotech, one must be nimble and realize that sometimes you need to anticipate change to stay ahead. I had a number of my colleagues at LIGAND who had been at three companies in 6 years, and this was and still is typical of biotech. However, in spite of the instability, the opportunities today I feel are still in biotech for the translational scientist. It is a great place to learn your craft, especially if you are in a company that has the mix of experienced industrial scientists who know how to do drug discovery. I knew I had to leave LIGAND when I saw the focus of the company shifting from Oncology to Metabolic Disease research. I had gotten feelers from one of the premier Oncology companies, and I jumped at the opportunity to work at Bristol-Meyers Squibb.

The Bristol days (BMS)

Bristol-Meyers Squibb had a large Oncology franchise that was based on the first billion dollar Oncology drug Taxol. The story of Taxol has been written about before, but it is a classic story of how all things fell into place to get a drug to market and how other companies passed on the same opportunity. The landscape of Big Pharma is strewn with examples of courageous individuals who make the bold and critical correct decisions, which change medical practice and course of treatment of a disease.

After I joined BMS as an associate director, it became apparent to me that BMS research was undergoing a large change in approach and scope for Oncology. The research group at BMS had not registered an in-house drug in over 10 years and they had hired, my VP of Research, Robert Kramer to turn things around. Rob was instrumental in my hire, and he taught me management of science in a large organization. I was fortunate to have Rob as my boss for almost the entire time I was at BMS and I felt the same kind of energy I felt wherever I had succeeded in the past. Our Oncology group became very productive, and it was because of our continued focus on selected areas of biology. In addition, Rob set the bar for us to judiciously hire scientists, which precipitated a change in culture that set us on a path for success. As hiring manager, it wasn't about the project a candidate was on, and it was their scientific skills and personality makeup that I focused on. In academia, I was taught to work in a team with boundaries by Craig, which is different from the "all-in" teamwork you have to have in industry. I looked for people who could collaborate and that I knew would adapt to industry quickly. I was fortunate to be able to hire many Ph.Ds. who, almost to the last, all succeeded in industry.

The most important lesson I learned at BMS was to adapt and reinvent oneself during a career in Big Pharma. It is important to manage one's career and to always visualize where you want to be 5 years hence. Self growth was a very important to me, and I prided myself in never asking a supervisor for a promotion in my entire career. I learned early on from others that my achievements would always speak for themselves. As a Director in Oncology Discovery, I never turned down opportunities for growth for myself or my reports. One of the best opportunities among these was being an early development leader for multiple assets in the clinic. In this role, you are the matrix leader of a multifunctional team that encompasses all the skills you need to drive compounds to Phase 2 in the clinic. Here, I learned much more about formulation, clinical trial design, regulatory sciences, and other disciplines. As a matrix leader, with the dotted line to your team, you have to have all these functional leaders on your team. In your capacity as their leader, you need to lead with deference to their skill sets. However, you must give them confidence that you can make the decisions to lead them to success. Matrix leadership is a prized talent in industry and is something that can be learned. It is one of the most rewarding positions you can have in industry.

Epilogue

During my last years at BMS, I rose to Executive Director and coled the Oncology Discovery Group. In the entire time I was at BMS, I always pushed myself and my group to take chances and to take on new opportunities in new areas of oncology science. I have not looked back. I took a matrix position as the Vice President of Oncology and Leader of Prostate Disease Strategy at Janssen Pharmaceuticals which I am greatly enjoying.

I hope that this narrative has given our new generation of scientific leaders some insight to what I have experienced. I believe there are few jobs in the world that have more pressure but more rewards than that of a medical researcher. As I have mentioned in this narrative, things are changing rapidly in our industry. There is consolidation that is still occurring in Big Pharma, and there is outsourcing of research jobs from Europe and the United States to emerging markets. It will be very important for those of you wanting to enter industry to understand this dynamics of this change and make yourself into the research scientist who has the skill sets, knowledge, and behaviors that are attractive to industry. I wish you all the best and much success.

Andreas Friedl, MD

I am honored to be able to contribute to this book on scientific survival. Declining resources and increasing competition have brought concerns about survival to the forefront of both research and clinical programs. I've been around long enough to know that research funding is cyclical and will eventually be more favorable. Nevertheless, in challenging times, it is easy to lose heart and to succumb to the temptation of moving to a safer career path that doesn't involve having one's life work placed at risk every 5 years. In such an environment, I believe researchers survive through perseverance and maintaining resilience, while keeping a steady eye on the goal.

I arrived in Madison when Craig had just turned 40 and was already a full professor and international leader in breast cancer research. My Professors, Maass and Jonat, from the University of Hamburg, Germany, sent me to the UW for research training, and I was expected to return after a year to complete a residency in Obstetrics and Gynecology. With a mixture of naiveté and excitement, I began work on my postdoc project on the role of "antiestrogens" in endometrial carcinoma. The goal was to test the hypothesis that tamoxifen stimulates rather than inhibits the growth of estrogen receptor positive endometrial carcinoma. To this end, we were trying to establish primary human endometrial carcinoma xenografts, which proved very difficult and frustrating. However, we obtained an endometrial carcinoma that could be serially passaged in immunodeficient mice. Curiously, the growth of this tumor was stimulated by estradiol and tamoxifen despite the fact that it was negative for estrogen receptors, which defied the model of how those agents work. This observation was reproducible in a slow-growing line of estrogen receptor negative breast carcinoma cells. Subsequently, we were able to show that the growth-promoting activity was due to hormone effects on the mouse host rather than the tumor cells directly. This experience triggered in me an interest in breast cancer—host interactions which my lab studies to this day.

The Jordan lab was a happy workplace. I remember fondly Marco, Cathy, Ethel, Chris, Mike, Meei-Huey, Shun-Yuan, Doug, and many others. We worked hard and played hard. There was a canoe trip on the Wisconsin River and many visits to the Memorial Union Terrace. A chaotic novice graduate student joined the group and ended up contaminating the entire lab with radioactivity. After this incident, he left the lab somewhat abruptly but not before introducing me to his sister Cathy, whom I married about a year later.

As planned, I returned to the University of Hamburg and began an Ob/Gyn residency. After a year, I decided to return to Madison for residency training in pathology and laboratory medicine, concluding that pathology would better allow me to continue meaningful research in the cancer field. Until Craig's departure for Northwestern University, I continued to spend elective time in his lab. After completing my residency, I signed up for another 2 years of postdoctoral work with Alan Rapraeger before becoming an assistant professor and starting my own research program at UW-Madison.

In 2011, I was appointed Chair of the Department of Pathology and Laboratory Medicine at UW-Madison and was charged with the task of leading the transition to a modern clinical department with a focus on molecular pathology, while maintaining and expanding a successful research enterprise. As a result, one of my main duties now focuses on mentoring junior colleagues and teaching them science survival skills. Here's my top 10 list of pearls of wisdom.

1. Choose your mentors wisely! Some of my mentors only reassured me how wonderfully I was doing, which didn't help me at all. In contrast, when one of my mentors, in particularly brutal fashion, pointed out the weaknesses in my work and in my grantsmanship, it wasn't pleasant, but it saved my science career. Be open to criticism and include mentors who are not afraid to tell you what you don't want to hear.

2. Be persistent! It is so easy to get discouraged and frustrated in the current science environment. As an assistant professor, I was down to my last dollars and ready to lay off my last technician when that first grant from the American Cancer Society came through. Don't give up!

3. Collaborate; seek help! Don't be shy to ask more experienced colleagues at your institution or elsewhere for help. Often, experts are right on your campus and willing to share expertise and resources.

4. Go deep! When planning a project or writing a grant, it is always tempting to cast your net wide and try to answer too many questions. Grants usually fare better if you decide to delve deep into a mechanism and focus on the most important pathway.

5. Keep it simple! Grant reviewers have a limited attention span. They will get lost in complex models and technical details. Keep it as simple as possible and get them as excited about your work as you are.

6. Seek out alternative funding sources! Creatively look for sources of funding outside the normal channels. A good friend of mine received funding from the regional Harley Davidson motorcycle club, which required him spending a weekend in a bar in Northern Wisconsin and getting drunk with a hoard of tattooed leather-clad guys and their significant others. The things we do to advance science!

7. Include translational aspects! The NIH wants to see clear evidence of diseases relevance and applicability. Try to integrate studies on human tissues or primary cells into your work. This may require talking to your local friendly pathologist.

8. Serve yourself! It is so easy to get sidetracked and sucked into time sinks like committees and other administrative tasks. For faculty with clinical responsibilities in particular, it is important to sequester time for your research. Try to come in early and work on a project for an hour or two before even opening your email or do all the other things you are supposed to accomplish that day. Maybe someday I will follow my own advice on this.

9. Review grants! I learned more about how to write a grant (and how not to write a grant) from serving on study sections for a number of years. Reviewing grants takes a lot of time, but it is time well spent.

10. Balance your life! Everybody needs something they are passionate about outside of work. For me, it's nature and photography. What is it for you?

Doug Wolf, Ph.D.

In thinking about what to include in a personal reflection on my training and career that would complement what Craig and others have contributed in the rest of this book, I decided to focus on the ways in which my experience has perhaps differed from the outline offered up in Craig's 12 survival suggestions, on some thoughts about how to recover from said deviations, and on perhaps some alternate pathways to consider that can provide personal and professional fulfilment. Be mindful that different people harbor different definitions of success (or survival), and success determined solely by alignment with external standards but devoid of personal satisfaction is scant survival.

I entered the University of Wisconsin as an academically capable, but highly distractible, undergraduate intending to pursue a premedical curriculum, which would be followed by medical school and then a career in some yet to be determined medical specialty. Early, guaranteed acceptance into medical school via UW's Medical Scholars Program afforded me significant flexibility, however, to tailor my academic studies—as long as I maintained a minimum acceptable GPA in my core premedical classes, I was free to pursue a wide range of academic interests, and forays first into theater production and then into philosophy followed. Some measure of practicality crept back in toward the end of my planned undergraduate years, and a tally of the classes I had completed added up to a major in zoology with an emphasis on genetics and biochemistry. This served as a suitable launch pad for the next phase of my academic career, although in reality, the next step owed less to my undergraduate studies than to my employment as an undergraduate research assistant in Gerry Mueller's lab at the McArdle Cancer Research Center at UW. Gerry was a pioneer in the field of estrogen and estrogen receptor research, and luckily for me, the relative of a childhood friend who arranged the connection when he found I was looking for a part time student job (never underestimate the importance of serendipity). My experience with Gerry opened my eyes to the prospect of a career in basic science research and also introduced me to Craig, who had a research collaboration with Gerry.

This led to a significant revision in the original plan, and following completion of my bachelor's degree, I entered the graduate program in Human Cancer Biology at the UW Comprehensive Cancer Center, and chose (or was chosen by—opinions vary) Craig as my mentor. It was to be a straightforward project (you can see where this is going) to describe the underlying mechanism of tamoxifen-stimulated growth that was occurring in the resistance model previously developed by Craig and Marco Gottardis. The prevailing hypothesis at the time was that resistant tumors were able to convert tamoxifen to a metabolite that was more estrogen than antiestrogen and that this directly stimulated the growth of estrogen receptor—positive tumors. Logically, if this conversion could be blocked, then this form of resistance would not occur. Due to a collaboration with a skilled synthetic chemist, Ray McCague in England, we had access to a number of interesting compounds, including an analog of tamoxifen that could not undergo isomerization to the hypothesized estrogenic metabolite, but still maintained the antiestrogenic function of the parent compound. Ultimately, this compound stimulated the growth of resistant tumors just like tamoxifen. Hypothesis disproved interesting paper published in the *Journal of the National Cancer Institute*, but original question still unanswered.

The next hypothesis to address was that tamoxifen-stimulated tumors acquired mutations in the estrogen receptor allowing them to "see" antiestrogens as estrogens. After an analysis of ER from multiple tamoxifen-stimulated tumors, we did find one mutant ER—which ultimately proved to be a valuable tool for understanding structure—activity relationships of estrogens and SERMs, but given that all of the other tumors contained wild-type ER, this clearly wasn't the prevailing mechanism for resistance. We now know that the ER must interact with a large number of protein cofactors to function, and that the distribution of cofactors expressed by a cell has a great deal to do with how the ER "sees" a particular molecule, but the determinants of estrogenicity versus antiestrogenicity are still not completely described. During the course of these experiments, we made probably the most important observation from my time in Craig's laboratory, which was that the resistant tumors that had been maintained for prolonged periods under tamoxifen exposure had changed to such a degree that estrogen was no longer a stimulus, but was rather lethal to a majority of the tumor cells. Apoptosis as a mechanism of cell death was just beginning to be understood at this time, and the full elucidation of the workings of estrogen-induced apoptosis would wait for the work of others, in newer iterations of Craig's Tamoxifen Teams.

The various and sundry publications from the work described above were judged sufficient for a thesis, though no single, compelling story thread could be constructed from my work alone. This reinforces Craig's point that it is key to publish important observations as soon as a "publishable unit" has been assembled, rather than waiting for the whole story and thus running the risk of never getting to the end, or being scooped by another group, at which point your work will struggle to see the light of day.

The next phase of my career was rather nondescript, and I won't share it in detail, other than to describe a couple of key lessons. Item 1 on Craig's list, regarding the careful choice of a mentor, is indeed key, but sometimes even if all of the initial criteria pass muster, sometimes circumstances will play out such that it is better to cut your losses and pursue plan B. Don't make such a decision lightly or too quickly, but don't waste too much time waiting for an untenable situation to improve before you yourself take action to change it. For all you know, the next pursuit will open up pathways you hadn't previously considered. Such was the case for me, when irreconcilable differences about the interpretation of a series of experiments led me to leave my postdoc to pursue additional graduate work in statistics, so that I would be better able to identify and address the root causes of such issues were I ever to be in a similar situation again. Little did I realize at the time that the combination of scientific knowledge and communication skills learned during my Ph.D., coupled with the statistical knowledge from my subsequent MS in that field had left me tailor-made for a medical affairs career in the pharmaceutical industry, where I have found a satisfying and rewarding home for the past decade.

To close, I'd add a 13th point to Craig's top dozen list. Take time out periodically for honest introspection—know what kind of person you are, and be honest enough with yourself to understand that your skills and knowledge alone won't determine your ability to succeed. There is serendipity (though Pasteur's adage about chance and the prepared mind should be recalled), and there is your mindset itself. Craig's laser-like focus on science from his early teen years of home chemistry experiments (and the attendant charred curtains, mangled gardens and sundry explosions) to his adult successes as a pharmacologist and translational scientist certainly outline one clear path for scientific survival, but there are other routes to be considered, and each person will find that there are differences in the choice of path that will suit them best. The analytical and intellectual skills that come from a high-quality Ph.D. and subsequent training can serve you well in a wide array of fields.

Survival alone should not be your goal—career satisfaction and self-fulfillment—are key. Early on in your career, be open to a wide variety of career prospects, and don't rule anything out simply because those choices weren't appropriate for your friends, colleagues, and mentors. Have a plan, but part of that plan should be to fully explore the unexpected, and take full advantage of it when your skills and temperament suit that newly discovered path.

I have recently been promoted to Global Lead—Field Excellence at Pfizer Oncology.

Shun-Yuan Jiang, Ph.D.
I am proud to be a member of the Tamoxifen Team

I joined the Wisconsin Tamoxifen Team to pursuit my Ph.D. at 1987. Tamoxifen had been used for the treatment of hormone responsive breast cancer for some years, and Dr. Jordan view was that drug resistance would be an unavoidable outcome for patients following long-term tamoxifen treatment. Therefore, establishing cell models that are either resistant to tamoxifen or independent of estrogens for growth was a high priority at that time. I had some experience in hybridoma cell culture back in Taiwan, therefore establishing of oestrogen-independent MCF-7 cells was part of my startup experiments in the lab. We did not know how long was required for the cells to gain independent growth following estrogen deprivation. So, MCF-7 cells were simply fed and split under estrogen-free environment with minimum attention. Thanks to all the efforts in the lab to maintain estrogen-free culture, cells slowly took up the speed to growth around 2 years after selection in an estrogen-free environment. Several clones derived from single cell were then selected and validated. Three representative clones, WS8, 2A, and 5C, were selected for further validation. The WS8 clone exhibits all the hormone-responsive phenotypes of the parental MCF-7 cells. Although the 2A cells were independent of estrogen for growth, the cells were growth inhibited by 4-hydroxytamoxifen and the pure antiestrogen ICI164384. To our surprise, the 2A cells expressed two forms of ER, the 65 kDa wild-type ER and the 80-kDa aberrant ER, and exhibited high gel shift binding capacity. However, 17β-estradiol was not efficient in activating the expression of the progesterone receptor in the 5C cells. Subsequent study carried out by a graduate student John J. Pink identified the structure and activities of the aberrant 80-kDa ER. In contrast to the 2A cells, the 5C cells were antiestrogen resistant and estrogen independent. They were markedly reduced in oestrogen-stimulated expression of progesterone receptor. It was quite disappointing that we did not identify any mutation in the ER of the 5C cells. Results related to the establishing and characterization of 2A and 5C cells were sent for publication. I did not anticipate at the beginning of my study that the establishing estrogen-independent cells would be part of my Ph.D. thesis, and I certainly did not expect that the 2A and 5C cells would be used extensively for future studies after my graduation. Therefore, I was thrilled to find that the poster presented by Dr. Jordan's team using 5C cells was in the same poster section as my poster at the AACR meeting in 2010. It was truly quite amazing and excited to see the WS8, 2A, and 5C cells, once nurtured in my hands for almost 4 years, have been used extensively in studies to gain ways to control breast cancer.

Other than establishing estrogen-independent 2A and 5C cells, I was also interested to establish ER stable cells from the ER-negative MDA-MB-231 cells, in the hope to use the stable cells as a model system to analyze the regulation of cell growth by estrogen in previously ER-negative cell environment. In addition to Northern and Southern blotting, techniques such as gene cloning, transfection, promoter, and gel shift assays were totally new to me and to the lab. Thanks to Dr. Jordan's encouragement and full support, the study was carried out. Instead of cotransfection with ER expression and neomycin-resistant plasmids, I decided to construct an ER expression plasmid that synthesizes a bicistronic mRNA coding for both ER and neomycin-resistant proteins. Initial screening using Northern blotting failed to identify ER-positive stable clones, the use of simple and easy ways for large scale of screening was therefore essential. So, one night, I decided to seed each clone cells into two wells in a 24-well plate and the next day refreshed with control or 17β-estradiol-containing medium, anticipating to look for active cell growth in some clones 2−3 days after estrogen supplementation. To my surprise, one clone had a bipolar structure with some cells rounding up after estrogen supplementation. The number of cells was progressively decreased with the increase in the length of estrogen exposure. I did not yet understand that this was the estrogen-responsive phenotype of ER stable cells derived from the ER-negative MDA-MB-231 cells. When I presented my finding in our lab meeting, Dr. Jordan immediately picked up the unique feature and hypothesized that estrogen addition may actually kill, instead of promote, cell growth in ER stable cells established from the ER-negative breast cancer cells. Coincidently the ER cDNA, a generous gift from Professor P Chambon, was identified to harbor a point mutation at codon 400. To confirm that the phenomenon of oestrogen-induced downregulation of cell growth was independent of the mutation at ER at codon 400, all the experiments including ER cDNA subcloning and establishment of stable cells were repeated using the real wild-type ER cDNA. The observation of estrogen supplementation downregulated the growth of ER stable cells was again confirmed in wild-type ER stable clones. When the stable transfectants that expressed the 400 codon-mutated ER were compared to the wild-type ER stable cells, the wild-type transfectants were more sensitive to estrogen and the change in morphology was much more evident and happened earlier after estrogen exposure. Since estrogen-stimulated cell growth was a well-established concept, the observation of estrogen-induced cell death rather than cell growth in ER-stable cells derived from ER-negative cells was revolutionary. I remembered we had a lot of debate regarding the observation and the hypothesis in the lab meetings. More than 60 clones were screened in 24-well plates for estrogen-responsive death in the wild-type ER transfected cells, and less than five wild-type ER-positive stable clones were selected. Low frequency of ER-positive clones selected may agree to the estrogen-induced cell death of ER-stable cells derived from MDA-MB-231 cells.

The wild-type ER stable clone S30 was considered to be a sensitive model to investigate estrogenecity of antiestrogens in further analysis during my Ph.D. program. Because transfectants are highly sensitive to estrogens that lead to cell death, the S30 cells have to be maintained in completely estrogen-free culture. Regrettably, this is also the key issue that prevented further exploration using the S30 cells for analysis.

With excellent training in the area of hormonal regulation of breast cancer growth, I started up my research in Taiwan beginning in the analysis of ER in the growth of hepatoma cells in 1992. The concept of nuclear receptor was subsequently adapted in my following research in the analysis of the role of retinoic acid signaling in the control of gastrointestinal cancer. We cloned and investigated the function of a type II tumor suppressor gene, retinoid acid inducible gene I (RIG1). Looking back in the years during my Ph.D. study, Dr. Jordan was a great mentor to me. Lots of my subsequent research approaches, like gene cloning, RNA in situ hybridization, and cell cycle and apoptosis analysis, are attributed to my training in Dr. Jordan's lab. Dr. Jordan had a very tight schedule; I used to simply put a hard copy of my draft manuscript in Dr. Jordan's mail box, and grasped whatever moment he had available to discuss the research. These personal interactions were enjoyable moments during my Ph.D. study. In addition to the training in research skills, Dr. Jordan very much emphasized writing and presentation skills, which had a great impact on my teaching career in medical school in Taiwan. I am very proud to be a member of the Tamoxifen Team.

I am a professor at the Buddhist General Hospital in Taiwan.

William H. Catherino, MD, Ph.D.
Jordan's Marines

"Join me if you want to succeed." Memorable words from my first meeting with Dr. Jordan. At the time, I was finishing my first year of medical school, and I was considering the diverse research opportunities at the University of Wisconsin–Madison. The vast majority of other potential mentors shared with me their compelling stories about the beauty of science and discovery. Craig's story is certainly no less compelling. However, he provided much more than a vague blueprint that hard work and good ideas will be a more than adequate salve for any challenge. Dr. Jordan provided a living model of how success involves intelligence, determination, sweat, charisma, marketing, and an absolute refusal to accept failure (you're a marine). A tough yard-stick to measure up to, and my story is a weak reflection of Dr. Jordan's life values, but I'm happy to share what I've learned along the way.

I completed my undergraduate training at the University of Michigan, and joined the first refurbished MD/Ph.D. class at the University of Wisconsin–Madison with three other students. After my fateful meeting described above 8 months later, I joined Dr. Jordan's laboratory. Within days of agreeing, Dr. Jordan was assisting me with a grant application that ultimately led to my first research project and presentation in Baltimore with the Fellowship Program in Academic Medicine for Minority Students, sponsored by Bristol-Myers Squibb Company and the Commonwealth Fund. Thus came the first pearl of academic success: Be fiercely loyal and supportive of those whom you teach. As Dr. Jordan can attest, his graduate students worked both hard and smart because he stood by us and supported us in every way. Aside from supporting me during my graduate student training, Dr. Jordan sponsored me, after I had completed my Ph.D. training, to attend a meeting with him in Cambridge, United Kingdom, to discuss future directions for cancer research. He has remained a stalwart supporter of my career from the moment I accepted his challenge to succeed.

For the sake of brevity, I will briefly outline my career and then provide a few thoughts that I hope the reader will find helpful. I completed my MD and Ph.D. degrees at the University of Wisconsin–Madison, completed a residency in Obstetrics and Gynecology at Duke University Medical Center, and completed a Clinical Fellowship at the Combined Federal Fellowship (National Institutes of Health, Walter Reed Army Medical Center, National Naval Medical Center, and the Uniformed Services University of the Health Sciences) before starting as junior faculty at the Uniformed Services University (As an aside, Dr. Jordan strongly encouraged and supported graduate student publication, and as a result, I had more than sufficient publications by the completion of my graduate studies to make a compelling argument for a hire at the Assistant Professor level). I was board-certified in both Obstetrics and Gynecology and Reproductive Endocrinology and Infertility, and earned tenure. I have maintained my laboratory with Federal, private, institutional, and foundation funding, and have been successful in maintaining a respectable publication record. I also maintain a clinical practice and serve as a Boards Examiner for the field of Reproductive Endocrinology and Infertility.

A few remaining thoughts/pearls:

1. Find a research topic that YOU are enthusiastic about.
2. Market yourself.
3. Decide what YOU define as success.
4. Never, ever give up; don't give the [expletive deleted] satisfaction.

I am Professor and Chair-Research Division, Department of Obstetrics and Gynecology USUHS, and Editor-in-Chief, Fertility and Sterility Science.

Anait S Levenson, MD, Ph.D.

I joined the Breast Cancer Program at the Robert H Lurie Comprehensive Cancer Center in 1994. I moved to Chicago that year from Charlottesville, Virginia, where my family started our new life in America.

I received my MD/Ph.D. degrees in Moscow, Russia, where I was subsequently leading my own research group in the Institute of Dentistry. After immigration to the United States, I had to start my career all over. My time at the University of Virginia were years of adaptation to a new language, culture, and science.

When my family moved to Chicago, I interviewed at several laboratories and decided to do my postdoctoral training in Dr. V Craig Jordan's lab. This decision was based on the quality of research as well as Dr. Jordan's reputation as a prominent scientist working in the breast cancer field.

The choice proved to be one of the best decisions in my life. It became clear that Dr. Jordan provides an outstanding range of opportunities for his junior colleagues, starting from high-quality day-to-day mentoring to confidence-building tasks such as writing scientific review articles for first-class scientific journals and giving presentations at international conferences. My years in Dr. Jordan's laboratory were extremely productive: 3 review articles, 2 book chapters, 13 scientific papers in peer-reviewed journals, and numerous presentations at scientific meetings. I learned to be enthusiastic and optimistic about the science, and I learned to believe in hard work and success.

I was in Dr. Jordan's lab from 1994 to 1998 as a postdoctoral fellow, and then I became a faculty member of the Department of Medicine at University of Illinois at Chicago for about a year after which I came back to the Breast Cancer Program Core Laboratory of Northwestern University as a junior faculty member. Dr. Jordan's unique attitude toward his junior colleagues was collaboration with building trust and self-confidence and a wide range of opportunities.

Aside of my scientific training, the most important skill Dr. Jordan furnished for me was the confidence to succeed.

I was promoted to Professor of the University of Mississippi Medical Center and Professor at the Arnold and Marie Schwartz College of Pharmacy and Health at Long Island University. I am currently President of the American Council for Medicinally Active Plants.

Debra A. Tonetti, Ph.D.

I have been in the Chicago area all of my life. After earning a Bachelor of Science degree from Northern Illinois University with a major in Biology, I took a laboratory technician position at Loyola University Medical School in the Biochemistry and Biophysics department. Despite volunteering in a research laboratory as an undergrad, I had no idea what it meant to do basic scientific research. As an undergrad, I worked in Dr. Arnie Hampel's lab, and at the time, his research on newly discovered ribozymes was truly cutting edge. Nothing about my duties was cutting edge. My job was to oc-

casionally help one of the grad students with a timed assay, wash the dishes and yes, wash the toluene out of scintillation vials. It is a miracle I'm still alive! As a technician working for Dr. Mary Manteuffel, I began to understand scientific investigation studying maternal undernutrition and alcohol on fetal brain development. I learned how to isolate rat brain synaptic plasma membranes, and once I realized how cool it was to perform experiments and actually obtain data to answer a specific question, I wanted to become a scientist. I began a master's program in Biology part-time at Loyola University Lakeshore Campus. Working with Dr. Howard Laten, I studied yeast genetics where I acquired classical biochemistry techniques and spent a lot of time in the cold room trying to isolate an enzyme. After finishing my master's degree, I was accepted into the Ph.D. program in the Biochemistry department where I previously worked as a technician. I joined Dr. Robert Miller's lab and undertook a bacterial genetics project. Specifically, I was trying to clone the gene for DNA gyrase from *Pseudomonas aeruginosa*. I spent a lot of time reading the Maniatis Molecular Biology bible, performing cloning techniques and pouring massive sequencing gels. Reading nucleotide sequences from autoradiographs was highly satisfying. When my dissertation committee finally declared that I was ABD (all but dissertation), I applied for the Enrico Fermi Postdoctoral Fellowship at Argonne National Laboratory and got it. I began my postdoc before finishing my dissertation—big mistake. I eventually successfully defended my Ph.D. 6 months after beginning my postdoc. I was extremely excited to make the switch to cancer biology in Dr. Eli Huberman's lab. As it turns out, this decision was pivotal to my career path. Eli was the Biology Division Director at Argonne at the time, and it was a very exciting place to work. I was investigating differentiation of the promyelocytic HL-60 cells and determined that protein kinase C (PKC) beta is required for PMA-induced macrophage differentiation. This is where I began to learn how to construct a scientific paper. At the time, Eli didn't use the computer (he certainly does now), but he would edit my manuscript using the "cut and paste" method. When returned to me for revision, my manuscript often looked like a ransom note, but I learned.

I remember attending AACR in 1992 and was very impressed with one of the plenary session lectures delivered by Dr. V Craig Jordan. I took lots of notes (which I still have) and was so pulled in by the fascinating work he presented about tamoxifen and breast cancer. Two years later, when it was time for me to move on from my postdoc position, I saw a job ad in Science for a Research Associate position in V Craig Jordan's laboratory that had recently moved to Northwestern University. I was really excited about this potential opportunity especially since I remembered well the energetic and interesting lecture he delivered at the AACR. I witnessed that same energy and enthusiasm during my interview with Dr. Jordan and I very much wanted to join the "Tamoxifen Team." I distinctly remember he asked if I would be disappointed to make a switch away from studying the PKC signaling pathway and focus instead on the estrogen receptor. I assured him that this would not be a problem. My first project involved performing a scanning mutagenesis of the estrogen response element and using the luciferase assay as a readout. In that first year, I learned so much not only involving the new technical skills that I needed to master, but also I was learning about breast cancer in a comprehensive way that I had never encountered before. Firstly because Craig's lab was diverse in the sense that there was always a mix of Ph.D. types (postdocs and research associates) and MDs (surgical and oncology residents and fellows) that forced us to learn from each other. Secondly, he provided us with a multidisciplinary learning environment in the form of a weekly journal club with presenters from all disciplines with an interest in breast cancer including basic scientists, epidemiologists, surgeons, oncologists, radiologists, radiation oncologists, etc. Thirdly, I was given the opportunity to write a review article on mechanisms of endocrine resistance. This was invaluable for me to immerse myself in the pertinent literature I needed to be able to pose scientifically and clinically relevant research questions. Fourthly, within my first year in the lab, I was given the opportunity to attend the San Antonio Breast Cancer Symposium for the first time. At that time, it was a relatively small meeting that was held at the Marriott Rivercenter hotel. I have attended this meeting almost every year since with the exception of a few and still regard this meeting as a key way to keep my research relevant and to instill this in my graduate students and postdocs. The most significant opportunity Craig gave to me was the permission to pursue my own research direction, ironically involving PKC signaling. I was able to convince Craig that there was compelling evidence in the literature that the PKC signaling pathway was relevant in endocrine resistance. This opportunity led me to the award of my first R01, and I will forever be grateful to Craig, as that is what launched my independent line of investigation and the faculty position at UIC that I have today. He generously promoted me to Research Assistant Professor and allowed me to pursue this research in his laboratory until I was offered a tenure—track position in the Biopharmaceutical Sciences department at UIC. The time I spent in the Jordan lab significantly positively influenced the way I direct my own students, technicians, and postdocs. I will forever remember his "work or die" speeches. We would all roll our eyes, especially when he told his group of mostly women to "be a marine." He was right, we needed to learn to ask clinically relevant questions, we needed to crank out the data, and we needed to know how to package the data into a manuscript that was publication quality, craft an oral presentation that told a story. and most of all, master the art of grantsmanship. He would tell us how to do this, and at the same time, because of the multidisciplinary environment, we knew we could potentially improve breast cancer survival. This is where I made lifelong friends and colleagues. It was exciting to be a part of this.

I now deliver my own version of the "work or die" speech. I always require my graduate students and postdocs stay in touch with current clinical thought. Since many of my collaborators are breast pathologists, breast surgeons, and medical oncologists, I carry on the tradition of the multidisciplinary approach. My lab continues to pursue the role of PKCα in endocrine resistance and is also interested in identifying gene signatures to predict pregnancy-associated breast cancers. I am now Professor of Pharmacology in Biopharmaceutical Sciences at UIC and very grateful to V Craig Jordan for providing and outstanding foundation for my scientific career.

Rita Dardes, MD, Ph.D.

I was 23 years old when I graduated out of medical school and went straight to the residence program in Ob/Gyn at the Federal University in São Paulo, Brazil (UNIFESP), which I completed in 1996. Shortly after, in 1997, I finished my master's degree focusing in female sex hormones and the pineal gland, also at UNIFESP.

I had decided to apply for a scholarship program with the official Federal student financing program offered by CNPQ (National Counsel of Technological and Scientific Development). This wasn't easy as only about 3% of applicants would make the cut for the foreign scholarship program. My medical school grades and the results of my master's degree were key in attaining a positive outcome. Well, sure enough came January 1998, and I was in Chicago. Once there, in 1998, I applied and was admitted as a Ph.D. student at the Robert H. Lurie Comprehensive Cancer Center at Chicago's Northwestern University. In Dr. Jordan's lab, I worked on my Ph.D. degree for 4 years. I was granted the first Avon Foundation scholarship to study breast cancer and adjuvant hormone therapies for my doctor degree. I obtained my Ph.D. degree from Chicago's Northwestern University as an Avon scholar in 2001.

I had attended 6 years of medical school plus 3 years of residence program where I developed a passion for research and academics. Granted I knew I was going to be a practicing physician at some point in the future, but I felt I would not have been as complete and assertive as I feel I am now, if it as not for my years as a researcher. In addition to practicing as a board certified obstetrician/gynecologist, I also specialized in Mastology having passed the certification exam in 2004. Yet, even nowadays with my own private clinic in São Paulo practicing as a physician, I continued my academic activities as an assistant professor at UNIFESP, where I have the opportunity to mentor students getting started as researchers—just as I have myself been at one point in my past life.

After joining the Federal University of São Paulo in 2002 as faculty, I developed and managed the Postmenopausal High Risk Breast Cancer Program, working in collaboration with the University's Gynecology and Mastology departments. Through this program, I am able to offer comprehensive care to the unique needs of high-risk patients and serve as an educator for issues pertinent to this group.

My current work includes researching prevention with SERMs in high-risk breast cancer patients and a collaborative project looking at secondary prevention for breast cancer in Brazil as an emerging country. I am a member of the Brazilian Federation of the Associations of OB/GYN (FEBRASGO) and the Brazilian Society of Mastology, where I served as a member of the Genetics and Molecular Biology Department. Currently, I am President of the Philanthropy Group of the Brazilian Society of Mastology.

Dr. Jordan was a mentor and a true professor at all times. I realize how cliché this may sound, but it is the simple truth. And not only to me, but to every single hard working fellow smart enough to grab on to the opportunity of working at his lab.

I like to think that Dr. Jordan also appreciated my hard work and dedication. He helped me secure financing for my research as an Avon Scholar—which would later also become an important and constant partner in my professional life. Avon's commitment to women's health is unchallenged and unmatched.

Through Avon's financing and Dr. Jordan's mentorship, I managed to complete my work in 2001. I presented my Ph.D. manuscript to the Board of academic postgraduate program at UNIFESP in November 2001. Among the academic revising body was an honourable guest—Dr. Jordan. My Ph.D. degree paved the way to several academic publications (http://lattes.cnpq.br/3773357188654076).

I continued with my academic activities, and in 2005, I attained my postdoctorate degree from FAPESP (Sao Paulo Research Foundation) working on high-risk breast cancer and raloxifen therapy.

Soon after getting my Ph.D. degree, I received an invitation from Avon in Brazil to act as medical director to their soon-to-be-established Avon Institute, based in São Paulo. I now know that Dr. Jordan had proposed this idea to senior Avon management. I have been their medical director since then, and in my technical capacity, I have reviewed numerous research applications for financing; assisted and approved the donation of dozens of mammography machines to hospitals and universities, participated in several awareness campaigns, Avon runs, and marathons. I have been interviewed—and still am on a regular basis—by various TV shows on national television, radio talk shows, and lead publications. What an opportunity.

I continue to be in close contact with Dr. Jordan, and he visits Brazil often as our special scientific guest. It couldn't be any different. I guess I have come to feel a part of an important few that have learned so much from him. I really feel indebted to him, but if I asked I think I know what he might ask in return. He would probably say "keep on working for the cause."

I am currently Adjunct Professor of Gynecology at the Federal University of Sao Paulo, and I am a member of the Global Avon Breast Cancer Advisory Board. I am Vice Chair of the Department of Gynecology.

Clodia Osipo, Ph.D.

I was born in Tehran, Iran, to two wonderful and very encouraging parents. We moved to the United States in 1972 and there began a lifelong dream to learn and explore all of the possibilities. You might even say that the move to the United States was a scientific project and many experiments were conducted during my adolescent, teen, and adult years. The love for science is based simply on curiosity. Curious minds ask questions and proceed to answer them. The most critical aspect in the lifelong training of a scientist is encouragement from your family and educators and importantly the confidence to believe that anything is possible. Many people are responsible for this training environment. One of the most important is your mentor.

I received my Ph.D. in Molecular and Cellular Biochemistry from Loyola University Chicago in 2001. Thereafter, I joined Dr. V Craig Jordan's laboratory at Northwestern University's Robert H. Lurie Comprehensive Cancer Center. This was the start of a lifelong love and commitment to breast cancer research. My experience in the Jordan laboratory provided me the important foundation and self-confidence to pursue an independent career in breast cancer research. I began my research career at Loyola University in September 2005 as a nontenure track Assistant Professor in the laboratory of Dr. Lucio Miele. In January 2008, I was transferred to a tenure-track Assistant Professor status after receiving my first peer-reviewed grant (ACS-IL). I published my first corresponding author publication in Oncogene in 2008 based on research that I developed and originated. From 2008 to 2010 as a tenure-track Loyola faculty, I spent the majority of my research time developing novel model systems of therapeutic resistance in breast cancer to specifically address questions of the role of Notch signaling in drug resistant breast cancer. Development of these model systems were time-consuming but laid the foundation for my independent research progress. As a result of my contributions, I have written an invited review article in 2010 on the role of Notch in Trastuzumab Resistance (Scientific World Journal). Furthermore, I have published two seminal, original articles in the field of Notch signaling and its critical role in Breast Cancer Therapeutics in 2011 (Pandya et al., Brit J Cancer; Clementz et al., Breast Cancer Res). My track record strongly indicates that the research generated in my laboratory will provide novel therapeutic strategies to prevent drug-resistant breast cancer with the ultimate goal of eradicating breast cancer in the future. I was promoted to Associate Professor with Tenure at Loyola University Chicago's Cardinal Bernardin Cancer Center. I have an independent research program that has trained Ph.D. and master's graduate students. I have three active grants that include an American Cancer Society Scholar award, an IDPH award, and a recently funded R01. The focus of my research career has been to elucidate critical mechanisms responsible for drug-resistant breast cancer. Currently, the laboratory is focused on the role and contribution of the Notch signaling pathway in drug resistance to antihormonal and anti-ErbB-2 therapies. My research objective is to identify, validate, and test novel therapeutics targeting Notch signaling with the expectation of preventing breast tumor resistance, recurrence, progression, and ultimately death-associated with Notch-mediated drug resistance. These successes are due to the strong and thorough training provided by Dr. Jordan and his team.

On a more personal note, Craig Jordan was not just a postdoctoral mentor while I was in his laboratory but a sincere and now lifelong friend. I actually consider him one of my dear extended family members. When you are a member of the Jordan team, you are treated like his family. When my father suffered a stroke and was ill for many months, Craig sat me down in his office and told me his own personal family struggles to provide me not just comfort but also resilience to complete my projects and know that life goes on during difficult times. This conversation has left a lasting impression on my life and career. I try my best to treat my trainees with the same respect and to provide confidence and comfort when needed.

In regard to the ultimate goal of curing breast cancer for the millions of women still enduring this disease, I think it is important for the research community to take notes from the Craig Jordan laboratory training manual: (1) Provide opportunities for open and creative thinking; (2) Form teams of research groups that work naturally together to achieve goals; (3) Allow mistakes to be made so that risks and high rewards are encouraged; and (4) Respect your trainees as scientists to give them the confidence to achieve their dreams.

I am an associate professor of Cancer Biology at Loyola University, Chicago.

Thank you Craig for the scientific opportunities, confidence to run my own laboratory, and the warm and friendly climate to succeed in a very competitive research environment.

Ruth O'Regan, MD

I started my postgraduate, junior doctor career in Dublin, and rapidly developed an interest in oncology. There was no opportunity to undertake research projects, particularly lab-based research, in Dublin at the time so I made a decision to come to the United States to do a Fellowship in Oncology. I was delighted when I was offered a position as a fellow at Northwestern University, given the protected research opportunities afforded during this fellowship. During the first very busy clinical year, I sought out a mentor for my research time during my second and third years of fellowship. Given my complete lack of experience in laboratory research, I strove to find a mentor who would provide me an environment to learn these skills toward my ultimate goal of becoming an academic oncologist. After speaking to several of my colleagues and mentors, Dr. Jordan's laboratory was recommended as a potential possibility.

Being principal investigator of a laboratory myself, I am now well aware of the enormous undertaking of mentoring someone who has no laboratory skills and I remain extremely grateful to Dr. Jordan for affording me that opportunity. Things started off slowly not surprisingly but thanks to Dr. Jordan and the extraordinary team he had built in his laboratory, I quickly got up to speed with laboratory activities. Dr. Jordan proposed experiments focused on unique mouse models that he had developed during his career. Initially, I was a little disappointed feeling that animal work was not perhaps as sexy as the bench work some of my predecessors had been involved in. However, it quickly became clear that being involved with these fascinating mouse models was much more in line with my goals of becoming a translational scientist. I can safely say, in retrospect, that the time spent in the mouse rooms formed the basis for my career as a breast cancer researcher. Close bonds were formed between the team of us who went down daily, sometimes even at the weekends, to administer tamoxifen and other agents to the mice. I will never forget the hours we spent transplanting and dissecting tumors. Though initially I was somewhat squeamish about dealing with these mice, particularly when it came time to sacrifice them, it didn't take long for me to develop nonchalance toward my visits to the mouse room. As a member of this volume of the Tamoxifen Team story, I believe we contributed several key findings regarding SERMs, which were ultimately translated directly into patient care. We noted that raloxifene is ineffective and potentially increases the risk of endometrial cancer when used after tamoxifen, which contributed to the fact that patients with early-stage breast cancer rarely, if ever, receive raloxifene after tamoxifen. Our findings that HER2 plays a role in acquired resistance to tamoxifen, and that trastuzumab can inhibit the growth of tamoxifen-resistant cancers, has been confirmed by other groups. In fact, I am currently the principal investigator of a clinical trial in which patients with endocrine-resistant, HER2-normal metastatic breast cancers are treated with trastuzumab with or without a mTOR inhibitor, in an attempt to reverse resistant to endocrine agents. The research that I was involved in when with Dr. Jordan formed the basis for this trial design, which we hope will provide a new therapeutic approach for patients with endocrine-resistant metastatic breast cancer.

Following my fellowship, I remained in Dr. Jordan's laboratory for 4 more years while I was a junior faculty member at Northwestern University. During this time, we published several important papers in the *Journal of the National Cancer Institute and Clinical Cancer Research*. Dr. Jordan mentored me on the art of writing scientific publications and reviews. Additionally, he gave me substantial opportunities to present our research at national and international venues, including a clinical symposium in Spain. One of the major advantages of working with Dr. Jordan is his ability to understand the clinical importance of the research we do in the laboratory. Though not perhaps a unique attribute, as a medical oncologist, this was of critical importance to my career development. I believe this intertwining of basic and clinical research led me to achieve two important achievements, which solidified my early career in academic oncology. The first was the chance to present my research evaluating the effect of raloxifene after tamoxifen, as an oral presentation, at an annual meeting of the American Society of Clinical Oncology. This is a primarily clinical meeting and, as such, the fact that this research was accepted for oral presentation is a true tribute to Dr. Jordan's standing in the clinical oncology community. This presentation gave me greater visibility in the academic arena and resulted in invitations to several other meetings at which I presented this and other research performed during my tenure with Dr. Jordan. The second was the award of a Young Investigator Award from the National Surgical Adjuvant Breast and Bowel Project (NSABP). This important award allowed me to continue my research with Dr. Jordan while I was a junior faculty member at Northwestern. The fruit of my research under Dr. Jordan's mentorship was my recruitment to direct the breast cancer program at Emory University. I became Professor and Vice-Chair for Educational Affairs in the Department of Haematology and Medical Oncology. There is no doubt that the publications and presentations that resulted from this research increased my visibility in the breast cancer community and directly resulted in my obtaining my position at Emory. My laboratory research continues to focus much on mouse models, although the focus is primarily on triple negative rather than hormone receptor-positive breast cancer. However, much of my clinical research continues to focus on endocrine resistance.

Another key attribute of Dr. Jordan is his ability to assemble subgroups of the Tamoxifen Team that continue to interact and collaborate even after they leave his laboratory. I was extremely fortunate to have such outstanding colleagues during my time in his laboratory. We continue to collaborate and interact by speaking at each other's institutions and working together on grants. We meet up regularly at national meetings to have lunch or a glass of wine. I believe these interactions continue to benefit all of our careers. Aside from the team I worked with during my time in Dr. Jordan's laboratory, I cannot count the number of times I have come across other investigators who were previously mentored by Dr. Jordan. This is the true testament to the Tamoxifen Team with so many graduates progressing to successful careers in breast cancer research. It is hard to imagine another team who has had such continuing success in academic breast oncology, and this success is, of course, thanks to the opportunities Dr. Jordan afforded each of us while and after we spent time in his laboratory.

I am Chair, Department of Medicine, Charles A Dewey, Professor of Medicine, University of Rochester, Rochester, NY.

David Bentrem, MD

I worked as a research fellow in the laboratory of V Craig Jordan, Ph.D., at Northwestern University School of Medicine from 1999 to 2001. I didn't have much additional training in basic research beyond that obtained in medical school, but Dr. Jordan took me in as long as I gave it "my all." Dr. Jordan's passion flowed through the lab. His work was always focused on the translational aspects of basic research. I was able to learn firsthand the practice of sound investigations using in vitro cancer cells and animal tumor models as well as the importance of asking clinically relevant research questions. I learned the rationale and value of targeted anticancer therapies. There was always a large engaged group of investigators in the lab ready to lend assistance to help advance the various projects.

During my 2-year fellowship, we evaluated novel antiestrogenic agents in preclinical models of tamoxifen-resistant breast cancer. Through this work, I learned my valuable skills, which I continue to use to this day such as routine histology, basic immunohistochemistry, and how to isolate and quantify RNA and protein from cancer cells and tumors. I gained extensive experience with animal models: animal surgery, heterotopic tumor development, and drug treatment trials. These skills have served me well in managing our human pancreatic tumor bank at Northwestern. In addition, our work focused on the molecular classification of novel agents under investigation for use against breast cancer. During this research 2-year fellowship, I developed skills necessary to design, conduct, analyze, document, and present research. I loved working in Dr. Jordan's lab because he was also relating what we were working on to the "big picture" namely advances in the fight against breast cancer. We felt like we were making a difference. Because of the quality of intellect, research, and productivity in that laboratory, I was able to establish a strong background in translational research, which I have utilized over my whole career.

After completing my fellowship at Memorial Sloan Kettering Cancer Center, I was recruited back to Northwestern University in the Division of Surgical Oncology focusing on the care of patients with GI malignancy and development of a translational research program. Thus far, this solid scientific foundation in cancer research and translational research enriches my current research and clinical care each day.

I am currently Professor of Surgery at Northwestern University Hospital in Chicago.

Joan Lewis-Wambi, Ph.D.

I am an associate professor with tenure in the Cancer Biology Department at the University of Kansas Medical Center in Kansas City, Kansas. My research focuses on understanding the mechanism by which breast cancer cells and tumors develop resistance to endocrine therapies such as tamoxifen and aromatase inhibitors and using that knowledge to develop alternative treatment options for patients with resistant and metastatic disease.

Lessons learned in the laboratory

As Louis Pasteur said, "Chance favors only a prepared mind." Serendipitous events reorienting the pathway of science often occur through the actions of dedicated individuals with unique cultural and educational backgrounds, an original sense of values, and firm principles. All scientific endeavors begin with observations, or facts. However, the real goal of research activity is to convert accumulated knowledge to something with new technological, economic, or social value.

After completing my Ph.D. at Rutgers University in 2002, I accepted a postdoctoral position in the laboratory of Dr. V Craig Jordan at the Robert H. Lurie Comprehensive Cancer Center at Northwestern University. In 2004, Dr. Jordan accepted the position of Vice President of Medical Research at the Fox Chase Cancer Center in Philadelphia, PA, and I agreed to move with his lab to Fox Chase where I completed my second postdoctoral fellowship from 2004 to 2006. My decision to join Dr. Jordan's laboratory, effectively becoming a member of the "tamoxifen team," was a tremendous learning experience for me and it gave me the opportunity to learn important lessons which have helped to positively shape my scientific career. Dr. Jordan was a great mentor to me. He supported and encouraged my individual learning and provided opportunities for me to maximize my technical laboratory skills, enhance my writing and presentation abilities, and network through traveling nationally and internationally. Through his mentorship, I was able to acquire all the necessary skills needed to successfully transition from being a mentored postdoc to being an independent faculty member. During my tenure in Dr. Jordan's lab, I published 15 peer-reviewed manuscripts (10 first-author publications), successfully applied for and was awarded a 5-year K01 Career Development Award, and was invited to present my work at national and international meetings. My experiences as a postdoc were truly positive and the training I received helped to prepare me for the academic rigors of being an independent faculty member. As I reflect back on my postdoc years in the lab, there are several lessons that I have learned. One important lesson I have learned is the importance of choosing the right mentor and the right lab. A very good mentor will stimulate intellectual independence, critical and analytical thinking skills, and foster professional growth in his/her student, which is what Dr. Jordan did for me and all of his trainees. Another important lesson I have learned is the importance of setting career goals and having a timeline and strategy for achieving those goals. Last but not least, trust your instincts regarding your research ideas; be meticulous about documenting your research to ensure that your findings can be reproduced in the lab, and pay close attention to experimental details to ensure that you do not overlook important findings.

Serendipitous discovery

As a postdoctoral fellow in Dr. Jordan's laboratory, my initial task was to evaluate breast cancer cell lines to understand the mechanisms of drug resistance to aromatase inhibitors. To address this clinical problem, Dr. Jordan's laboratory had previously developed many models of antihormone resistance using transplantable models in animals (see Marco Gottardis and Doug Wolf); however, his laboratory did not have any good in vitro models to study long-term estrogen deprivation. Soon after joining Dr. Jordan's lab, I was able to classify the first in vitro models of AI resistance based on Shun-Yuan Jiang's original Ph.D. and ancillary MCF-7: 2A and 5C. I should note, however, that during the course of developing the AI-resistant cell models, I discovered that the AI-resistant cells exhibited an unusual phenotype in that they grew robustly in the absence of endogenous estrogen, the female hormone that stimulates the proliferation of breast cancer cells, but died through apoptosis when treated with physiologic levels of estradiol. In addition, I found that the AI-resistant cells spontaneously formed tumors when injected in athymic mice and that these tumors completely regressed when the animals were treated with estradiol. Even more interesting was my discovery that the apoptotic effect of estradiol in AI-resistant breast cancer cells was highly influenced by the serum composition of the media the cells were cultured in. Additional experiments indicated that the mechanism by which estradiol induced apoptosis in the AI-resistant cell models involved activation of the mitochondrial death pathway and endoplasmic reticulum stress. I should note that the discovery that estradiol kills AI-resistant breast cancer cells was a serendipitous finding and was initially overlooked by me and by Dr. Jordan. We both thought that my experimental design was flawed and that I had made a critical mistake when culturing the cells. However, after several repeated experiments with multiple controls, we realized that my findings were indeed correct and that I had made an important laboratory observation with potential clinical significance. This is the hallmark of Dr. Jordan's scientific approach: reasonable skepticism, repeat the experiments, and then integrate what nature is telling you into a new model. This was the same process as occurred with the first ER transfectants. This experience taught me the importance of following my instincts and paying close attention to experimental details and it gave me the confidence I needed to think big and explore more "high-risk/high reward" experiments. This experience also demonstrated to me that I had the full support of Dr. Jordan and that he trusted me and my abilities and was willing to let me fully explore the project. These important findings were published in a pivotal paper in the *Journal of the National Cancer Institute* (2005: 97: 1746−59), and this discovery opened the door for me to successfully apply and obtain a 5-year K01 Career Development Grant to study the new biology of estrogen action in AI-resistant breast cancer cells. This pivotal finding was also instrumental in helping Dr. Jordan apply successfully for a $10M Center of Excellence grant, studying mechanisms of actions and clinical applications of estrogen-induced apoptosis in breast cancer. Patient care was improved, and a new biology of oestrogen-induced apoptosis is now accepted.

Philipp Y. Maximov, MD, Ph.D., MBA

Some people believe that his or her stars seal the fate of a person. One of those stars for me was Dr. V Craig Jordan. Dr. Jordan is one of those extraordinary people, whose perseverance and enthusiasm have changed the lives of millions including my own. I met Dr. Jordan for the first time in late 2005, when I was a graduate student in another lab at the Fox Chase Cancer Center in Philadelphia, PA. I arrived at Fox Chase in February 2005 as a participant of an exchange program between my alma mater the N. I. Pirogov Russian National Medical Research University in Moscow, Russia, Department of Molecular Biology, and Medical Biotechnology. I was assigned to a lab to study an ovarian tumor suppressor protein OVCA1, but there was no opportunity for me to continue my work as a Ph.D. student in the same laboratory. I really wanted to stay as I really wanted to continue to gain knowledge and experience in cancer research. I was applying to a number of labs, in Philadelphia area, including Fox Chase, and one job ad for a postdoctoral position caught my eye. It was an ad for a position in Dr. Jordan's lab. I immediately wrote up a cover letter and printed out my CV and walked over to Dr. Jordan's office on the opposite side of the Center. I found that Dr. Jordan was a VP for Medical Sciences at Fox Chase and at first I thought that "maybe it's not such a great idea," but it doesn't hurt to try. I gave my documents to Dr. Jordan's secretary Marge and told her that "I know that Dr. Jordan is looking for a postdoc, but I can do the same job for less money." Half an hour later I received a phone call to my desk and I was invited to meet Dr. Jordan immediately. Very anxiously, I went back to his office and that's when I met Dr. Jordan for the first time. All my worries dissolved as soon as I met Dr. Jordan. Before me appeared a calm, very cheerful, and a very intelligent scientist. I knew at that very moment that his advice would be either way very valuable and helpful. He asked me a few questions about myself and told me about himself, and said that he liked my enthusiasm and that he always had graduate students in his lab before at previous universities. Fox Chase, however, at that time was not affiliated with any university and was not an educational institution, and thus had no students of its own except for those that came from anywhere else, like me. He told me that he would gladly train me under one condition that I successfully complete my current program and graduate, and then the job was mine. I was on cloud number nine, except I had never heard of tamoxifen or other SERMs before. I agreed and informed my department head in Moscow, that I have found a lab to work on my Ph.D., and ran to read up what was tamoxifen, as I needed to explain what Dr. Jordan did. The Department Head was reluctant at first, because in Russia the research tradition at the time was that a change of labs was irregular. However, my professor agreed that it would be a very good opportunity to work in Dr. Jordan's lab, especially since there was already another master's student that was due to start working in Dr. Jordan's lab in early 2006. That year I graduated with a medical degree in medical biochemistry and joined Dr. Jordan's lab in October 2006. I should say that one could not ask for a better mentor, considering that I was doing completely novel research at that time on structure—functional relationships between Estrogen Receptor bound with a nonsteroidal estrogens and estrogen-induced apoptosis in the estrogen-independent MCF-7:5C human breast cancer cell line that was also developed in Dr. Jordan's lab. I was working on the project very enthusiastically. I will always remember the great years spent at Fox Chase, until disaster stuck. Our lab was closed in Fox Chase and everyone was fired, including myself, a student whose success and immigration status depended on the completion of my thesis. I had completed my thesis with the help of another wonderful friend and scientist Dr. Joan Lewis-Wambi who stayed with her own new lab at Fox Chase. I invited Dr. Jordan for my thesis defense in Moscow and Dr. Jordan agreed to come "and fight beside me." There was not a single instance that Dr. Jordan ever has left his "marines" on the battlefield. His presence was not mandatory for my defense in Moscow; however Dr. Jordan felt that he had to be there with me. It was truly an honor, and I will never forget that. Subsequently, I was invited by Dr. Jordan as a Susan G Komen for the Cure International postdoctoral fellow in his lab at Georgetown University Medical Center Lombardi Comprehensive Cancer Center. I was doing the most interesting projects in breast cancer, and I couldn't be happier doing the work on the role of endoxifen in the treatment of breast cancer patients with various CYP2D6 genotypes. Also we continued to work further on structure—function relationship studies with nonsteroidal estrogens and the estrogen receptor. Now I am completely in love with medicinal chemistry, and my dream now is to participate and facilitate development of new anticancer drugs. Eventually, I received an invitation from Dr. Jordan to move to the MD Anderson Cancer Center in Houston, TX, as a junior faculty, which I accepted. As a junior faculty, I learned a lot about leadership, courage, and the value of mentorship that Dr. Jordan possesses. I am proud to be a member of such an exceptional team as the "Tamoxifen Team," and all this wouldn't be possible without a good mentor, a good friend, and an exceptional leader. I will never forget our great times with D. Jordan and all the adventures we have shared in over the past 15 years.

I am an assistant professor at the Department of Breast Medical Oncology-Research, University of Texas MD Anderson Cancer Center, Houston, TX.

Ping Fan, MD, Ph.D.

I earned my MD and Ph.D. degrees at the Nanjing Medical University in China. Then, I worked as a postdoc in Dr. Richard Santen's lab at the University of Virginia in Charlottesville, Virginia. My research focused on the mechanisms underlying tamoxifen resistance in breast cancer. During my 4 years in Charlottesville, I found that long-term tamoxifen treatment translocated estrogen receptor α to extranuclear areas and increased its interactions with epithelial growth factor receptors, ultimately leading to tamoxifen resistance. By 2008, due to a funding deficiency in the Santen lab, I embarked on a job search.

At that moment, my dream was to work under the guidance of the Father of Tamoxifen. Following this dream, I wrote an email to Dr. Jordan and requested a position in his team. Unexpectedly, he quickly replied to me and arranged an interview. After the interview, Dr. Jordan recruited me as a Staff Scientist in the Fox Chase Cancer Center, where his lab was located at the time. Under his direction, we got many paradoxical research results, which were confounding but illuminating of a truth in nature. First, we tried to increase estrogen-induced apoptosis in long-term estrogen-deprived breast cancer cells by treating these endocrine-resistant cells with estrogen plus the oncogene c-Src inhibitor. The reason why we targeted c-Src is because it is overexpressed in 80% of breast cancer. Paradoxically, the c-Src inhibitor blocked estrogen-induced apoptosis and recovered estrogen stimulation in a newly discovered cell line, MCF-7:PF cells, PF being my initials. It is a tradition in Tamoxifen Team that if you create a new cell line, your initials become part of the name forever. When Dr. Jordan's lab moved to Georgetown University, I was promoted to faculty as a research assistant professor. Our major accomplishments were finding that estrogen induces apoptosis through accumulation of stress responses including endoplasmic reticulum stress, oxidative stress, and inflammatory stress. Particularly, three sensors of endoplasmic reticulum stress are quickly activated by estrogen with different functions when coping with stress. Specifically, PERK is critical for estrogen to induce apoptosis. The other two sensors, IRE1 and ATF-6 are involved in the endoplasmic reticulum-associated degradation of PI3K/Akt/mTOR pathways. In 2014, Dr. Jordan's lab moved to MD Anderson Cancer Center. I continued my research work as a research associate professor. We further found that the PERK increased NF-κB DNA-binding activities and subsequently TNFα expression, leading to estrogen-induced apoptosis. The transcription factor NF-κB has wide interactions with other transcription factors in the nucleus. Therefore, the critical role of NF-κB in estrogen-induced apoptosis created more opportunities to improve therapeutic effects of estrogen-induced apoptosis on endocrine-resistant breast cancer. Based on this, we found that the mechanism of medroxyprogesterone acetate (MPA) used in traditional hormone replacement therapy (HRT) has glucocorticoid activity and suppresses NF-κB DNA-binding activity to inhibit estrogen-induced apoptosis. Thus, traditional HRT increases breast cancer incidence in postmenopausal women compared with treatment with estrogen alone. Many translational research studies that are currently under investigation in Dr. Jordan's Tamoxifen Team work toward saving the lives of women. I am now an Associate Professor at the MD Anderson Cancer Center, Department of Breast Medical Oncology.

As time passes so quickly, I have been working with Dr. Jordan for more than a decade. His guidance for me in research is the same as wings for a bird. My experience working in his laboratory will benefit me for my whole life.

Balkees Abderrahman MD, Ph.D.

The day Professor V Craig Jordan's path and I crossed is a watershed in my life. I walked into his laboratory as an MD, and, 5 years later, I walked out as an MD, Ph.D., with a decorated curriculum vitae, and a set of invaluable skills and character traits, which would allow me to thrive in an ever-changing world. His altruistic mentorship style significantly improved my career and character, and, as a result, I am improving others' lives through a similar mentorship style. This is his legacy of perpetual excellence, and perpetual contribution.

My story of meeting Professor Jordan highlights the butterfly effect of simple interactions, and the legacy of good-hearted individuals; something that we all can experience if we were more receptive to what life has to offer, especially when its what we need, not what we want. The clinical supervisor of my elective training, next to Professor Jordan's office, fortunately, was late to our meeting. Professor Jordan was heading to his office, and I recognized him as the world-renowned "Father of Tamoxifen," whose research continues to influence the lives of so many women and breast cancer patients. "You are the father of tamoxifen!" I enthusiastically said. This was followed by a conversation, in which I expressed my interest in translational research, and being part of his team. He gave me a lot of reading that day and then interviewed me twice. At the end of the second interview, he shook hands with me and said: "welcome to my Tamoxifen Team." Before that hand shake, everyone encouraged me to pursue clinical practice, and I gave into that notion as I could not see another path at the time (i.e., what I wanted), but after that hand shake, I was able to become a physician-scientist with a prolific contribution profile: a bibliography of more than 40 publications, being listed in Forbes 30 Under 30 (science category), being 1 of 10 finalists for the Rolex Award of Enterprise (science and health), among others (i.e., what I needed). As the leader he is, he took a risk and invested in someone with potential not experience, which was paid back in dividends, for his laboratory and for my life.

Professor Jordan always goes the extra mile for his mentees. Revolutionizing the landscape of breast cancer treatment and prevention did not happen because he "employed" researchers, but because he "mentored" them, and then invited them to be part of making history. In my case, he established an educational exchange program between MD Anderson Cancer Center and the University of Leeds, under which I was accepted into a split-site high-merit Ph.D. program. Without his philanthropy, I would not have been able to pay the costly tuition fees. My graduation made me the first successful candidate under this program, which would allow it to grow to benefit many others.

Professor Jordan, through the most challenging times, always put his mentees first, remained enthusiastic about experimentation and discovery, and gave us many opportunities to grow and become. He often said: "I can give you many opportunities, and only you can fail, by not accepting them." He sponsored me to attend conferences, invited me to contribute to articles, introduced me to world experts in the field, and gave me the space to lead and innovate as a young minority woman. In the many interactions we had, he taught me to say truth and do right no matter what the pressures are, to give and not expect anything in return, to be more understanding of the human predicament and not rush into judgment, and to take genuine interest in fulfilling others' needs not only ours.

Professor Jordan and I have many things in common: we were born in Texas and raised outside the United States only to return back to Texas; my roots are from Jordan and his family's name is Jordan; Leeds is our alma mater; and we were invited to the Lindau Nobel Laureate Meeting (considered the world's second largest congregation of Nobel Prize winners after the Nobel Prize ceremony), but couldn't make it (in his case, his father's death, and in mine, COVID-19 travel restrictions). Nevertheless, in 2021, I was invited by the Nobel Foundation to be a member of a 90-minute Zoom discussion panel to consider the proposition "Trust in Science." The Chair of the panel was the President of the Nobel Foundation. I was invited to prepare a document for publication of my opinions of our topic. The links to the session and the paper are https://www.lindau-nobel.org/blog-6-tools-to-supercharge-your-science-communication and https://www.mediatheque.lindau-nobel.org/videos/39161/why-trust-science/meeting-2021.

Now, looking back down memory lane, I realize that being part of his Tamoxifen Team is being part of a movement and that his handshake is his bond and our future.

Index